ADVANCES IN GENDER AND COMMUNICATION RESEARCH

Edited by

Lawrence B. Nadler
Miami University

Marjorie Keeshan Nadler
Miami University

William R. Todd-Mancillas
California State University, Chico

UNIVERSITY
PRESS OF
AMERICA

Lanham • New York • London

Copyright © 1987 by

University Press of America,® Inc.

4720 Boston Way
Lanham, MD 20706

3 Henrietta Street
London WC2E 8LU England

Printed in the United States of America

British Cataloging in Publication Information Available

"The Gender Shift in Journalism Education" © 1987
by Maurine H. Beasley

"Teaching the College Course on Gender Differences" © 1987
by Deborah Borisoff and Lisa Merrill

Library of Congress Cataloging-in-Publication Data

Advances in gender and communication research.

Based on selected papers presented at the 1984 and
1985 Communication, Language, and Gender Conferences,
sponsored by the Organization for the Study of
Communication, Language and Gender.
   Includes bibliographies and index.
   1. Communication—Sex differences—Congresses.
I. Nadler, Lawrence B., 1954-   . II. Nadler,
Marjorie Keeshan, 1954-   . III. Todd-Mancillas,
William R., 1948-   . IV. Communication, Language,
and Gender Conference (1984 : Miami University)
V. Communication, Language, and Gender Conference
(1985 : University of Nebraska) VI. Organization for
the Study for Communication, Language, and Gender.
P96.S48A38 1987   305.3   87-13350
ISBN 0-8191-6477-1 (alk. paper)
ISBN 0-8191-6478-X (pbk. : alk. paper)

All University Press of America books are produced on acid-free
paper which exceeds the minimum standards set by the National
Historical Publication and Records Commission.

ACKNOWLEDGMENTS

No undertaking of this magnitude could be successfully completed without the assistance and support of many people. We would like to thank the Department of Communication at Miami University for the varied forms of support which made this volume possible. In particular, we wish to extend out deepest thanks to Janet Lowitz, whose skilled typing and patience truly brought this book together. Also, we would like to express our appreciation to Diana Askea and Noelle Brown for their support efforts. Finally, we wish to thank all the contributing authors, whose research has enlightened us in the area of gender communication.

TABLE OF CONTENTS

INTRODUCTION

Increasingly, communication scholars are recognizing the importance of gender issues across interaction settings. Some theorists have attempted to document differences (and less often, similarities) in the ways in which men and women communicate. Other researchers have focused on the impact which these differences have upon various interaction outcomes, such as interpersonal perceptions, relational development and satisfaction, organizational effectiveness, and even the quality of one's life experiences. In either event, these gender communication theorists and researchers are united by their efforts to enhance awareness of gender-related issues on the part of students, scholars, and the general public. This objective is the guiding light for this book.

The various articles in this volume are based upon papers presented at the 1984 and 1985 Communication, Language and Gender Conferences. These conferences, which were sponsored by the Organization for the Study of Communication, Language and Gender, were held at Miami University in Oxford, Ohio, and the University of Nebraska in Lincoln, Nebraska. These articles were competitively selected and represent up-to-date research in topical areas which possess currency and practical significance for interpersonal interaction. These topical areas include gender issues in the organizational environment, interpersonal relationships, the cultural milieu, the classroom, sales and bargaining situations, and the political realm. As gender communication is such a broad subject area, the book incorporates diverse methodological approaches to study this area and to provide insight regarding communication between and about men and women. The methodological approaches adopted include rhetorical methods, survey techniques, experimental procedures, and meta-analytic techniques. While the book's breadth is certainly one of its strongest features, each chapter, authored by an expert or experts in the particular subject matter, also offers an in-depth examination of specific gender-related communication issues. The following paragraphs provide further information regarding each chapter as well as the overall organization of the book.

The book is divided into five sections. Section I, "The Role of Gender in Organizational Communication," examines the importance of gender issues in the business/professional environment. As career success and satisfaction are vitally important to most members of our society, and as women are often treated differently and receive lesser compensation, the organizational environment represents a key area of application in terms of gender communication issues. In chapter 1, Fink, Heintz, Lowy, Seebohm, and Wheeless explore how women managers are perceived and the implications of these perceptions in the organizational setting. These researchers found that women generally hold more favorable attitudes toward women as managers than do men. They also discovered that perceptions of female managers are mediated by organizational type and prior experience with women managers. In chapter 2, Dallinger examines men's and women's networks in various work organizations. She discovered that men were more integrated into task networks, while females were more integrated into social networks of organizations. Other dimensions, such as organizational type, masculine versus non-masculine climate, and male dominated versus female dominated organizations were found to mediate these results. The organizational perspective is broadened to encompass other cultures in chapter 3, where Rossi and Todd-Mancillas provide a comparison of Brazilian men and women managers in terms of how they manage conflicts with employees. While no sex differences were obtained for explicit or ambiguous disputes, the authors noted that these findings differed somewhat from results obtained in studying the behavior of American men and women. Specifically, Brazilian women managers were more likely than American women managers to use power in ambiguous conflict situations. In chapter 4, Booth-Butterfield examines sex differences in perceptions of sexual harassment, an issue of growing concern in organizational environments. While females are generally more aware of sexually harassing communication, the author notes that the communication script analysis approach and the four-part model she developed are explanatory for male and female perceptions. This model, which delineates factors that contribute to perceptions of sexual harassment, includes the immediacy of the communication, employment in a field dominated by or balanced with members of the opposite sex, information about anti-harassment guidelines, and prior experience with harassment. Finally, in chapter 5, Beasley examines the gender shift in journalism education and the journalism field. She reports that, despite the fact that women account for about 58 percent of all journalism school enrollments, they encounter more difficulty than males in finding media-related jobs and, due to salary discrimination, may be depressing pay scales in the journalism field. This concern regarding "velvet" or "pink" ghettos is an important one for many types of organizations.

Section II, "Gender Issues in Interpersonal and Professional Relationships," explores sex differences in a variety of interaction settings. In chapter 6, S. Parrish Sprowl examines sex differences in the experience of jealousy. She reports an interaction between sex and self-esteem, such that females with high esteem experienced the least amount of jealousy. A multidimensional view of relationships is advanced to account for men and women's jealous reactions. In chapter 7, Deakins, Osterink, and Hoey look at topic selection in same and mixed sex interaction. In contrasting studies performed in the 1920's with the results of their own research, the authors note that the assumption of "unyielding innate divergence" which was advanced to account for sex differences in the earlier research, was not supported in the present set of studies. The authors offer some interesting observations regarding topic selection in contemporary society. In chapter 8, Beinstein-Miller explores sex differences in interaction management and interaction goals. She reports that when their competencies have been criticized by valued others, women's concerns for self-presentation lead them to increase their efforts at interaction management. In fact, the author notes that, overall, women are more responsive to situational variations in interpersonal situations. Finally, in chapter 9, Indvik performs a meta-analysis of gender as a moderator of leader behavior-subordinate outcome relationships. She reports that the examination of extant research indicates that female subordinates prefer supportive leader messages. Further, the author notes that the results of this meta-analytic study point to the need for future research to delineate more fully the nature and impact of sex differences in leader-subordinate communication in the workplace.

Section III, "Gender and Advocacy: Negotiation, Persuasion and Argumentation," explores the nature and impact of sex differences in persuasive communication. In chapter 10, Rancer and Baukus look at men and women's belief structures regarding arguing behavior. Their findings suggest that females view arguing as a more hostile and combative communication encounter than do males. The authors contend that as recent research has revealed that organizational outcomes are more favorable when a woman is high versus low in argumentativeness, perhaps sex-role development and training should be geared toward promoting a positive view toward arguing, particularly for men and women who are low in argumentativeness. In chapter 11, Henzl and Turner examine whether men and women rationalize conflict choices in a similar or different manner. In contrast to prior research, the authors report no significant differences between men and women in terms of types of decision reached or reasons used to support decisions. The researchers identify methodological and theoretical explanations to account for these disparate results. In chapter 12, Nadler and Nadler examine sex differences in negotiation success in asymmetric power situations. Using role play simulations, the authors report that the lowest outcomes regarding negotiated salary increases occurred in the male supervisor-female subordinate condition. As this pairing most frequently typifies the organizational setting, the researchers assert that additional research should be performed in this area. In chapter 13, Womack questions whether female negotiators are more cooperative than men and whether their behavior maximizes or fails to maximize utility. Employing a used car sales scenario, the author reports that female subjects did not exhibit verbal and nonverbal behaviors associated with powerlessness and that women were not more cooperative than men in this situation. Further,

Womack astutely observes that negotiation behaviors, such as equivocal language, which is often associated with women's speech, could just as easily serve as an effective bargaining tactic as represent powerless behavior. Finally, in chapter 14, J. Parrish Sprowl explores sex differences in compliance gaining behavior in personal sales situations. While sex of target person produced no significant differences, men and women salespersons did differ in certain ways regarding their communication behavior. Although the findings did not entail a clear, consistent pattern, the author indicates that, overall, males utilized a larger number of compliance gaining strategies than did females when attempting to sell a product

Section IV, "The Communicative Influence of Gender on Politics and Culture," provides rhetorical and empirical analyses of the role of sex in the political and cultural realms. In chapter 15, Miller focuses upon the link of sex and language in political discourse. The author reports that female politicians are aware of their language behavior and are not making major changes in this regard in public or private situations. Further, female politicians did not mention double bind situations, suggesting that they can be themselves without necessarily encountering the negative reactions which other researchers have suggested they might experience. In chapter 16, Davey and Mayer explore the role of gender issues in Geraldine Ferraro's 1984 campaign for vice-president. They conclude that, despite Ferraro's desire to focus on content issues during the election campaign, she was forced to devote significant time to gender-based matters, including sexism from the media, political organizations, and some members of the electorate. While Ferraro revolutionized the political process, the authors assert that she also encountered many gender-based problems not experienced by male candidates. In chapter 17, Allen, Long, O'Mara, and Judd explore candidate image, voter values, and gender as determinants of voter preference in the 1984 presidential campaign. The researchers report that candidate image was significant in predicting voting preference and that George Bush was evaluated more favorably than Geraldine Ferraro. The authors discuss the importance of gender issues in the political realm, particularly given the increasing number of women seeking elective office. In chapter 18, Kingsolver and Cordry examine editors' perceptions of sexist and non-sexist language usage in print journalism. They note that while most editors have reservations regarding the use of phrases such as "he or she" and "his or her," these concerns are based upon the cumbersome and unwieldy nature of these language forms, rather than reflecting disagreement with the feminist argument against sexist language. The authors indicate that sentence restructuring is recognized as a viable method of addressing feminists' concerns while maintaining stylistic consistency with The Associated Press Stylebook and Libel Manual. Finally, in chapter 19, Cox explores the impact of sex and black identification on evaluations of communicator style in the organizational setting. The author reports that black males rate themselves as mostly dramatic and argumentative communicators, whereas black females see themselves primarily as attentive. Further, Cox observes that for black males, black identification may dilute communicative activity in organizational settings, while it may have an intensifying effect for black females.

Section V, "Gender Communication Pedagogy," focuses upon instructional considerations and applications of gender-related theory and research. In chapter 20, Borisoff and Merrill discuss teaching the college course on gender differences as barriers to conflict resolution. The authors provide a concise review of the literature regarding sex differences in the management of conflict situations and delineate the benefits of adopting an androgynous style for becoming a good negotiator. Further, Borisoff and Merrill offer a basis for promoting understanding of sex differences in conflict situations. In chapter 21, Stewart explores the influence of participant sex and sex role on participativeness in organizational situations. Using an organizational simulation model, the author reports that men and women did not differ in their desire to participate or in the amount of participation they perceived in their work environment. In terms of sex roles, a significant difference was that high instrumental respondents had a greater perception of the amount of participation in their work environment. In chapter 22, Valentine examines the use of videotape to teach about women's communication. The historical development of an innovative educational program is traced. Also, useful instructional materials for providing such gender communication education are described. Finally, in chapter 23, West discusses the development of a unit on sex roles in the communication classroom. The steps involved in such instructional development, including researching sex roles, instigating self-analysis and assessing student perceptions, are delineated. Suggested readings, films, exercises, and paper topics are also described.

SECTION ONE

THE ROLE OF GENDER IN ORGANIZATIONAL COMMUNICATION

CHAPTER 1

PERCEPTIONS OF WOMEN AS MANAGERS:
INDIVIDUAL AND ORGANIZATIONAL IMPLICATIONS

Cynthia Berryman-Fink
University of Cincinnati

Mary A. Heintz
Procter and Gamble Company

Marc Steven Lowy
University of Cincinnati

Monica Louise Seebohm
Xerox Corporation

Virginia Eman Wheeless
West Virginia University

As the number of women entering managerial positions steadily climbs (Powell, 1980), social and behavioral scientists increasingly are examining factors affecting the integration and success of women in organizations. One such factor, which has been the focus of considerable research, is attitudes toward women as managers (Bass, Krusell, & Alexander, 1971; Bowman, Worthy, & Greyson, 1965; Crino, White, & DeSanctis, 1981; Guissippi & Forgionne, 1977; Matteson, 1976; Peters, Terborg, & Taynor, 1974; Powell & Butterfield, 1979; Schein, 1975; Terborg, Peters, Ilgen, & Smith, 1977). Negative societal or organizational attitudes toward women as managers seemingly would impinge upon the career success of women in managerial positions.

The field of management is perceived as a masculine activity (Evangelist, 1981; Moore & Rickel, 1980; Powell & Butterfield, 1979), and although more women are assuming management positions, they are perceived as being less competent than their male counterparts (Basil, 1973; Bass et al., 1971; Bowman et al., 1965; Brenner & Bromer, 1981; Guissippi & Forgionne, 1977; Orth & Jacobs, 1971; Powell & Butterfield, 1979; Rosen & Jerdee, 1974; Schein, 1973, 1975).

The purpose of this paper is to explore variables affecting attitudes toward women managers and perceptions of their communication competencies. This paper will present the results of several studies which cumulatively provide information on three variables affecting attitudes toward and perceived communication abilities of women managers: (1) gender of respondent; (2) type of organization in which the respondent is

3

employed; and (3) respondent's work experience with women managers. Additionally, individual and organizational implications of these variables on perceptions of women managers will be discussed.

Gender

Previous research on the relationship of gender of respondent and perceptions of women managers indicates that females generally hold more positive attitudes toward women as managers (Crino et al., 1981; Matteson, 1976; Peters et al., 1974; Terborg et al., 1977). Some studies show no difference between male and female respondents' attitudes toward women in management (Brenner & Bromer, 1981; Ellis, 1983; Powell & Butterfield, 1979).

Organizational type

Though intuitively we would expect the type of organization in which a person is employed to influence that person's perception of women managers, this variable has not been examined by researchers. We can predict that an organization's culture would affect the attitudes of its members; thus, in this investigation, we will empirically examine the effect of "organizational type" on respondents' attitudes toward women as managers.

Work experience

There is evidence to posit a relationship between an individual's work experience with women managers and that person's attitude toward and perception of the communication of women in management. Newcomb's (1961) research on interpersonal attraction shows that with physical proximity comes favorable information and a tendency toward liking the other person. Likewise, the contact hypothesis of Amir (1969) predicts that when minority and majority groups come into contact with each other, all individuals come to know each other better, and this contact helps reduce prejudice and tension between the groups. Amir (1969) provides support for this phenomenon with Black and White groups, while Caspi (1984) has documented it with children and older persons.

While much research has examined attitudes toward women as managers, less research has focused on perceptions of the communication abilities of women managers. Women managers have been perceived as more interpersonally-oriented (Baird & Bradley, 1979), less influential (Brass, 1984), and less assertive (Baron & Witte, 1980) than male managers. Therefore, in addition

4

to examining how the variables of gender, organizational type, and work experience affect attitudes toward women managers, we also will investigate the effect of these variables on perceptions of women managers' communication competencies.

By synthesizing the results of several studies by these authors, we will attempt to explicate the relationship between three independent variables (gender, organizational type, and work experience with women managers) and two dependent variables (attitudes toward women as managers and perceived communication competencies of women managers).

METHOD

Study 1

One-hundred and seventy-eight employees (98 males and 80 females) of various types of organizations participated in this study in the Fall of 1983. Sample organizations included hospitals, banks, insurance companies, the auto industry, a railroad company, and federal and city government. All S's participated in this research while enrolled in business administration courses in the Evening College of a large Midwestern metropolitan university. All were employed full-time during the day. One-hundred and thirty S's indicated that they had experience working for or with women managers. Attitudes toward women as managers were measured by the Women As Managers Scale (WAMS) (Peters et al., 1974), a 21-item measure of general acceptance of women managers, "feminine barriers" to employment, and personality traits ascribed to women managers. Subjects' perceptions of women managers' communication were measured by the Communication Competencies of Women Managers Scale (CCWMS) (Wheeless & Berryman-Fink, 1985), a 30-item measure of perceived communication abilities of women managers.

Study 2

One-hundred and forty-six employees (73 males and 73 females) from five different organizational types in a large Midwestern metropolitan area participated in this research during the Winter of 1984. The five organizational types included: a national accounting firm (n=28), a community hospital (n=26), a national chain hotel (n=33); city government (n=36); and a food service organization (n=22). Each subject completed the WAMS. The personnel manager in each organization administered the research instrument. All responses were anonymous.

Study 3

Eighty-seven subjects (28 males and 59 females) from three Midwestern metropolitan hospitals participated in this study during the Spring of 1985. The hospitals included: a large state university-affiliated hospital (n=27), a medium-sized Catholic supported hospital (n=33), and a small private hospital (n=27). All but one of the subjects had had work experience with/for women managers. Respondents completed the WAMS and the CCWMS. A member of the research team administered the instruments in hospital one, while department heads distributed the questionnaire booklet in the remaining two hospitals. All responses were anonymous.

RESULTS

Gender

All three studies resulted in a significant gender effect. In Study 1, male and female subjects' responses were significantly different on the WAMS (t = 8.89, df = 176, $p <$ .0001) with women demonstrating more positive attitudes ($\bar{X}$ = 128.41) than men ($\bar{X}$ = 108.58). Subjects' responses on the CCWMS differed significantly according to gender (t = 4.24, df = 176, $p <$ .0001) with women reporting more positive perceptions ($\bar{X}$ = 121.41) than men ($\bar{X}$ = 111.71).

In Study 2, analysis of variance revealed a significant difference between male and female respondents on the WAMS (F = 11.84, df = 144, $p <$ .008). Females reported more positive attitudes toward women as managers ($\bar{X}$ = 127.89) than did males ($\bar{X}$ = 106.90).

Study 3 resulted in significant differences between male and female respondents on both the WAMS (t = 17.13, df = 85, $p <$ .01) and the CCWMS (t = 20.68, df = 85, $p <$ .01). Females scored higher on the WAMS ($\bar{X}$ = 130.15) than did the males ($\bar{X}$ = 115.79). Females reported more positive perceptions of the communication abilities of women managers than did males (for females, $\bar{X}$ = 164.61; for males, $\bar{X}$ = 141.61).

Organizational type

Study 2 examined the effect of type of organization in which the respondent was employed on attitudes toward women as managers. t-tests revealed that scores on the WAMS did differ significantly according to organizational type from which respondents were drawn. The accounting industry differed significantly from the hotel industry (t = 2.90, $p <$ .005), city government (t = 3.22, $p <$ .002), and the food service industry (t = 3.16, $p <$ .003). The hospital differed significantly from

6

the hotel industry (t = 2.09, p < .041), city government (t = 2.36, p < .022), and the food service industry (t = 2.05, p < .046). Three organizations did not differ significantly in attitudes toward women managers. Respondents from the hotel organization, city government, and the food service organization had essentially similar attitudes toward women as managers. The overall means for the five organizations, in descending order indicating most to least favorable attitudes toward women managers, are as follows: city government $\bar{X}$ = 128.4, hotel $\bar{X}$ = 126.3, food service $\bar{X}$ = 124.8, hospital $\bar{X}$ = 104.4, and accounting $\bar{X}$ = 99.6.

Work experience

Studies 1 and 3 examined the effect of work experience with/for women managers on attitudes toward and perceptions of the communication of women managers. In Study 1, there was a significant difference on the WAMS between subjects with and without work experience with/for women managers (t = 2.83, df = 167, p < .005). Those who had worked with/for women managers demonstrated higher scores on the WAMS ($\bar{X}$ = 119.49) than those without such experience ($\bar{X}$ = 110.39). There was no significant effect of this variable on the CCWMS in Study 1.

Study 3 attempted to examine this variable more specifically by soliciting the subject's actual number of years of work experience either with or for women managers. Thus, the number of years experience as a colleague ("with") or as a subordinate ("for") were related to WAMS and CCWMS scores.

Pearson Product Moment Correlations revealed a significant relationship between a subject's years working as a subordinate to women managers and perceptions of women managers' communication competencies (r = .2924, p < .01). This indicates that the longer one works for women managers, the more positive one's attitude will be toward the communication abilities of women managers. The relationship between years working as a colleague with women managers and the CCWMS approached significance (r = .2304, p < .06). No significant relationship was found between work experience with or for women managers and the WAMS scores in Study 3.

DISCUSSION

These three studies produced a consistent finding of a gender effect in attitudes toward women as managers and perceptions of the communication abilities of women managers. That female respondents hold more favorable attitudes toward women as managers than male respondents corroborates previous research (Crino et al., 1981; Matteson, 1976; Peters et al. 1974; and Terborg et al., 1977). Because of the positive relationship of attitudes toward another and perceived behavior of the other, it is not surprising that female respondents also attributed greater communication competence to women managers than did male respondents.

Clearly, this research shows a gender bias among employees from numerous organizations in perceptions of "women as managers" as a general phenomenon. This may mean that judgments of women managers' general ability and specific communication ability could contain an inherent bias. These results show such judgments to be favorably biased in the same-sex condition and unfavorably biased in the opposite-sex condition. Should a woman manager expect more favorable perceptions of her managerial abilities from other women in the work environment? Should she expect less favorable perceptions of her managerial abilities from males in the workplace? If gender of evaluator mediates judgments of the managerial and communicative competence of women managers, as it did in these studies, then workplace evaluations and decisions inherently may be biased.

This implication must be interpreted cautiously, however, for several reasons. First, these investigations analyzed perceptual data in relation to the general concept of "women managers." We do not know if the same gender effect would emerge when making perceptions of actual women managers in one's work environment. Perhaps a stereotype emerges which polarizes men and women when making attributions of women in the hypothetical role of manager. Secondly, we do not know the relationship between perceptions and behavior on these variables. A gender bias in attitudes toward women managers may not result in biased evaluations or decisions. Subsequent investigations should examine the effect of gender of evaluator on actual evaluations concerning selection, performance review, and promotion decisions in organizations.

This investigation found significant differences in attitudes toward women as managers according to organizational type. Some types of organizations seem more favorable to the concept of women managers than others. These researchers found attitudes toward women as managers to be more favorable in the city government, hotel, and food services organizations than they were in the hospital and accounting organizations. It is difficult to explain such a finding. Numerous factors contributing to the organization's culture may account for this finding. Subsequent researchers might explore, for example, the ratio of males to females in the organization, the number of women in top level positions in the organization, and the educational levels, personality traits, and aptitudes needed to be employed in that occupation. Because only five organizational types were studied, it is too early to comment on occupations or professions which are more or less favorable to women as managers. But this line of research may provide information for women in making career decisions. Likewise, organizations may benefit from knowing the stereotypical predilections within their industry type. Such information could be useful in affirmative action, organizational development, and career counseling efforts.

These studies confirm the effect of familiarity and proximity on attitude formation. Those subjects who had experience with women managers held more favorable attitudes than those without such experience. This may mean that individuals with negative attitudes toward women managers may change their attitudes as a result of working directly with women managers. Stereotypes seem to exist because of a lack of information. Gaining information through direct experience with women managers may be the best means of reducing stereotypes. Organizations may consider this strategy for dealing with gender and other stereotypes. The findings from this research imply that employees' familiarity with different races, cultures, or departments in an organization, for example, may improve attitudes toward those who are different from oneself.

This investigation found that the longer one's experience as a subordinate to women managers, the more favorable is one's perception of the communicative competence of women managers. This may be a function of women managers' actual improved communication abilities with time in the role affecting subjects' perceptions. Or it may mean that initially unfavorable perceptions of women managers will dissipate over time.

This study attempted to locate and explain factors affecting perceptions of women managers. It has shed light on three such factors. Subsequent investigations should continue to examine perceptual attributions toward the woman manager which ultimately impinge on her career success.

REFERENCES

Amir, Y. (1969). Contact hypothesis in ethnic relations. Psychological Bulletin, 71, 319-342.

Baird, J. E., & Bradley, P. H. (1979). Styles of management and communication: A comparative study of men and women. Communication Monographs, 46, 101-111.

Baron, A. S., & White, R. L. (1980, August). The new work dynamic: Men and women in the workforce. Business Horizons, 56-60.

Basil, D. C. (1973). Women in management. New York: McGraw-Hill.

Bass, B. M., Krusell, J., & Alexander, R. A. (1971). Male managers' attitudes toward working women. American Behavioral Scientist, 15, 221-236.

Bowman, G. W., Worthy, N. B., & Greyson, S. A. (1965). Problems in review: Are women executives people? Harvard Business Review, 43, 52-67.

Brass, D. J. (1984). Women and networks: A study of informal interaction patterns and influence in an organization. Unpublished manuscript, Pennsylvania State University.

Brenner, O. C., & Bromer, J. A. (1981). Sex stereotypes and leaders' behavior as measured by the agreement scale for leadership behavior. Psychological Reports, 48, 960-962.

Caspi, A. (1984). Contact hypothesis and inter-age attitudes: A field study of cross-age contact. Social Psychology Quarterly, 47, 74-80.

Crino, M. D., White, M. C., & DeSanctis, G. L. (1981). A comment on the dimensionality and reliability of the women as managers scale (WAMS). Academy of Management Journal, 24, 866-876.

Ellis, L. K. (1983). An empirical investigation of sex-characteristic stereotypes and sex-role stereotypes affecting women in management. Unpublished Master's Thesis, Texas Tech University.

Evangelist, M. A. (1981). Managerial aptitude as a function of sex-role orientation (Doctoral dissertation, Fordham University, 1981). Dissertation Abstracts International, 41, 4903-A.

Guissippi, A., & Forgionne, I. (1977). Male attitudes toward women. Business Review, 3, 23-28.

Matteson, M. T. (1976). Attitudes toward women as managers: Sex or role differences? Psychological Reports, 39, 166.

10

Moore, L. M., & Rickel, A. U. (1980). Characteristics of women in traditional and nontraditional managerial roles. Personnel Psychology, 33, 317-333.

Newcomb, T. M. (1961). The acquaintance process. New York: Holt, Rinehart & Winston.

Orth, C. D., & Jacobs, F. (1971). Women in management: Pattern for change. Harvard Business Review, 49, 139.

Peters, L. H., Terborg, J. R., & Taynor, J. (1974). Women as managers scale: A measure of attitudes toward women in management positions. JSAS Catalog of Selected Documents in Psychology, 4, 27. (Ms. No. 585).

Powell, G. N. (1980). Career development and the woman manager--a social power perspective. Personnel, 57, 22-32.

Powell, G. N., & Butterfield, D. A. (1979). The "good manager": Masculine or androgynous? Academy of Management Journal, 22, 395-403.

Rosen, B., & Jerdee, T. H. (1974). Effects of applicant's sex and difficulty of job on evaluations of candidates for managerial positions. Journal of Applied Psychology, 59, 511-512.

Schein, V. E. (1973). The relationship between sex role stereotypes and requisite management characteristics. Journal of Applied Psychology, 57, 95-100.

Schein, V. E. (1975). Relationships between sex role stereotypes and requisite management characteristics among female managers. Journal of Applied Psychology, 60, 340-344.

Terborg, J. R., Peters, L. H., Ilgen, D. R., & Smith, F. (1977). Organizational and personal correlates of attitudes toward women as managers. Academy of Management Journal, 20, 89-100.

Wheeless, V. E., & Berryman-Fink, C. (1985). Perceptions of women managers and their communicator competencies. Communication Quarterly, 33, 137-148.

11

CHAPTER 2

AN ANALYSIS OF MEN'S AND WOMEN'S NETWORKS

Judith M. Dallinger, Western Illinois University

Sex differences in both attitudes and behaviors related to communication have become a major focus of study in recent years. Though many studies have been completed, results have often been inconsistent and some areas have not produced adequate examination to support any concrete conclusions about possible sex differences or similarities.

This paper represents an attempt to provide information about possible sex differences in one specific area of communication—task and social communication networks in organizations. Though the correlation between organizational member sex and network placement has not been commonly studied, there is some evidence that sex differences do occur in social interaction (Shaw, 1981). Some support has been found for the customary idea that women talk more than men, at least in dyads (Ickes & Barnes, 1977), though other studies have supported the opposite results (Eakins & Eakins, 1976). Further, in his literature review, Baird (1976) concluded that males generally communicate to fulfill a task function, while females normally communicate to fulfill a social-emotional function.

Though it would be dangerous to generalize these findings to the organizational setting, they do suggest that an examination of sex differences in that situation may be useful. Both amount and function of communicative acts are important in communication networks. Different networks are developed for different functions in the organization, and network members' ties with one another are generally defined in terms of number and importance of interactions.

The following study attempts to provide a preliminary answer to the following research questions. R1: Do males and females differ in their placement in task and social organizational communication networks? R2: Do different types of organizations mediate the possible sex differences in communication network placement?

Method

Subjects Subjects were 224 employees of six small businesses located in a small midwestern city. Organizations included a grocery store (N = 30), a retail store (38), a bank (60), a real estate agency (18), and city (30) and state (51) police organizations. Response rates varied among the organizations from 79% to 94% resulting in an overall rate of 86%.

Of the 224 subjects included in the hypothesis test, 47% were male and 53% were female. Two organizations were dominantly male (city police = 90% male, and state police = 78% male); two were dominantly female (bank = 82% female, and the retail store = 81% female) and two were about equally divided between males and females (grocery store = 57% female, and the real estate agency = 53% male). Ages ranged from 17 to 66 with a mean age of 33.4. Forty-five percent had attained a high school degree or less, while only 4% had achieved a more than a bachelor's degree. Fifty-nine percent of the employees had worked for their respective organizations for 5 years or less, and 30% reported that they supervised at least one other person in the organization.

Procedures Organizations used in this study were selected according to size and availability. Only organizations employing 20 - 75 employees were included, and organizations made up primarily of volunteers were not used. Top manager/executives of each organization included in the study provided a list of employee names which were used to develop the network analysis questionnaire. All employees of every organization received an individualized questionnaire packet including the task and social network questionnaires and a question asking them to indicate their sex (among other items).

Employees of each organization were identified by name or identification number and were assured that their individual responses would not be made available to any other member of their organization and that only summary information would be returned.

In all organizations, each employee received his/her questionnaire at work and was asked to complete it alone in his/her free time. They were asked to return the questionnaires (in sealed envelopes) either to the contact person in the organization or to mail it directly back to the author within a two week time period.

Communication Network Analysis Measurement The NEGOPY network analysis program was used to identify task and social network participation (Richards, 1974, 1975; Richards & Rice, 1980). All organizational members were asked to indicate with whom they interact for both task and social purposes by estimating approximately how many times they interact with every other individual for each function (based on a 1 to 4 scale from "once or twice a month" to "several times a day"), and by indicating how important each relationship was to them (on a 1 to 4 scale from

14

"slightly important" to "crucial to survival"). Both frequency of interaction and importance of the relationship were used in the NEGOPY analyses. Following Richards (1975), frequency ratings were cubed to approximate a ratio scale based on how often members talked to one another in a month, and then multiplied by the importance rating. Because analyses using reciprocated links failed to produce any differentiation among organizational members, the reciprocated only links solution was used in subsequent analyses.

NEGOPY network analysis produces both role indications for each network member (liaisons, group members, isolates, and others) as well as integrativeness scores. Both indicants of network membership were used in the analyses for this study. An isolate is an organizational member who has few relationships within the organization. Groups consist of several people who have indicated that they have more ties with each other than with other organizational members outside the group, and a liaison is an organizational member who has linkages with members of two or more groups, but who does have enough ties within a group to be one of its members. Others are members who have some ties with one group but not enough to be counted as a regular member. Integrativeness scores represent the number of links that a member has with other members in the organization divided by the number of possible links that s/he could have. Scores range from 0 (no links) to 1 (links with every other member) (Farace, et al., 1977; Richards, 1975).

Results

Task networks for the total sample included 8 employees classified as liaisons, 13 isolates, 148 group members and 57 others. Seventeen task groups were identified. For social networks, there were 20 employees classified as isolates, 185 as group members, 1 liaison, and 17 others. Altogether, seven social groups were identified.

Members of these organizations were far more closely connected in their social networks than they were in their task networks. For task networks, two organizations (the grocery and the real estate agency--the smallest organizations) produced only one group each, comprised of nearly all organization members. Each of the remaining four organizations produced at least two groups each, and three had at least one liaison (police--3 groups, 3 liaisons; retail--4 groups, 3 liaisons; state police--4 groups, 4 liaisons; and bank--4 groups, 0 liaisons). For social networks, however, five of the six organizations produced only one comprehensive group including nearly all organizational members, and only the state police produced two separate groups (with one liaison).

The first research question was examined by computing a series of t-tests, using gender as the independent variable. First, t-tests were done using roles in the task and the social networks as dependent variables. Neither produced a significant t value (task: $t = -.40$, $p = .688$, df = 221; social: $t = -.86$, $p = .392$, df = 221). However, t-tests for sex using integrativeness scores for both task and social networks produced somewhat different results. The t-test using task integrativeness was significant (task: $t = 1.93$, $p = .05$, df = 221, with males more integrated) while the t-test for social integrativeness was not (social: $t = -1.62$, $p = .106$, df = 221). Means and standard deviations for sex groups on integrativeness scores are included in Table 1.

Table 1

Means, and Standard Deviations for Integrativeness Scores
for Males and Females (n=221)

Task Integrativeness Scores

	Overall	City Police	State Police	Grocery	Bank	Retail	Real Estate
MALES	.551	.600	.482	.573	.544	.452	.566
	.23	.21	.22	.22	.14	.30	.28
FEMALES	.492	.296	.550	.506	.541	.373	.605
	.22	.28	.20	.28	.18	.20	.29

Social Integrativeness Scores

	Overall	City Police	State Police	Grocery	Bank	Retail	Real Estate
MALES	.495	.387	.509	.570	.551	.308	.881
	.27	.30	.88	.20	.64	.23	.06
FEMALES	.572	.528	.089	.570	.644	.470	.760
	.43	.26	.15	.24	.59	.16	.31

For further analysis of research question 1 and a partial answer to question 2, the author wished to determine if any particular organization was contributing more to the sex differences noted for social integrativeness than others. Therefore, a series of t-tests, focusing on each organization separately, were conducted using males and females as the independent variable and social integrativeness as the dependent variable. Of those, the tests for the retail store and the city police were significant and the others were not (see Table 2). Means for male and females groups on social integrativeness scores are included in Table 1.

Table 2

T-test Results For Sex Differences by Each Organization
Task Communication Networks

	City Police	State Police	Grocery	Bank	Retail	Real Estate
t value	.83	-.93	.70	.05	.85	-.28
Prob level	.01	.36	.49	.96	.40	.78
df	28	47	28	58	35	15

Social Communication Networks

	City Police	State Police	Grocery	Bank	Retail	Real Estate
t value	3.39	-1.43	.01	-.52	-2.23	1.14
Prob level	.00	.16	.99	.53	.03	.27
df	28	47	28	58	35	15

Finally, for question 1, a series of t-tests for sex were conducted using task integrativeness as the dependent variable in order to determine if particular organizations did have sex differences, though as noted above, taken together the groups did not. Results indicated that one organization did indeed have a sex difference on task integrativeness (city police), though the remaining five did not. T-test results are included in Table 2, and means and standard deviations are in Table 1.

To examine further research question 2--do different types of organizations mediate sex differences in network placement-- another series of t-tests was conducted. Initially, organizations were divided into two types, police and non-police. This division is based on the author's observation of a particularly masculine climate in both police organizations, due no doubt to their para-military nature. Therefore, the police and state police were combined into one group (n = 79), and the remaining four organizations comprised the second group (there is no reason to suppose that these four organizations were female dominated, n = 145). Police and non-police organizations were compared on both task and social integrativeness scores. Though task integrativeness was not significantly different for organization

17

types (t = 1.25, p = .21, df = 222), social integrativeness was (t = −3.39, p = .003, df = 222, with non−police organizations having higher levels of social integrativeness). Means for integrativeness scores for the two types of organizations are included in Table 3.

Table 3

Means, and Standard Deviations for Integrativeness Scores
for Police and Other Type Organizations (n=222)

Task Integrativeness Scores

	POLICE	NON−POLICE	FEMALE DOMINATED
Mean	.545	.506	.483
Standard Deviation	.23	.22	.20
Sample Size	79	145	98

Social Integrativeness Scores

	POLICE	NON−POLICE	FEMALE DOMINATED
Mean	.437	.588	.553
Standard Deviation	.27	.39	.44
Sample Size	79	145	98

A different version of this difference between organizations might divide organizations between those that were primarily made up of male employees and those that were primarily made up of females. In this sample, the police and state police were primarily male (police = 90%, state police = 78%) and the bank and retail store were primarily female (bank = 82%, retail = 79%). These constituted the two groups for a final set of t−tests using task and social integrativeness as dependent variables. This time both tests were significant (task: t = 1.91, p = .05, df = 175 with police showing more integrativeness, social: t = −2.15, p = .03, df = 175 with female dominated groups showing more integrativeness). Means for task and social integrativeness for both groups are included in Table 3.

Discussion

There is some evidence in the present data to provide a positive answer for research question 1--males and females do differ in their placement in task and social organizational communication networks. It is not surprising that network role comparisons did not support a difference because with so many of the organizational members classified as group members and so few as liaisons or isolates, all groups of any type will be made up primarily of group members, so differences between them would be hard to find. However, the t-tests for sex, using all organizations combined, indicated that there is indeed a difference between males and females on their social integrativeness scores. Males were more integrated into organizational communication networks than females. However, the task results indicated no sex differences in integrativeness.

Sex differences were dependent on organization though. The city police showed clear differences between men and women on integrativeness scores in both the social and task networks. However, the direction of differences differed. Females were more integrated in the social network while males were more integrated in the task network. The retail store also produced a sex difference for the social network. Here females were again more integrated than males.

Apparently males and females participate differently in communication networks in at least some circumstances. Specifically, females seem to be more fully integrated in the social network and males more fully integrated in the task network.

Though the preceeding discussion applies to research question 2 (do different types of organizations mediate the possible sex differences in communication network placement?) further information is available. There is some evidence that masculine climates differ from other climates in network makeup. The t-test indicated that social integrativeness was different in masculine organizations (police) than in non-masculine climates, with organizational members being more integrated with one another in the non-masculine climates. Task networks did not produce significant climate results.

More clear evidence resulted from the comparison between female dominated and male dominated organizations (based on percentage of male or female members). Both task and social networks differed in these two types of organizations, though in opposite directions. For task networks, the male dominated organizations were more integrated, but for social networks, the female dominated organizations were more integrated.

Taking all the sets of results together, males seem to be more integrated in the task networks, while females are more integrated into the social networks of organizations. This finding agrees with Baird's (1976) conclusions that males

19

generally communicate to fulfill a task function while females communicate to fulfill a social-emotional function. These results support and perhaps reflect the general cultural stereotype that men are the workers in society while women are more socially oriented. Though these stereotypes may be breaking down in recent years, this study supports the notion that they are still in existence in some situations.

A second explanation of the results may be that it takes too much time to become highly involved in both task and social networks, so it will be unlikely that members will be highly integrated in both. But then the question arises--why are females more integrated in the social networks and men more integrated in the task networks? Three reasons present themselves. First, it may be by choice. Men and women may choose to participate more in these respective types of networks--maybe because of their stereotypical upbringing. Second, perhaps there are barriers to women becoming highly involved in the task network. "Old boy" networks and the lack of women in top management positions might seem to inhibit women's abilities to become ingrained in task networks. Finally, there may be barriers which would keep men from becoming highly involved in social networks. Coffee breaks for secretaries or sales clerks (often female) might lead to strong female social ties that would be difficult for men to break in to. Any or all of these are possible explanations of the results of this study. Additional information is necessary to determine if these results would replicate, and to determine why they occur.

Further investigation into the nature of sex differences in organizational communication networks should begin by re-examining the questions pursued in this study. More organizations of different sizes and different types need to be examined. A priori decisions about male and female domination need to be made and then organizations should be selected specifically to match those categories, in order to determine the climate/domination effects on network integration. Further, other indicants of network involvement should be examined for sex differences. Finally, if such differences are found consistently, an analysis of their effects on outcome variables, such as member satisfaction and productivity would be useful for future application.

REFERENCES

Baird, J. E. (1976). Sex differences in group communication: Review of relevant research. The Quarterly Journal of Speech, 62, 179–192.

Eakins, B. W. & Eakins, R. G. (1976). Verbal turn-taking and exchanges in faculty dialogue. In B. L. DuBois & I. Crouch (Eds.), Papers in southwest English IV: Proceedings of the conference on the sociology of the languages of American women (pp. 53–62). San Antonio: Trinity University Press.

Farace, R. V., Monge, P. R. & Russell, H. M. (1977). Communicating and organizing. Reading, MA: Addison-Wesley.

Ickes, W., & Barnes, R. D. (1977). The role of sex and self-monitoring in unstructured dyadic interactions. Journal of Personality and Social Psychology, 35, 315–330.

Richards, W. E., Jr. (1974). Network analysis in large complex systems: Techniques and methods--tools. Paper presented at the meeting of the International Communication Association, New Orleans, LA.

Richards, W. D., Jr. (1975). A Manual for network analysis (Using the NEGOPY network analysis program). Stanford University: California Institute for Communication Research.

Richards, W. D., Jr. & Rice, R. E. (1980). The negopy network analysis program. Paper presented to the meeting of the American Cybernetics Society, Philadelphia, PA.

Shaw, M. E. (1981). Group dynamics: The psychology of small group behavior. New York: Mc Graw Hill Book Company.

CHAPTER 3

DIFFERENCES BETWEEN BRAZILIAN MEN AND WOMEN MANAGERS IN THEIR MANAGING OF CONFLICTS WITH EMPLOYEES

Ana Maria Rossi, University of Nebraska-Lincoln
William R. Todd-Mancillas, California State University, Chico

Many scholars have been concerned with comparing and contrasting communication strategies used by men and women managers. Recent research indicates consistent differences, with women managers tending to be more open, responsive, and communicative than men managers (Baird and Bradley, 1979; Todd-Mancillas and Rossi, 1985). However, these findings have been drawn from research done on American men and women managers and, therefore, may not apply to communication differences between men and women managers in other countries.

This study attempts to expand our understanding of communication strategies used by Brazilian men and women managers. By contrasting the communication strategies of American and Brazilian managers, one may better appreciate the differences culture makes in sanctioning certain norms and communication strategies (Lannon, 1977).

The first author is a native of Brazil, with many business contacts in Porto Alegre. Accordingly, the first author was able to collect a considerable amount of data about Brazilian men's and women's managerial communication behavior. Further, in a previous study the authors had already collected and analyzed systematically a large body of data contrasting American men's and women's managerial communication when attempting to resolve disputes with subordinates (Todd-Mancillas and Rossi, 1985). For the purpose of this study, a similar data collection effort was undertaken in Porto Alegre, with 40 men and 40 women managers interviewed to identify their preferred communication strategies when attempting to resolve disputes with employees. This data was then compared with the previously collected data on American men and women managers. This comparison proved useful for answering the basic research question of this study: In what ways (if any) do Brazilian men and women managers differ from one another in their communication strategies when resolving disputes with subordinates?

Procedures

Interviewees

All 80 managers (40 Brazilian men, 40 Brazilian women)

participating in this study worked in middle and top-management positions. All of them lived and work in Porto Alegre, an economically progressive coastal city.

Data Collection Procedure

Each manager was asked to read a packet of four scripts describing various problems that a manager might have with an employee or another manager of equal status as themselves. Each of these scripts described critical incidents validated by previous research personnel problems frequently encountered by managers (Rossi and Wolesensky, 1983). While these scripts were initially constructed on the basis of interviews conducted with American managers (Wolesensky, 1981), they were also representative of personnel problems encountered by Brazilian managers.

Script A describes an instance in which an employee expresses reluctance to do an assigned task not included in his/her job description (see Appendix A). Script B describes an instance in which an employee violates (apparently inadvertently) the established chain of command (see Appendix B). Script C involves a dispute in which an employee challenges the manager's competence to give correct instructions on how to do an assigned task (see Appendix C). Script D is different from the others in that it involves a dispute between a newly hired high-level employee and other high-level employees (managers), who challenge the former's authority to introduce a change in termination policy (see Appendix D). Script D contains sufficient ambiguity to make less than clear whether the newly hired high-level employee has the authority to impose changes in personnel policy on the managers.

Four versions of each script were utilized, matching all possible combinations of men and women managers with male and female employees. After reading the scripts, interviewees were asked to explain how they would resolve the problems.

Coding Procedures

Using previously established and validated coding procedures (Rossi and Todd-Mancillas, 1985), the responses were read and assigned to one of three classifications. Responses were assigned a Communication classification if they indicated that the primary means of resolving the dispute was through discussion with the employee which, at least to some extent, considered objectively the employee's perspective and used neither coercion nor threat, but rather nonmanipulative persuasion in obtaining compliance (see Appendix E).

24

Responses were assigned an <u>Organizational Power</u> classification if they indicated that the employee would be forced to follow the manager's directives (or sanctioned for presumably not having followed them in the first place). Usually, responses received organizational power classifications for one of two reasons: (1) the respondent made an explicit comment to the effect that the employee would be reprimanded or threatened with dismissal; (2) the respondent did not imply in any way that she would consider objectively the employee's reasons for objecting to or possibly having inadvertently violated the managerial directive in question (see Appendix E).

Lastly, responses were assigned a <u>Mixed Approach</u> classification if they included both an indication to discuss objectively the problem with the employee, coupled with either an implicit or explicit threat of sanction should the employee refuse to comply with the manager's directives (see Appendix E).

Data Analysis Procedures

For the purposes of this paper, only the results of scripts A and B have been analyzed. The results of Scripts C and D will be analyzed and discussed in a later paper.

After the responses were coded into communication, organizational power, and mixed approach categories, 2 X 3 contingency tables were constructed. Preliminary to the analysis of the data using X^2, tests were then conducted to determine what managerial styles predominated in each of the scenarios. First, 2 X 3 X ^{2} tests were conducted separately for men and women managers to determine whether they responded differently to male employees than to female employees. If both tests were found nonsignificant and, therefore, it appeared that men and women managers responded similarly to male and female employees, the data for male and female employees were combined and an X^2 test was then conducted to determine whether men managers differed from women managers in their overall response styles (see Tables 3 and 4). If it appeared that men and women managers did not differ in their response profiles, then the data for American and Brazilian managers were combined and a one-way (1 X 3) X^2 test was conducted to determine whether one response type was preferred over the others (see Tables 5 and 6). In general, significant X^2 tests were followed by simpler X^2 tests to tease out the conceptually meaningful relationships attributable to managerial gender, response style, and gender of employee.

All X tests were considered significant if the obtained X exceeded 5.99 the critical X^2 needed at the .05 level of significance, with df = 2 (Siegel, 1956).

Results

All Scripts: Tests for Significant Gender of Manager by Gender of Employee Interactions

In none of the scenarios was there obtained evidence of either men or women managers intending to behave differently toward men than women employees (see Tables 1 and 2).

Script A: Employee Reluctantly Complies With Manager's Order To Do Task Not Included in Current Job Description

Analysis of the data indicated that Brazilian men and women managers did not differ significantly in the ways in which they would attempt to resolve disputes with employees disgruntled because they were being asked to do something not in their job descriptions (see Table 3). Further, when combining data across gender of manager, neither did there appear to predominate a particular response style (see Table 5). Brazilian men and women managers were nearly equally divided in their preferences for using communication, power, or some combination thereof in attempting to resolve disputes with employees.

Script B: Employee Goes Beyond Boundaries of Authority and Violates Chain of Command

Analysis of the data indicated that Brazilian women were somewhat more likely than men to use some form of communication when attempting to resolve disputes with employees who had apparently violated chains of command (see Table 4). Nonetheless, it is also important to note that both women and men managers identified power as the preferred mechanism for resolving this particular dispute (see Table 6).

Discussion

There appears, then, considerable similarity in the management styles of Brazilian men and women managers, at least as indicated by the data analyzed for this paper. Both Brazilian men and women managers appear equally divided in their use of communication and power strategies to resolve disputes with employees contesting (apparently legitimately) tasks assigned to them but which are not specifically included in their job descriptions. Moreover, while, in general, Brazilian women managers appear somewhat more inclined than Brazilian men managers to use some form of communication when resolving disputes with employees who have violated the chain of command, the majority of Brazilian men and women managers identify power

26

strategies as the preferred means of resolving this dispute as well.

These findings are both similar and different from those obtained in a previous investigation in which 80 American men and women managers responded to the same two scenarios described in this study (Rossi and Todd-Mancillas, 1985). They are similar in that the previous investigation also found that American men and women managers were nearly equally divided in their use of communication and power strategies to resolve disputes with employees who had objected to doing something not included in their job description (Scenario A).

This may suggest that there may be a pancultural norm operating in management contexts, which requires communication and negotiation to clarify what is or is not the responsibility of an employee. However, this study yielded different results form the previous investigation in that when an employee has violated a chain of command, Brazilian women managers appear more similar to Brazilian men managers than American women managers in their reliance on power usage as a preferred means of resolving the problem.

What explains the finding that Brazilian women managers appear somewhat more prone to use power than American women managers? Perhaps the answer lies in recognizing that there are available to American managers, particularly American women managers a greater variety of managerial role models than what exist in Brazil for Brazilian women managers. In Latin America, and to a far greater extent than in the United States, nearly all organizations have a long history of male stewardship (Aguiar, 1975; Ball, 1984). Further, the machismo tradition also strongly influences the way in which managers (usually male) supervise their employees (Taylor, 1984). Basically, a tradition of machismo predisposes a manager to be highly concerned about their image as a superior and to behave in a hostile manner when their position is threatened (Christensen, 1975; Paz, 1962). In a society, such as Brazil, where there are few women managers to begin with, and even less diversity in management styles, it may not be surprising that women managers have simply adopted the macho model of management, calling for liberal use of power (and punishment) when sanctioning employees ostensibly challenging their authority.

No such similar tendency may occur in the United States, because there exists in this country a greater variety of role models to follow and because the culture is more attuned to the problems women encounter as they struggle to advance themselves in the market place. (Note, for instance, the plethora of trade

27

books and talk shows focusing on some or another problem that women must surmount to succeed in business.)

This study is one of the first to be done by communication researchers, which focuses on intercultural factors affecting communication between managers and their employees. Efforts are under way to expand this line of research by translating scenarios used in this study into Chinese and French, so that similar studies can be done in China and France. This additional research, as well as research undertaken by others (e.g., Korzenny, Korzenny, & Sanchez de Rota, 1985), will help us to develop a fuller appreciation for the role culture plays in affecting managerial communication.

Appendix A
(Script A)

Employee Reluctantly Complies With Manager's Order
To Do Task Not Included in Current Job Description

(Marge/Mario) is the supervisor of several employees in the stock room at an organization. Just recently, the position of inventory control clerk was eliminated. Marge's employees are now responsible for controlling and monitoring the amount of inventory on hand. Marge says, "When an order came in, I assigned the task of doing the inventory work to one of the clerks. She appeared angry, but did do the inventory control work. I found out later, via the grapevine, that the clerk felt she should not have had to do the inventorying. She felt that it was my responsibility to do it with her, after the fact, that it was now her responsibility to inventory the stock unpacked. I was met with lots of resistance, because it was her expectation that this was my responsibility and vice versa."

(Maria/Mario) supervisiona diversos funcionários no setor de estoque de uma companhia. Recentemente, a posição do empregado que fazia o balanço das mercadorias foi eliminada na companhia. Agora os empregados de Maria são responsáveis pelo controle e balanço do estoque. Maria diz que "quando recebemos um carregamento, eu solicitei a uma das funcionárias para fazer o balanço das mercadorias. Ela ficou braba, mas terminou por fazer. Descobri mais tarde, através de boato no escritório, que a funcionária disse que não deveria ser obrigada a fazer o balanço, pois acreditava que isto era minha responsabilidade. O problema nesta situação foi o de persuadi-la, depois do facto ter ocorrido, de que de agora em dianta ela seria responsável pelo balanço das mercadorias. Encontrei muita resistencia de sua parte, pois ela achava que era minha obrigação fazer o balanço e vice-versa."

Employee Goes Beyond Boundaries of Authority
and Violates Chain of Command

(Jean/Joseph) is the supervisor of a senior clerk and several entry-level clerks in an organization, but she and the senior clerk have experienced difficulties in defining the boundaries of authority in the department. "For example," Jean says, "She had been given responsibility for calculating the statistics of a report that is published by another department. When he encountered an error in some of this data, rather than coming to me with it, he went to the other department manager. This angered the other manager, since he felt that my subordinate should have checked with me before coming to him. I also felt that this was the case, so it was very difficult for me to support my subordinate when the angered department manager contacted me to complain about the senior clerk's "uppity" behavior. If he (the senior clerk) had just come to me first, we could have gone together to the department manager, and none of the anger would have occurred, and lots of time would have been saved in clarifying the error."

(Nara/Nilo) supervisiona um datilógrafo e vários outros funcionários em uma companhia. Entretanto, ela e o funcionário tiveram alguma dificuldade em estabelecer o parâmetro de autoridade do datilógrafo no departamento. "Por exemplo," disse Nara, "o datilógrafo era responsável pelo cálculo de um relatório estatístico que era publicado por um outro departamento. Quando encontrou um erro nos dados fornecidos pelo outro departamento, em vez de me comunicar sobre isto, foi direto ao supervisor do outro departamento. O supervisor ficou irritado, pois achava que meu funcionário deveria ter me consultado antes. Eu também achei que o funcionário nao agiu corretamente e por isso foi difícil para mim dar-lhe apoio quando o outro supervisor veio reclamar. Se meu datilógrafo tivesse me consultado, nos teríamos ido juntos falar com o supervisor e assim nada disto teria ocorrido e nos teríamos poupado tempo e energia, esclarecendo a atitude do datilógrafo."

Employee Challenges Manager's Competence to Give Correct
Instructions on How To Do an Assigned Task

(Kathy/Ken) was hired by a local company not only to manage the office, but also to check the accuracy of the work being done by the employees. In this capacity, she not only instructs people in the office about how certain procedures are to be carried out, but also is responsible for giving them feedback when they make mistakes. One of the female employees in the office repeatedly made the same mistake in completing a form. When Kathy went to her for the third time to explain how the form was to be completed, she "told me that she didn't think I was right. She suggested that I call the head office and make sure that my instructions were correct. I walked away knowing that I was right, but I called the office anyway. As I suspected, I was right. Only after she had seen me call the head office and get their information did she accept the fact that she was doing something wrong and that my suggestions were right. My feedback alone was not enough, though."

(Lisa/Luiz) foi admitida em uma companhia local nao apenas para chefiar o escritório, como também para checar a precisão do trabalho executado pelos empregados. Neste sentido, tinha que instruir os funcionários daquele setor sobre a maneira como certos procedimentos deveriam ser executados a fazer comentários quando encountrasse erros. Uma funcionária no escritório, continuamente, cometia o mesmo erro ao completar um formulário. Quando Lisa a abordou pela terceira vez para explicar como o formulário devaria ser preenchido, a empregada disse que "ela achava que eu estava errada e sugeriu que em chamasse o escritório central para confirmar minha informação. Afastei-me da funcionária, sabendo que estava correta, mas chamei o escritório de qualquer maneira para satisfazê-la. Como achava, eu estava correta. Apenas depois de presenciar meu telefonema e que a funcionária admitiu estar errada. Portanto, minha instrução por si só não foi suficiente para convencê-la a preencher o formulário como eu estava dizendo."

Appendix D
(Script D)

High-Level Employee's Authority is Challenged
by Other High-Level Employees (Managers)

(Jane/John) was hired by her employer to develop personnel
policies and procedures. The organization had tripled in size
since its creation, and the need for someone in this capacity was
apparent to her employer. As Jane familiarized herself with the
organization, she realized the need for reports which specified a
supervisor's reason(s) for terminating an employee. All of the
supervisors in the organization were men. They reacted to Jane's
procedure by telling her that the forms were unnecessary, and
since they hadn't done this type of reporting before, why did
they need to now. Jane said, "I had to persuade them of the
importance of this type of documentation. Two of the supervisors
even went to my boss and asked about the necessity of such
reports. It was fortunate that my boss endorsed me. However, a
great deal of time was wasted in persuading the supervisors. I
felt as if I had to defend not only the credibility of the
reporting, but also my credibility."

(Jane/Juca) foi admitida por seu patrão para desenvolver
procedimentos e mormas involvendo problemas de demissão no
departamento de pessoal. A companhia em que trabalhava havia
triplicado em tamanho desde sua criação e a necessidade de
re-organização nesta área era aparente ao empregador. Enquanto
Jane se familiarizava com os procedimentos e normas em vigor na
companhia, ela se deu conta da necessidade de relatórios
especificando a razão ou razões para deemissão de funcionários.
Os gerentes da companhia reagiram as modificações sugeriada por
Jane dizendo que os formulários que ela queria implementar não
eram necessários e, como eles nunca precisaram preencher tais
formulários antes, nao viam qualquer razão para fazê-lo agora.
Jane disse, "eu tive que persuadir aqueles gerentes da
necessidade deste tipo de documentação. Dois dos gerentes
inclusive foram perguntar ao meu patrão sobre a necessidade de
tais formulários. Felizmente, meu patrão me deu apoio.
Entretanto, muito tempo foi disperdiçado persuadindo os gerentes.
Neste caso, tive que defender não apenas a credibilidade dos
formulários, como também minha própria credibilidade."

Appendix E

Example of Communication as the Predominate Response Mode

Female Manager

I'd involve all supervisors in my decision so it would be easier to persuade them about the need for change.

Male Manager

I'd involve the other supervisors in my decision. It'd take longer, but in the long run we would save time.

Examples of Use of Power as the Predominate Response Mode

Female Manger

I'd be very angry with my clerk. I'd take him to the other manager to explain himself and would warn him about similar situations in the future.

Male Manager

I'd apologize to the other manager and terminate the clerk. I'd ask that a memo would be sent out to all employees clarifying the lines of communication in the organization.

Examples of Combined Use of Power and Communication as Predominate Response Mode

Female Manager

I'd explain the situation to my employees and I'd try to find a volunteer to do the job. If I couldn't find a volunteer, I'd choose someone everytime the task had to be done.

Male Manager

I'd inform the employee of her new duty and would emphasize her qualities to perform the job.

33

Table 1

Script A

(Employee Reluctantly Complies with Manager's Order
to Do Task Not Included in Current Job Description)

Women Managers

Response Style

	Communication	Power	Mixed
Male Employees	6	6	8
Female Employees	7	9	4

$X^2 = 2.02$

Men Managers

Response Style

	Communication	Power	Mixed
Male Employees	9	7	4
Female Employees	4	9	6

$X^2 = 2.55$

Table 2

Script B

(Employee Goes Beyond Boundaries of Authority and
Violates Chain of Command)

Women Managers

Response Style

	Communication	Power	Mixed
Male Employees	1	14	5
Female Employees	3	11	5

Men Managers

Response Style

	Communication	Power	Mixed
Male Employees	1	19	0
Female Employees	1	17	2

NOTE: In each of the above tables, at least two of the six cells have expected frequencies less than 5. Accordingly, it was not appropriate to compute X^2 values (Siegle, 1956). However, inspection of the tables makes apparent that both women and men managers identified power usage as the preferred option, and, further, that neither women nor men managers indicated they would treat male employees differently from female employees.

Table 3

Script A

Women Managers Contrasted With Men Managers

(Employee Reluctantly Complies with Manager's Order
to Do Task Not Included in Current Job Description)

Women Managers

Response Style

	Communication	Power	Mixed
Women Managers	13	15	12
Men Managers	13	16	10

$X^2 = .20$

36

Table 4

Script B

Women Managers Contrasted With Men Managers

(Employee Goes Beyond Boundaries of Authority
and Violates Chain of Command)

Response Style

	Communication	Power	Mixed
Women Managers	4	25	10
Men Managers	2	36	2

X^2 = 7.25 (significant at alpha = .05; df = 2).*

*Because two cells had expected frequencies less than 5, the communication and mixed cells were combined, thereby meeting appropriate criteria for the computation of X^2 values, while at the same time allowing one to determine whether one or the other gender had a significant preference for using power.

37

Table 5

Script A

Data From Women and Men Managers Combined

(Employee Reluctantly Complies With Manager's Order to Do
Task Not Included in Current Job Description)

Response Style

	Communication	Power	Mixed
	26	31	22

$X^2 = 1.54$

Table 6

Script B

Data From Women and Men Managers Combined

(Employee Goes Beyond Boundaries of Authority
and Violates Chain of Command)

Response Style

	Communication	Power	Mixed
	6	61	12

X^2 = 69.15 (significant at alpha = .05, df = 2).

References

Aguiar, N. (1975). Impact of industrialization on women's work role in northeast Brazil. Studies in Comparative International Development, 10, 78–94.

Baird, J. E. and Bradley, P. H. (1979). Styles of management and communication: A comparative study of men and women. Communication Monographs, 46, 101–111.

Ball, R., (1984, April). Italy's most talked-about executive. Fortune, 99–102.

Christensen, E. W. (1975). Counseling Puerto Ricans: Some cultural considerations. Personnel and Guidance Journal, 53, 349–356.

Korzenny, B. A., Korzenny, F. and Sanchez de Rota, G. (1985). Women's communication in Mexican organizations. Sex Roles, A Journal of Research, 12, 867–876.

Lannon, J. M. (1977). Male vs female values in management. Management International Review, 17, 9–12.

Paz, O. (1962). The labyrinth of solitude. New York: Grove.

Rossi, A. M. and Todd-Mancillas, W. R. (1987). Communication differences in managing conflict with male and female employees: Does context make a difference? In L. Stewart and S. Ting-Toomey (Eds.), Communication, gender and sex roles in diverse interaction contexts (pp. 96–104). Norwood: Ablex.

Rossi, A. M. and Wolesensky, B. (1983). Women in management: Different strategies for handling problematic communication interaction with subordinates. Proceedings of the Annual Meeting of the American Business Communication Association. 79–93.

Siegel, S., (1956). Nonparametric statistics for the behavioral sciences (pp. 42–47 104–111), New York: McGraw Hill.

Taylor, F. (1984). Women grab management in home of machismo. International Magazine, 24–27.

Todd-Mancillas, W. R. and Rossi, A. M. (1985). Gender differences in the management of personnel disputes. Women's Studies in Communication, 8, 25–33.

Wolesensky, B. (1981). Communication problems encountered by supervisory and managerial women in their interactions with subordinates. Unpublished manuscript. University of Nebraska-Lincoln, Department of Speech Communication, Lincoln.

CHAPTER 4

COMMUNICATION SCRIPT ANALYSIS:
A FOUR-PART MODEL FOR PREDICTING PERCEPTION OF
SEXUAL HARASSMENT

Melanie Booth-Butterfield, West Virginia University

Four variables appear strong in predicting why one
person may label behavior "sexual harassment" while
others are less inclined to interpret communication as
harassing: 1) the immediacy of the communication, 2)
employment in a field dominated by or balanced with
members of the opposite sex, 3) information about
anti-harassment guidelines, and 4) prior experience
with harassment. Communication scripts provide a useful framework for examining how potentially threatening
information is processed and the impact these four
elements have on interpretation of communication
interactions.

Reports on the phenomenon of sexually harassing communication have occupied substantial journal space in recent years.
Incidence surveys tend to be most numerous (Collins & Blodgett,
1981; Glamour, 1979; Kelber, 1975; Safran, 1976; Verba, DiNunzio,
& Spaulding, 1983). In addition social science researchers
investigate the personal impact of sexual harassment (Crull,
1979; Josefowitz, 1982), organizational concerns with its
prevention (Driscoll, 1981; Hoyman & Robinson, 1980; Linenberger
& Keaveny, 1982; Neugarten & Shafritz, 1980), and implications
for litigation (Faley, 1982; Goldberg, 1978; Somers, 1982).
Others attempt to define sexually harassing communication (Booth-
Butterfield, 1983; Reilly, Carpenter, Dull, & Bartlett, 1982) or
explore reasons for its occurrence (Gutek & Morasch, 1982, Kansas
City Times, 1981; Remland & Jones, 1984; Tangri, Burt, & Johnson,
1982).

Yet the fact remains that there is very little consensus on
the communication behavior which will be labeled sexually
harassing. Men are often less likely than women to consider
sexual innuendo, joking, or certain nonverbal actions as sexual
harassment (Tangri et al., 1982; U.S. Office of Merit Systems,
1981) and may disagree on the frequency of such occurrences as
well (Collins & Blodgett, 1981).

However, all women do not perceive sexually harassing
communication uniformly either. Collins and Blodgett (1981),
Booth-Butterfield (1983), and Linenberger and Keaveny (1982) all
describe wide discrepancies in subjects' perceptions of sexual
harassment, both between and within the sex groupings. There-

fore, what is needed is a model to predict who is most likely to interpret communication behaviors as harassing and an explanation of factors leading to this interpretation. In other words, given two individuals facing the same situation, what conditions will make one more likely than the other to interpret communication as "sexual harassment?"

Four components appear strong in predicting perception of sexual harassment: 1) the immediacy of the communication behavior, 2) employment in a profession dominated by or balanced with members of the opposite sex, 3) information concerning harassment guidelines, and 4) prior experience in a harassing situation. The scripts concept is useful in showing the relationship of each of these variables to the labeling of sexually harassing communication. As each component adds comparison information and detail to existing employment scripts, it increases the likelihood that sexual communication will be recognized as an inappropriate part of that script and labeled "harassment."

THE SCRIPT CONCEPT

Scripts are those sets of expectations and rules which guide us in enacting and interpreting routine communication interactions (Abelson, 1976, 1981; Schank & Abelson, 1977; Berger & Douglas, 1982). Specifically, a script is a "hyopthesized cognitive structure that when activated organizes comprehension of event-based situations" (Abelson, 1981, p. 717). Thus, when a script is activated we tend to perceive and enact communication according to the pattern established by that script. For example, if our "mother" or "father" script is activated we tend to send and interpret messages according to the expectations of a parent.

Although the schema/script concept has received criticism for being "mushy" and broad enough to explain almost any behavior (Fiedler, 1982; Fiske & Linville, 1980), it can be a sound tool when implemented with a cognitive construct such as information processing (Fiske & Linville, 1980; Shaklee, 1983). This approach produces a more precise explanation of the way scripts are developed and the impact of existing scripts on subsequent information processing. The central tenet of the information-processing approach is that "the organism actively seeks out information in the environment, operates on this information, and adjusts its behavior according to some internal representation of this knowledge" (Markus & Sentis, 1982, p. 43). The "script" is just such an internal representation. Accordingly, it is not sufficient to observe communicative actions in order to understand someone's responses, but we must also understand how those actions fit into the individual's overall pattern of "knowledge of the world." Markus and Sentis further explain that these schemata or scripts are central cognitive units in this human information processing system. If we examine the way information is interpreted, organized, and acted upon in explaining script application, the construct becomes tighter and more appropriate for use in predicting behavior.

Most individuals have many cognitive structures, scripts, which facilitate functioning in day-to-day communication situations. A frequently cited example is Schank and Abelson's typical "restaurant script" for entering, ordering, and eating in a restaurant (1977). This script provides the individual with a set of rules and expectations so that when a new restaurant is entered it is not necessary to completely re-learn appropriate behaviors.

Along similar lines, Bem explains many sex role-associated behaviors and ideas in terms of gender schemas or scripts (1981). Langer describes certain overlearned and automatic behaviors, such as complying with small requests, as a type of scripted behavior (Langer, Blank & Chanowitz, 1978; Langer & Imber, 1978). Douglas (1983) uses a script approach to compare high and low self-monitors' communication in initial interactions. In each instance comparisons are drawn between communication behaviors which are congruent with a script and those which are not. Communication which is congruent with an operative script does not receive special attention and tends to be processed almost automatically. However, when behaviors are recognized at a conscious level as inconsistent with the ongoing script performance, special action must be undertaken to deal effectively with the new event. This model of analysis can be implemented in explaining how sexually harassing communication is processed.

Two aspects of scripts are particularly important for understanding how we function in a scripted situation: action rules and commitment (Abelson, 1981). First, a particular script is activated when we encounter the situation. At that time a set of "action rules" guides our interaction (Abelson, 1981; Cushman, 1977; Pearce, 1973). Such rules may serve to a) guide specific communicative behavior or b) form sets of expectations for interpreting the interaction. The handshake/greeting is a simple example of the guidance function. Action rules dictate that in most professional settings a handshake is the expected form of greeting. Therefore, we don't have to think extensively about it or try to interpret the action.

Second, when we have initiated a script performance we typically feel committed to carry through with it unless the rules are violated or something unusual or atypical distracts us (Langer et al. 1978; Abelson, 1981). To illustrate, when we

45

enact our restaurant script by entering the restaurant, we typically comply with situational rules without comment. It may only be when the host leads us far to the rear of the dining area next to the restrooms and kitchen that we put a halt to the automatic compliance with this script. For some people even this violation is insufficient to warrant breaking out of the routine. The concept of commitment to the action script is particularly important in understanding perception of sexually harassing communication. As long as coercive behaviors are labeled part of the work routine people exhibit commitment to complete the working script.

We have cognitive scripts for most communication situations which occur regularly and repeatedly. These constitute "abstract summaries of recurring events," (Berger & Douglas, 1982, p. 44) and employment routines fall within this definition for most of us. "Behavior at work" scripts guide day-to-day communication so that interactions are conducted in an expected and predictable manner. For some people low-level sexually harassing communication is incorporated as part of their routine script. For others the harassment draws attention to itself and breaks into the scripted communication. It is this process which we next examine.

MODEL COMPONENTS

#1 Immediacy

The more direct and immediate the sexually harassing communication, the more likely it is to break through the scripted routine and be labeled "harassment."

Booth-Butterfield (1983) found a strong relationship between the immediacy of the behavior and the intensity and frequency with which it was labeled harassing.[1] That is, if the behavior was gazing or innuendo rather than direct touching or verbal threat to the harassee, the communication was less likely to be recognized and interpreted as harassment. Low-level harassing behavior tends not to interrupt the "behavior at work" script by emerging as an atypical situation. Instead it is often easier for such ambiguous communication to be processed as a "mistake" or incorrect perception of intent. For example, Reilly et al. reported that although much disagreement existed concerning ambiguous, suggestive behavior, an instructor's explicit threat to a student that her grades could suffer if she didn't cooperate was the best predictor in determining perception of sexual harassment (1982). In addition, situations which threatened physical force were rated higher in perceived harassment than threat without use of force.

46

The directness and immediacy of such threats allows little room for alternate interpretations when processing information into the script. Few people mistake direct, immediate coercion for a routine part of their "behavior at work" script. When sexual behavior or communication rises above the threshold of awareness, it draws attention to itself and becomes information to be processed separately from the script. Thus, the phenomenon is increasingly likely to be labeled as harassing.

#2 Occupation

Sexually harassing communication is more likely to be recognized and labeled harassment if the target is employed in a field populated by the opposite sex.

When targets receive social-sexual communication at work, a phenomenon Gutek and Morasch term sex-role spill-over (1982), it is readily apparent that their co-workers of the opposite sex are not treated in the same way. The background provided by opposite sex co-workers sets off recognition of the action. Targets of harassment become aware through social comparison, that they are being singled out for attention as individual women or men rather than functional employees. Wicklund and Frey (1980) report that heightened self awareness leads to less conformity to scripts. In other words, the recognition that others are not treated as you are, leads to re-evaluation of the script. An employee might decide that "behavior at work" scripts should be similar for all employees regardless of gender.

Such contrasts are typically most pronounced in opposite-sex dominated occupations such as architect, machinist, or coal miner for women or nursing and secretarial jobs for men. Gutek and Morasch (1982) report that females in male-dominated work were more likely to report receiving social-sexual behaviors. In comparison, people employed in a same-sex dominated field such as female secretaries or waitresses appear to incorporate harassing communication into their overall perception of the job. For example, females in traditional work such as waitress or stenographer were less likely to report being the target of sexual comments or harassment. Instead they referred to such communication as "part of the job" (Gutek & Morasch, 1982). Such behavior is processed as part of the "behavior at work" script because employees have no clear background (i.e. co-workers of the opposite sex) against which to compare questionable behavior.

#3 Information

The more a person is educated about harassment the more likely he or she is to recognize and label harassing communica-tion as an inappropriate part of the work script.

Bargh (1982) discusses "active scripts" which can be elicited to overcome an already established, passive behavioral script. By changing specific instructions for a task and thereby inducing an active script for the situation, the passive script can be over-ridden by the new information. A useful example is the "women's consciousness-raising" groups active in the 1970's. Their goal was to cause people to analyze and consider sex role concepts which previously had remained unquestioned.

Nevertheless, illustrative of Langer's (1978) "mindless" processing of information many people never question sexist or coercive communication behaviors because such behaviors are part of the regular routine. However, in Bargh's terms an "active" script has been implemented when an employee "raises his or her consciousness" about legal or ethical guidelines against harassing communication. Subsequently, if coercive communication occurs it is more likely to be recognized and labeled harassment. While such active scripts are relatively short-lived, it seems logical that repetition and practice with the information would lead to incorporation of the short-term "active" script into the more stable "behavior at work" script. This is presumably one of the intentions of descriptive/advisory articles and EEOC published guidelines against harassment.

In contrast, as long as a worker remains uninformed those coercive or unethical behaviors are likely to be assimilated into the overall "behavior at work" script. Again the result would be non-recognition of sexually harassing communication. Behavior which legally and ethically falls within the category of "sexual harassment" may not be perceived as such until the employee has new information and is made specifically aware through induction of a new script.

#4 Previous Experience

People who have previous experience with recognized harassment are more likely to interpret subsequent communication as harassing.

Fazio and Zanna (1978) found that attitudes learned through direct experience correlate more strongly with behavior than do attitudes learned without direct involvement. One's attitudes toward harassment may not be as strong a predictor of actual labeling or interpretation of behavior if the labeler has never directly experienced harassing communication. The naive person's script remains intact until he or she becomes directly involved in the threatening interaction. Education ABOUT harassment is probably not as salient as direct exerience WITH harassment.

This aspect may explain why men often don't perceive harassment in communication situations where women do (Booth-Butterfield, 1983; Collins & Blodgett, 1981; Reilly et al., 1982). Whether because of cultural inequities, sex-role stereotyping, or asymetrical power, women are more likely to be in a position to directly experience harassment. Most studies agree that women are still the primary targets of harassment. However, a man's perception of the problem may be heightened in the event that it is his wife, daughter, friend, or even himself who is the target. At that point harassing communication becomes a salient part of the man's environment as well, and the possibility of harassment occurring is added to his "behavior at work" script (Graesser, Gordon, & Sawyer, 1979; Graesser, Woll, Kowalski, & Smith, 1980). It is interesting to note that while female students saw the most harassment in situations presented by Reilly and associates, male students who are also potential targets of instructor harassment perceived more harassment than did faculty members (Reilly et al., 1982). According to Abelson (1981), the expectation of such a potential outcome facilitates organization of the script. Awareness of harassing phenomena is enhanced, increasing the likelihood that an observer will label behavior "harassment." Without comparable direct experience others might not recognize sexually harassing communication.

IMPLICATIONS

Each of the elements of the model, 1) immediacy, 2) employment in occupations populated by both sexes, 3) information about harassing behaviors, and 4) prior experience with sexually harassing communication, may operate individually to interrupt scripted communication. The elements may also converge and overlap to more strongly predict perception of sexual harassment. For example, a woman working in a male-dominated profession who had a former employer threaten her sexually is probably more likely to label subsequent behavior harassing than is a female teacher in a private school who has never encountered direct harassing cues. In the former case low level sexual communication may be interpreted as harassment, while in the latter example breaking through the "behavior at work" script might be contingent upon more direct, immediate, and unambiguous harassing communication.

A final note is in order concerning the environment in which the scripted behavior is enacted. Organizations may transmit subtle cues regarding appropriate "behavior at work" scripts, including organizational agendas and suitable interpretation of communication cues (Booth-Butterfield, 1984). While it is not the primary focus of this paper, the importance of context cannot be ignored when examining perception of communication behavior.

This model of predicting response to potentially harassing communication cues has several important implications for understanding why some people see coercion in situations where others do not. First, this approach avoids making harassing communication a women's issue. The script model is explanatory for both male and female perceptions.

Second, instead of labeling non-perceivers as hostile, ignorant, or supportive of sexually harassing norms, this perspective focuses on a person's script of work communication. Thus the perception of sexual harassment becomes more amenable to "consciousness-raising" or education in order to alter the script and increase individuals' awareness of communication which is unethical although not blatantly sexual.

Further, this 4-part model has implications for training workers to recognize and deal with potentially harassing situations. Active scripts can be developed to provide alternative "work scripts." Such scripts might emphasize women and men in more equalitarian work roles and thus sensitize employees to communicative violations. This aspect in turn could help avert harassment in organizational settings rather than dealing with it after the incident occurs. This has been a key concern in personnel management in recent years (Driscoll, 1981; Faley, 1982).

Finally, the next logical step with this model is direct empirical testing of the effects of immediacy, career choice, prior experience and topical knowledge on the perception of sexual harassment. Results from existing empirical analyses offer some support for the model. Booth-Butterfield (1983), Collins and Blodgett (1981), Tangri et al. (1982), and Reilly et al. (1982) all report differences in perception of harassment based on the extremity and immediacy of the behavior. Behaviors at extremes of coercion are consistently regarded as harassment, but as the immediacy declines so does agreement.

Several organizations suggest workshops or other educational settings to increase workers' information on what constitutes "harassment" (Collins & Blodgett, 1981; Kroenenberger & Bourke, 1981; Livingston, 1982). However, the direct impact of such information on potential targets of harassment has yet to be assessed.

Most incidence studies support the third component of the model, prior experience with harassment, as a predictor of perception (Reilly et al., 1982; Tangri et al., 1982; US Merit Systems, 1981). Reilly and colleagues specifically noted that a) males exhibited less agreement on harassing communication than did females and b) that there was more agreement among respondents who had been victims of sexual harassment than among nonvictims.

Finally, the gender balance of work environment has also received limited support. Tangri et al. (1982) and Gutek and Morasch (1982) report increased recognition of sexually unethical communication when the male-female ratio in the work population was balanced or dominated by the opposite sex.

While these results are promising, the four central components have not been the primary independent variables of research. Future studies need to examine the direct impact of each element of the model on labeling of sexual harassment. Nevertheless, communication script analysis currently offers a coherent model for predicting circumstances under which people are most likely to perceive communication behaviors as sexually harassing.

NOTES

1. The development and validation of the Perception of Sexual Harassment Scale was reported by Booth-Butterfield in 1983. Over the course of two years the scale was administered to over 500 undergraduate students at three separate universities. The 24-item scale reports internal reliabilities between .85 and .91. It exhibits no relationship with the need for social approval (Crowne-Marlowe), self-monitoring, or communication apprehension. Females have consistently scored significantly higher than males on the perception of sexually harassing communication. Additional testing is in progress. For further information on the scale contact the author.

Abelson, R. (1976). Script processing in attitude formation and decision-making. In J. S. Carroll & J. W Payne (Eds.). Cognition and Social Behavior. Hillsdale, N.J.: Erlbaum.

Abelson, R. (1981). Psychological status of the script concept. American Psychologist, 36, 715-729.

Bargh, J. (1982). Attention and automaticity in the processing of self-relevant information. Journal of Personality and Social Psychology, 43, 425-436.

Bem, S. (1981). Gender schema theory, a cognitive account of sex typing. Psychological Review, 88, 354-64.

Berger, C. & Douglas, W. (1982). Thought and talk: "Excuse me, but have I been talking to myself?" in F. Dancc (Ed.) Human Communication Theory, 42-60. New York: Harper & Row Publishers.

Booth-Butterfield, M. (1983). An empirical investigation of sexually harassing communication. Paper presented at Speech Communication Association convention. Washington, D.C.

Booth-Butterfield, M. (1984). Communication strategies in harassment-prone organizational climates. Paper presented at Central States Speech Association, Indianapolis.

Brewer, M. (1982). Further beyond nine to five: An integration and future directions. Journal of Social Issues, 38, 149-158.

Collins, E. & Blodgett, T. (1981). Sexual harassment: Some see it, some won't. Harvard Business Review, 59, 76-96.

Cushman, D. (1977). The rules perspective as a theoretical basis for the study of human communication. Communication Quarterly, 25, 30-45.

Douglas, W. (1983). Scripts and self monitoring: When does being a high self monitor really make a difference? Human Communication Research, 10, 81-96.

Driscoll, J. (1981). Sexual attraction and harassment: Management's new problems. Personal Journal, 60, 33-57.

Faley, R. (1982). Sexual Harassment: A critical review of legal cases with general principles and preventative measures. Personnel Psychology, 35, 583-600.

Fazio, R. & Zanna, M. (1978). Attitudinal qualities relating to the strength of the attitude-behavior relationship. Journal of Experimental Social Psychology, 14, 398-407.

Fiedler, K. (1982). Causal schemata: Review and criticism of research on a popular construct. Journal of Personality and Social Psychology, 42, 1001-1013.

Fiske, S. & Linville, P. (1980). What does the schema concept buy us? Personality and Social Psychology Bulletin, 6, 543-557.

Glamour (1979). How working women feel now about jobs, men, and salaries. February, p. 149.

Goldberg, A. (1978). Sexual Harassment and Title VII: The foundation for elimination of sexual cooperation as an employment condition. Michigan Law Review, 76, 1007-1035.

Graesser, A., Gordon, S., & Sawyer, J. (1979). Recognition memory for typical and atypical actions in scripted activities: Tests of a script pointer plus tag hypotheses. Journal of Verbal Learning and Verbal Behavior, 18, 319-32.

Graesser, A., Woll, S., Kowalski, D., & Smith, D. (1980). Memory for typical and atypical actions in scripted activities. Journal of Experimental Psychology: Human Learning and Memory, 6, 503-515.

Gutek, B. & Morasch, B. (1982). Sex-ratios, sex-role spillover, and sexual harassment of women at work. Journal of Social Issues, 38, 55-74.

Hoyman, M. & Robinson, R. (1980). Interpreting the new sexual harassment guidelines. Personnel Journal, 59, 996-1000.

Josefowitz, N. (1982). Sexual relationships at work: Attraction, transference, coercion, or strategy. Personnel Administrator, 27, 91-96.

Kansas City Times (1981). Mrs. Schlafley calls it "body language"; others call it sexual harassment. April 22, p. A-1.

Kelber, M. (1975). The UN's dirty little secret. Ms. 5, 51.

Kronenberger, G. & Bourke, D. (1981). Effective training and the elimination of sexual harassment. Personnel Journal, 60, 879-883.

Langer, E., Blank, A., & Chanowitz, B. (1978). The mindlessness of ostensibly thoughtful action. Journal of Personality and Social Psychology, 36, 635-42.

Langer, E. & Imber, L. (1979). When practice makes imperfect: Debilitating effects of overlearning. Journal of Personality and Social Psychology, 37, 2014-2024.

Livingston, J. (1982). Responses to sexual harassment on the job: Legal, organizational, and individual actions. Journal of Social Issues, 38, 5-22.

Markus, H. & Sentis, K. (1982). The self in social information processing. In J. Suls (Ed.) Psychological Perspectives on the Self. Hillsdale, N.J.: Erlbaum.

Neugarten, D. & Shafritz, J. (1980). Sexuality in Organizations. Oak Park, Illinois: Moore Publishing.

Pearce, B. (1973). Consensual rules in interpersonal communication: A reply to Cushman and Whiting. Journal of Communication, 23, 160-168.

Reilly, T., Carpenter, S., Dull, V. & Bartlett, K. (1982). The factorial survey: An approach to defining sexual harassment on campus. Journal of Social Issues, 38, 99-110.

Remland, M. & Jones, T. (1984). Sex differences, communication consistency, and judgements of sexual harassment. Paper presented at Central States Speech Association, Indianapolis, IN.

Safran, C. (1976). What men do to women on the job. Redbook, November, 149.

Schank, R. & Abelson, R. (1977). Scripts, Plans, Goals, and Understanding. Hillsdale, N.J.: Erlbaum.

Shaklee, H. (1983). Causal schemata: Description or explanation of judgement process: A reply to Fiedler. Journal of Personality and Social Psycology, 45, 1010-1012.

Somers, A. (1982). Sexual harassment in academe: Legal issues and definitions. Journal of Social Issues, 38, 23-32.

Tangri, S., Burt, M., & Johnson, L. (1982). Sexual harassment at work: Three explanatory models. _Journal of Social Issues_, _38_, 33-54.

U.S. Merit Systems Protection Board (1981). Sexual harassment in the federal workplace: Is it a problem? Washington D.C.; USGPO.

Verba, S., DiNunzio, J., & Spaulding, C. (1983). Unwanted attention: Report on a sexual harassment survey. Report to the faculty council of the faculty of arts and sciences, Harvard University.

Waks, J., & Starr, M. (1982). The "sexual shakedown" in perspective: Sexual harassment in its social and legal contexts. _Employee Relations Law Journal_, _7_, 567-586.

Wicklund, R. & Frey, D. (1980). Self-awareness theory: When the self makes a difference. In D. M. Wegener & R. R. Vallacher (Eds.), _The Self in Social Psychology_. New York: Oxford University Press.

CHAPTER 5

THE GENDER SHIFT IN JOURNALISM EDUCATION

Maurine H. Beasley, University of Maryland

What happens when an academic field within communications changes from predominantly male to female? In 1977 the percentage of women students enrolled in journalism nationally surpassed that of men students. Today about 60 percent of all journalism students are women. Yet this is a development that has received almost no attention from educators.

It is the purpose of this paper to analyze the situation and to raise the issues involved for discussion. It ends with a proposed research agenda on this subject.

I. Historical Background

As the 1960s opened, the position of women in higher education was weaker than it had been three decades before. In 1960, women received 35 percent of all bachelors' degrees awarded; in 1930 they had received 40 percent. American women were pictured in the media as affluent housewives, fulfilled by their husbands, homes and children, although 36 percent of all women worked for pay. But the myth of the "happy homemaker" soon was challenged by a movement for women's liberation that had widespread impact on colleges and universities (Deckard, 1983).

As an outgrowth of the civil rights struggle for Black Americans, women became increasingly politicized. Linked to the New Left, which opposed the Viet-Nam war, women's groups waged their own fight for equality. An odd coalition of feminists, who sought passage, and southerners, who wanted to ridicule the bill to death, were behind 1964 civil rights legislation that outlawed sex discrimination under Title VII, the equal employment section of the measure. When the bill took effect in 1965, it became illegal to discriminate against women in hiring and promotions (Deckard, 1983).

Journalism education, long considered a male bastion, was forced to look at the composition of its faculties in light of the new federal law. What emerged was widespread evidence of prejudice against women. Roberta Applegate (1965), who had left an outstanding newspaper career as a political reporter to teach journalism at Kansas State University, found that 76 women faculty members, representing 56 schools or departments of journalism, belonged to the Association for Education in Journalism, the umbrella organization for all journalism educators. Of the 76, only seven had attained the full professor rank. Most were so isolated from participation in AEJ that only nine had attended the association's convention that year.

In fact, Applegate discovered, male dominance of the educator ranks had not changed much since the 1930s. She noted that "thirty-five years ago, two Helens -- Hostetter [Kansas State] and Patterson [Wisconsin] stuck together for moral support whenever they attended conventions of journalism educators. At the start, they didn't have much trouble finding each other because frequently they were the only women college faculty members present.

Applegate also reported two observations from male department heads about the lack of women faculty members. Charles E. Rogers, former head at Kansas State, cited "the fact that prejudice against women is still present to some degree." Grant M. Hyde, director at the University of Wisconsin, called for token hiring at least since one-third of the students were women.

Although the percentage of women students increased during the 1960s along with total enrollments, journalism education did not change dramatically. In 1968 the percentage of women stood at 41 percent of the student total. By 1970 there were 33,000 journalism majors in colleges and universities and the majority was male. The largest single group was in news-editorial. But old barriers for women were breaking down.[1]

In view of equal employment legislation, the Columbia University Graduate School of Journalism did away with its long-standing quota on women students, previously limited to 10 percent of the class. "Since there were few jobs on large newspapers for women, we had (we felt) no business making women qualified to be unemployed," recalled Professor Melvin Mencher. "My recollection is that The Wall Street Journal broke its sex barrier in 1970 when it hired Ellen Graham, but we stopped the quota system two years before," he continued. "The surprising thing is that though the women were 10 percent, they usually walked off with more than half the prizes. But perhaps it wasn't surprising: They were carefully selected."[2]

In 1972 three women journalism faculty members at Kansas State, Ramona Rush, Carol Oukrop and Sandra Ernst, presented results of the first formal study of women journalism educators at the annual convention of the Association for Education in Journalism. Key findings:

o For the year 1970-71, there were 131 women members of the association, representing 11 percent of the membership of 1,200.

These women were almost invisible within the organization. The official program of the annual meeting in 1971 did not show any woman on the convention program.

o No women were listed in the 1970-71 AEJ Directory as officials or even members of the association executive committee or its co-founding affiliates, advisory board or standing committees. Thus, women were not represented at all in the organization's official structure. No woman had ever been president of the association.

o The percentage of women involved in Journalism Quarterly, the main professional journal for journalism educators, was low. From 1960 to 1971, only seven percent of the contributors of major articles were women, with 59 women compared to 886 men having articles published in the journal. The percentage of women contributing to the "Research in Brief" section was slightly higher, with 10 percent of the articles (30 out of 290) written by women.

o The number of women faculty members nationally in journalism education was less than the number of women members of AEJ (which included professional journalists and students as well as teachers). In 1971-72, women constituted about eight percent of the total employed on journalism faculties. Only 10 were identified as having Ph.D. degrees (Rush, 1973).

o The lack of women faculty meant few role models for women graduate students in journalism and communication, Rush, Oukrop and Ernst found. Questionnaires sent by them to 101 women working on doctorate degrees at 16 universities elicited comments on the role conflicts faced by those preparing to be journalism educators. Fifty-seven percent out of 72 responding stated they had to "do more" than men to earn the respect of their professors and male graduate counterparts. Sample comments:

- "I feel that I am assumed to be dumb (because I'm female and look young) and must prove myself to be competent. Men, on the other hand, are automatically assumed to be competent unless proven stupid."

- "Both professionally and personally, women are suspect. It seems we must be better students than men and more womanly than non-student females."

- "I find that as a single woman one must be particularly careful to cultivate the wives and make it apparent I'm no threat to them -- that I am interested in their husbands only professionally" (Rush, 1973).

As a result of the report, AEJ appointed a committee on the Status of Women, which is still in existence. One of its first tasks was to follow up a study made by Women in Communications, as Theta Sigma Phi had renamed itself following a decision to admit men in 1972. (This came one year after Sigma Delta Chi had added the title of Society of Professional Journalists to its name and voted to accept women.) The Women in Communications study showed that 81 percent of 170 journalism schools had one or no woman on the faculty. Women in Communications called for an affirmative action program to increase the number of women faculty.[3]

In 1973, for the first time in the history of AEJ, the organization held a plenary session to spotlight the status of its women members. A survey of 60 schools led to the following conclusions: "If you teach journalism in a college or university which has a sequence accredited by the American Council on Education in Journalism and you are a woman, you tend to be ranked lower, promoted more slowly and paid less than your colleagues who are male." Of the eight percent of journalism faculty members who were female, two-thirds of them were in the lowest ranks: Instructor, lecturer or assistant professor. By contrast only one-third of the males were at the lower levels. (Marzolf, 1977).

The creation of the Committee on the Status of Women led to more research about the position of women within journalism education. A 1974 study showed that the number of women in journalism education took a funnel shape. At the undergraduate level it was large with women making up about half of the enrollment, but the number of women decreased at the master's level and represented only 10 percent of the doctoral candidates (Marzolf, 1977).

A shortage of qualified women to teach journalism was stressed in responses by 29 department heads to the effort by Women in Communications to urge employment of more women faculty members. They cited both lack of women with advanced degrees in communications and lack of authority from academic institutions to recognize extensive practical experience as a valuable substitute for advanced degrees. Since Ph.D. degrees were required for most positions leading to the prestige and pay of a full professorship, women with distinguished professional careers were limited to jobs on the lower levels, instructor or assistant professor, which paid significantly less than nonacademic positions (Daly, 1972-73).

Interest in the position of women on journalism faculties marked only one aspect of attempts by women to elevate their role in the media during the late 1960s and 1970s. Women's groups attacked the content of women's publications. They followed the lead of Betty Friedan, whose best-selling book, The Feminine Mystique, published in 1963, accused traditional magazines of depicting women only as sex objects or subservient housewives (Magid, 1977).

Women's portrayal and participation in the media became a well-publicized issue in March of 1970 in New York when feminists staged a sit-in at the Ladies Home Journal. The same week as the sit-in, women at Newsweek filed a complaint with the Equal Employment Opportunity Commission, the enforcement arm of the Civil Rights Act. They charged discrimination in employment because they were restricted to jobs as researchers while men held reporter-editor positions. An agreement between Newsweek and the women subsequently settled the complaint.

As the women's liberation movement spread, women became more assertive in demanding different treatment both as consumers of media and as working journalists. Feminist publications, ranging from Ms., a national monthly, to mimeographed newsletters, sprang up. After the National Organization of Women challenged a license renewal for WABC-TV in New York in 1972 on grounds the station discriminated against women, feminist groups obtained agreements with stations in Pennsylvania, Colorado, New York, Tennessee, and California. These contained promises to improve employment opportunities for women, and to take women's groups into account in programming. Newspapers did away with their traditional women's pages, replacing them with lifestyle sections aimed at readers of both sexes.⁴

More and more women poured into journalism schools. Lady Bird Johnson, the wife of President Lyndon B. Johnson, who held office from 1963 to 1968, helped publicize the major. Although she had never worked as a journalist, she held a degree in journalism from the University of Texas. "Not a day passes that I am not confronted with a situation, a group, a question that causes me to be grateful that I picked journalism for my major," she wrote in 1965 (Johnson, 1965). In 1967-68, journalism enrollment rose for the eighth consecutive year with a total of 24,445 students enrolled in courses at 118 schools. This represented an enrollment increase of 9.4 percent, which exceeded the over-all college enrollment gain of 8.3 percent (*Matrix*, 1968, February).

Upon graduation women journalists still faced the prospect of lower pay and fewer chances for promotions than men. A 1970 survey of 616 members of Theta Sigma Phi showed that the women, many of whom had lengthy experience, made an average of $838 per month compared to $578 monthly for beginning journalism graduates. By far, the majority said they felt, or knew, they were not paid as well as their male counterparts for equal work (Quinn, 1971).

The Matrix reported, "In spite of laws against discrimination, some employers frankly tell their women employees that they cannot expect to make as much as men. Many women feel that they would be in serious trouble with their bosses if they openly insisted on equal pay for equal work" (Quinn, 1971).

To help women cope with discrimination, women's studies courses were added to the curriculum in some journalism schools. The first began as a seminar for seniors and graduate students taught by Marion Marzolf, an assistant professor, at the University of Michigan in 1971. "Do women in journalism have a history?" Marzolf wrote on a sign posted on her office door, inviting students to explore the subject with her. Out of Marzolf's course came the first bibliography on women in journalism. Six years later she published the first history of women journalists (Rush, 1973, and Marzolf, Rush and Stern, 1974-75).

Women who were graduated with journalism degrees in 1966 and 1971 from three state universities, Louisiana, Missouri and Nebraska, were surveyed in 1977 on their careers and personal lives. The study found the majority both married and employed and committed to the successful mixing of marriage and family with a lifetime career (Crumley, Patterson and Sailor, 1977).

Their continued enthusiasm for journalism supported results of an earlier study which concluded that "...female (students) considered journalism more interesting than did males." That study reported in 1974 that men with journalism degrees were more likely to pursue non-journalism careers than women (going on to law school, for example). It concluded "...women students are more likely to be committed to pursue journalism careers than men" (Bowers, 1974).

Yet observers of journalism education overlooked the growing numbers of women students. In a 1977 attack on journalism schools that appeared in the _Atlantic_, Ben H. Bagdikian, a media critic, attributed the swell in enrollment, which reached 64,000 students that year, to youth eager to emulate Carl Bernstein and Bob Woodward. These two young _Washington Post_ reporters were credited with exposing the Watergate scandal that toppled President Nixon in 1974. While stressing their fame may have drawn students to journalism, Bagdikian ignored the fact that percentage increases in journalism enrollment were larger in the 1960s than in the 1970s (Bagdikian, 1977).

In an 11-page article, Bagdikian contended many journalism schools taught trivial trade skills "imbedded in a curriculum that discourages intellectual growth, prevents depth of knowledge, and denies the future journalists a broad perspective on society." He also argued journalism education was flooding the market with far more graduates than could find newspaper jobs. Nowhere in his critique did he refer to the changing nature of the student body, made up of an increasing number for whom Woodward and Bernstein were unlikely role models (Bagdikian, 1977).

The same year Bagdikian's article appeared the percentage enrollment of women in journalism schools surpassed that of men for the first time. According to Paul V. Peterson, journalism professor at Ohio State University and the compiler of the major annual journalism enrollment survey, the proportion of women represented slightly more than 50 percent in 1977. In 1978 it reached 53.1 percent, compared with only 41.1 percent a decade before (Peterson, 1979, and 1985).

II. Present Situation

Since then the percentage of women has continued to increase. In 1983 it stood at 58 percent compared with 57.5 percent in 1981. While the comparable figure for 1982 was 58.6 percent, Peterson did not see the 1983 figure as representing a downward turn (Peterson, 1984).

"At best these figures are only estimates since some schools don't keep figures broken down by sex," Peterson said. His survey of 1983 enrollments showed a total of 82,649 journalism students listed by sex with 47,961 women and 34,688 men. In the 1984 survey, Peterson found the female majority to be about 59.2 percent out of a total of about 86,000 students. The minority enrollment was about 8 percent.[5]

In terms of graduates, women represented 61.5 percent of the 14,274 persons receiving journalism degrees in 1981-82, the most recent year for which figures are available from the United States Department of Education. By contrast the percentage of women obtaining degrees in other professional fields traditionally considered male-dominated was far smaller for 1981-82. Women represented 33.4 percent of law school graduates, 25 percent of medical school graduates and 11.4 percent of engineering school graduates. As expected women continued to dominate in traditionally female fields, receiving 75.9 percent of all degrees given in education and 82.3 percent of all degrees given in library science, for example.[6]

The new predominance of women in journalism schools reflected the growing numbers of women college students in general. While higher education long had been the domain of men, women constituted the majority of undergraduates by 1982. According to Betty Vetter of the Scientific Manpower Commission, which made an annual statistical study of the numbers of women going into professions, it was not surprising that journalism had drawn an increasing percentage of women students.[7]

"When women started to get the option to do what they pleased, they went to college and they went into those non-traditional fields where they had been before," she explained in 1984. She pointed out women as a group tended to select fields where other women had gone before them, although in fewer numbers. Vetter projected the percentage of women in law schools would soon increase to the 50 percent mark.

Peterson's surveys linked the growing percentage of women journalism students to the increase of enrollments in public relations and advertising sequences. In 1980 Peterson first observed, "...when sequences are analyzed, there is a clear indication that a growing percentage of students are enrolling in the advertising and public relations sequences, while the number of news-editorial is declining. The first two sequences are more heavily female-populated as well" (Peterson, 1980).

Peterson concluded this shows "more females looking at non-traditional forms of journalism for careers." He also saw a reflection of the past. "I still think they see the newsroom as an all-male bastion," he said.[8]

The influx of women students did not bring an equal influx of women faculty members. In 1983 researchers at Syracuse University determined there was a striking imbalance between the percentage of women students and women faculty members. Based on a national survey, they found women students constituted 59 percent of enrollment at the undergraduate, 52 percent at the masters, and 36 percent at the doctorate level. But women represented only 20 percent at the faculty level. Only two accredited journalism programs were headed by women (Turk, Sharp, Hollenbeck, Schamber and Eisiedel, 1984).

The study also found 43 percent of women faculty viewed sex discrimination as a problem. Those who perceived it gave the following areas of concern: Salary, 44 percent; appointment to administrative positions, 53 percent; tenure and promotion, 34 percent. Subtle discriminatory attitudes were cited by 59 percent who said they had to do more than their male colleagues to earn respect from male faculty and administration.

Responding to inquiries from the National Federation of Press Women in 1983, male heads of eight journalism programs said they wanted more women on their staffs but that they received relatively few applications from qualified women when openings were advertised. Most said few applicants had the required doctorate or master's degree and strong professional experience (*PW*, 1983, February).

64

"In addition to teaching strengths, women faculty are needed as role models and as advisers and counselors," commented Herbert Strentz, dean at Drake University. "We're presently conducting a search for two assistant professors and received only four applications from women in this national search," Walter Bunge, director at Ohio State University, noted. "The response from such a small number of women is not unusual in our previous searches, but it's disappointing" (*PW*, 1983, February).

In terms of employment, women graduates appeared to experience somewhat more difficulty than male graduates in finding media-related jobs. The Dow Jones Newspaper Fund/Gallup survey completed in 1984 showed differences in the employment patterns of men and women who received bachelor's degrees in the spring of 1983. Among them:

o While women represented 64.1 percent, or 11,326 of the total of 17,670 graduates surveyed, they were less likely than male graduates to find media-related jobs. While 14.6 percent of the graduates as a whole found jobs in the print media, only 11.8 percent of the women did so.

o Although 9.4 percent of the graduates found jobs on daily newspapers, women were less likely than men to be in this category, with only 6.9 percent of the women reporting jobs on daily papers. An almost equal percentage of men and women, 4.8 and 4.7 respectively, found jobs on weekly newspapers.

o A higher percentage of women were unemployed than the graduates as a whole, with 14.2 percent of the women continuing to seek media-related work compared to 11.8 percent for the total group.

o A higher percentage of women than graduates as a whole were employed in two categories -- advertising and magazines -- with 7.7 percent of the women finding jobs in advertising compared with 6.8 percent of the total and 2.5 percent of the women finding jobs on magazines compared with 1.9 percent of the total. In public relations 6.8 percent of the women found jobs compared to 7.3 percent for the total.

o In broadcasting 6.1 percent of the total found work in radio and 5.8 percent in television, while the comparable percentages for women were 5.5 percent in radio and 5.6 percent in television.

The figures suggested women were less successful than men in moving from journalism school into the field. Were too many women fighting for too few jobs confronted by employers who preferred men? Was journalism education becoming a "pink-collar ghetto" field? What effect was the predominance of women graduates having on salaries in the field?

General sex discrimination in pay has been a well documented fact. According to the U.S. Census Bureau, on the average women who worked full-time, year-round were paid approximately 61 cents for every dollar paid to men in 1982. Median earnings in professional occupations with large concentrations of women fell short of median earnings in nonprofessional occupations with large concentrations of men. Registered nurses, for example, had a median income of $18,980, librarians $17,992 and elementary school teachers $18,148, compared to $21,840 for mail carriers, $17,732 for meat cutters and $21,944 for plumbers and pipefitters (National Committee on Pay Equity, 1983).

The salary picture for male and female journalism graduates in 1983 showed no clear pattern of discrimination. The Newspaper Fund/Gallup survey broke down the weekly salaries of 1983 graduates into 12 ranges varying from $130 or less to more than $400. The percentage of women being paid in the lowest range was exactly the same as the percentage for the group as a whole -- .9 percent. In the highest range, however, the percentage for the group as a whole was 5.5 compared to 3.9 percent for the women. In the middle range of salaries of $231 to $250 a week, women fared somewhat better than the group as a whole, with 14.3 percent in this category compared to 13.5 percent of the total.

Yet journalistic salaries in general were not high and fears that women depressed pay scales did not appear unrealistic. Peterson commented, "Is it important that women dominate the field? I don't think so. But as males began to look at the salaries, they may give journalism another thought. Traditionally females have been willing to accept lower salaries than males."[10]

A 1982 study of women in educational communications, a branch of public relations, for example, showed that salary discrepancies existed between men and women respondents with comparable years of experience. Even at the lowest level of experience, two or fewer years in the field, men had a mean salary of $23,090 compared to $19,397 for females, a difference of almost $4,000 (VanSlyke, 1982).

This suggested that journalism schools might be turning out an increasing number of graduates who would encounter sexual bias in their careers. Were they being properly prepared to recognize sexism and to overcome it? How adequate was mentoring? Academic and career advisement? Were women students being prepared to see themselves as potential managers, editors and policy-makers not simply as technicians or entry-level editorial assistants? Were they being discouraged from careers in news-editorial work and counseled to go into public relations and advertising on the grounds that these areas were more appropriate for women? Were appropriate role models being provided? And, perhaps most important, what sort of attitudes and expectations did the women students bring with them into journalism schools? Did these differ from the attitudes and expectations of the male students to whom journalism schools so long were geared?

III. Implications for the Future

If journalism education is not able to successfully prepare women to gain jobs traditionally given to men, then the future of the field seems uncertain. In January, 1984, a national conference on journalism education was held at the University of Oregon as part of a two-year program to explore new directions for journalism education at a time of radical change in the mass communication industry. Participants, including both educators and journalism professionals, grappled with issues including curriculum, relationships between academia and professionals, faculty qualifications and the status of journalism units within university structures. After debate the group reaffirmed the traditional liberal arts tradition in journalism education, which required students at accredited schools to take 75 percent of their coursework in liberal arts and sciences and only 25 percent in journalism skills courses (Talevich, 1984).

The conference drew attention to the explosive growth in journalism programs and mass communications in the past two decades, which outstripped efforts to develop coherent academic models. It pointed out the changing employment picture for journalism graduates: Whereas newspapers once were the prime employer of graduates, this certainly was no longer true. Figures showed that advertising and public relations each claimed about one-fourth of the students enrolled in journalism, while another quarter did not remain in the communications field (Friendly, 1983).

The remaining quarter, about the same proportion as 20 years ago, entered news organizations, with expansion in radio and television offsetting decreases in jobs on newspapers and magazines. Yet newspapers apparently continued to depend on journalism graduates. In 1974 the Newspaper Fund discontinued its study of the percentages of new college graduates being hired by daily newspapers who had either journalism majors and minors. It found the figures so lopsided in favor of those with journalism backgrounds -- 77.2 percent -- that it decided against continuing to collect these figures (Genovese, 1980).

The Oregon conference did not consider the impact of the gender shift in enrollment. But no more pressing question confronts journalism educators. Since formal licensing requirements do not exist for journalists (unlike lawyers, doctors and some other professionals), employers are under no obligation to hire journalism graduates rather than individuals with college preparation in other fields. Some evidence already exists that employers are concerned about the declining percentage of male journalism graduates. In a report on a 1983 conference on professional support of journalism education, the American Newspaper Publishers Association Foundation drew attention to the dwindling proportions of men in journalism schools. "In the broadcast area it is becoming difficult to find male -- especially black male -- journalists," the report stated.[11]

In public relations, a woman-dominated field, the percentage of those employed who majored in journalism apparently dropped during the period that journalism enrollments changed from predominantly male to predominantly female. According to the International Association of Business Communicators, the percentage of women communicators in its membership is growing -- moving from 50.8 percent in 1977 to 59.8 percent in 1983. Yet over this same period the percentage of journalism graduates among its membership has declined -- from 53 percent in 1977 to 38 percent in 1983. Journalism, however, has remained the single most common major for communicators (International Association of Business Communicators, 1979 and 1983).

In view of this situation it is vital for educators to address the implication of the gender shift in journalism school enrollment. Therefore the following research agenda is proposed:

o Journalism educators should take action immediately to recognize the importance of the gender shift by calling for a national conference to bring together administrators, faculty members, representatives of professional organizations, and experts in the education of women to address the issue.

o Journalism educators should undertake a national survey of the socio-economic characteristics of journalism students and alumni, similar to one recently undertaken on medical students, as a way of assessing changes in the student body. Only by analyzing the present population can efforts be made to develop programs that meet its needs.

o Journalism educators should set up a series of pilot programs at selected schools, including predominantly minority institutions, to determine the career expectations of women entering the program and to discover whether these decline, remain the same or rise as the women leave college and enter the labor market.

o Journalism educators should make sure that women students have accurate information about the position of women in the labor force today and encourage them to make realistic long-range plans.

o Journalism educators should survey communications employers to discover their perception of changes in modes of work and skills needed on the local level for the future.

o Journalism educators should research the introduction of new technology into communications industries with emphasis on their responsiveness to needs of women workers.

NOTES

[1]This point was made by Paul V. Peterson in a telephone interview (1984, March 26).

[2]M. Mencher to M. Beasley (1985, February 25).

[3]For a full discussion see article entitled, "Journalism Faculties - Where Do We Stand." *The Matrix* (1972, Fall), pp. 20-21.

[4]Documents related to broadcast challenges appear in M. Beasley and S. Gibbons (1977), *Women in media: A documentary sourcebook*. Wash., D.C.: Women's Institute for Freedom of the Press, pp. 119-137, 142-146.

[5]Telephone interviews with P. Peterson (1984, March 26 and 1985, April 11).

[6]Telephone interview with Tom Snyder, National Center for Education Statistics, U.S. Department of Education (1984, March 26).

[7]See paper entitled, "The classroom climate: A chilly one for women?" (1982). Project on the Status and Education of Women. Wash., D.C.: Association of American Colleges, p. 1; materials also gained in a telephone interview with B. Vetter, Scientific Manpower Commission (1984, March 26).

[8]Peterson telephone interview (1984, March 26).

[9]Final tabulation (1984, January). Dow Jones Newspaper Fund/Gallup survey of 1983 journalism graduates obtained from the Dow Jones Newspaper Fund, Princeton, N.J.

[10]Peterson telephone interview (1984, March 26).

[11]Report on 1983 conference for professional support of journalism education (1983). Reston, VA.: American Newspaper Publishers Association Foundation, p. 2.

REFERENCES

Applegate, R. (1965, June). Women as journalism educators. *The Matrix*, pp. 4-5.

Bagdikian, B. (1977, March). Woodstein U.: Notes on the mass production and questionable education of journalists. *Atlantic Monthly*, pp. 80-92.

Bowers, T. (1974, Summer). Student attitudes toward journalism as a career. *Journalism Quarterly* 51, 265-70.

Crumley W., Patterson, J. and Sailor, P. (1977, October). Journalism career patters of women are changing. *Journalism Educator* 31, 50.

Daly, A (1972-73, Winter). Journalism faculty women. *The Matrix*, pp. 20-21.

Deckard, B. (1983). *The women's movement: Political, socio-economic, and psychological issues.* New York: Harper & Row.

Enough women on the faculty? (1983, February). *PW (Press Woman)*, pp. 103.

Friendly, J. (1984, January 23) Journalism educators debate strategies, technology and ties to the media. *The New York Times*, p. A-11.

Genovese, M. (1980, September). J-schools try to keep up with change. *Presstime*, p. 4.

International Association of Business Communicators (1979). *Profile '79: A survey of business communication and business communicators.* Syracuse, N.Y.: Syracuse University, p. 7.

International Association of Business Communicators (1983). *Profile '83: A survey of business communication and business communicators*, p. 4.

J-schools continue to grow (1968, February). *The Matrix*, p. 8.

Johnson L. (1965, April). Woman's tomorrow is here. *The Matrix*, p. 3.

Magid, N. (1977). Women's magazines in the sixties. In M. Beasley and S. Gibbons, *Women in Media: A documentary sourcebook.* Wash., D.C.: Women's Institute for Freedom of the Press.

Marzolf, M., Rush, R. and Stern, D. (1974-75, Winter). The literature of women in journalism. *Journalism History I*, 117-128.

Marzolf, M. (1977). *Up from the footnote.* New York: Hastings House.

National Committee on Pay Equity (1983). *The wage gap: Myths and facts.* Wash., D.C.

Quinn, D. (1971, Summer). Are we going for a discount price? *The Matrix*, pp. 14-15.

Peterson, P. (1979, January). Enrollment surged again, increases 7% to 70,601. *Journalism Educator* 33, 3.

Peterson, P. (1980, January). J-school enrollments reach record 71,594. *Journalism Educator* 34, 3.

Peterson, P. (1984, Spring). Survey indicates no change in '83 journalism enrollment. *Journalism Educator* 39, 3.

Peterson, P. (1985, Spring). 1984 survey: No change in mass communication enrollment. *Journalism Educator* 40, 3-9.

Rush, R. (1973, August). *Women in academe: Journalism education viewed from the literature and other memorabilia*. Paper presented to the Association for Education in Journalism annual convention, Ft. Collins, Colo., pp. 13-20.

Talevich, T. (1984, February). Liberal arts tradition backed at j-education 'summit'. *Presstime*, pp. 38-39.

Turk, J., Sharp, N., Hollenbeck, L., Schamber, L., and Einsiedel, E. (1984, April). Results of survey of women journalism faculty members. Syracuse University.

VanSlyke, Jr. (1982, July). *Women in educational communications: Profile of case members, 1982*. Paper presented to the Committee on the Status of Women, Association for Education in Journalism annual convention, Athens, Ohio.

SECTION TWO

GENDER ISSUES IN INTERPERSONAL AND PROFESSIONAL RELATIONSHIPS

COGNITIVE, AFFECTIVE, AND BEHAVIORAL CORRELATES OF
ROMANTIC JEALOUSY: AN ANALYSIS OF GENDER DIFFERENCES

Susan Parrish Sprowl, University of Massachusetts

For decades scholars have argued that because of feelings of
dependency and low self-esteem, females are more prone to jealousy
than males. Margaret Mead (1931), for example, reminds us that
for centuries females have been viewed not only as the "insecure
sex" but the "jealous sex" as well. Mead (1931) captures the
essence of the traditional female's romantic jealousy experience
when she notes:

> The wife threatened with the loss of her
> husband's affection, fidelity, interest, or loyalty,
> whichever point her society has defined as the pivot of
> wifely tenure, sees the very roots of her existence
> being cut from beneath her. She has been in the
> position in which a man would be if he had to read in
> his wife's averted shoulder, the depreciation of all his
> stocks, a loss of his business reputation, eviction from
> whatever position he holds, both social and political as
> well as the loss of his home and possibly of all control
> over his children.

One of the few consistent findings in the jealousy literature
is that males and females differ in their cognitive constructions
of the romantic jealousy situation which in turn influences their
affective and behavioral responses. These differing cognitive
constructions are based on traditional sex role socialization
processes (Clanton & Smith, 1977). The male sees jealousy as
occurring in response to a perceived sexual infidelity by his
partner. The language describing the male jealousy experience is
almost exclusively sexual. For example, Clanton and Smith (1977)
report that when confronted with their partner's infidelity,
"jealous men are more apt to focus on the outside sexual activity
of the partner and they often demand a recital of the intimate
details" (p. 11). White (1981a) has found that "sexual motives
[for extrarelationship involvement] were rated by partners as more
important for males than for females" (p. 29). In a study of
jealous conflict in dating couples, Teismann and Mosher (1978)
discovered that, when asked to assume a distancing role based on
jealousy in a role-playing situation with their partner, males
were more likely than females to select sexual issues to elicit
jealousy. Finally, several studies have suggested that sexual

acumen is a more fundamental aspect of male self-esteem than female self-esteem (Bartell, 1970; Constantine & Constantine, 1971; Denfeld, 1974; Gottschalk, 1936; Varni, 1974; White, 1981a).

Research indicates that when men are jealous, they display a variety of affective and behavioral responses. For example, they may experience feelings of anger, intropunitiveness, inadequacy, humiliation, and/or despondency (Bryson, 1976, 1977; Clanton & Smith, 1977; Ray, 1978). Behavioral responses to the jealousy-evoking situation reflect a tendency to "externalize the cause of jealousy" by blaming the partner, the interloper, or circumstances (Clanton & Smith, 1977, p. 11). Responses are often confrontational, i.e., verbally threatening the interloper and/or becoming violent with partner and/or interloper (Bryson, 1976, 1977; Clanton & Smith, 1977). When the interloper is attractive, supposedly posing a greater threat, males display a tendency to seek other relationships in response to their feelings of jealousy (Shettel-Neuber, Bryson, & Young, 1978). Bringle (1981) concludes that, in general, males tend to respond to jealousy-evoking situations with behaviors designed to maintain and protect their self-esteem.

While males focus on sexual infidelity, the essence of the female jealousy experience lies in emotional (nonsexual) infidelity. The female seems to be more concerned with the emotional involvement between her partner and the third party than their sexual relationship (Clanton & Smith, 1977). In a study examining the motivation behind extrarelationship involvement, White (1981a) found that "females were more likely to stress nonsexual qualities of the rival relationship (rival's personality, good communication, etc.)" as the motivation for their partner's infidelity (p. 29). In addition, he reports that "perception of partner's attraction to nonsexual aspects of the rival relationship" was more related to female than male jealousy (p. 29). White (1981a) argues that "the ability to be interpersonally sensitive and to provide mate with a supportive relationship is a more salient part of female than male self-esteem" (p. 24). This view is consistent with past theoretical and empirical work which indicates that for females, the primary threat of a partner's infidelity is the potential loss of the relationship (Bernard, 1977; Bringle, 1981; Clanton & Smith, 1977).

Perhaps even more so than men, women display a wide range of affective and behavioral responses when jealous. Jealous females may experience feelings of emotional devastation, anger, intropunitiveness, frustration, betrayal, inadequacy, and/or disgust (Bryson, 1976, 1977; Clanton & Smith, 1977; Ray, 1978).

While the behavioral responses of the male to the jealousy-evoking situation reflect an external attribution, the responses of females indicate a tendency to blame themselves (Clanton & Smith, 1977). Behavioral responses include attempts to make themselves seem more desirable to their partners, e.g., making themselves more attractive (Bryson, 1976). In addition, they are more likely to try to induce jealousy in their partner in an effort to strengthen or test their relationship or to achieve a particular outcome, e.g., to get more attention from their partner (Bryson, 1976; White, 1980). Finally, females are more likely than males to express a need for social support when they experience jealousy. Bringle (1981) argues that, unlike males who respond to a jealousy-evoking situation with behaviors designed to maintain self-esteem, females react with behaviors designed to maintain the relationship. In other words, the primary threat of infidelity is what distinguishes male and female jealousy; men fear loss of face while women fear loss of place.

While there is a plethora of evidence supporting the cognitive differentiation of jealousy for males and females, research examining sex differences in the intensity of jealousy has produced mixed results. No consistent pattern of sex differences can be found in the available literature (Bringle, 1981; Mathes & Severa, 1981; White, 1981a, 1981b). Stereotypical assumptions hypothesizing higher levels of jealousy for females because of their insecurity and low esteem have not been fully supported. The rationale for assuming that women are more jealous than men because of low esteem is problematic since research indicates no differences in male and female self-reports of global self-esteem (Kaplan & Sedney, 1980). Indeed, the interpretation of the jealousy/gender relationship becomes more difficult when one examines the role of self-esteem in that relationship. Numerous studies have supported the relationship between self-esteem and jealousy (Bringle, Roach, Andler, & Evenbeck, 1977; Bringle, 1981; Jaremko & Lindsey, 1979; Manges & Evenbeck, 1980; White, 1977). Other studies have failed to support this relationship (White, 1981b; White, 1981c). Finally, White (1981b) and Buunk (1980) report a correlation between self-esteem and jealousy for males but not for females, while Buunk (1982) obtains the opposite result in a separate study. The purpose of the current study was to more fully explore the interaction between gender and self-esteem as it relates to romantic jealousy. Specifically, the following research questions were posited: 1) Is there a significant difference in the chronic jealousy level of males and females high and low in self-esteem?, and 2) Are there significant differences in the feelings and behaviors of males and females high and low in self-esteem in jealousy-evoking situations?

Method

Subjects and Procedure

Subjects were 199 males and 294 females (N=493) enrolled in communication courses at a medium-size midwestern university. Each subject was given a packet containing ten self-report scales, three of which are analyzed in the current study. Scales were randomized to control for order effects.

Operational Definitions

Chronic Jealousy. This construct was measured via a 6-item Likert-type scale referred to as the Chronic Jealousy Scale. The scale measures a person's "tendency to view self as chronically jealous in romantic relationships" (White, 1981b, p. 301). The scale measures a unidimensional jealousy construct and includes items such as "How jealous a person are you generally?" and "How much have jealous feelings been a problem in your romantic relationships?." Cronbach's alpha for the unidimensional scale in the current study was .89.

Affective & Behavioral Responses to Jealousy-Evoking Situations. These responses were measured via a Likert-type scale which taps "actions and feelings we may experience when we believe that someone with whom we are romantically involved is, or is becoming, attracted to or by another person" (Bryson, 1976, p. 2). The scale is composed of actions and feelings usually associated with jealousy and subjects are asked to indicate how well each of these feelings and actions describes what they feel and do when jealous.

Factor analysis of the scale in the current study produced seven orthogonal factors. Factor one, emotional devastation, included items such as "I feel helpless" and "I feel depressed." The second factor, anger, was defined by items such as, "I feel angry toward my partner" and "I feel angry toward the other person." Factor three, reactive retribution, included items such as "I feel like getting even" and "I do something to get my partner jealous." The fourth factor, labeled loss of control, included items such as "I feel like I'm in a daze" and "I feel less able to cope with other aspects of my life." Factor five, arousal, included items like "I feel more sexually aroused by my partner" and "I become more sexually aggressive with my partner." The sixth factor, need for social support, was defined by items such as "I talk to close friends about my feelings" and "I check with others who might confirm or disconfirm my feelings." Finally, factor seven was defined by items like "I feel guilty about being jealous" and I feel angry toward myself," and was labeled intropunitiveness. Reliabilities for the seven factors were .88, .84, .76, .70, .62, .59, and .70, respectively.

It should be noted that the factor structure obtained in the current analysis differed slightly from that reported in the original study (Bryson, 1976). The "loss of control" factor did not emerge in the original study and "confrontation," a factor present in the original study failed to emerge in the current analysis. These differences in factor structure are probably reflective of the embryonic stage of development of the scale. The decision to use the scale, despite its brief history was based on several considerations. First, it is the only available measure of affective and behavioral responses to jealousy-evoking situations. Secondly, there were only slight shifts in the factor structure of the scale in the current study. Finally, preliminary evidence indicates support for the validity of the scale (Bryson, 1977; Parrish, 1983).

Self-Esteem. This variable was measured by the Rosenberg (1965) self-esteem scale. This scale is composed of 10 five-point Likert-type statements that measure a single dimension of self-acceptance. Cronbach's alpha for the scale in the current study was .82.

Statistical Analysis

The first research question was analyzed via a 2 X 2 analysis of variance (ANOVA) with biological sex and level of self-esteem as the independent variables and chronic jealousy as the dependent variable. Categorization of subjects on the self-esteem variable was accomplished via a median split. The second research question was analyzed via a 2 X 2 multivariate analysis of variance (MANOVA) with biological sex and self-esteem as independent variables and the dimensions of the Bryson (1976) scale as the dependent variables. Scheffe and multiple discriminant analysis (MULDIS) were used as post hoc tests to locate group differences. Procedures found in SPSS (Version 9) were used for all statistical analyses. All items were reflected such that higher scores on each scale indicate a greater incidence of the construct being measured. The .05 level of significance was used for all statistical tests.

Results

Research question one asks if there is a significant difference in the chronic jealousy level of individuals based on a gender/self-esteem interaction. The results of the ANOVA reveal a significant interaction (F= 4.10, df= 3/489, p< .04). Post hoc analysis indicates a significant difference between females with high self-esteem ($\overline{X}$ = 17.12) and all other groups. There are no significant differences among the other groups: low self-esteem females ($\overline{X}$ = 23.02), low self-esteem males ($\overline{X}$ = 23.64), and high self-esteem males ($\overline{X}$ = 21.84).

Research question two asks if there are significant differences in the feelings and behaviors of males and females, high and low in self- esteem in jealousy-evoking situations. The results of the MANOVA show a significant interaction between gender and self-esteem (Wilks' F=1.91, df= 8/482, p< .05). The post hoc MULDIS reveals two significant discriminant functions (Table 1). The first discriminant function is labeled "need for social support." Analysis of group centroids reveals that females with high self-esteem score highest on this function (1.00), followed by females with low esteem (.84), males with low self-esteem (-1.14), and males with high self-esteem (-1.58). The second significant discriminant function is labeled emotional devastation. Females with low self-esteem score highest on this function (.70), with low esteem males following close behind (.66). High self-esteem females score lowest on this function (-.80), followed by high esteem males (-.64).

Discussion

A significant finding in the current study is that females with high self-esteem seem to experience less jealousy than females and males low in self-esteem, as well as males high in self-esteem. At first glance, this finding seems somewhat counterintuitive; after all, aren't females supposed to be more jealous than males? An examination of the roots of this commonly held view may provide insight into the seemingly counterintuitive result obtained in the current study.

As mentioned previously, one reason females have been labeled the "jealous sex" is based on the assumption that females have also been the "insecure sex." "Given the strong evidence that stereotypes of men are more favorable than stereotypes of women, we might expect that the self-concepts of men and women would reflect these same norms" (Deaux, 1976, p. 37). However, research has failed to support a relationship between gender and self-esteem (Deaux, 1976; Kaplan & Sedney, 1980). Deaux (1976) offers one explanation for this finding based on role expectations. She suggests that males and females may evaluate themselves against different standards. The criteria an individual uses for evaluation of self could be a function of the role society has bestowed upon him/her. "While these roles may be different, and

TABLE 1

Discriminant Analysis of Affective and Behavioral Responses to Jealousy-Evoking Situations

| | Loadings | |
Variable	DF_1	DF_2
Need for Social Support	.77	-.18
Arousal	-.40	.05
Emotional Devastation	.28	.68
Loss of Control	-.01	.48
Intropunitiveness	.33	.40
Reactive Retribution	-.05	.50
Anger	-.03	.07

Centroid Values		
Males/Low Self-Esteem	-1.14	.66
Males/High Self-Esteem	-1.58	-.64
Females/Low Self-Esteem	.84	.70
Females/High Self-Esteem	1.00	-.80

Tests of Significance

DF_1: $\chi^2 = 204.02$, df=24, $p < .00001$; Wilks' Lambda= .576

DF_2: $\chi^2 = 70.154$, df=14, $p < .00001$; Wilks' Lambda= .945

in fact unequal, women may be as satisfied with their role as are men" (Deaux, 1976, p. 37). For traditional females, that role would be wife/mother. This would suggest that, at least historically, a female's self-esteem has been dependent on her performances as wife and mother. Of course, the person who provides the most feedback, whether verbally or nonverbally, on her performance in this role is her husband. Since a female's self-esteem is dependent on her husband's evaluation of her performance in the relationship, she becomes more relationally oriented out of a sheer survival motive if nothing else. In other words, because her self-esteem is dependent on the relationship, she must become astute at understanding the dynamics of the relationship in order to accurately gauge her behavior. This relational focus is characteristic of what Schaef (1981) refers to as the "Female System." She argues that this is markedly different from the "White Male System."

> In the White Male System, the center of the universe is the self and the work . . . . Other things in life may be important . . ., but they are never of equal importance; they always occupy positions on the periphery of the man's life, on the outside circle. . . In the Female System, however, the center of the universe is relationships. Everything else must go through, relate to, and be defined by relationships. (p. 108)

It is not surprising that an individual who spends a great deal of time analyzing his/her relationships comes to eventually realize that romantic relationships are complex and multidimensional, characterized by sexual as well as nonsexual qualities. This multidimensional view of relationships is also characteristic of the Female System. Schaef (1981) suggests that males and females differ in the level of saliency placed on sexuality. "In the Female System, sex is seen as important, fun, and sacred. It is not used to define the world, individuals, or relationships, however." (Schaef, 1981, p. 115). Whereas males tend to "sexualize the universe," including their relationships, females see relationships as more complex and dynamic (Schaef, 1981, p. 114).

This multidimensional view of relationships, however, has potential "negative" side effects. Since females see a variety of factors as being important in a healthy relationship, partner's dissatisfaction with respect to any of these factors might result in an increased fear of loss of the relationship and, therefore, higher levels of jealousy. If an individual defines a relationship unidimensionally (i.e., sexually), any threat to the relationship must be grounded in that dimension for it to be perceived as a threat. As discussed previously, this unidimensionality is reflected in the male's view of infidelity. The behavior must be a violation of sexual exclusivity to be perceived as infidelity. However, if one views relationships as multidimensional, each of those dimensions represents a domain for potential threat to the relationship. Since the traditional female's self-esteem is dependent on her husband's approval of her performance, it is necessary for her to be aware of even subtle changes in her partner's satisfaction in any of these areas. An analysis of the results of a 1981(a) study by White reveals that females report a wider range of perceived motives for their partner's infidelity than males. Potential motives include rival attractiveness, good communication, troubles in the primary relationship, as well as sexual variety. Interestingly, White (1981a) had predicted that "perception of a sexual motive would be more strongly linked to male than to female jealousy" (p. 29) because "sexual ability or prowess is a more salient aspect of male self-esteem than of female self-esteem" (p. 24). However, he failed to confirm this hypothesis. His prediction reflects a lack of understanding for the Female System's view of relationships. Females do not necessarily consider sexual infidelity unimportant, but rather as simply one type of infidelity. Just as relationships are multidimensional, so is infidelity.

Armed with this multidimensional view of relationships characteristic of her Female System, the contemporary woman may find herself in a unique position. More so than any other time in history, women are not obligated to define themselves via their relationships with men. This is perhaps particularly true for the young, educated, middle to upper-middle class females used as subjects in the current study. While their self-esteem might be influenced by their relationships with men, it is highly likely that a female college student's self-esteem is also influenced by her academic performance. Females whose self-esteem is not tied exclusively to their role as wife/mother/girlfriend and who have higher esteem overall would experience less jealousy since their relationship is not the only measure of their "performance" in life. Based on this reasoning, one might conclude that males with high self-esteem should experience the least jealousy, or certainly no more than the high esteem female. However, such was not the case in the current study. Perhaps the answer lies in the multidimensional view of relationships characteristic of the Female System. Because of this multidimensional view, no one factor is the measure of the relationship. Unlike the female whose self-esteem is dependent on her partner's approval of her performance, the female who has high self-esteem, based on a variety of factors, is not as threatened by subtle changes in her partner's behavior. However, like her traditional counterpart, she uses several barometers to assess her relationship. Males, on the other hand, preoccupied with the sexual dimension of their relationships, place "all their eggs in one basket." This may have been a safe and effective technique for the traditional male whose traditional partner was very unlikely to violate this "right of sexual exclusivity." However, females, especially on college campuses, are enjoying greater sexual freedom than ever before. When you place all your eggs in one basket, and the person holding that basket decides s/he likes turning it upside down, you end up with broken eggs. In this case, this translates into higher levels of jealousy.

The discussion thus far has painted a positive picture of the female with high self-esteem. The picture becomes more positive when one examines the affective and behavioral responses of males and females to jealousy-evoking situations. The results indicate that most females, high or low in self-esteem, tend to use their social support systems more than males when they are jealous. This is not terribly surprising and is consistent with past research on male/female differences in disclosiveness (Chelune, 1979). However, it is possible that females high in self-esteem are not using their support systems for the same purpose as females low in esteem. The results reveal that when jealous, females with high esteem experience the least amount of emotional devastation of all groups studied. Females with low self-esteem, however, experience the greatest amount of emotional devastation. It could be that while most females talk about their relational conflict, females with high esteem do so in an effort to find a rational, viable solution to their problem, while low esteem females use members of their support systems as "lay crisis counselors." Future research should address the issue of how these two groups use their support systems.

Contrary to past research (Bryson, 1976), the results of the current study reveal that males do not necessarily experience less emotional devastation when jealous than females. High esteem males scored low on this function; however, not as low as high esteem females. Further, low esteem males scored high on this function, very close in fact to low esteem females. This finding is consistent with the analysis provided thus far. First, high esteem females, even when they do experience jealousy, are not devastated since it is unlikely that their jealousy encompasses every aspect of the relationship that they consider salient. In addition, since their esteem is not totally dependent on their relationship, fear of loss of the relationship is troublesome but not devastating. On the other hand, when males are jealous, it is probably based on a perceived sexual infidelity. Since this is the defining dimension of their relationship as well as an important component of their self-esteem, the odds are greater that they would feel more devastation with respect to that relationship. This is especially true for males low in self-esteem. Sexual exclusivity is supposedly their "right." When even that is taken away from them, it is understandable for them to feel devastated. Females low in esteem score lowest on this function. It could be that these females still depend on their relationships with men to define themselves and thus are more fearful that they will lose their partner to another. This would result in greater feelings of devastation when they do experience jealousy.

Summary & Conclusions

This study reports several new and exciting findings for researchers interested in gender and jealousy. There appears to be an interaction between gender and self-esteem, such that females with high esteem experience the least amount of jealousy. A tentative explanation for this finding is offered; future research should attempt a more systematic effort with an adult population other than college students to determine the reliability of the finding as well as the reasons behind it. If the explanation provided here is supported, it could have important implications for the treatment of men and women who have problems with jealousy in their romantic relationships. The explanation offered would suggest helping females broaden their definitions of themselves beyond their relationships with men and helping males understand the multidimensional nature of relationships. In addition, future research should attempt to discover how females high and low in self-esteem differ in the use of support systems when they experience jealousy. Further, since males do not seem to use support systems to cope with their jealousy, attention should focus on what they do use and how this is affected by their esteem level. Clearly, past research has not adequately explained the gender/self-esteem/jealousy relationship. Future research should respond to this critical need.

References

Bartell, G. (1970). Group sex among Mid-Americans. Journal of Sex Research, 6, 113-130.

Bernard, J. (1977). Jealousy and marriage. In G. Clanton and L. Smith (Eds.), Jealousy,(pp. 141-150). Englewood Cliffs, N.J.: Prentice-Hall, Inc.

Bringle, R. (1981). Conceptualizing jealousy as a disposition. Alternative Lifestyles, 4, 274-290.

Bringle, R., Roach, S., Andler, C., & Evenbeck, S. (1979). Measuring the intensity of jealous reactions. Journal Supplement Abstract Service, 9.

Bryson, J. (1976). The nature of sexual jealousy: An exploratory study. Paper presented at the 84th Annual Convention of the American Psychological Association, Washington, D.C.

Bryson, J. (1977). Situational determinants of the expression of jealousy. Paper presented at the 85th Annual Convention of the American Psychological Association, San Francisco.

Buunk, B. (1980). Intieme relaties met derden. Een sociaal-psychologische studie. Alphen a/d Rijn: Samsom.

Buunk, B. (1982). Strategies of jealousy: Styles of coping with extramarital involvement of the spouse. Family Relations, 31, 13-18.

Chelune, G. (1979). Self-Disclosure. San Francisco: Jossey-Bass Publishers.

Clanton, G., & Smith, L. (1977). Jealousy. Englewood Cliffs, N.J.: Prentice-Hall, Inc.

Constantine, L. & Constantine J. (1971) Sexual aspects of multilateral relations. Journal of Sex Research, 1, 204-255.

Deaux, K. (1976). The behavior of women and men. Belmont, CA: Wadsworth.

Denfeld, D. (1974). Dropouts from swinging: The marriage counselor as informant. In J. Smith and L. Smith (Eds.), Beyond monogamy. (pp. 260-267). Baltimore: Johns Hopkins University Press.

Gottschalk, H. (1936). Problems of jealousy (Skinsygens problemer). Copehagen: Fremad.

Jaremko, M., & Lindsey, R. (1979). Stress-coping abilities of individuals high and low in jealousy. Psychological Reports, 44, 547-553.

Kaplan, A., & Sedney, M. (1980). Psychology and sex roles: An androgynous perspective. Boston: Little, Brown and Co.

Manges, K., & Evenbeck, S. (1980). Social power, jealousy, and dependency in the intimate dyad. Paper presented at the annual meeting of the Midwestern Psychological Association, St. Louis.

Mathes, E., & Severa, N. (1981). Jealousy, romantic love, and liking: Theoretical considerations and preliminary scale development. Psychological Reports, 49, 23-31.

Mead, M. (1931). Jealousy: Primitive and civilized. In S. Schmalhausen & V. Calverton (Eds.), Women's coming of age. New York: Horace Liveright.

Parrish, S. (1983). Toward an understanding of romantic jealousy: A psychometric assessment of seven scales. Unpublished Doctoral Dissertation, Bowling Green State University.

Ray, L. (1978). The emotional components of jealousy: A multivariate investigation. Paper presented to the Speech Communication Association.

Rosenberg, M. (1965). Society and the adolescent self-image. Princeton, N.J.: Princeton University Press.

Schaef, A.(1981). Women's reality. Minneapolis: Winston Press.

Shettel-Neuber, J., Bryson, J., & Young, L. (1978). Physical attractiveness of the "other person" and jealousy. Personality and Social Psychology Bulletin, 4, 612-615.

Teismann, M., & Mosher, D. (1978). Jealous conflict in dating couples. Psychological Reports, 42, 1211-1216.

Varni, C. (1974). An exploratory study of spouse swapping. In J. Smith & L. Smith (Eds), Beyond monogamy, (pp. 246-259). Baltimore: Johns Hopkins University Press.

White, G. (1977). Inequity of emotional involvement and jealousy in romantic couples. Paper presented at the annual meetings of the American Psychological Association, San Francisco.

White, G. (1980). Inducing jealousy: A power perspective. Personality and Social Psychology Bulletin, 6, 222-227.

White, G. (1981a). Jealousy and partner's perceived motives for attraction to a rival. Social Psychology Quarterly, 44, 24-30.

White, G. (1981b). A model of romantic jealousy. Motivation and Emotion, 5, 295-310.

White, G. (1981c). Some correlates of romantic jealousy. Journal of Personality, 49, 129-142.

CHAPTER 7

TOPICS IN SAME SEX AND MIXED SEX CONVERSATIONS

Alice H. Deakins, Carole Osterink, and Timothy Hoey

Columbia University Teachers College

Topic selection[1]--who talks about what to whom and where--is a clue to the social rules, roles, and values of the people who are speaking. Eavesdropping, a "rapid and anonymous"[2] method of collecting data, is suited to study topic selection in populations found in public places because eavesdropping permits the collection of a large amount of data from naturally occurring, spontaneous interactions. If locations for eavesdropping are carefully selected, reliable data about groups (not individuals) can be collected. In this study, topic selection data obtained by eavesdropping shows variation by sex composition of the dyads, by setting, by social class, and by ethnic group. Further, topic selection patterns have changed over time.

The use of eavesdropping in public places to study gender differences in topic selection began during the 1920's.[3] In the face of the evidence from "mental" tests that men and women differ insignificantly in cognitive ability ("something that common sense and universal experience refuse to allow" Moore, 1922, p. 210), Henry T. Moore of Dartmouth College set out to prove that men and women differ in their "strong personal interests" as revealed by the topics of their conversations as they walk down the street in the evening. Such differences in interests are critical, according to Moore, for " a ctual mental achievement will always depend more on one's interests and enthusiasms than on one's downright native capacity" (Moore, 1922, p. 210).

Moore collected his data on conversation topics while "walking slowly up Broadway from 33rd Street to 55th Street at about 7:30 every evening" and jotting down "every bit of audible conversation" (Moore, 1922, p. 212). The frequencies of the topics he collected in 174 fragments of conversation are reported in Table 1 (Moore, 1922, p. 212).

Moore's study revealed that the subjects that men talked about most frequently--money, business and amusements--were the very subjects that women talked about least. A total of 62% of all conversations among men dealt with money and business or amusements, whereas only 7% of the conversations among women dealt with these topics. Similarly, the subjects that women talked about most frequently--men, or people of the opposite sex, and clothing and interior decorating--were the topics that men talked about least. Between women, 67% of all the conversations were about men, clothing, buildings, and interior decorating

89

while these were the topics of only 10% of the conversations between men.

Table 1

Topic Frequency: 1922
(in percent)

	M/M	F/F	M to F	F to M
Money and business	48	3	22	12
Amusement	14	4	25	10
Persons of same sex	13	16	13	13
Clothes, buildings, interior decoration	2	23	3	17
Persons of opposite sex	8	44	10	22
N=	80	30	32	32

The conversations between men and women showed that both men and women adapted to a degree when speaking to a person of the opposite sex, but women made the greater effort. Women quadrupled their interest in money and business and more than doubled their interest in amusements, the two favorite topics among men. Men´s effort to adapt consisted only of talking less about money and business--their favorite topics--and more about amusements--their second favorite topic. The increase in their interest in clothing, interior decorating, or people of either sex was negligible.

From this data, Moore concluded that

> there are very considerable and ineradicable differences in the original capacities of the two sexes for certain types of enthusiasm, and this difference must of necessity set the ultimate limit to woman´s success in assimilating male spheres of interest, regardless of the apparent equality of capacity often indicated by mental tests (Moore, 1922, p. 214).

Moore´s study inspired a similar one in 1923 by M. H. Landis and H. E. Burtt of Ohio State University. Their purpose was threefold: (1) to test Moore´s general results in a different section of the country and with a larger number of cases and to add as variables (2) the social status of the participants and (3) the physical setting of the conversations.

Landis and Burtt did their study in Columbus, Ohio. The method of collecting data was similar to that used by Moore. However, in addition to the conversation fragment and the sex of the persons involved, the time and place and an estimate of the speaker's social status were also recorded. In all, 481 conversations were recorded in a variety of places. The results of this study pertaining to sex differences are reported in Table 2 (Landis and Burtt, 1924, p. 84).

Table 2

Topic Frequency: 1924
(in percent)

	M/M	F/F	M to F	F to M
Business and money	49	12	19	10
Men	12	22	11	14
Women	4	15	5	10
Clothes and decoration	5	19	7	17
Sports	6	3	3	1
Other amusements	9	8	22	23
College work	3	4	2	4
Health	2	2	6	3
Self	7	13	17	15
Weather	3	2	8	3
N=	195	155	63	87

The later study confirmed the results of Moore's study. Men and women in Columbus, Ohio, showed essentially the same trends in conversation as men and women in New York City. Men talked to other men most frequently about money and business and about amusements. Women talked to other women most frequently about men, clothing, and interior decorating. It must be noted, however, that the women of Columbus, Ohio, showed only half as much interest in men as the women of New York City did and four times as much interest in money and business. When speaking to people of the opposite sex, both men and women in Columbus showed a fairly strong tendency to talk about amusements and about themselves.

When the data were coded for social status, there were sufficient numbers for three "classes": business people, industrial
workers, and students. All doubtful cases were listed as "unclassified." "The majority of the industrial workers and business
people were men and the majority of the unclassified group were
women. The students were about equally divided between the two
sexes" (Landis and Burtt, 1924, p. 85). The results showed that
business people talked about business (70%); industrial workers
talked about business (43%), men (21%), and self (13%); students
talked about sports and amusements (31%), men (21%), and self
(13%); and unclassified talked about clothes and decoration (20%),
with business and money, men, and self tied for second place
at 15%.

When the data were coded for gender and situation, Landis
and Burtt concluded that " t he situation in which the conversation takes place colors it to some extent but is not sufficient
to obscure the more fundamental trends" (Landis and Burtt, 1924,
p. 89). Men´s most frequent topic was still business and money
except when they were at the theatre or engaged in some form
of amusement. Women´s most frequent topics were still clothes,
men, and, to a lesser degree, women. Together they talked about
amusements, men, and themselves.

Both of the earlier studies confirm that if the topics in
conversation indicate the individuals´ "fundamental interests
and enthusiasms" (Landis and Burtt, 1924, p. 89), men´s greatest
interests are business and money, followed by sports and amusements. Women´s main interests are men and clothes. People are
a major focus for women but not for men.

Three studies done in 1980, 1983, and 1985 replicated those
of Moore and of Landis and Burtt, with some changes. Although
the Landis-Burtt assumption that "the natural trend of an indivi-
dual´s conversation is to quite an extent an indication of his
or her fundamental interests and enthusiasms" (Landis and Burtt,
1924, p. 89) needs modification; nevertheless, researchers in
this area still assume that what people talk about in naturally
occurring situations does reflect, in some undefined way, their
interests, both as individuals and as members of the group "man"
or "woman," that is, as exemplars of social roles. The three
contemporary studies added not only the variable of a later historical time but also setting, social class, and ethnic group.

METHODOLOGY

Coding

Each of the researchers followed the same peripatetic method
used by Moore, that is, they listened to conversations taking
place on public streets. The method of recording data differed

92

in two ways, however. First, the researchers coded data into 11 topic categories established by grouping 35 topics into the general categories: (1) business and money (including professional "shop talk," inflation, investments, and interest rates); (2) men; (3) women; (4) self and personal experience; (5) entertainment and recreation (including professional sports and recreational sports, leisure-time interest, and restaurants and food); (6) personal appearance concerns (clothing, hairdos, weight loss); (7) household concerns (furniture and decorating, food shopping and preparation, apartment hunting); (8) current events (including metropolitan, national, international); (9) children; (10) weather; and (11) serious discussion of general topics. All topics were coded into one of these 11 categories; no exact words were recorded.

Second, based on the difficulty of determining which member of a dyad had initiated a topic in mixed sex conversations, the previous categories used by Moore and Landis and Burtt of "man to woman" and "woman to man" were collapsed into "man and woman." Only the cross sex nature of the conversation was recorded, not who was speaking. This procedure also made possible the recording of more than one speaker on the same topic without distorting the data.

Study A (Osterink, 1980) recorded the topics of nearly 1,100 conversations in 40 hours; Study B (Hoey, 1983) recorded 800 conversations in 39 hours; and Study C (Richmond, 1985) recorded 72 conversations in 5 hours.[4]

Subjects

Study A looked at two populations: people on the street at lunchtime on weekdays in midtown Manhattan on the east side. This is a diverse population united by the concept of a "work setting." The second population, defined as "leisure setting," were people on Manhattan's upper west side on the weekends. This population is also diverse in demographics but inclined to be middle to upper income and single or married without children.

Study B also looked at two populations: a middle class and a working class neighborhood in Queens, New York. The neighborhoods were distinguished on occupations, mean income per household, average mean value of a house, and average mean rent.[5] A large number of the residents of the middle class area were working at the managerial or professional level, as technicians, or in sales. In the working class neighborhood, residents were chiefly employed as skilled or unskilled laborers, in the service industries, or as clerical workers.

Study C looked at one population: in a Bronx working class

neighborhood. The West Fordham Road area of the Bronx is characterized by a high degree of enclosure, with approximately 40%
Black, 40% Hispanic, 15% Asian and 5% White population. Most
(90-95%) of the subjects used in this study were Black, as most
of the Hispanics spoke in Spanish amd most of the Asians spoke
in Chinese, Korean, or Vietnamese.

Location and Time

Study A took place on various Manhattan streets. The midtown
Manhattan lunch hour conversations were overheard on Lexington,
Third, and Second Avenues between 47th and 57th streets. This
is an area which combines business with department stores (Bloom-
ingdales, Alexanders). During the week, it is an "at work" setting. The weekend conversations were heard on Broadway between
86th and 72nd, on Columbus Avenue beween 79th and 72nd, on 72nd
between Broadway and Central Park West, and around the West 81st
Street entrance to Central Park. This area contains unique cultural and recreational attractions, including restaurants, thea-
tres, and Central Park. People from both the immediate neighborhood and diverse areas of the metropolitan area congregate
here for recreational reasons. On the weekends, it is an "at
leisure" setting.

Study B was done on two streets in Queens. The middle class
data was collected along Queens Boulevard from Yellowstone Boulevard to 62nd Drive. The working class data was collected along
Jamaica Avenue from Lefferts Boulevard to Forest Parkway. Both
of these neighborhoods can be characterized as "at home" settings,
that is, they are the home neighborhoods for many of the people
on their streets.

Study C was done on West Fordham Road in the Bronx on weekend
afternoons. Although this was a neighborhood in commercial dis-
trict, it was also the home neighborhood for many of the people
on the street; it also is an "at home" setting.

RESULTS

Study A (setting variable)

Study A shows that data collected in a work setting differs
from data collected in a leisure setting. Further, work setting
topics for men today closely ressemble those found by Moore 60
years ago in what he might have defined as a leisure setting.
Table 3 displays the work setting data and Table 4 compares the
relevant categories to Moore´s study.

Table 3

Topic Frequency: Work Setting
(in percent)

	M/M	F/F	M/F
Business and money	43.0	8.5	24.5
Men	19.0	19.5	16.0
Women	9.5	24.0	12.5
Self and personal experience	3.5	5.5	8.25
Entertainment and recreation	14.5	15.0	22.75
Personal appearance	2.5	17.0	3.5
Household concerns	2.5	6.0	4.0
Current events	5.0	2.5	6.0
Children	---	---	---
Weather	---	1.5	2.0
Serious discussions of general topics	.5	.5	.5
N=	244	185	146

Table 4

Topic Frequency: 1922 and 1980 Work Setting
(in percent)

	M/M		F/F		M/F	
	1922	1980	1922	1980	1922	1980
Business and money	48.0	43.0	3.0	8.5	17.0	24.5
Amusements	14.0	14.5	4.0	15.0	17.0	22.75
Men	13.0	19.0	44.0	19.5	17.0	16.0
Women	8.0	9.5	16.0	24.0	11.0	12.5
Clothing, interior decoration	2.0	5.0	23.0	23.0	10.0	7.5

The results show that the patterns of conversation for men have not changed a great deal since Moore´s study in 1922. Business and money, amusements, and other men are still the topics of about 75% of all conversations among men. However, some interest has shifted from business and money to people as topics, mostly to men but a little to women as well. A greater change is seen in the conversations that women have with other women. Women talked about men only half as much as they did in Moore´s study, while their interest in other women is 50% greater. Women´s interest in recreation and entertainment has quadrupled since 1922; women show as much interest in amusement as men do. The results also show that in conversation with other women, women talk about clothing and personal appearance almost three times as much as they talk about money and business.

Contemporary conversations that involve men and women together in the work setting show an almost equal amount of interest in people, money and business, and entertainment and recreation. Women and men together discuss business considerably less frequently than men do with each other but almost three times more often than women do with each other. Men and women together discuss entertainment and recreation more than either women or men. Conversations between men and women show less interest in people than conversations among women and about the same amount of interest in people as conversations among men.

The sharp distinctions between men´s and women´s interests that were found in the studies done in the 1920´s have lessened in the 1980´s. Although a comparatively large percentage of M/M talk is about subjects (business and money) that appear to interest women very little and a fair amount of F/F talk is about subjects that seem to interest men hardly at all (clothing, hairdo´s, weight loss), the results from the work setting do show a trend toward convergence.

The communality of interest that is suggested by the data from the work setting is dramatically apparent in the data from the leisure setting. Table 5 compares the contemporary work and leisure settings.

In a leisure setting, men talk about entertainment and recreation, other men, and themselves; women talk about entertainment and recreation, other women, and themselves; and women and men together talk about entertainment and recreation, other women and men, and themselves. These topics constitute 66.5% of the conversations among men, 56.25% of the conversations among women, and 66.25 % of the conversations between men and women. Both men and women talk about themselves more in the leisure setting than in the work setting, with women doing so more frequently. Of 69 cases of a person talking about themselves, 42 were women and 27 were men.

In the leisure setting, men have as many conversations about business and money as they have serious discussion on such topics as education, literary criticism, and military history (in each case the figure is 6.25%). Women in the leisure setting show less than half as much interest in clothing and personal appearance than they do in the work setting.

Table 5

Topic Frequency: Work and Leisure Settings
(in percent)

	M/M		F/F		M/F	
	Work	Leisure	Work	Leisure	Work	Leisure
Business and money	43.0	6.25	8.5	3.5	24.5	6.25
Men	19.0	18.5	19.5	13.5	16.0	10.5
Women	9.5	9.0	24.0	18.0	12.5	1.0
Self and personal experience	3.5	10.5	5.5	14.75	8.25	13.75
Entertainment/ recreation	14.5	37.5	15.0	23.5	22.75	31.00
Personal appearance	2.5	3.5	17.0	8.0	3.5	6.25
Household concerns	2.5	4.5	6.0	6.75	4.0	8.5
Current events	5.0	2.0	2.5	1.25	6.0	4.5
Children	---	1.0	---	6.75	---	3.0
Weather	---	1.0	1.5	2.0	2.0	.5
Serious discussion of general topics	.5	6.25	.5	2.0	.5	4.75
N=	244	112	185	149	146	255

The conversations in the work setting reveal traditional role-influenced patterns, which are especially apparent in the M/M interactions. In the leisure setting, however, the "spontaneous choice of topics" and the "natural trend of easy conversation" that Moore counted on to betray woman´s mental shortcomings show that the interests common to men and women are greater than the interests peculiar to either men or women.

Study B (social class variable)

The study done in Queens was also in non-work setting, with the addition of an at-home, neighborhood environment. Social class was the independent variable. Table 6 displays the results of the study.

Compared to Study A, Study B shows a decline in the topics of business and money, other people (men or women), entertainment and recreation, and current events. It shows a sharp rise in the topics self and personal experience and household concerns and a slight rise in the topics personal appearance (especially among middle class males), children (across a variety of dyads), and serious discussion of general topics (especially among women). Some of these general differences may be due to the at-home setting of Study B, in contrast to the at-work or at-leisure settings of Study A.

Table 6

Topic Frequency: Middle Class and Working Class
(in percent)

	M/M		F/F		M/F	
	MC	WC	MC	WC	MC	WC
Business/money	5.0	4.3	1.2	1.8	6.5	1.9
Men	8.4	11.9	5.5	7.5	4.5	8.9
Women	5.0	3.2	12.4	10.4	11.7	5.7
Self and personal experience	52.5	52.1	33.5	38.3	38.5	45.2
Entertainment/ recreation	6.7	9.7	6.2	8.5	12.4	5.0
Personal appearance	6.7	3.2	16.1	11.3	6.5	8.2
Household	10.1	8.6	14.9	15.1	13.0	17.8

	M/M		F/F		M/F	
	MC	WC	MC	WC	MC	WC
Current events	1.6	---	0.6	0.9	---	---
Children	---	1.0	3.1	2.8	3.2	2.5
Weather	---	2.1	2.4	1.8	0.6	---
Serious discussion of general topics	3.3	3.2	3.7	0.9	2.6	4.4
N=	59	92	161	211	53	157

Comparing across the two classes of Study B, self and personal experience dominate all the dyads, comprising more than half the topics for both M/M groups. Household concerns were the second most popular topic across most dyads; for F/F and M/F dyads, it was the second most popular topic ("men" was the second most popular topic for M/M dyads).

Of particular interest is the result that men are talked about more in the working class and women in the middle class in all the dyads. Table 7 shows that middle class dyads talk about women and men in the reverse proportions of working class dyads.

Table 7

Topic Frequency "Men" and "Women"
(in percent)

	M/M	F/F	M/F	Total
Middle class				
"men"	8.4	5.5	4.5	18.4
"women"	5.0	12.4	11.7	29.1
Working class				
"men"	11.9	7.5	8.9	28.3
"women"	3.2	10.4	5.7	19.3

Entertainment and recreation again show a merger of interests in the cross sex middle class dyads but not in the working class. Personal appearance is higher for women than for men and more middle class than working class except in the cross sex dyads. Serious discussion of general topics takes place infrequently across all dyads but is most common in the cross sex working class group.

Children are discussed by five of the six dyads, the exception being middle class M/M. The infrequency of children as a topic is somewhat surprising as these neighborhoods are family-oriented, with children under 18 comprising 25% of the population of the middle class neighborhood and 13% of the working class neighborhood. The lack of discussion of children contrasts sharply with the saliency of household concerns as a topic.

Another point of interest is that women, as a group, discuss a wider range of topics than men; they discuss topics outside of their own personal experience about 2/3rds of the time whereas the men do so less than 1/2 the time.

This study, like Study A (leisure), does not find the sharp topic differences characteristic of the earlier studies and the work setting. Smaller differences in topic preferences still separate the same sex and mixed sex groups, however.

Study C (ethnic group variable)

The study of a multi-ethnic predominately black working class neighborhood adds some interesting information to the area of topic. Table 8 displays the results of the study.

Again, self and personal experience surface as the most frequently discussed topics. The second most popular topic among the men was women, in sharp contrast to the other two studies. For women, women and personal appearance tied for second place as most popular topics with men and children tied for third. In mixed sex groups, children were the second most popular topic after self and personal experience.

In contrast to all the other studies, children in this study were discussed across all dyads, being the third favorite topic for women and the second for mixed groups. The Bronx neighborhood which was surveyed had many toddlers through preteens accompanied by adults walking the streets on one day of the survey, possibly because of unusually hot weather, which is reflected in the more frequent occurrence of weather as a topic than in the other studies. The greater talk about children by the mixed gender group could also result from the fact that more married couples were overheard than mixed dyads of single people.

The least favored topics were business and money (dominant among men in Study A); household concerns (popular in Study B); and current events and serious discussion of a general topic (not of high saliency in the other studies either).

Certain topics--men, women, self and personal experience, personal appearance, and children--reveal differences between same sex and mixed sex dyads.

Table 8

Topic Frequency: Black Working Class
(in percent)

	M/M	F/F	M/F
Business and money	---	---	3.8
Men	10.5	11.1	---
Women	31.6	14.8	3.8
Self and personal experience	47.4	29.6	50.0
Entertainment/ recreation	5.3	7.4	7.7
Personal appearance	---	14.8	3.8
Household	---	---	3.8
Current events	---	3.7	3.8
Children	5.3	11.1	15.4
Weather	---	7.4	7.7
Serious discussion of general topics	---	---	---
N=	19	27	26

DISCUSSION

A comparison of topics across time shows some some continuities and some discontinuities with the past. In comparing the
top three topics in all dyads across the studies, continuities
appear in the frequent discussion of men and amusements and infrequent discussion of women. Discontinuities appear in the loss
of money and business as a frequent topic across dyads and the
addition of self and personal experience and household concerns.
Table 9 displays the data.

In relationship to the past, Study A shows a maintenance,
in the work sphere, of M/M topics, some change in F/F topics,
and the beginnings of topic convergence in M/F dyads. In the
leisure setting there is a startling convergence of topics with
"entertainment" coming first across the three dyads and "same
sex" and "self" second and third in the same sex dyads. In the

mixed dyads,"self" was second and "women" and "men" were in a
close race for third.

Table 9

Topics: 1920´s and 1980´s

	1920´s	1980´s
continuities		
"men"	3/3	10/15
"amusements/		
entertainment"	2/3	8/15
"women"	1/3	4/15
discontinuities		
"money and business"	2/3	2/15
"self and personal		
experience"	0/3	12/15
"household concerns"	0/3	5/15

Study B shows clearly that "self and personal experience"
have high frequency; it was the most frequent topic across the
six dyads surveyed. "Household concerns" was second in four
dyads and third in two. "Men" was second in one and third in
two.

Study C continues the dominance of "self"; it was first
in all three of the dyads studied. "Women" was second in two,
and "men" was third in two. The prominence of "self and personal
experience" as a topic discussed on the street is a clear break
with the past and an indication of a change over time. Study
C also revealed the presence of "children" as a topic in certain
groups.

Context, class, and ethnic group differences emerged in
the frequency of "men" and "women" as topics. In Studies A and
B, "men" are discussed more than "women" in M/M dyads and "women"
more than "men" in F/F dyads. In mixed sex dyads in Study A,
"men" are discussed more in the work setting and "women" in the
leisure setting. In mixed sex dyads in Study B, the middle class
discusses "women" more and the working class discusses "men"
more. In Study C, in contrast, ""women" are discussed more than
"men" in both the M/M and F/F dyads, and "men" are not discussed
at all in the mixed dyads.

The visibility and invisibility of "men" and "women" as
topics is correlated to their differential visibilty and availability for eavesdropping on the streets (see Table 10). The visibility of M/M dyads in the 1924 study and in the 1980 work context

is remarkable in comparison to their relative invisibility in
the leisure context and in both the at-home, neighborhood studies.
One possible explanation is that men socialize together in sex
segregated areas like golf courses, basketball courts, billiard
halls, and other recreation-oriented places. It is also possible
that they meet in bars. Other research has noticed that the
corner bar is an invaluable area for sociolinguistic research
on male working-class speech and topic patterns.

> Typically, groups of men have their own corner bar, a public
> drinking establishment which has been claimed by them as
> their `turf,´ a territory to which outsiders are not invited
> or welcomed. Working class men seek out other men of like
> identity, in well-established locations, and these are the
> situations in which it is most appropriate and proper for
> a man to produce a great quantity of talk (Philipsen, 1975,
> p. 15).

The data from this study raise the possibility that this pattern
extends beyond the working class.

Table 10

Numbers of Conversations

	M/M	F/F	M/F
Landis and Burtt (1924)	195	155	150
Study A (1980)			
Work	244	185	146
Leisure	112	149	255
Study B (1983)			
Middle class	59	161	153
Working class	92	211	157
Study C (1985)	19	27	26

As a methodology, eavesdropping has both limitations and
advantages. This study is limited by the anonymity of the individuals who are its subjects. While variables of sex, setting,
social class, and ethnic group have been roughly controlled,
education, age, and degree of intimacy of the relationship are
unknown. Further, all the data has been collected in a public
domain, "the street"; what people talk about in boardrooms or
in bedrooms is not accessible via this methodology.

A further limitation to eavesdropping studies is that the

categories of M/M, F/F and M/F hide the dynamics of conversation, that is, while they reveal what topics are discussed in such dyads, they do not show who introduces each topic and the mechanisms which support or suppress its continuation.[6] An understanding of the dynamics of single sex and mixed sex conversation is only hinted at by eavesdropping studies.

Eavesdropping studies have the advantages of using naturally occurring data, accessible to replication. A variety of group variables may be studied: age, sex, social class, ethnic group, and setting. This study has shown that topic is sensitive to variables of historical time, sex of partner, work-leisure context, social class, and ethnic group.

In the last 60 years, there have been two sets of topic selection studies using eavesdropping to gather the data, from the 1920´s and the 1980´s. It is not within the scope of this paper to examine why eavesdropping was abandoned for 60 years, but the two sets of studies, separated by more than half a century, show vivid contrasts. Eavesdropping studies in the 1920´s were based on the assumption of an "unyielding innate divergence" (Moore, 1922, p. 211) between the two sexes in the "enthusiasms" of men and women, which "must of necessity set an ultimate limit to woman´s success in assimilating male spheres of interest, regardless of the apparent equality of capacity often indicated by mental tests" (Moore, 1922, p. 214). The recent studies show not "unyielding innate divergence" but topic convergence, especially in non-work settings, while sex distinct patterns (M/M, F/F, and M/F) are less strongly maintained in fewer areas. Topic selection patterns reveal a growing equality between men and women without loss of distinct sex differences.

[1]The definition of "topic," which is theoretically complicated, was not a problem for the researchers. In grammatical
theory, the notion of topic is related to subject, and efforts
to understand this relationship have resulted in the labels grammatical (superficial) subject, logical subject, psychological
subject, theme, emphasis, focus, given, in addition to subject
and topic (Gundel, 1977, passim; Li, 1976).

In discourse theory, a distinction needs to be made between
what is being talked about (overt topic) and what proposition
the participants may actually be arguing (covert topic). For
example, discussion about a "china closet" (overt topic) may
actually be negotiating a marital relationship (covert topic)
(Hill and Varenne, 1986, p. 18). These distinctions were not
pertinent to this study, which collected overt topics as data.

[2]Labov's 1966 study of three New York City department stores
established the rapid and anonymous survey as a reliable sociolinguistic methodology (Labov, 1972, chap. 2).

[3]Other methods used to study topic selection have been self-
report (Aries and Johnson, 1983; Haas and Sherman, 1982; Johnson
and Aries, 1983; and Sollie and Fischer, 1985); participant observation (Derber, 1979); and audiotaping (Fishman, 1977, 1978,
and 1980; Hill and Varenne, 1986; Labov and Fanshel, 1977; Soskin
and John, 1963; Tannen, 1984; West, 1979; and Zimmerman and West,
1983). Self-reporting is vulnerable to inaccuracy in reporting
one's own behavior (Labov, 1972, pp. 131-132) and to gender differences in self-disclosure (Pearson, 1985, p. 114).

[4]Study C (Richmond, 1985) has a small population, the significance of which is not clear in sociolinguistic analysis. Landis
and Burtt in 1924 enlarged Moore's 1922 sample from 174 to 500
without changing Moore's conclusions. The problem of what constitutes an adequate sample has not been resolved for sociolinguistic
data; therefore, Study C has been included in this paper with
a caution concerning the small sample.

[5]Figures were taken from the U.S. Department of Commerce,
Bureau of the Census (1982).

[6]Initiation and maintenance of topic are critical to understanding the dynamics of interaction (Derber, 1979; Fishman,
1978; Hill and Varenne, 1986; Tannen, 1984; and Zimmerman and
West, 1983). A bibliography of topic control studies is found
in Thorne, Kramarae, and Henley, 1983, p. 287.

REFERENCES

Aries, E. J. and Johnson, F. L. (1976). Close friendship in adulthood: Conversational content between same-sex friends. Sex Roles, 9(12), 1183-1196.

Derber, C. (1979). The pursuit of attention. Cambridge, MA: Schenckman.

Fishman, P. M. (1978). What do couples talk about when they´re alone? In Douglas Buturff and Edmund Epstein (Eds.), Women´s language and style (pp. 11-22). Akron, OH: L & S Books.

Fishman, P. M. (1983). Interaction: The work women do. In Barrie Thorne, Cheris Kramarae, & Nancy Henley (Eds.), Language, gender and society (pp. 89-101). Rowley, MA: Newbury.

Gundel, J. K. (1977). Role of topic and comment in linguistic theory. Bloomington: Indiana University Linguistics Club.

Haas, A. & Sherman, M. A. (1982). Reported topics of conversation among same-sex adults. Communication Quarterly, 30(4), 332-342.

Hill, C. and Varenne, H. (1986). Talk and topic. Unpublished manuscript.

Hoey, T. (1983). Class and environmental influences on leisure-time conversation. Unpublished manuscript.

Johnson, F. L. and Aries, E. J. (1983). Conversational patterns among same-sex pairs of late-adolescent close friends. The Journal of Genetic Psychology, 142, 225-238.

Labov, W. (1972). Sociolinguistic patterns. Philadelphia: Univ. of PA Press.

Labov, W. and Fanshel, D. (1977). Therapeutic discourse. N Y : Academic Press.

Landis, M. H. and Burtt, H. E. (1924). A study of conversations. Journal of Comparative and Physiological Psychology, 4, 81-89.

Li, C. C.(Ed.). Subject and topic. NY: Academic Press, 1976.

Moore, H. T. (1922). Further data concerning sex differences. Journal of Abnormal Psychology and Social Psychology, 17 (2), 210-214.

Osterink, C. (1980). What men and women talk about at work and at play. Unpublished manuscript.

Pearson, J. C. (1985). Gender and communication. Dubuque, IA: Wm. C. Brown.

Philipsen, G. (1975). Speaking "like a man" in Teamsterville: Culture patterns of role enactment in an urban neighborhood. Quarterly Journal of Speech, 61, 13-22.

Richmond, A. (1985). A study of the effect of class and gender based variables on the selection of conversation t o p i c s . Unpublished manuscript.

Sollie, D. L. and Fischer, J. L. (1985). Sex role orientation, intimacy of topic, and target person differences in self-disclosure among women. Sex Roles, 12(9/10), 917 929.

Soskin, W. F. and John, V. P. (1963). The study of spontaneous talk. In Roger Barker (Ed.), The stream of behavior (pp. 228-281). NY: Appleton Century Crofts.

Tannen, D. 1984). Conversational style: Analyzing talk among friends. Norwood, NJ: Ablex Publishing Company. U.S.

Department of Commerce, Bureau of the Census. (1982). Washington, DC: U.S. Government Printing Office.

West, C. (1979). Against our will: Male interruptions of females in cross-sex conversations. In Judith Orasanu, Miriam K. Slater, and Leonore Loeb Adler (Eds.), Language, sex, and gender (pp. 81-97). NY: New York Academy of Sciences.

Zimmerman, D. H. and West, C. (1975). Sex roles, interruptions and silences in conversation. In Barrie Thorne and Nancy Henley (Eds.), Language and sex: Difference and dominance (pp. 105-129). Rowley, MA: Newbury.

CHAPTER 8

SEX DIFFERENCES IN INTERACTION MANAGEMENT AND GOALS

Judi Beinstein Miller, Oberlin College

Studies of interaction management have generally found that men attempt to control interaction more than women do. Yet significant exceptions suggest that these differences may not be transsituational and, in fact, may depend on their respective goals in interaction. The purpose of this chapter was to review the literature on sex differences in interaction management and compare patterns of control among men and women as a function of their conversational situation. The first part of the chapter addresses measures that have been used in previous studies to index control of interaction and summarizes findings regarding sex differences. The second part reports a two-part study in which comparisons are made 1) between the control moves of men and women whose interaction goals have been indirectly manipulated in a set of hypothetical social situations and 2) between their control moves in these situations and a roleplay conversation.

Interaction Management

Attempts to control interaction have been measured in a variety of ways. One has been the coding of efforts to manage speaking roles (i.e. to hold or get the conversational floor). Interruptions are one example, even though it is questionable whether all interruptions amount to domineering behavior. Interruptive questions, for example, may function to support and encourage the speaker, rather than to take the floor away from him/her. Still, in the majority of studies that have compared interruptions by men versus women, men have been found to interrupt their partners more often than have women (Hall, 1984); their interruptions have also been found to be longer than those of women (Natale et al., 1979).

Exceptions to these findings suggest that there may be circumstances in which men do not consistently produce the largest number of interruptions. In one study, where same and mixed sex dyads had to solve a murder mystery, women and men differed only in their interruptions of opposite sex partners; men interrupted women more than women interrupted men (McMillan et al., 1977). In a study by Zimmerman and West, where same and mixed sex dyads were asked to have acquainting conversations, men initiated more interruptions but did not contest challenges to their interruptions as often as women did (Smith, 1985). In still another study, where married, dating, and previously unacquainted couples discussed human relations problems, women interrupted their partners more often than the reverse (Shaw and Sadler,

1965). And in another, women produced the larger number of interruptive questions while discussing college experiences and a debatable issue (LaFrance and Carmen, 1980).

When efforts to hold the floor are measured by speech quantity, men are generally found to participate more than women (Duncan and Fiske, 1977; Hall, 1984; Strodtbeck et al., 1957), but in one study women talked considerably more in same sex dyads than did men (Hall, 1984). In another they produced longer utterances in both same and mixed sex dyads (Markel, Long, and Saine, 1976). In still another there were no differences in the average duration of utterances by men and women (McMillan et al., 1977). In studies where the differences favored men, these differences were not sizeable. Consequently, it can also not be concluded that men talk consistently longer than women.

When floor holding is measured by filled pauses, findings are relatively consistent. Men use more filled pauses (presumably to hold the floor while collecting their thoughts) than women, regardless of whether their partners are the same or opposite sex (Duncan and Fiske, 1977; Hall, 1984; LaFrance and Carmen, 1980). Fewer studies have been made of filled pauses though, and in one these appeared to reflect anxiety on the part of males and were associated with low self-rated dominance (Frances, 1979).

Two other measures of floor getting and holding have been employed in studies of women's and men's dialogic behavior: loudness and silence breaking. In both cases men exceed women (Hall, 1984).

Another way in which attempts to control interaction have been measured is through efforts to manage the topic or task under discussion. Here, such utterances as suggestions, statements of orientation, and opinions are considered to be task-oriented and directive (Bales, 1950). Early studies of mixed sex mock juries found that men offered more opinions and statements of orientation than women, who offered more agreements (Strodtbeck et al., 1957; Strodtbeck and Mann, 1956). More recently, in discussions of 3 human relations cases, opinion and information giving occurred most often among males in same sex groups and least often among women in same sex groups (Pilliavin and Martin, 1978). In mixed sex groups, opinion and information giving increased among females and decreased among males. Suggestions also have been found to be offered most often in all male groups and least often in all female groups, with predominantly male and predominantly female groups falling in-between (Mabry, 1985). These differences occurred primarily in structured groups (those with a rank-ordering task), not in relatively unstructured ones (those discussing a human relations problem).

When attempts to manage interaction in general (i.e. both speaking roles and topics) have been measured, fewer differences have been found between men and women. In a study of newly-weds discussing minor agreements, for example, women defended their opinions, disagreed, and criticized their husbands' viewpoints or character as often as their husbands did theirs (Doherty and Ryder, 1979). In conversations regarding a lawsuit over which same and mixed sex dyads agreed or disagreed, women attempted to control interaction (e.g. by one-up moves) as often as men (Fisher, 1983). In four-person discussion groups, men and women were equally assertive in same sex groups, and in mixed sex groups only the second woman to talk proved to be less assertive (Kimble et al., 1981). Yet when women and men were instructed to compete for a minor, hypothetical reward in same sex dyads, women proved to be significantly more acquiescent (e.g. by moving down) than men (Beinstein Miller, 1985).

Interaction Goals

The balance of findings suggests a competitive edge for men but sufficient exceptions to raise questions regarding the circumstances under which men and women attempt to control interaction. Of particular interest in this regard is that participants in these studies have been placed in relatively unstructured conversational situations (e.g. to have acquainting conversations or discuss any topic) or in structured ones (e.g. to reach decisions, offer arguments, or exchange opinions about a specific issue), where interaction goals besides the presumable purpose of the encounter could have been salient. Acquainting and freewheeling conversation, for example, may make self-presentational goals more salient than structured conversations do. In studies of acquainting and freewheeling conversations, men appear to produce more controlling behavior than women, regardless of the measure used to index conversational control (Aries, 1976; Duncan and Fiske, 1977; Natale et al., 1979; Smith, 1985). Findings from two studies may be exceptions. In one, verbal assertiveness did differ in mixed sex groups, but not in same sex groups (Kimble et al., 1981). In the other, women produced longer utterances than men but were talked to longer by both women and men (Markel, Long, and Saine, 1976).

Structured conversational situations, in contrast, appear to produce more exceptions, which may indicate differences in the extent to which they make different interaction goals salient. Mabry (1985) found, for example, that relatively structured tasks produced more dominant behavior than relatively unstructured ones, especially among all male groups. Fisher (1983) found that women and men did not differ in controlling responses when discussing differences of opinion; rather, it was the extent of disagreement between them that made a difference. Adams (1980) and Doherty and

111

Ryder (1979) also found no differences in the extent to which men and women sustained challenges to their opinions.

It is possible that the relative salience of self-presentational goals may make a difference in the behavior of men and women. Women have been found to score higher in interpersonal orientation than men (Swap and Rubin, 1983). They report being more responsive to interpersonal aspects of their relationships with others, more interested in and reactive to variations in the behavior of others, and taking the behavior of others perhaps unduly personally. In acquainting conversations it would not be surprising for them to be more concerned with establishing mutuality (e.g. through agreement and politeness) than with managing speaking roles and discussion of topics. Men, in contrast, might be less concerned with others' impressions of their mutuality and more concerned with impressions of their autonomy in the situation.

In such relatively structured situations as issue disagreements, instructions to argue points of view or reach consensus may increase controlling behavior only if the issue is important. When the issue or disagreement is not important, relational and self-presentational goals may override instructions by the experimenter. Unfortunately, such comparisons have not been made in previous research on conversations.

The Present Study

The present study attempted to compare the control responses of men and women undergraduates in a variety of situations where self-presentational concerns had or had not been manipulated to be salient. Participants were asked how they would respond in a series of 9 hypothetical conflict situations, 3 posing minor threats to their goals, 3 to their opinions, and 3 to their competencies. While this technique did not permit examination of conversational data (only the initial response to each situation was of interest), it did provide a set of targets that were expected to structure the students' responses. To determine the validity of these responses, a subset of students was engaged in a roleplay situation regarding a moral dilemma (they had to reach consensus regarding passengers to save on a sinking ship) and their control moves compared with those they indicated in the hypothetical situations. Based on findings regarding opinion disagreements and the expectation that this roleplay situation would make differences in opinion salient, it was anticipated that the responses of women and men in same sex dyads would be equally controlling. Moreover, it was hoped that correlations between their control moves in the roleplay situation and in the 3 hypothetical situations challenging their opinions would validate the use of self-reported response style. Moderately strong positive correlations would attest the usefulness of this technique.

The salience of self-presentational goals was manipulated indirectly by having one set of students respond to the hypothetical situations privately and a second set respond in an interview situation. It was expected that the presence of an interviewer would make self-presentational goals salient (as has been demonstrated by other manipulations of public self-awareness, for example, Carver and Scheier, 1981) and that women, in particular, would be susceptible to this manipulation. Specifically, it was expected that differences between the control moves of women responding privately and women responding publicly (to an interviewer) would be greater than those between the control moves of men responding privately and publicly (to an interviewer), although the direction of these differences was not predicted.

METHOD

Subjects

Two hundred, forty-seven male and female undergraduates responded to 9 hypothetical conflict situations that posed minor threats to their competencies, opinions, and goals. One hundred, thirty-three responded privately on a questionnaire in their dormitory rooms; 114 responded publicly to trained student interviewers. Unfortunately, equal numbers of male and female interviewers could not be recruited. Eight were women and only two were men. The 23 interviews that had been conducted by men were dropped from subsequent analysis so that the sex of the interviewer could be held constant.

Procedure

The students were asked to imagine themselves with a friend in each situation and indicate precisely what they might say.

Three of the situations were intended to challenge their competencies. One, for example, was described as follows.

> You have been taking a course that is of great interest to you and in which you frequently make comments and raise questions. One day a friend, who is also taking the course, comes up to you after class and says, "You really ought to save your comments for after class...they take up too much time."

> What would you say to your friend?

113

Similarly they were asked to indicate what they would say after being told that they'd done poorly on an exam due to careless reading of a question and after being accused of having told a bad joke. Three other situations were intended to challenge their opinions. One, for example, was described as follows.

> You are chatting with a friend about a movie
> you've both seen. You liked the movie but
> your friend says, "It was simple-minded,
> trite, really stupid."
>
> What would you say to your friend?

They were also asked to indicate what they would say in response to being told a new acquaintance they liked was 'weird' and in response to being told the major they had declared was poor.

The final 3 situations were intended to challenge their goals. One, for example, was described as follows.

> You have an important job interview in an hour
> and a friend of yours has promised to lend you
> his/her car to get there. When you arrive at
> your friend's for the keys your friend says,
> "Oh...I was going to let my roommate use the
> car for an hour."
>
> What would you say to your friend?

They were also asked to indicate what they would say in response to being prevented from finishing a termpaper in their dormitory room because their roommate was planning a party there and in response to a friend wanting to take the only place left in a course that they also wanted to take.

Scoring

Their responses to the situations were coded as one-up, one-down, or one-across moves, according to a previously validated relational control coding system (Rogers and Farace, 1975; Courtright, Millar, and Rogers-Millar, 1979; Rogers-Millar and Millar, 1979). One-up moves are considered to be attempts to control or define interaction, one-down moves requests for or acceptance of the other's definition, and one-across moves relatively noncommittal responses. The number of times they moved up was used to estimate their assertiveness in these situations, the number of times they moved down their acquiescence, and the number of times they moved across their noncommittalness. The potential range for each estimate was therefore 0 to 9. Similar

114

sums were computed for the control direction of their responses to the 3 situations in which their competencies had been challenged, to the 3 in which they were faced with an opinion disagreement, and to the 3 in which their goals had been threatened. The potential range for each of these estimates was therefore 0 to 3. Coding agreement was estimated at .95, pi (Scott) at .91.

Validation Procedure

Sixteen of the men and 18 of the women who had responded privately to the hypothetical social situations also participated in a roleplay exercise that was intended to make differences in opinion salient. These previously unacquainted men and women were paired into same sex dyads and asked to imagine themselves at a small party where most of the people were strangers. At the party someone suggests that they break the ice by trying to reach consensus on a moral dilemma. The dilemma required roleplayers to save three out of six passengers on a sinking ship. There followed descriptions of 6 passengers, 3 women and 3 men, each with a different occupation and set of family circumstances. Students were permitted to study the situation prior to roleplaying. They did not discuss the situation with their partners, however, prior to its enactment. All conversations were tape-recorded and transcribed. All but one produced at least one disagreement over who should be saved.

The same coding instrument as was used to code responses to the hypothetical situations was used to code all exchanges in the roleplay conversations. Coding agreement was estimated at .92, pi (Scott) at .87.

Public Self-Consciousness Scores

Finally, because similar findings have been reported for manipulations of self-awareness and differences in dispositional self-consciousness (Carver and Scheier, 1981), a subset of students (those who responded publicly to the hypothetical social situations) were also asked to fill out the self-consciousness questionnaire reported by Fenigstein, Scheier, and Buss in 1975. This instrument contains 3 subscales, one for private self-consciousness, one for public self-consciousness, and one for social anxiety. It was the public self-consciousness subscale that was of interest here because it measures concern with reactions of others to the self. Specifically, it was expected that if differences in private and public response to the 9 hypothetical social situations were greater among women than among men, then these differences would also be manifest among men and women who scored high (scale scores of 21-28) and low (scales scores of 4-15) in dispositional public self-consciousness.

115

Separate ANOVA's were run to compare the total number of one-up, one-down, and one-across moves, according to the sex of the students and whether they had responded privately or publicly. Separate ANOVA's were also run to compare their responses to situations in which their competencies, opinions, and goals had been challenged.   ·

T-tests were used to compare the control moves and interacts of the 16 men and 18 women who also participated in the roleplay exercise. Correlations (r) were computed between their responses in the roleplay exercise and their responses to the hypothetical social situations.

Finally, because only 2 of the 10 trained interviewers had been men, the responses of participants interviewed by men were compared with those interviewed by women in a separate set of ANOVA's to determine whether the sex of the interviewer could have made a difference in control moves.

RESULTS

Control Moves in the Hypothetical Social Situations:
Differences among Private and Public Responders

Comparisons of control moves among men and women who responded privately and publicly to the 9 hypothetical situations yielded two interaction effects (See Table 1). Women who responded publicly and men who responded privately moved up most often ($F=5.955$, $df=1,220$, $p<.05$) and women who responded privately and men who responded publicly moved down most often ($F=6.461$, $df=1,220$, $p<.01$).

When competencies were target, public responders moved up more often than private responders ($F=5.981$, $df=1,220$, $p<.05$). A marginally significant testing condition X sex interaction indicated that this was due primarily to the greater difference in women's private and public responses than to the men's ($F=3.727$, $df=1,220$, $p<.10$). In contrast, private responders moved down more often than public responders ($F=15.606$, $df=1,220$, $p<.001$). A testing condition X sex interaction indicated that this too was due primarily to the greater difference in the women's than men's private and public responses ($F=5.934$, $df=1,220$, $p<.05$).

When goals were target, women moved across somewhat more often than men ($F=3.670$, $df=1,216$, $p<.10$). No other differences proved to be statistically significant.

Control Moves in the Hypothetical Social Situations:
Differences according to Public Self-Consciousness

Comparisons of control moves by men and women who had been
interviewed and categorized as low or high in public self-
consciousness substantiated most of the above findings (See Table
2).   Since the self-awareness of these men and women had been
increased by the presence of an interviewer, it should come as no
surprise that differences in their self-consciousness widened the
differences in their control moves. Across all 9 situations women
moved up more than men (F=7.699, df=1,54, p<.01); men moved down
more than women (F=14.566, df=1,54, p<.001). Those who scored
high in public self-consciousness moved up more than those who
scored low (F=5.128, df=1,54, p<.05). High scorers moved across
less than low scorers (F=10.653, df=1,54, p<.01).

A   posteriori contrasts (Student-Newman-Keuls procedure)
indicated that women who scored high in public self-consciousness
had moved up more than any other group and that men, regardless of
their public self-consciousness scores, had moved down more than
these women.

Differences in response to attacks on competencies were
similar. Men moved down more often than women (F=13.187,
df=1,54, p<.001) but the greater number of one-up moves on the
part of women was only marginally significant (F=2.688, df=1,54,
p<.10).   Both men and women who scored high in public self-
consciousness moved up more often than those who scored low
(F=9.211, df=1,54, p<.01). They also moved across less often
(F=11.753, df=1,54, p<.001).

Responses to Male and Female Interviewers

Comparisons of responses to male and female interviewers
should be regarded cautiously due to the relatively small number
of students, especially men, interviewed by men. Still, results
suggest that the sex of the interviewer may have made little
difference in responses to opinion disagreements but may have made
a difference in responses to attacks on competencies and goals.
When competencies were target, both men and women moved up more in
response to female than to male interviewers (F=3.683, df=1,110,
p<.10) and moved down more in response to male than female
interviewers (F=2.938, df=1,110, p<.10). But women moved up more
(F=3.234, df=1,110, p<.10) and men down more (F=5.776, df=1,110,
p<.05) regardless of who happened to interview them.

When goals were target, differences in response appeared to
depend primarily on the sex of the interviewer. Men who had been
interviewed by men moved up most often and women who had been
interviewed by men least often (F=17.908, df=1,110, p<.001).

Conversely, men who had been interviewed by men moved down least often and women who had been interviewed by men most often (F=11.964, df=1,110, p<.001).

Thus the differences in response to attacks on competencies among self-aware and publicly self-conscious men and women were probably not due to the sex of the interviewer. Differences in response to attacks on goals may have emerged had there been equal numbers of male and female interviewers.

Control Moves in the Roleplay Situation

As anticipated, the men and women who roleplayed the moral dilemma produced similar proportions of one-up, one-down, and one-across moves. They also did not differ in responses to their partner's moves. They were similarly inclined to move up, down, and across in response to their partner's one-up moves. The same held true of responses to their partner's one-down and one-across moves. Presumably, differences in opinion had been made salient and, as in the hypothetical situations challenging their opinions, they differed little in their attempts to control the situation or acquiesce.

Correlations between their control moves in the conversations and in the hypothetical social situations, however, were not similar. Among the men, these correlations were positive and moderately strong. The more often they indicated moving up in the hypothetical social situations, the more often they moved up in the conversations (r=.57, p<.05) and the less often they moved down (r=-.59, p<.01). The more often they indicated moving down in the hypothetical social situations, the more often they moved down in the conversations (r=.68, p<.01) and the less often they moved up (r=-.70, p<.001). Correlations between their responses to the situations challenging their opinions and their responses in the conversations were similar, although of slightly less magnitude.

In contrast, correlations between the women's responses to the hypothetical social situations and in the conversations were negative. The more often they moved up in the hypothetical social situations, the less often they moved up in the conversations (r= -.38, p<.10) and the more often they moved down (r=.53, p<.01). The more often they moved down in the hypothetical social situations, the less often they moved down in the conversations (r=-.51, p<.05) and the more often they moved up (r=.28, p=.13). Correlations between their responses to the situations challenging their opinions and their responses in the conversations were similar, but small and statistically insignificant. Consequently, the men's responses in the hypothetical situations and in the roleplay conversation were consistent; those of the women were not.

DISCUSSION

At the outset it was proposed that significant exceptions to findings regarding male dominance in conversations might be a function of goals made salient by the conversational situation. In studies of freewheeling or acquainting conversations, women appear to exercise fewer controlling behaviors than men, whereas in relatively structured situations they do so less consistently. It was suggested that the absence of task-related goals in the former types of situations made relational or self-presentational goals salient and that differences in control behaviors among men and women might reflect social norms for men to be autonomous and dominant and women to be cooperative and polite. In the latter types of situations, differences in control behaviors might depend on the importance of the task or issue at stake. The more important the task or issue, the more its resolution might compete with self-presentational concerns, thereby affecting interaction management. For important matters, women might attempt to control the situation as much as men.

What was needed, it was argued, was a method by which responses of men and women in a variety of situations could be compared, when their concerns for self-presentation were manipulated to be relatively high or low. The 9 hypothetical conflict situations were constructed to discover how men and women would respond in public and in private when their competencies, opinions, and goals were targets of social attack. It was expected that public testing conditions would enhance the salience of self-presentational concerns and would influence the behavior of women more than the behavior of men. It was also expected that women with chronically high levels of concern for their self-presentation (those who scored high in dispositional public self-consciousness) would be most susceptible to such verbal attacks.

These expectations were largely confirmed by the responses of men and women in this study, but primarily when their competencies were target. They responded similarly in private and in public when their opinions were target. Women, in general moved across more than men when their goals were target. This is a move that women have previously been found to prefer in a goal-oriented roleplay exercise (Beinstein Miller, 1985). When their competencies were target, women who responded publicly did not behave more acquiescently than their privately responding counterparts; rather, they behaved more assertively.

These findings were not altered substantially when the sex of the interviewer was taken into consideration; nor were findings regarding attacks on opinion. Only in situations where goals were at stake did the sex of the interviewer appear to make a

119

difference. Here, men responded more assertively with male interviewers and women more assertively with female interviewers. In other words, when differences in opinion were made salient, men and women responded similarly, regardless of self-presentational concerns. While there were no differences in assertive and acquiescent responses among men and women when their goals were at stake, such differences may have emerged had there been equal numbers of male and female interviewers. Men may have then acted more assertively and women more acquiescently. But when competencies were target, situational, self-presentational concerns affected the behavior of women more than men, and did so especially among women chronically concerned with reactions of others to themselves.

It is significant, then, that correlations between the men's responses in the roleplay conversations and in the hypothetical social situations were positive and moderately strong, whereas no such correlations were found among the women responses. Since these students had responded privately to the hypothetical social situations, the absence of positive correlations among women's responses may have been due, in part, to differences in their chronic levels of public self-consciousness and to the dissimilar testing situations (one private, in which only initial response was examined, and one public, the roleplay conversation, in which self-presentational concerns were not assessed). Had comparisons been made between responses in the roleplay conversations and public responses to the hypothetical social situations, correlations among the women's responses may have also been positive. It is also possible that the absence of positive correlations among the women's responses could have been due to their greater flexibility or adaptability in the roleplay situation. But then a random relationship, not a negative one, might have been expected between their roleplay responses and their responses to the hypothetical situations.

The results of this study suggest there may be circumstances in which concerns for self-presentation increase attempts by women to manage interaction....when their competencies have been criticized by valued others. This may be because they are more interpersonally oriented than men and therefore place a higher priority on esteem from valued others. The origin of the Interpersonal Orientation Scale, in fact, was in observations that the bargaining behavior of women differed considerably when their partners played competitively versus cooperatively, while similar differences did not occur among men (Swap and Rubin, 1983). It has been previously noted that, according to this scale, women are more reactive than men to variations in the behavior of others and take the behavior of others towards themselves more seriously. Public self-consciousness may serve to intensify their reactivity.

This interpretation is in accord with a control theory of behavior (Carver and Scheier, 1981). Put simply, people regulate their behavior according to standards that they have internalized or have been made appropriate in a situation. When they become aware of discrepancies between their behavior (or information about their behavior) and these standards, they act to reduce the discrepancy. In this study, 3 different types of standards had been made salient by the hypothetical social situations and in each case a discrepancy was created by a verbal attack. Students were asked to imagine situations in which their competencies were considered inadequate, where their opinions might be inappropriate, and in which their achievements or goals might be blocked. Since publicly self-conscious women, in particular, should be concerned with the reactions of others to their behavior, they should have been especially motivated to reduce the discrepancies. The specific line of action they chose, however, would depend also on their outcome expectancies: whether they believed a specific line of action could actually reduce the discrepancy.

Now consider again the targets in question. One set concerned their opinions. Some opinions may be more appropriate than others, but one is not necessarily more correct than another. People are, after all, entitled to their own opinions. Reducing discrepancies in opinion may entail changing one's own as well as changing another's. It may be simpler to justify such discrepancies by the belief, "To each his/her own." In each of the situations that challenged the students' goals, the challenger had as much right to the goal in question as did the student, whether to take the course, use the dormitory room, or take the car. Here too, the students' ability to reduce the discrepancy between what they wanted and what they were apparently going to get was not certain. In the situations challenging their competencies, however, their jokes, comments in class, and performance on an examination had come under harsh criticism. In each case the criticism could have been construed as socially inappropriate, if not rude and insensitive. Bringing the self into alignment by countering such attacks might not only be appropriate but also effective, since it is socially inappropriate to be rude. Thus it may be socially inappropriate attacks on their competencies that motivate publicly self-conscious women to assert control in interaction. In contrast, when they are treated politely or complimented by others, it is advantageous for them to let their complimentors manage interaction. Indeed it is likely, though speculative, that the freewheeling and acquainting conversations in which women have been found to be less controlling than men entailed few or no insults and many civilities.

Table 1.   One-Up, One-Down, and One-Across Responses by Men and
           Women in Private versus Public Testing Situations

	In all 9 situations		In situations regarding competencies	
	Private response	Public response	Private response	Public response
Mean Number of One-up Responses				
Men	4.90	4.36	1.42	1.45
Women	4.61	5.28	1.28	1.83
Mean Number of One-down Responses				
Men	2.78	3.05	1.16	1.02
Women	2.92	2.17	1.28	.57
Mean Number of One-across Responses				
Men	1.26	1.55	.42	.52
Women	1.42	1.55	.45	.60

Note: Male private responders = 50
      Female private responders = 83
      Male public responders = 44
      Female public responders = 47

Table 2.   One-Up,   One-Down, and One-Across Responses by Men   and
            Women   who Scored High and Low in Public   Self-
            Consciousness

	In all 9 situations		In situations regarding competencies	
	Low Self-conscious (4 - 15)	High Self-conscious (21 - 28)	Low Self-conscious (4 - 15)	High Self-conscious (21 - 28)
	Mean Number of One-up Responses			
Men	4.08	4.27	1.23	1.64
Women	4.71	6.41	1.35	2.41
	Mean Number of One-down Responses			
Men	3.23	3.55	1.23	1.09
Women	2.06	1.71	.59	.35
	Mean Number of One-across Responses			
Men	1.62	1.18	.54	.27
Women	2.24	.88	1.06	.24

Note: Low self-conscious men = 13
      Low self-conscious women = 17
      High self-conscious men = 11
      High self-conscious women = 17

REFERENCES

Adams, K. A. (1980). Who has the final word? Sex, race, and dominance behavior. Journal of Personality and Social Psychology, 38, 1-8.

Aries, E. (1976). Interaction patterns and themes of male, female, and mixed groups. Small Group Behavior, 7, 7-18.

Beinstein Miller, J. (1985). Patterns of control in same-sex conversations: Differences between women and men. Women's Studies in Communication, 8, 62-69.

Carver, C.S. and Scheier, M.F. (1981). Attention and self-regulation: A control-theory approach to human behavior. New York: Springer-Verlag.

Courtright, J., Millar, F., and Rogers-Millar, L. E. (1979). Domineeringness and dominance; replication and expansion. Communication Monographs, 46, 177-192.

Doherty, W.J. and Ryder, R.G. (1979). Locus of control, interpersonal trust, and assertive behavior among newly-weds. Journal of Personality and Social Psychology, 37, 2212-2220.

Duncan, S. and Fiske, D.W. (1977). Face-to-face interaction: Research, methods, and theory. Hillsdale, New Jersey: Lawrence Erlbaum Associates.

Fenigstein, A., Scheier, M.F., and Buss, A.H. (1975). Public and private self-consciousness: Assessment and theory. Journal of Consulting and Clinical Psychology, 43, 522-527.

Fisher, B.A. (1983). Differential effects of sexual composition and interactional context on interaction patterns in dyads. Human Communication Research, 9, 225-238.

Frances, S.J. (1979). Sex differences in nonverbal behavior. Sex Roles, 5, 519-535.

Hall, J.A. (1984). Nonverbal sex differences: Communication accuracy and expressive style. Baltimore: Johns Hopkins University Press.

Kimble, C.E., Yoshikawa, J.C., and Zehr, H.D. (1981). Vocal and verbal assertiveness in same-sex and mixed-sex groups. Journal of Personality and Social Psychology, 40, 1047-1054.

LaFrance, M. and Carmen, B. (1980). The nonverbal display of psychological androgyny. Journal of Personality and Social Psychology, 38, 36-49.

Mabry, E.A. (1985). The effects of gender composition and task structure on small group interaction. Small Group Behavior, 16, 75-96.

Markel, N.N., Long, J.F., and Saine, T.J. (1976). Sex effects in conversational interaction: Another look at male dominance. Human Communication Research, 2, 356-364.

McMillan, J.R., Clifton, A.K., McGrath, D., and Gale, W.S. (1977). Women's language: Uncertainty or interpersonal sensitivity and emotionality. Sex Roles, 3, 545-559.

Natale, M., Entin, E, and Jaffe, J. (1979). Vocal interruptions in dyadic communication as a function of speech and social anxiety. Journal of Personality and Social Psychology, 37, 865-878.

Pilliavin, J.A. and Martin, R.R. (1978). The effects of the sex composition of groups on style of social interaction. Sex Roles, 4, 281-296.

Rogers, L.E. and Farace, R.V. (1975). Relational communication analysis: New measurement procedures. Human Communication Research, 1, 222-239.

Rogers-Millar, L. E. and Millar, F. (1979). Domineeringness and dominance: a transactional view. Human Communication Research, 5, 238-246.

Shaw, M.E. and Sadler, O.W. (1965). Interaction patterns in heterosexual dyads varying in degree of intimacy. Journal of Social Psychology, 66, 345-351.

Smith, P. M. (1985). Language, the sexes and society. Oxford, United Kingdom: Basil Blackwell.

Strodtbeck, F.L., James, R.M., and Hawkins, C. (1957). Social status in jury deliberations. American Sociological Review, 22, 713-719.

Strodtbeck, F.L. and Mann, R.D. (1956). Sex role differentiation in jury deliberations. Sociometry, 19, 3-11.

Swap, W.C. and Rubin, J.Z. (1983). Measurement of interpersonal orientation. Journal of Personality and Social Psychology, 44, 208-219.

Zimmerman, D. H. and West, C. (1975). Sex roles, interruptions and silences in conversation. In B. Thorne and N. Henley (eds.), Language and sex: Difference and dominance. Rowley, Massachusetts: Newbury House.

A META-ANALYSIS OF GENDER AS A MODERATOR OF
LEADER BEHAVIOR-SUBORDINATE OUTCOME RELATIONSHIPS

Julie Indvik
California State University-Chico

Interest in the gender-structuring of organizations and in gender differences in work behavior has spawned a huge literature (recent reviews include Bartol, 1978; Dobbins & Platz, 1986; Fairhurst, 1986; Foss & Foss, 1983; Hearn & Parkin, 1983; Heilman, 1983; LaFrance & Mayo, 1979; Nieva & Gutek, 1981; Putnam, 1979; Terborg, 1977; Wallston & O'Leary, 1981; White, Crino, & DeSanctis, 1981). Among the most researched gender differences are those found in superior-subordinate relationships because of this dyad's centrality in organizational information flows and because of this dyad's direct influence on participants' organizational outcomes (e.g., Bass, 1981; Cashman, Dansereau, Graen, & Haga, 1976; Likert, 1961). For example, concern with superiors' and subordinates' career progress has resulted in a large literature on gender differences in managerial evaluations of subordinates (e.g., Deutsch & Leong, 1983; Heilman & Stopeck, 1985; Izraeli & Izraeli, 1985; Mai-Dalton, Feldman-Summers, & Mitchell, 1979; Peters, O'Connor, Weekley, Pooyan, Frank, & Erenkrantz, 1984; Pulakos & Wexley, 1983; Shore & Thornton, 1986; Wexley & Pulakos, 1982) and in subordinates' reactions to managerial behavior (e.g., Baird & Bradley, 1979; Liden, 1985; Nieva & Gutek, 1980; Rice, Instone, & Adams, 1984; Terborg & Shingledecker, 1983; Trempe, Rigne, & Haccoun, 1985; Wexley & Pulakos, 1983; Wheeless & Berryman-Fink, 1985). Because the interpretation of message behavior is more prominent in research on subordinates' reactions to managers, this body of literature is more pertinent for organizational communication scholars and will be the focus of this paper.

While the studies in this area have usually lacked a conceptual rationale for hypothesizing gender differences (notable exceptions include discussions of the congruence, the gender context, and the similarity hypotheses; see, for example, Schein, 1975; Schneer, 1985; and Wexley & Pulakos, 1983, respectively), the use of a contingency approach holds promise for developing explanations of superior-subordinate relationships in general (Jablin, 1979) and of gender differences within them in particular (Putnam, 1979). A contingency approach would place gender within the configuration of contextual factors that can affect message behavior and interpretation in work settings, rather than treating gender as an isolated explanatory variable as has been the case in much of the past research. Contingency

approaches to the study of superior-subordinate relationships
have been developed within the rubric of leadership theory.

The general trend in leadership research has been to view
leadership as an interpersonal influence process moderated by
contingent, situational factors (e.g., Ashour, 1982; Barrow,
1977; Davis & Luthans, 1979). Three major leadership approaches
have addressed the contingent nature of the superior-subordinate
relationship: Fiedler's (1967) Contingency Theory, Vroom and
Yetton's (1973) model of leader decision-making, and House's
(1971) path-goal theory. Of these three approaches, path-goal
theory is more useful for the study of superior-subordinate
relationships and of potential gender differences therein for
several reasons. Path-goal theory's conceptualization of leader
behavior explicitly includes message behavior (House, 1971). Its
dependent variables comprise a range of subordinate outcomes
(House & Mitchell, 1974), and it assumes that behavior varies
situationally (House & Mitchell, 1974) which is consistent with
communication (e.g., Smith, 1984) and with gender (e.g., Schneer,
1985) research in other areas.

Of particular relevance to the study of gender differences,
path-goal theory includes subordinate characteristics as one of
two major categories of situational contingencies (House &
Dessler, 1974). Subordinate characteristics are seen as
determining how the work environment and leader message behavior
are interpreted and, therefore, as important for influencing the
impact of a particular leader behavior on subordinate outcomes.
While gender was not studied as a subordinate characteristic in
early path-goal work, the theory was left explicitly open to the
incorporation of additional variables (House & Mitchell, 1974).

Path-goal theory uses several types of leader message
behavior to predict subordinate affect and performance. According
to path-goal theory, the function of a superior's communication
is to enhance a subordinate's goal attainment by supplementing
the informational cues and rewards found in the work environment.
In general, this is accomplished when a leader clarifies the
behaviors (or paths) that a subordinate can adopt to attain goals
and the outcomes of such attainment. The particular leader
behavior that will effectively enhance goal attainment is
determined by situational contingencies, namely work environment
structure and subordinate characteristics. Work environment
structure (organizational formalization, work group norms, task
structure) determines the type of leader message behavior
required as a complement if subordinate outcomes are to be
maximized. Subordinate characteristics influence the
effectiveness of leader behavior since they affect the degree to
which leader behavior appears immediately satisfying or

instrumental to future satisfaction. Figure 1 illustrates the relationships among path-goal variables. If gender were to shed light on superior behavior-subordinate outcome relationships, then, it would mean that male and female subordinates would find particular leader behaviors differentially helpful in complementing the work environment.

To date, path-goal theory has included four types of leader message behavior that function to provide structure and/or reward to subordinates (House & Dessler, 1974; House & Mitchell, 1974). A directive superior "lets subordinates know what is expected of them, gives specific guidance as to what should be done and how it should be done" (House & Mitchell, 1974, p. 83), and asks that they follow performance standards and organizational rules. These kinds of messages provide explicit structuring of subordinate goals and the paths (behaviors) to goal attainment. Interpreted as rewarding (Graen, Dansereau, Minami, & Cashman, 1973), supportive leader behavior creates a friendly climate, verbally recognizes achievement, and expresses support in stressful times (Hammer & Dachler, 1975; House, 1971; House & Dessler, 1974; House & Mitchell, 1974; Mawhinney & Ford, 1977).

Participative leader behavior entails "consult(ing) with subordinates, solicit(ing) their suggestions and tak(ing) these suggestions seriously into consideration before making a decision" (House & Mitchell, 1974, p. 83). Such messages from a superior function to clarify goals and their attainment but do so by asking for input from subordinates. An achievement-oriented superior "sets challenging goals, expects subordinates to perform at their highest level, continuously seeks improvement in performance and shows a high degree of confidence that the subordinates will assume responsibility, put forth effort and accomplish challenging goals" (House & Mitchell, 1974, p. 83). Achievement-oriented messages can clarify changing goals and paths in response to a subordinate's past success at goal attainment and thus may be interpreted as a form of both indirect structure and reward.

Because path-goal theory's stated intention was to identify the "precise psychological mechanisms underlying the effects of leaders on others" (House & Dessler, 1974, p. 30), the theory's dependent variables include intrinsic job satisfaction, the expectancy that effort leads to effective performance (expectancy one), the expectancy that performance leads to valued rewards (expectancy two), role clarity (House, 1971); satisfaction with extrinsic rewards (House & Dessler, 1974); and satisfaction with the superior (House & Mitchell, 1974). Subsequent revision of the theory included performance and overall satisfaction as dependent variables (House & Mitchell, 1974), although a leader's effect on these variables was conceptualized as indirect.

Path-goal theory would hypothesize that gender moderates the relationship between leader communication and subordinate outcomes if men and women differentially interpret direction, support, participation, or achievement-orientation as providing helpful structure or reward. In other words, to the degree that a superior's communication clarifies goals and the paths needed to attain them differently for male and female subordinates, gender constitutes a significant moderator. Males' and females' differential interpretation of leader communication would be seen in varying levels of affect and performance.

The direction of gender-moderated hypotheses depends on additional reasoning about males and females that is outside the purview of path-goal theory. A modified sex-role congruency hypothesis (e.g., Schein, 1975) would suggest that subordinates would prefer leader behaviors consistent with stereotypes of the subordinates' own gender roles. In that case, male subordinates should prefer direction and achievement-orientation, while female subordinates should prefer support and participation. Support for the sex-role congruency hypothesis has been mixed (e.g., Burgoon, Dillard, & Doran, 1983; Falbo, Hazen, Linimon, 1982; Petty & Bruning, 1980; Weimann, 1985).

Alternatively, the attribution theory literature has suggested that females are more likely to attribute success to external causes than are males (Deaux, 1979; Deaux & Farris, 1977). Information from a superior that is clearly structuring or rewarding may then be more useful to female subordinates for clarifying paths and outcomes (cf., Lenney, Browning, & Mitchell, 1980). If male subordinates are more confident about the internal sources of their success, then less direct leader messages may be more appropriate for conveying structure and reward without appearing excessive. This reasoning would suggest that male subordinates would prefer participative and achievement-oriented leader messages, while female subordinates would prefer directive and supportive messages. The evidence on females' lower self-confidence is also mixed (e.g., Lenney, 1977; Shore & Thornton, 1986).

These two bodies of literature would both predict that supportive leader messages would do more to enhance female than male goal attainment and that achievement-oriented leader messages would be more effective with male than with female subordinates. Conflicting predictions arise, however, for directive and for participative leader messages.

The means chosen for testing the above hypotheses in this

study was meta-analysis (Glass, McGaw, & Smith, 1981; Hunter, Schmidt, & Jackson, 1982; Rosenthal, 1978). "Meta-analysis is the quantitative cumulation and analysis of descriptive statistics across studies" (Hunter et al., 1982, p. 137). Because a substantial number of path-goal studies have already been done and because the findings have been "mixed," a narrative review of the literature could not adequately assess the level of support for the theory. Until the strength of path-goal relationships can be ascertained, further data collection would be premature.

The present meta-analysis differs from another that treated gender differences (Dobbins & Platz, 1986) in several ways. The present meta-analysis is testing hypotheses within a theoretical framework and thus offers a conceptual rationale for examining gender differences. The present meta-analysis treats gender as a moderating variable rather than as an independent variable having separate relations with leader behavior, with satisfaction, and with leader effectiveness. Finally, the present meta-analysis corrects for attentuation due to reliability differences as well as for sampling error. A more detailed description of meta-analytic procedures follows in the next section.

METHOD

Two approaches to meta-analysis have been used most frequently. Glass et al.'s (1981) approach accepts the variance of effect sizes at face value and seeks to explain this variance with a variety of study characteristics. Glass et al. suggest coding all possible study characteristics to permit testing with regression until effect size variance can be accounted for. This approach capitalizes on chance and suffers from low statistical power because the sample size for testing study characteristics is the number of studies rather than the number of respondents in the studies (Hunter et al., 1982, pp. 32-33).

In contrast, Hunter et al.'s (1982) approach does not accept effect size variance at face value. Hunter et al. initially hypothesize that the variance is due to various statistical artifacts: sampling error, study differences in the reliability of independent and dependent variable measures, study differences in range restriction and in instrumental validity, and computational, typographical, and transcription errors. Only if a significant amount of variance remains after these artifacts have been subtracted are moderators tested. Hunter et al. emphasize moderator choice based on theoretical reasoning rather than on empirical trial and error.

Hunter et al.'s (1982) approach was chosen for this meta-analysis for two reasons. First, sampling error is large in comparison to outcome values when sample size is small (i.e., less than 1000 respondents) as it often has been in the path-goal literature. Consequently, correction for sampling error is especially important for path-goal studies in order to avoid major statistical errors. Secondly, path-goal theory specifies situational moderators that must receive priority if variance remains after statistical artifacts have been removed from effect size variance. The need to use study characteristics as moderators would suggest that path-goal theory has failed to receive support.

Identification of Studies

Four articles have been identified as forming the foundation of path-goal theory's conceptualization: Evans (1970), House (1971), House and Dessler (1974), House and Mitchell (1974). It was presumed that any work predicated on path-goal theory would cite one of these articles. Based on this presumption, the relevant literature was identified with a computer-assisted search of the Social Science Citation Index (SSCI). SSCI reports every article that cites a specified reference. In this case, the four articles just listed were the specified references.

When the repeated listings of articles that cited more than one of the specified references were subtracted from the initial total of 295 articles, 227 remained. The 227 articles represented the widest possible parameters for work done within the path-goal rubric since any author even mentioning one of the four early path-goal references was included. This method of identifying studies ensured that the studies included were those that explicitly acknowledged a conceptual linkage to path-goal theory.

Selection of Studies

In order to be included in the meta-analysis, a study had to meet several criteria. A study had to be published, to report a relationship relevant to path-goal theory, to report a statistic amenable to meta-analysis, to report a unique sample (to avoid statistical dependence), and to refrain from using the Supervisory Behavior Description Questionnaire (SBDQ; Fleishman, 1957) which is inconsistent with path-goal conceptualization (Schriesheim & Von Glinow, 1977; Szilagyi & Keller, 1976). The vast majority of these articles either contained no data or no path-goal variables. When this was the case, one of the four early path-goal articles was simply cited in a very general way as an example of taking a contingency approach to organizational behavior. A total of 44 articles reporting 48 studies met all five criteria.

132

Unpublished studies were not included because effect sizes and methodological quality vary significantly between published and unpublished studies (Rosenthal & Rubin, 1978; Smith & Glass, 1977). Additionally, systematic sampling from unpublished sources is difficult. To determine the extent to which the exclusion of unpublished studies might affect the results of this meta-analysis, a "fail-safe n" was computed for each relationship. The fail-safe n indicated the number of unpublished or "hidden" studies with effect sizes of zero that would be needed to invalidate the cumulative size of a particular relationship (Rosenthal, 1979). For all but one of the available relationships, more studies with relationships of zero would be required to invalidate the effects than were used to establish them (Tables 1-4, column 3).

Coding the Studies

In order to make general statements about the relationships of interest, data were aggregated initially at the highest possible level (Hunter et al., 1982, p. 126). In order to test the path-goal proposition that leader behavior is situationally moderated, total sample correlations were used when available or subsample correlations were averaged. When an article contained data from multiple independent samples, each sample was coded separately (Hunter et al., 1982, p. 116).

Sample Characteristics

Sample sizes in individual studies ranged from 34 to 2422 with a mean of 247 in each study for a total of 11,862 respondents. A typical respondent in this sample was employed at a high job level (30%), in a large organization (67%), in the private sector (88%). This indicates that a trend in extant path-goal research has been to study large organizations in the private sector, particularly with workers in high level jobs. The percentage of studies mixing job levels (56%), organizational sizes (23%), and organizational types (5%) prevented a clear delineation of many samples.

Reliability of Variables

In 83% of the findings, leader behavior was measured with the Leader Behavior Description Questionnaire (LBDQ; Halpin, 1957), the revised LBDQ XII (Stogdill, 1963), or some subset of these items (House & Dessler, 1974). Most of the remaining 17% included participative or achievement-oriented leader behavior or were measured with Schriesheim's (1978; cited in Jermier & Berkes, 1979) scales. Across the studies in this meta-analysis the reliabilities of directive (.80), supportive (.86), and participative (.81) leader behavior were acceptable. The reliability of achievement-oriented leader behavior (.69) was borderline but based on only two studies.

Performance was included when rated by the subordinate's superior or peers or when determined from organizational records using indices such as salary increases or daily output. Acceptable reliabilities were found for all subordinate outcomes: role clarity (.79); expectancies one (.72) and two (.82); intrinsic (.76), extrinsic (.82), overall (.87) satisfaction; satisfaction with the superior (.86); and performance (.87).

Analysis of Relationships of Interest

Tables 1-4 present the number of studies and sample size for each of the relationships included in the meta-analysis of zero-order relationships. In general, two studies is the minimum number necessary for a meta-analysis (Hunter et al., 1982, p. 28). Consequently, only 26 of the 32 possible relationships could be analyzed. This was due primarily to the relatively infrequent investigation of achievement-oriented leader behavior in path-goal studies. The number of studies reporting a given relationship ranged from 26 to two, with sample sizes ranging from 4,993 to 272.

The data analysis consisted of two phases. The first phase followed procedures suggested for bodies of literature in which individual studies do not report enough information to correct all effects prior to cumulation (Hunter et al., 1982, pp. 73-87). The strategy in this instance is to compute the mean and variance of the uncorrected correlations as well as of the artifacts. The distribution of correlations is then corrected using the distributional information about the artifacts. Of the four types of artifacts mentioned by Hunter et al., sampling error and differences in reliability were corrected in this meta-analysis. Researcher error can never be assessed without access to the raw data. Range restriction could not be determined because insufficient information was available to compute reference populations against which to compare the study populations.

When two studies reported a relationship, a significance test for the difference between two independent correlations was performed. If the two correlations were not significantly different, any variance was attributed to sampling error (Hunter et al., 1982, p. 29).

When three or more studies reported a relationship, a distribution was calculated for each relationship being analyzed. When the variance of each relationship was corrected for sampling error and attenuation, the significance of the remaining variance was assessed. A small corrected variance indicated that the primary sources of variance were artifactual, whereas a large corrected variance indicated the existence of subpopulations as defined by moderator variables. Greater interpretive errors would be made by attributing false variation to nonexistent moderators because of capitalization on chance than by ignoring potential moderators of true variation (Hunter et al., 1982, pp. 31-32). Consequently, three (related) indices were computed to ascertain the size of the corrected variance.

First, the corrected variance was tested with a chi square. An insignificant chi square provided strong evidence of no true variation across studies because the test has very high statistical power (Hunter et al., 1982, p. 47). A significant chi square was a tentative indication of the presence of moderators. A second indicator of the advisability of testing for moderators was a large corrected standard deviation (Hunter et al., 1982, pp. 31-32). The 95% confidence interval around the corrected mean correlation indicated the variability of the correlation. Third, when sampling error and reliability differences comprised 75% or more of the mean correlation's variance (Hunter et al., 1982, p. 139), the small residual variance was attributed to uncorrected artifacts (e.g., researcher errors) rather than to real moderators (Hunter et al., 1982, p. 40). A finding of large corrected variance supported the path-goal proposition that superior-subordinate relationships are moderated.

Moderator Coding and Analysis

In the second phase of the data analysis, those relationships with significant corrected variance and more than four studies were recoded and tested for moderator variables. As part of the larger meta-analysis of path-goal research, the analysis of gender differences was undertaken at this point. A minimum of four zero-order relationships was needed for any gender difference tests in order to have at least two studies reporting a particular leader behavior/subordinate outcome relationship for males and two for females. Of the 48 studies that could be used in the larger meta-analysis, five studies reported either the gender of the entire sample or that of subsamples (Abdel-Halim, 1981; Osborn & Vicars, 1976; Petty & Bruning, 1980; Petty & Lee, 1975; Szilagyi & Keller, 1976). This small number meant that only for the relationships between supportive leader behavior and two outcomes (intrinsic satisfaction and satisfaction with the superior) could meta-analytic tests be performed (see Table 5).

Since the small number of cases available precluded the use of regression, studies were grouped in two subsamples (Hunter et al., 1982, p. 32). For each subsample, the meta-analytic procedures just described were repeated (Hunter et al., 1982, p. 36). A moderator was indicated when the mean correlation varied among subsamples, when the corrected variance was lower in the subsamples than in the entire sample (Hunter et al., 1982, p. 48), and/or when the chi square was insignificant. When these indices were reversed, the need for a second moderator was suggested. Hypothesis tests were performed by examining the direction of the mean effects.

RESULTS

Only the results relevant to testing the gender difference hypotheses will be discussed in this section. Both relationships permitting gender difference tests did indeed require moderators (see Table 2). Summary statistics for the gender tests may be found in Table 6. These results indicate that while gender does moderate the relationship between supportive leader behavior and satisfaction with the superior, it does not moderate the relationship between supportive leader behavior and intrinsic satisfaction. Another moderator would be required for that relationship and has been reported elsewhere (Indvik, 1985).

Both sets of hypotheses predicted that female subordinates would prefer supportive leader behavior more than would male subordinates. If this were supported, satisfaction with the superior and intrinsic satisfaction would be significantly higher for female than for male subordinates. The results in Table 6 indicate that there is essentially no difference between male and female subordinates in their reaction to supportive leader behavior; both groups react quite favorably to this type of leader message.

DISCUSSION

This paper proposed two alternative sets of hypotheses to predict the moderating effect of gender in superior-subordinate relationships. One set of hypotheses, based on the concept of sex-role congruency, predicted that male subordinates would find directive and achievement-oriented leader messages more conducive to goal attainment than would female subordinates, and that female subordinates would experience more favorable outcomes as a result of supportive and participative leader messages. The second set of hypotheses, based on the attribution and self-evaluation literatures, predicted that male subordinates would prefer less direct forms of structure and reward, i.e., participation and achievement-orientation, while female subordinates would react more favorably to directive and supportive leader messages.

The available data in a meta-analysis of path-goal research permitted a partial assessment of only one of these hypotheses, namely, that female subordinates would prefer supportive leader messages. Although supportive leader messages enhanced two types of satisfaction for both male and female subordinates, few conclusions can be drawn about the validity of the hypotheses discussed in this paper since the results were based on only five studies. Furthermore, since only two relationships could be examined out of a possible 32 included in path-goal theory, a pattern of gender differences, even an imperfect one, could not really be explored in this study. It may be that one of the two sets of hypotheses may apply to most, even if not all, leader message-subordinate outcome relationships, and that the relationships examined in this meta-analysis were exceptions rather than the rule.

One purpose of a meta-analysis is to establish when further research would or would not make a real addition to the human knowledge base. While some meta-analyses, particularly those examining isolated relationships (e.g., Dobbins & Platz, 1986), conclude that further data are unnecessary, this meta-analysis concludes emphatically that more samples need to be collected. Only two out of a possible 32 relationships could be examined for gender differences in this meta-analysis. There were no gender data available whatsoever for participative or achievement-oriented leader messages or for performance or expectancies one and two. Indeed, the positive side to the missing data in extant path-goal research is the plethora of research opportunities available to investigators. Future samples, however, will be useful to the extent that they fill the gaps uncovered by this meta-analysis.

Similarly, future attention to gender differences can increase our understanding of work life only if there are genuine conceptual reasons for expecting men and women to differ. Findings of "no significant difference" are becoming more common in gender difference studies in part, perhaps, because of actual changes in work behavior and attitudes, and in part, perhaps, because atheoretical stabs can not be expected to reach solid empirical targets. Future work that incorporates gender as one of the contingencies of path-goal theory might consider how gender operates as an interpretive filter in combination with work environment structure. In other words, gender could be used as a joint moderator to refine hypotheses about subordinates' reactions to the work environment and leader messages much as other subordinate characteristics (preference for external structure and need for achievement) are currently used to refine hypotheses about the ways in which participative and achievement-oriented leader messages complement the work environment (Indvik, 1985). Such a conceptualization, although more complex than simply using gender as an independent variable, is more likely to yield fruitful results. The construct of gender must be integrated with other constructs just as men and women have been integrated in the workplace.

Table 1

Directive Leader Behavior Summary Statistics

Criterion variables				Statistics				
	Number of studies	Sample size	Fail safe n	Mean effect	Corrected mean effect	% artifact variance	Corrected s.d.	Chi Square
Role clarity	15	2377	1613	.34	.43	58%	.08	28.37*
Expectancy one	2	633	---	.08	.11	---	---	---
Expectancy two	3	494	26	.23	.28	43%	.11	7.16*
Intrinsic satisfaction	17	3355	302	.12	.15	63%	.07	27.81*
Extrinsic satisfaction	9	666	99	.14	.17	47%	.10	19.67*
Superior satisfaction	17	3482	2385	.32	.39	14%	.20	134.84***
Overall satisfaction	24	4344	1229	.18	.22	43%	.10	56.93***
Performance	9	1715	0	.03	.04	23%	.16	39.95***

*p<.05. ***p<.001.

Table 2

Supportive Leader Behavior Summary Statistics

Criterion variables	Statistics							
	Number of studies	Sample size	Fail-safe n	Mean effect	Corrected mean effect	% artifact variance	Corrected s.d.	Chi Square
Role clarity	14	2178	1458	.35	.42	45%	.10	32.94**
Expectancy one	3	868	70	.27	.34	25%	.13	13.87***
Expectancy two	2	423	--	.39	.46	--	--	--
Intrinsic satisfaction	20	4318	2027	.25	.31	49%	.09	47.59***
Extrinsic satisfaction	11	2113	239	.17	.20	41%	.10	27.56**
Superior satisfaction	18	4207	18154	.67	.78	8%	.17	341.48***
Overall satisfaction	26	4993	8464	.40	.46	12%	.21	253.64***
Performance	12	2489	349	.18	.21	19%	.16	66.28***

**p<.01. ***p<.001.

140

Table 3

Participative Leader Behavior Summary Statistics

Criterion variables		Statistics						
	Number of studies	Sample size	Fail-safe n	Mean effect	Corrected mean effect	% artifact variance	Corrected s.d.	Chi Square
Role clarity	4	585	77	.30	.38	9%	.31	47.96***
Expectancy one	1	409	--	.41	.54	--	--	--
Expectancy two	2	640	--	.38	.47*	--	--	--
Intrinsic satisfaction	8	1646	360	.27	.34	18%	.19	54.20***
Extrinsic satisfaction	5	819	109	.27	.33	15%	.18	34.62***
Superior satisfaction	8	1612	743	.38	.46	28%	.12	32.46***
Overall satisfaction	10	1864	553	.28	.33	17%	.17	63.07***
Performance	3	765	109	.35	.41	55%	.06	6.28*

*$p < .05$. ***$p < .001$.

Table 4

Achievement-oriented Leader Behavior Summary Statistics

Criterion variables	Statistics							
	Number of studies	Sample size	Fail-safe n	Mean effect	Corrected mean effect	% artifact variance	Corrected s.d.	Chi Square
Role clarity	2	459	---	.48	.65*	---	---	---
Expectancy one	0	---	---	---	---	---	---	---
Expectancy two	0	---	---	---	---	---	---	---
Intrinsic satisfaction	1	129	---	.12	.17	---	---	---
Extrinsic satisfaction	0	---	---	---	---	---	---	---
Superior satisfaction	2	459	---	.52	.68	---	---	---
Overall satisfaction	1	129	---	-.06	-.08	---	---	---
Performance	2	272	---	.27	.35*	---	---	---

*$p < .05$.

Table 5

Path-Goal Relationships Available for Gender Difference Analyses

Criterion variables	Directive Messages Gender		Supportive Messages Gender		Participative Messages Gender		Ach.-Oriented Messages Gender	
	Male	Female	Male	Female	Male	Female	Male	Female
Role clarity	2	0	2	0	0	0	0	0
Expectancy one	0	0	0	0	0	0	0	0
Expectancy two	0	0	0	0	0	0	0	0
Intrinsic satisfaction	4	1	5	2	0	0	0	0
Extrinsic satisfaction	1	0	1	0	0	0	0	0
Superior satisfaction	3	1	4	2	0	0	0	0
Overall satisfaction	2	0	3	1	0	0	0	0
Performance	0	0	0	0	0	0	0	0

Table 6

Summary Statistics for Gender Analyses with Supportive Leader Behavior

Criterion variables	Gender	Number of studies	Sample size	Mean effect	Corrected mean effect	% artifact variance	Corrected s.d.	Chi Square
Intrinsic satisfaction								
	Male	5	874	.69	.85	14%	.11	47.06***
	Female	2	2138	.70	.86	--	--	--
Superior satisfaction								
	Male	4	785	.73	.85	64%	.04	6.40
	Female	2	2138	.70	.81	--	--	--

***p<.001.

Figure 1

Household and Mitchell's (1974) Original Path-Goal Relationships

Leader Behavior and Contingency Factors	Cause	Subordinate attitudes and behavior
1. Directive		1. Job satisfaction
2. Supportive		2. Acceptance of leader
3. Participative		3. Motivation Expectancy one Expectancy two
4. Achievement-oriented		
1. Environmental factors Task Work group norms Organizational formalization	Influence → Personal perceptions	
2. Subordinate characteristics Authoritarianism Locus of control Self-perceived ability	Influence → Motivational stimuli Constraints Rewards	

145

REFERENCES

Abdel-Halim, A. A. (1981). Personality and task moderators of subordinate responses to perceived leader behavior. Human Relations, 34, 73-88.

Ashour, A. S. (1982). A framework of a cognitive-behavioral theory of leader influence and effectiveness. Organizational Behavior and Human Performance, 30, 407-430.

Baird, J. E., Jr., & Bradley, P. H. (1979). Styles of management and communication: A comparative study of men and women. Communication Monographs, 46, 101-111.

Barrow, J. C. (1977). The variables of leadership: A review and conceptual framework. Academy of Management Review, 2, 231-251.

Bartol, K. M. (1978). The sex structuring of organizations: A search for possible causes. Academy of Management Review, 3, 805-815.

Bass, B. M. (1981). Stogdill's handbook of leadership. New York: Free Press.

Burgoon, M., Dillard, J. P., & Doran, N. E. (1983). Friendly or unfriendly persuasion: The effects of violations of expectations by males and females. Human Communication Research, 10, 283-294.

Cashman, J., Dansereau, F., Jr., Graen, G., & Haga, W. J. (1976). Organizational understructure and leadership: A longitudinal investigation of the managerial role-making process. Organizational Behavior and Human Performance, 15, 278-296.

Davis, T. R., & Luthans, F. (1979). Leadership reexamined: A behavioral approach. Academy of Management Review, 4, 237-248.

Deaux, K. (1979). Self-evaluation of male and female managers. Journal of Sex Roles, 5, 571-580.

Deaux, K., & Farris, E. (1977). Attributing causes for one's own performance: The effects of sex, norms, and outcome. Journal of Research in Personality, 11, 59-72.

146

Deutsch, F. M., & Leong, F. T. (1983). Male responses to female competence. Sex Roles, 9, 79-89.

Dobbins, G. H., & Platz, S. J. (1986). Sex differences in leadership: How real are they? Academy of Management Review, 11, 118-127.

Evans, M. G. (1970). The effects of supervisory behavior on the path-goal relationship. Organizational Behavior and Human Performance, 5, 277-298.

Fairhurst, G. T. (1986). Male-female communication on the job: Literature review and commentary. In M. McLaughlin (Ed.), Comunication Yearbook 9 (pp. 83-116). Beverly Hills: Sage.

Falbo, T., Hazen, M. D., & Linimon, D. (1982). The costs of selecting power bases or messages associated with the opposite sex. Sex Roles, 8, 147-160.

Fiedler, F. E. (1967). A theory of leadership effectiveness. New York: McGraw-Hill.

Fleishman, E. A. (1957). A leader behavior description for industry. In R. M. Stogdill and A. E. Coons (Eds.), Leader behavior: Its description and measurement. Columbus: Bureau of Business Research, The Ohio State University.

Foss, K. A., & Foss, S. K. (1983). The status of research on women and communication. Communication Quarterly, 31, 195-203.

Glass, G., McGaw, B., & Smith, M. (1981). Meta-analysis in social research. Beverly Hills: Sage.

Graen, G., Dansereau, F., Jr., Minami, T., & Cashman, J. (1973). Leadership behaviors as cues to performance evaluation. Academy of Management Journal, 16, 611-623.

Halpin, A. W. (1957). Manual for the leader behavior description questionnaire. Columbus: Bureau of Business Research, The Ohio State University.

Hammer, T. H., & Dachler, P. H. (1975). A test of some assumptions underlying the path-goal model of supervision: Some suggested conceptual modifications. Organizational Behavior and Human Performance, 14, 60-75.

Hearn, J., & Parkin, P. W. (1983). Gender and organizations: A selected review and a critique of a neglected area. Organization Studies, 4, 219-242.

Heilman, M. E. (1983). Sex bias in work settings: The lack of fit model. In L. Cummings & B. Staw (Eds.), Research in Organizational Behavior, Vol. 5 (pp. 269-298). Greenwich, CT: JAI Press.

Heilman, M. E., & Stopeck, M. H. (1985). Attractiveness and corporate success: Different causal attributions for males and females. Journal of Applied Psychology, 70, 379-388.

House, R. J. (1971). A path-goal theory of leader effectiveness. Administrative Science Quarterly, 16, 321-338.

House, R. J., & Dessler, G. (1974). The path-goal theory of leadership: Some post hoc and a priori tests. In J. G. Hunt & L. L. Larson (Eds.), Contingency approaches to leadership (pp. 29-59). Carbondale, IL: Southern Illinois University Press.

House, R. J., & Mitchell, T. R. (1974). Path-goal theory of leadership. Journal of Contemporary Business, 5, 81-94.

Hunter, J., Schmidt, F., & Jackson, G. (1982). Meta-analysis: Cumulating research findings across studies. Beverly Hills: Sage.

Indvik, J. (1985). A path-goal theory investigation of superior-subordinate relationships. Unpublished doctoral dissertation, University of Wisconsin, Madison, WI.

Izraeli, D. N., & Izraeli, D. (1985). Sex effects in evaluating leaders: A replication study. Journal of Applied Psychology, 70, 540-546.

Jablin, F. M. (1979). Superior-subordinate communication: The state of the art. Psychological Bulletin, 86, 1201-1222.

Jermier, J. M., & Berkes, L. J. (1979). Leader behavior in a police command bureaucracy: A closer look at the quasi-military model. Administrative Science Quarterly, 24, 1-23.

LaFrance, M., & Mayo, C. (1979). A review of nonverbal behaviors of women and men. Western Journal of Speech Communication, 43, 96-107.

Lenney, E. (1977). Women's self-confidence in achievement settings. Psychological Bulletin, 84, 1-13.

Lenney, E., Browning, C., & Mitchell, L. (1980). What you know can hurt you: The effects of performance criteria ambiguity on sex differences in self-confidence. Journal of Personality, 48, 306-322.

Liden, R. C. (1985). Female perceptions of female and male managerial behavior. Sex Roles, 12, 421-431.

Likert, R. (1961). New patterns of management. New York: McGraw-Hill.

Mai-Dalton, R. R., Feldman-Summers, S., & Mitchell, T. R. (1979). Effect of employee gender and behavioral style on the evaluations of male and female banking executives. Journal of Applied Psychology, 64, 221-226.

Mawhinney, T. C., & Ford, J. D. (1977). The path-goal theory of leader effectiveness: An operant interpretation. Academy of Management Review, 2, 398-411.

Nieva, V. F., & Gutek, B. A. (1980). Sex effects on evaluation. Academy of Management Review, 5, 267-276.

Nieva, V. F., & Gutek, B. A. (1981). Women and work: A psychological perspective. New York: Praeger.

Osborn, R. N., & Vicars, W. M. (1976). Sex stereotypes: An artifact in leader behavior and subordinate satisfaction analysis. Academy of Management Journal, 19, 439-449.

Peters, L. H., O'Connor, E. J., Weekley, J., Pooyan, A., Frank, B., & Erenkrantz, B. (1984). Sex bias and managerial evaluations: A replication and extension. Journal of Applied Psychology, 69, 349-352.

Petty, M. M., & Bruning, N. S. (1980). A comparison of the relationships between subordinates' perceptions of supervisory behavior and measures of subordinates' job satisfaction for male and female leaders. Academy of Management Journal, 23, 717-725.

Petty, M. M., & Lee, G. K., Jr., (1975). Moderating effects of sex of supervisor and subordinate on relationships between supervisory behavior and subordinate satisfaction. Journal of Applied Psychology, 60, 624-628.

Pulakos, E. D., & Wexley, K. N. (1983). The relationship among perceptual similarity, sex, and performance ratings in manager-subordinate dyads. Academy of Management Journal, 26, 129-139.

Putnam, L. L. (1979). Women in management: Leadership theories, research results, and future directions. Paper presented at the annual meeting of the Central States Speech Association, St. Louis.

Rice, R. W., Instone, D., & Adams, J. (1984). Leader sex, leader success, and leadership process: Two field studies. Journal of Applied Psychology, 69, 12-31.

Rosenthal, R. (1978). Combining results of independent studies. Psychological Bulletin, 85, 185-193.

Rosenthal, R. (1979). The "file drawer problem" and tolerance for null results. Psychological Bulletin, 86, 638-641.

Rosenthal, R., & Rubin, D. B. (1978). Interpersonal expectancy effects: The first 345 studies. Behavioral and Brain Sciences, 3, 377-415.

Schein, V. E. (1975). Relationship between sex role stereotypes and requisite management characteristics among female managers. Journal of Applied Psychology, 60, 340-344.

Schneer, J. A. (1985). Gender context: An alternative perspective on sex differences in organizations. Paper presented at the annual meeting of the Academy of Management, San Diego.

Schriesheim, C. A. (1978). Development, validation, and application of new leadership behavior and expectancy research instruments. Unpublished doctoral dissertation, Ohio State University, Columbus, OH.

Schriesheim, C. A., & Von Glinow, M. A. (1977). The path-goal theory of leadership: A theoretical and empirical analysis. Academy of Management Journal, 20, 398-405.

Shore, L. M., & Thornton, G. C., III (1986). Effects of gender on self- and supervisory ratings. Academy of Management Journal, 29, 115-129.

Smith, M. J. (1984). Contingency rules theory, context, and compliance behaviors. Human Communication Research, 10, 489-512.

Smith, M. L., & Glass, G. V. (1977). Meta-analysis of psychotherapy outcome studies. American Psychologist, 32, 752-760.

Stogdill, R. M. (1963). Manual for the Leader Behavior Description Questionnaire-Form XII. Columbus: Bureau of Business Research, The Ohio State University.

Szilagyi, A. D., & Keller, R. T. (1976). A comparative investigation of the Supervisory Behavior Description Questionnaire (SBDQ) and the revised Leader Behavior Description Questionnaire (LBDQ-Form XII). Academy of Management Journal, 19, 642-649.

Terborg, J. R. (1977). Women in management: A research review. Journal of Applied Psychology, 62, 647-664.

Terborg, J. R., & Shingledecker, P. (1983). Employee reactions to supervision and work evaluation as a function of subordinate and manager sex. Sex Roles, 7, 813-823.

Trempe, J., Rigny, A., & Haccoun, R. R. (1985). Subordinate satisfaction with male and female managers: Role of perceived supervisory influence. Journal of Applied Psychology, 70, 44-47.

Vroom, V. H., & Yetton, P. W. (1973). Leadership and decision-making. Pittsburgh: University of Pittsburgh Press.

Wallston, B. S., & O'Leary, V. E. (1981). Sex makes a difference: Differential perceptions of women and men. In L. Wheeler (Ed.), Review of personality and social psychology, Vol. 2 (pp. 9-41). Beverly Hills: Sage.

Weimann, G. (1985). Sex differences in dealing with bureaucracy. Sex Roles, 12, 777-788.

Wexley, K. N., & Pulakos, E. D. (1982). Sex effects on performance ratings in manager-subordinate dyads: A field study. Journal of Applied Psychology, 67, 433-439.

Wexley, K. N., & Pulakos, E. D. (1983). The effects of perceptual congruence and sex on subordinates' performance appraisals of their managers. Academy of Management Journal, 26, 666-677.

Wheeless, V. E., & Berryman-Fink, C. (1985). Perceptions of women managers and their communicator competencies. Communication Quarterly, 33, 137-148.

White, M. C., Crino, M. D., & DeSanctis, G. L. (1981). A critical review of female performance, performance training and organizational initiatives designed to aid women in the work-role environment. Personnel Psychology, 34, 227-248.

SECTION THREE

GENDER AND ADVOCACY: NEGOTIATION, PERSUASION AND ARGUMENTATION

CHAPTER 10

DISCRIMINATING MALES AND FEMALES ON BELIEF STRUCTURES ABOUT ARGUING

Andrew S. Rancer   Robert A. Baukus
Emerson College

Argumentative communication is a ubiquitous form of social interaction, found in interpersonal, small-group and public contexts. Recently, a psychological approach to understanding argumentative communication has been advanced by Infante and Rancer (1982). They define argumentativeness as a generally stable personality trait which predisposes an individual in communication situations to advocate positions on controversial issues and to attempt refutation of the positions which other people take on those issues. Argumentativeness has been differentiated conceptually and empirically from verbal aggressiveness, attacking a person's self-concept instead of, or in addition to, his or her position on an issue (Infante & Rancer, 1982).

This psychological approach to studying arguing has focused on what it means to be argumentative with regard to individual motivation and perceptions, and how people respond to the person's argumentative behavior (Infante, 1981, 1982, 1985a, 1985b; Rancer & Infante, 1985; Infante, Trebing, Shepherd & Seeds, 1984; Infante, Wall, Leap & Danielson, 1984). This emerging body of research has also revealed several differences in the communicative behavior of individuals who differ in this trait predisposition (Infante, 1981, 1982; Rancer & Infante, 1985; Infante, Trebing, Shepherd & Seeds, 1984; Infante, Wall, Leap & Danielson, 1984).

One area of concern to researchers attempting to understand arguing and argumentative communication from this psychological approach concerns the question of sex differences in argumentativeness. This is an area of concern to researchers because of the potential important consequences of one group of individuals being less argumentative than another. Infante (1985a) suggests that on a global level, if a group argues less, then it has less potential for achieving social influence. Schultz (1982) found that argumentative individuals in a group situation were selected as leaders more often than less argumentative members, and exerted a stronger influence on group

decisions.   Schultz and Anderson (1982) suggest that
skill   in   argument is essential   in   the   negotiating
process.

Johnson   and Johnson (1979) have found arguing to
be related to numerous favorable outcomes such as: a
positive   effect   on learning due to   stimulation   and
curiosity;   improved   accuracy in social   perspective-
taking   which facilitates self-concept development and
social   intelligence;   a   reduction   in   ego-centric
thinking;   greater   creativity;   and enhanced problem-
solving and decision-making ability.

Recent   research   exploring   sex   differences   in
argumentativeness has produced inconsistent findings.
Rancer   (1979) found that males were higher   in   trait
argumentativeness than females.   Infante (1982) found
that   males are significantly more argumentative   than
females.   Schultz and Anderson (1982) administered the
Argumentativeness Scale (Infante & Rancer,   1982) to a
large group of individuals and found that females were
consistently over-represented in the low argumentative
tail   of the distribution.   While conceptually   quite
different from argumentativeness, contentiousness, one
dimension   of Communicator Style (Norton,   1978)   has
been   investigated   with regard   to   sex   differences.
Montgomery and Norton (1981) exploring sex differences
and   similarities   in   communicator style   found   that
males   and   females did not   differ   significantly   on
contentiousness.

In an effort to better understand sex differences
in argumentativeness, Rancer and Dierks-Stewart (1985)
found   that   previous research classified   individuals
solely   by   biological   sex   when   investigating
differences   in   the trait predisposition.   Noting   a
decade of research which points to the impact sex-role
orientation   has   on   a wide   range   of   communication
behaviors, they sought to explore how sex and sex-role
orientation   influence   trait   argumentativeness.
Results   of   their   study   indicated that   males   and
females   did   not   differ   significantly   on   trait
argumentativeness,   but that individuals classified by
sex-role   orientation,   regardless of biological   sex,
did   differ.   Individuals classified as Instrumental
(masculine)   were   significantly   higher   in   trait
argumentativeness than those classified as Expressive
(feminine),   Androgynous or Undifferentiated.   Further
analyses   revealed that feminine and undifferentiated
individuals tend to avoid arguing, while masculine and
androgynous individuals do not.

156

The contradictory findings of these studies make it difficult to assess the role of sex in influencing an individual's motivation to argue, their perceptions of arguing, and their actual argumentative behavior. In order to investigate these often confusing and contradictory findings, it was reasoned that a more profitable approach might be to study the beliefs that males and females have about arguing.

Two reasons are offered for this approach to understanding the role of sex in arguing. First, studies attempting to investigate the influence of sex and/or sex-role orientation on trait argumentativeness have produced conflicting findings. Some studies (Infante, 1982, 1985a; Schultz & Anderson, 1982) found that males are more argumentative than females. Other studies (e.g., Rancer & Dierks-Stewart, 1985) found no sex (biological) differences, but found differences in argumentativeness by sex-role orientation. It does not appear that further research along these lines will significantly clarify our understanding of the role of sex in arguing. A second reason for studying the beliefs that people have about arguing, rather than examining the trait predisposition alone, is that a framework already exists which could provide a valuable research direction. This framework (Fishbein & Ajzen, 1975) maintains that a predisposition is controlled by the set of beliefs which the individual has learned to associate with the object of the predisposition. Since argumentativeness has been conceptualized as a predisposition to respond in a particular way, this framework seems appropriate to study the beliefs about arguing that contribute to the development of the predispostion.

According to this framework, additional insight into argumentativeness would be gained by determining the beliefs that people have about arguing. If beliefs control predispositions, insight into sex differences in argumentativeness should be achieved by determining the beliefs which differentiate males and females, and the beliefs which differentiate males and females who differ in trait argumentativeness. This research focus, of course, is consistent with the psychological perspective of the argumentativeness model and research.

A major undertaking in this effort to explore differences in the beliefs about arguing of males and females is to identify the beliefs that people have about arguing and argumentative communication. A recent study accomplished that task. Rancer, Baukus and Infante (1985) attempted to enhance our understanding of argumentativeness by determining the particular beliefs which differentiate high, moderate and low argumentative individuals. In their study, participants were asked to elicit beliefs they have about arguing and argumentative communication. Content analytic procedures were used to classify the beliefs into a set of categories identified as beliefs about arguing. Eight beliefs emerged: Hostility, Activity/ Process, Control/ Dominance, Conflict/ Dissonance, Self-Image, Learning, Skill and Situational.

With a sound and novel theoretical framework to draw upon, and a set of belief structures about arguing already developed, it was the purpose of this study to differentiate males and females on the beliefs about arguing in an effort to clarify and enhance our understanding of sex differences in argumentativeness. Specifically, this investigation posited the following research question:

> Q1: Do high argumentative males and females, and low argumentative males and females differ on belief structures about arguing?

METHOD

Subjects

Participants were 138 students enrolled in basic undergraduate communication courses at a small, Eastern college. The subjects participated in this study voluntarily, and received extra-credit toward their respective course. There were 81 females and 57 males represented in the sample.

Procedures

At the beginning of the semester, the Argumentativeness Scale (Infante & Rancer, 1982) was administered to the subjects. The scale has demonstrated reliability and validity through a series of studies during its development and subsequent usage (Infante & Rancer, 1982; Infante, 1981, 1982; Rancer & Infante, 1985; Rancer, Baukus & Infante, 1985).

Participants were classified into one of three groups on the basis of norms established for the scale

(Infante & Rancer, 1982): high argumentatives (ARGgt >
13), moderate argumentatives (ARGgt $\leq$ 13, $\geq$ -5), and
low argumentatives (ARGgt < -5). The respective $\underline{n}$'s
for the three groups were 47, 53, and 38.

A second questionnaire was administered to
participants about four weeks later. Participants
were told that the researchers were interested in
learning more about people's feelings about engaging
in argumentative communication. The questionnaire
asked the participants to explain: "Why do you feel
the way you do about arguing?" Participants were then
given ten minutes to write their responses to the
question.

Units of Analysis

The content provided by each participant was
divided into sentences which were treated as the units
of analysis for this investigation. Sentences were
employed as the units of analysis because they are
natural units of distinction made by the source. Each
sentence was assumed to represent a perception about
arguing provided by the participants. A total of 483
units were produced by the 138 participants.

Assignation of Units of Analysis to Categories

Previous research (Rancer, Baukus & Infante,
1985) provided the researchers with a set of eight
belief structure categories about arguing: Hostility,
Activity/Process, Control/Dominance, Conflict/
Dissonance, Self-Image, Learning, Skill and
Situational.

This study also provided a codebook which included
examples of units assigned to each belief category,
and a list of key descriptors for each category code.

The Hostility belief (category) is represented by
beliefs about arguing where aggressiveness,
combativeness and emotional intensity are highlighted
in the communication act. The Activity/Process
category is representative of the participants'
reference to statements concerning their affective
response to arguing as an activity. The
Control/Dominance category represents beliefs about
arguing as a mechanism for controlling and/or
dominating another individual. In the
Conflict/Dissonance category, participants beliefs
were concerned with their perceptions of arguing as a
159

communication event where social conflict is the most salient characteristic of the encounter.

The Self-Image category is representative of the participants' reference to statements about argumentative communication's impact on their self-perception, on their adversary's self-perception, and on the meta-perceptions between adversaries. The Learning category is representative of the participants' reference to statements reflecting their beliefs about arguing as a communication event where information acquisition and dissemination are the most salient characteristics. The Skill category represents participants' beliefs concerning argumentative communication as a communication event where the display, or lack of, verbal and rhetorical skill is most evident.

The Situational category represented statements made by participants where their perceptions of arguing were inextricably bound to various situational factors such as aspects of the adversary (sex, status, relational considerations), aspects of the environment (time, location, setting), aspects of the topic (salience, ego-involvement, relevance), or unspecified aspects of the topic.

The categories of Hostility, Activity/Process, Control/ Dominance as well as the Conflict/Dissonance, Learning and Skill belief structure categories allowed for dichotomous coding of both positive and negative beliefs for the units of analysis assigned to those categories. The coding for the Self-Image category allowed for four types of beliefs: beliefs that arguing enhances one's self-image, beliefs that arguing is threatening to one's self-image, personal statements concerning self-image not directly related to arguing, and one code for statements where the participant perceives arguing as a threat to an adversary's self-image.

The Situational belief category also allowed for four types of beliefs to be coded in it. It contained codes for statements where the participant linked arguing to aspects of the adversary, environment, topic and unspecified situational aspects of argument.

All 483 units of analysis (sentences) obtained from the participants were coded into the aforementioned categories by a trained team of three coders who were aware of the general purpose of the study.

Reliability of the Argumentativeness Scale

Coefficient alpha was computed as a measure of the internal consistency of the Argumentativeness Scale. Coefficient alpha was .86 for the ARGap dimension, and .84 for the ARGav dimension.

Coding Reliability

Three randomly selected subsets of questionnaires were used to assess the reliability of the coding procedure. Each subset consisted of seven questionnaires from subjects who represented the three levels of trait argumentativeness, high, moderate and low. Scott's (1955) pi formula was selected as the method of assessing reliability of coding because it accounts for chance co-occurrences. The pi values for each consistency test are: .69, .78, and .74 respectively. Considering the wide variance attributed to open-ended responses, the consistency results obtained seemed adequate.

Test of the Research Question

The hypothesis was tested via multivariate analysis of variance (MANOVA) with sex (male, female) and level of trait argumentativeness (high, low) as the independent variables. The vector of eight belief scores was dependent. The means for each of the belief structure categories are presented in Table 1 (see Table 1).

A significant main effect for sex was found, F=7.6638, df=9/73, p <.01, Wilks' lambda criterion. The univariate ANOVA results suggest that sex differences in beliefs about arguing originate along several dimensions. Table 2 presents the results of the univariate F-tests (see Table 2). Females tended to believe to a greater extent than males that arguments were hostile communicative acts and a means to assert control. They also believed to a greater extent than males that arguments serve as a means to assert control and/or dominate an adversary.

A significant main effect for level of trait argumentativeness was also observed based on Wilks' lambda, F=7.0808, df=9/73, p < .001. The univariate pattern for the argumentativeness treatment conditions suggest differences in the beliefs concerning hostility, activity/process, learning and skill. No significant interaction effects were found.

While an argument is conceived as at least two people defending different positions on an issue while attacking the positions of one another (Infante, 1981), the results of this study suggest that males and females have different belief structures that they bring to such an encounter. The MANOVA results indicate that cognitive differences between the treatment groups exist that can exacerbate, augment and therefore increase the probability that arguments can escalate into verbal aggression.

Females tended to believe more than males that an argument was a hostile, combative communication act highlighted by a strong degree of emotional intensity. In addition, females, to a greater degree than males, believed that an argument is a mechanism for controlling and/or dominating another individual. Table 1 reflects this result (See Table 1).

Beliefs about arguing were also found to differ contingent upon individuals' general trait to be argumentative. People high in trait argumentativeness held beliefs that suggest arguments are less hostile communication acts than low argumentative individuals. As noted above, this trend held when sex was accounted for. High argumentative females believed that arguing was more aggressive than high argumentative males. Low argumentatives believed arguing to be more aggressive in general, with low argumentative females possessing the strongest belief that an argument is an aggressive and hostile communication act. In terms of the belief that arguing is a means to control and dominate another, low argumentatives held this belief to a greater degree than high argumentatives. Females in both levels of argumentativeness held stronger beliefs that arguing is used as a means of dominating another individual.

No sex differences were noted in the five remaining significant belief structure categories. High argumentatives believed an argument to be an activity that encourages social interaction. In addition, high argumentative individuals believed that arguing is a learning situation where information acquisition and dissemination are the most salient characteristics. Highly argumentative individuals

162

also believed arguments are a demonstration or show of their communication and rhetorical skills. Individuals low in argumentativeness believed that the situation in which an argument occurs has a great impact on the argument in general, and their motivation to argue in particular.

Multiple discriminant structure coefficients were produced to examine the degree of separation among the treatment conditions and to provide an indication of the magnitude of the differences. The four group analyses provided two significant discriminant functions. Prior to the extraction of the functions, Wilks' lambda was .5604, indicating that a considerable power exists in the beliefs to discriminate among the groups defined by sex and trait argumentativeness. A summary of the discriminant functions is provided in Table 3 (see Table 3).

The structure coefficients for each of the beliefs that produced significant main effects in the MANOVA procedure are reported in Table 4 (see Table 4). Function I was primarily represented by the learning belief structure, and was therefore labelled Cultivation. The second function was influenced by the situational and hostility beliefs, and was labelled Antagonism.

A summary of the four treatment groups on the two discriminant functions is provided in Table 5 (see Table 5). The high argumentative male and high argumentative female groups had a moderately high positive correlation with respect to the Cultivation function. This indicates that both groups believed arguing to be a valuable learning experience, with the male high argumentatives having the greatest positive correlation. The low argumentative males and low argumentative females clustered with a moderately low negative correlation. Thus, both low argumentative males and low argumentative females believe that arguing is not a good means of learning about their adversary. Low argumentative females had the strongest negative correlation. Therefore, the greatest contrast on the Cultivation dimension was between highly argumentative males and low argumentative females.

The Antagonism function provides a significant, yet smaller, magnitude of separation among the four groups. Low argumentative males and high argumentative males were maximally separated on the

163

Antagonism dimension. The high argumentative males were the only group with a negative correlation on the dimension, and thus viewed arguing as the least antagonistic. Both low and high argumentative females had a low positive correlation indicating a somewhat negative view of arguing as a hostile communication act or encounter.

DISCUSSION

The major purpose of this study was to clarify and enhance our understanding of the influence of sex in argumentative communication. Previous research (e.g., Infante, 1981, 1982; Rancer & Dierks-Stewart, 1985) explored the issue of sex differences in argumentative communication by utilizing trait argumentativeness primarily as a dependent variable, then determining how individuals classified by biological sex, psychological gender, or both differed in the trait predisposition.

This research study sought to explore how the variables of sex and level of trait argumentativeness influence individuals' beliefs about arguing. It was reasoned that this approach would be more profitable in understanding the reported sex differences in motivation to argue.

The theoretical framework advanced by Fishbein and Ajzen (1975) was used to guide the current study. That belief framework asserts than an individual's predispositions are controlled by a set of beliefs which the person has learned to associate with the object of the predisposition. This belief structure framework has received considerable support in a wide range of contexts, and with several diverse predispositions (Fishbein & Ajzen, 1975; Ajzen & Fishbein, 1980).

Thus, this research effort was deemed valuable in helping develop greater understanding regarding the reported sex differences in motivation and performance in argumentative communication contexts. If a person's beliefs about arguing heavily influence their motivation and performance in argumentative encounters, then determining if males and females differ in their underlying belief structures about arguing should do much to clarify the disparate findings of previous studies.

The results of this study support the contention

that males and females, in general, differ in their belief structures about arguing. The current findings suggest that females to a greater degree than males, hold the belief that arguing is a hostile, combative communication encounter. In addition, females to a greater degree than males, hold beliefs about arguing which suggest it is a communication act employed as a means of controlling and/or dominating another.

This study also revealed that beliefs about arguing were found to differ contingent upon an individual's level of trait argumentativeness. In general, individuals high in argumentativeness hold beliefs that arguing is a functional, albeit assertive form of communication, in which individuals can learn a great deal about each other and positions on issues. Low argumentative males and females apparently do not share as strongly in this belief.

Moreover, this study discovered that an individual's sex and level of argumentativeness both appear to influence beliefs about arguing. Females high in argumentativeness were greater than high argumentative males in their beliefs that arguing is a hostile and aggressive communication act. Females and males low in argumentativeness held beliefs that arguing is a hostile, aggressive and potentially dysfunctional communication act. This finding was revealed by the results of the discriminant analysis. On the Antagonism function, low argumentative and high argumentative males were maximally separated, with low argumentative males holding the greatest belief that arguing is antagonistic. Low argumentative males were closely followed by low argumentative females and high argumentative females respectively, who also held beliefs that arguing is an antagonistic and hostile communication act.

Females in both levels of trait argumentativeness held greater beliefs than males that arguing is used for, and consequently results in, the control and domination of one individual over another. Males and females high in argumentativeness seem to hold beliefs that arguing with another individual is a valuable learning experience, although males had a greater correlation on the Cultivation function. The greatest contrast on the Cultivation function was between high argumentative males and low argumentative females.

One assumption of the argumentativeness construct is that arguing is a functional communication

165

behavior, and argumentativeness is a positive communication trait. This conceptualization is consistent with the assumptions that the communication discipline has advocated since antiquity. The ability to support and defend one's position on controversial issues is a key skill in personal and professional contexts. A recent study by Infante and Gorden (1985) revealed that organizational outcomes were more favorable when a woman was higher in argumentativeness.

Infante (1985a) suggests that the credibility of an individual in social and professional contexts may also be enhanced by greater levels of motivation to argue and argumentative behavior. Along those lines, both Infante (1985a) and Anderson, Schultz and Staley (1986) have explored methods of influencing and training women to increase their argumentative motivation and behavior. Infante (1985a) utilized a "cued argument procedure" to enhance females' argumentativeness. Anderson, Schultz and Staley (1986) employed training sessions with material on conflict and conflict management, along with practice in conflict management techniques in order to favorably influence females to be more argumentative.

The results of this study suggest that these "remediation" programs may be quite valuable in altering low argumentative females' argumentative behavior. In addition, the findings of this study that females have less favorable beliefs about arguing than males also suggests another possible direction for remediation. Utilizing the Fishbein and Ajzen framework , one could posit that the alteration of an individual's belief structure framework about arguing could ultimately affect their argumentative behavior.

A first step in enhancing an individual's argumentative skill and behavior might be directed at adding to, or reinforcing their positive beliefs about this communication activity. Efforts at altering individuals' cognitive associations about arguing and argumentative communication should favorably impact on their argumentative predisposition (ARGgt), and ultimately influence their behaviors relative to that predisposition. In fact, cognitive restructuring techniques previously advocated for the treatment of communication apprehension (Fremouw, 1984) could be applied to alter an individual's unfavorable beliefs about arguing. Introductory courses in argumentation theory could also stress the positive benefits of

166

arguing on an interpersonal level, as well as developing individuals' skill in argument.

The findings indicating sex differences in beliefs about arguing also suggest that, as a society, more sensitivity may be needed in the socialization and sex-role development process. Females, in particular, should be presented with appropriate female role models whose personal and professional lives depend upon high levels of motivation and skill in argumentative communication.

Although current emphasis appears to be placed on enhancing females' beliefs and abilities to argue, it must also be recognized that all individuals would appear to profit from enhancing their beliefs and behavior regarding argumentative communication.

TABLE 1

BELIEF STRUCTURE MEANS

	Host	Act/Pro	Con/Dom	Learn	Skill	Sit
Condition						
High ARG	.042	.276	.340	1.276	.361	.021
Females	.740	.296	.555	1.111	.296	.000
Males	.000	.250	.050	1.500	.450	.050
Low ARG	.684	.105	.368	.026	.342	.236
Females	.920	.160	.400	.000	.280	.120
Males	.230	.000	.307	.076	.461	.461

Belief Structure Categories

Host=Hostility
Act/Pro=Activity/Process
Con/Dom=Control/Dominance
Learn=Learning
Skill=Skill
Sit=Situational

TABLE 2

UNIVARIATE F TESTS

Effect

Argumentativeness	Belief Structure	F	Sig.
	Hostility	16.73	.00
	Activity/Process	3.68	.05
	Learning	38.32	.00
	Skill	5.05	.02

Effect

Sex	Belief Structure	F	Sig.
	Hostility	6.54	.01
	Control/Dominance	6.24	.01

----

df=1,8

TABLE 3

SUMMARY STATISTICS OF CANONICAL DISCRIMINANT FUNCTIONS

Individuals Classified By Sex and Trait Argumentativeness

Rank-Order Function I Cultivation

Eigenvalue=.5693   Relative % of Variance=81.00

Canonical R=.6023   Canonical R^2 =.36 Wilks' lambda=.560

Rank Order Function II Antagonism

Eigenvalue=.0989   Relative % of Variance=14.08

Canonical R=.3001   Canonical R^2 =.09 Wilks' lambda=.879

TABLE 4

STRUCTURE COEFFICIENTS

Belief Categories	I Cultivation	II Antagonism
Learning	.7616*	.0336
Skill	.0599	-.2649
Situational	-.1886	.6888*
Self-Image	.1753	.2650
Hostility	-.4416	.4844*
Activity/Process	.1812*	.2140
Control/Dominance	.0168	.2527

*=variables with the greatest relative power to distinguish the groups.

TABLE 5

GROUP CENTROIDS IN DISCRIMINANT SPACE

Discriminant Functions

Groups	I Cultivation	II Antagonism
Low ARG Males	-.62605	.66075
High ARG Males	.84986	-.14431
Low ARG Females	-.83457	.23657
High ARG Females	.61220	.17201

REFERENCES

Ajzen, I., & Fishbein, M. (1980). Understanding attitudes and predicting social behavior. Englewood Cliffs, N.J.: Prentice-Hall, Inc.

Anderson, J., Schultz, B., & Staley, C.C. (April, 1986). Training in argumentativeness: New hope for nonassertive women. Paper presented at the Eastern Communication Association, Atlantic City, New Jersey.

Fishbein, M., & Ajzen, I. (1975). Belief, attitude, intention, and behavior: An introduction to theory and research. Reading, MA: Addison-Wesley Publishing Company.

Fremouw, W.J. (1984). Cognitive-behavioral therapies for modification of communication apprehension. In J.A. Daly and J.C. McCroskey (Eds.). Avoiding communication. Beverly Hills, CA: Sage Publications.

Infante, D.A. (1981). Trait argumentativeness as a predictor of communicative behavior in situations requiring argument.Central States Speech Journal, 32, 265-272.

Infante, D.A. (1982). The argumentative student in the speech communication classroom: An investigation and implications. Communication Education, 31, 141-148.

Infante, D.A. (1985a). Influencing women to be more argumentative: Source credibility effects.Journal of Applied Communication Research, 13, 33-44.

Infante, D.A. (1985b, November). Response to high argumentatives: Message and sex differences.Paper presented at the annual convention of the Speech Communication Association, Denver, Colorado.

Infante, D.A., & Gorden, W.I. (1985). Benefits versus bias: An investigation of argumentativeness, gender, and organizational communication outcomes. Communication Research Reports, 2, 196-201.

Infante, D.A., & Rancer, A.S. (1982). A conceptualization and measure of argumentativeness. Journal of Personality Assessment, 46, 72-80.

Infante, D.A., Trebing, J.D., Shepherd, P.E., & Seeds, D.E. (1984). The relationship of argumentativeness to verbal aggression. Southern Speech Communication Journal, 50, 67-77.

Infante, D.A., Wall, C.H., Leap, C.J., & Danielson, K. (1984). Verbal aggression as a function of the receiver's argumentativeness. Communication Research Reports, 1, 33-37.

Johnson, D.W., & Johnson, R.T. (1979). Conflict in the classroom: Controversy and learning. Review of Educational Research, 49, 51-70.

Montgomery, B.M., & Norton, R.W. (1981). Sex differences and similarities in communicator style. Communication Monographs, 48, 121-132.

Norton, R.W. (1978). Foundation of a communicator style construct. Human Communication Research, 4, 99-112.

Rancer, A.S. (1979). An examination of the influence of interpersonal and situational variables on argumentativeness. Unpublished doctoral dissertation, Kent State University.

Rancer, A.S., & Infante, D.A. (1985). Relations between motivation to argue and the argumentativeness of adversaries. Communication Quarterly, 33, 209-218.

Rancer, A.S., & Dierks-Stewart, K. (1985). The influence of sex and sex-role orientation on trait argumentativeness. Journal of Personality Assessment, 49, 69-70.

Rancer, A.S., Baukus, R.A., & Infante, D.A. (1985). Relations between argumentativeness and belief structures about arguing. Communication Education, 34, 37-47.

Schultz, B. (1982). Argumentativeness: Its effect in group decision-making and its role in leadership perception. Communication Quarterly, 30, 368-375.

Schultz, B., & Anderson, J. (1982). Learning to negotiate: The role of argument. Paper presented to the Eastern Communication Association,Hartford, Connecticut.

Scott, W.A. (1955). Reliability of content analysis: The case of nominal scale coding. Public Opinion Quarterly, 19, 321-375.

CHAPTER 11

RATIONALIZING CONFLICT CHOICES: DO MEN AND WOMEN SPEAK THE SAME LANGUAGE?

Sally Henzl, Northwestern University
Lynn Turner, Marquette University

Much social science research attention in the past has focused on male/female differences. Specifically in the field of communication, long lists of variables have been examined with regard to their differential employment by males and females. This approach continues to be a research model despite the fact that many scholars have expressed dissatisfaction with gender research and pointed to several problems associated with it (e.g., Putnam, 1982).

One major problem has been that the results of gender difference studies have been ambiguous. Researchers have found that in conflict women tend to use more accommodation strategies (Frost and Wilmot, 1978); learn to avoid conflict situations (Bardwick, 1971); learn to use more expressions of support and solidarity (Strodtbeck and Mann, 1956); use more facilitative behaviors (Zimmerman and West, 1975) than males do. However, in a review of the literature on conflict behavior, Terhune (1970) observed women appear to be more accommodative than men in some experimental situations, but less cooperative in others. Recent research on sex differences in argumentativeness has also produced inconsistent results (e.g., Rancer and Baukus, 1984).

Self-disclosure research has indicated both that females engage in more self-disclosure than males (e.g., Jourard and Lasakow, 1958; Morgan, 1976; Pedersen and Higbee, 1969; Rivenback, 1971) and that there is no difference between male and female disclosure patterns (e.g., Certner, 1973; Ricker-Ousiankina and Kusmin, 1958; Weigel, Weigel, and Chadwick, 1969). These findings are further complicated by Chelune's (1976) observation that observers consistently overestimate the amount of males' self-disclosure while underestimating the amount of females' self-disclosure behavior.

In studies examining verbosity a similar problem exists. Some research has found females to be more verbose than males (e.g., Konsky, 1978; Mabry, 1976). Some research has yielded the opposite finding (Swacker, 1975), and still other research has failed to isolate verbosity effects (Brower, Gernitsen, and Dellaan, 1979; Martin and Craig, 1980).

In response to these mixed findings, researchers began considering the possibility that merely looking at anatomical sex is

175

insufficient as a predictive variable. For, in addition to the biological given of anatomical sex, individuals also acquire, through social interactions, psychological sex. Interest in psychological sex type produced numerous measuring instruments (Bem, 1974; Berzins, Welling, and Wetter, 1978; Heilbrun, 1976; Spence, Helmreich, and Stapp, 1975).

Many studies then examined the relationship between psychological sex-type and other variables (e.g., Baggio and Neilson, 1976; Bem, 1975, 1976; Greenblatt et al., 1980; Montgomery and Burgoon, 1977; Pearson, 1981).

However, after initial enthusiasm concerning the predictive power of psychological sex-type, several critiques have pointed to troubling issues in relation to the conceptual validity of the construct. Lott, Spence, and Helmreich, (1979) note that conceptually androgyny relies on an a priori definition of masculinity and femininity. They contend that this reinforces verbal habits which emphasize masculinity and femininity as two categories and thus contradict the essence of the androgyny construct. As Putnam (1982) observes:

> Our reliance on sex-stereotypic traits to define androgyny locks us into the very dilemma we seek to escape. By measuring masculinity versus femininity and using statistical tests of difference to uncover sex differences, we often perpetuate the inequities of the status quo by arguing tautologically for dualism. (p. 2)

Additionally, the psychometric adequacy of the instruments purporting to measure psychological sex-type poses a problem to the researcher. Analyses of the factor structure of the Bem Sex Role Inventory, the Personal Attributes Questionnaire, and Heilbrun's Masculinity and Femininity Scales (e.g., Gaudreau, 1977; Gross, Batlis, Small, and Erdwins, 1979; Pearson, 1980) have yielded a variety of different results. The emergence of more than two factors in most of these studies suggests a more complex situation than that invited by the masculine-feminine dichotomy and calls into question the psychometric adequacy of the instruments.

Thus gender research using biological sex yields contradictory findings and gender research based on psychological sex-type is plagued with problems of validity. Additionally, regardless of which approach one takes to the independent variable, researchers have been concerned by an evaluative bias in gender research that affects females negatively both by devaluing female characteristics and by establishing male characteristics as the norm. In a study exploring the premise that the masculine stereotype is the more rewarded in our culture, Rosenkrantz,

Vogel, Bee, Broverman, and Broverman (1969) found that more stereotypically masculine traits than feminine traits were rated as socially desirable by college students of both sexes. Gilligan (1982) notes that it is difficult to say "different" without connoting "better" or "worse".

Kramarae (1981), in offering the muted group theory as explanatory of male/female language differences, says that "females are 'inarticulate' because the language they use is derivative, having been developed largely out of male perception of reality" (p. 2). In psychology, McClelland (1975) observes that the tendency is to regard male behavior as the norm and female behavior as a deviation.

Finally, gender research has been criticized for its atheoretical nature. Konsky and Murdock (1982) point out that most variables in gender based language research are chosen largely on the basis of previous research without regard to theory. And Putnam (1982) notes that:

theorizing about male-female communications is . . . limited by our status as a disconnected array of investigators unified by the use of one variable, gender. (p. 3)

Many researchers believe that the lack of theoretical grounding ultimately renders gender research insignificant.

Taken together, these problem areas pose serious obstacles to proceeding with gender research in the future under the same assumptions as in the past. Fortunately several researchers (e.g., Gilligan, 1982; Kramarae, 1981; Putnam, 1982) have suggested new directions for gender research. Kramarae (1981) observes that we have theoretical analyses available to us that would be useful as a "quilting pattern" to organize contradictory results and guide future directions in gender research. In an influential recent publication, Gilligan (1982) addresses the critical problem of lack of theory by developing a theoretical framework that can be applied to female/male language differences. Gilligan theorizes that women's moral domain is informed by an interpersonal logic while men's moral domain develops from a justice approach derived from the formal logic of fairness. These two separate approaches are expressed in two different "voices" and point toward different understandings of morality.

To develop her theory, Gilligan conducted studies of (1) elementary school children, (2) college students, and (3) women considering an abortion. Gilligan's methodology involves analyzing subjects' responses generated during open-ended interviews. In each study, subjects were presented one of Kohlberg's (1969) well-known dilemmas designed to measure the stages of moral development. Particularly striking results were obtained in the study where children were told Kohlberg's (1969) "Heinz" story about a man who cannot afford to pay for a drug to save his dying wife. Gilligan (1982) reports that boys often see the story in terms of the man's individual moral choice, and conclude that the man should choose life over property and steal the drug. On the other hand, girls often take an overview: they wonder what will happen to the relationship if the man gets caught and goes to jail, or they focus on the morality of the druggist, seeing the problem as one of communication -- persuading the druggist to do the right thing.

Although the approaches to the problem are simply different, Gilligan (1982) states that in the past the girls' responses have been considered wrong. Further, according to Kohlberg's (1969) scale, girls appear to be deficient in moral development, since their judgments exemplify the third stage of Kohlberg's six-stage sequence. At this stage morality is conceived in interpersonal terms and goodness is equated with helping and pleasing others. A primary objective of a Stage 3 respondent is to be thought of as a "nice" person. Kohlberg and Kramer (1969) imply that mature women function well at this stage of moral development insofar as their lives take place in the home. Kohlberg and Kramer further suggest that only if women enter traditional areas of male activity will they recognize the inadequacy of this "good girl" orientation and progress like men to higher stages where relationships are subordinated to rules (stage four) and rules to universal principles of justice (stages five and six).

Gilligan (1982) stresses that her theory discusses the differential access of the genders to certain kinds of understanding, not the superiority of one gender over the other. Thus in Heinz's dilemma, boys and girls see two very different moral problems -- the boys a conflict between life and property that can be resolved by logical deduction, the girls, "a fracture of human relationship that must be mended with its own thread" (p. 31). By asking different questions arising from different conceptions of morality, the children arrive at fundamentally divergent answers. Gilligan states that arranging these answers according to Kohlberg's (1969) invariant successive stages of moral development misses the truths revealed by girls, since the stages are "calibrated" by the logic of boys' responses. According to Gilligan, Kohlberg's theory can answer the question, "What does he see that she does not?" but has nothing to say to the question, "What does she see that he does not?" In Gilligan's view, then, the contrasting images of a hierarchical logic of justice and an interpersonal network of relationships illustrate two views of morality which are "complementary rather than sequential or opposed" (p. 33).

An earlier study (Turner and Henzl, 1984) attempted to test the validity of Gilligan's theory in the specific moral domain of conflict resolution and rationale for decisions. In this study, subjects were given an imaginary conflict scenario to resolve, and it was hypothesized that two different languages would emerge in the rationales for the solutions to the problem. Women's choices would be defended in language referring to the relationships described in the scenario, while men's choices would be explained with a language indicative of a justice approach based on rights and rules. However, the results of this study were equivocal since although a justice voice and a networking voice emerged from the data, these voices were not related to the biological sex of the respondent. Turner and Henzl (1984) speculate that the two voices may be related to power position rather than biological sex since the relational voice was used to describe the employee's concerns and the hierarchical voice informed the employer's concerns in the data. However, this study had several methodological problems that limit acceptance of its findings. First of all, the sample did not represent a wide cross-section of the population, but rather was comprised of the traditional subject of social science research, the college sophomore. Secondly, the study used a priori categories (those defined by Gilligan, 1982). It is possible that the data were manipulated to fit these categories, and that other categories which might have arisen in the perusal of the data were obscured. Finally, the study relied on subjects' responses to a printed scenario. The scenario revolved around a work conflict where an employee had family obligations and a supervisor had business related concerns. Perhaps the nature of this situation itself predisposed the respondents to speak in an interpersonal language with regard to the employee and a justice language with regard to the employer.

The current study is an attempt to further test Gilligan's (1982) theory remediating the potential sources of confounding in our previous study. The following research question is explored:

R.Q. Will males and females justify conflict resolution decisions differently?

Methods

Subjects and Procedures -- Subjects were 44 employed adults (21 females, 23 males; 22 married, 16 single, 4 divorced, 2 widowed, ranging in age from 20 to 75) from a large metropolitan area. One-half of the subjects were drawn from a university community, and one-half from a liberal suburban church. The subjects were randomly assigned one of the two scenarios (See Appendices I and II) and asked how the conflict should be

179

resolved, what were the rationales for their choices, and what were the concerns of each character. The scenarios were devised to reflect an interpersonal context and a work related context in order to test the influence of the situation on the respondents.

Analysis

The data were coded by a coder blind to the purposes of the study and trained during a two-hour session. The coder first classified the decisions made by the respondents into one of two categories: siding with one character or the other, or reconstructing the problem. In order to assess reliability, two secondary coders also classified the decisions. 100% agreement was reached among the coders.

The primary coder then read the responses and identified 41 distinct decision rationales from the data. Guetzkow (1950) states that when research asks the question why people hold particular attitudes, each reason should be treated as a separate entity. The coder then sorted the rationales into groups based on their theme, following Holsti (1969):

> For many purposes the theme, a single assertion about some subject is the most useful unit of content analysis. It is almost indispensable in research on . . . values, attitudes, beliefs, and the like. (p. 116)

We intentionally avoided utilizing Gilligan's (1982) categories as the Turner and Henzl (1984) study had done, since the goal of this study was to describe as adequately as possible the different "voices" as they were articulated by our respondents. To have used a priori categories might have obscured other categories and resulted in needless fractionation of the data.

Initial analysis of the data revealed five distinct categories (economic concerns, relationship concerns, moral concerns, personal development concerns, and communication process concerns). The degree of coding agreement between a secondary judge and the primary judge for distinguishing five categories was calculated, and served as a unitizing (U) reliability estimate (Guetzkow, 1950). This analysis revealed that $U = .05$ (- .01), indicating that unitizing disagreements among the coders exceeding .05 occurred by chance only once for each one hundred units coded.

The five categories were then collapsed to form three categories: recourse to a higher principle, relationship concerns, and communication process concerns. The categories were formed following basic rules for category sets as outlined by Selltiz, Wrightsman, and Cook (1976):

1. The set of categories should be derived from a single classificatory principle.
2. The set of categories should be exhaustive, that is, it should be possible to place every response in one of the categories of the set.
3. The categories within the set should be mutually exclusive; it should not be possible to place a given response in more than one category within the set. (p. 466)

The coded data were analyzed by the chi square test to determine the differences. In order to retard inflation of Type 1 error, the .01 significance level was utilized.

Results

Analysis of the data by chi square revealed that there was no significant difference between men and women in this sample in either situation as to whether a decision was made within the problem as presented or whether the problem was reconstructed (Situation 1: X^2 obs = 2.86, X^2 crit = 6.64, $p > .01$; Situation 2: X^2 obs = .818, X^2 crit = 6.64; $p > .01$). Additionally, there was no significant difference between men and women in either situation as to the type of decision reached (Situation 1: X^2 obs = .15, X^2 crit = 9.21, $p > .01$; Situation 2: X^2 obs = .99, X^2 crit = 9.21, $p > .01$). Further, there was no significant difference based on sex of respondent or situation as to the type of reason used to support decisions (sex of respondent: X^2 obs = 4.88, X^2 crit = 15.09, $p > .01$; Situation: X^2 obs = 4.73, X^2 crit = 9.21, $p > .01$). Finally, collapsing the categories into two to resemble Gilligan's model (relationship and communication process were combined) did not yield significant differences between males and females (X^2 obs = 1.28, X^2 crit = 6.64, $p > .01$.

Discussion

We undertook this research in order to examine the power and generalizability of Gilligan's (1982) theory. Again, our results yielded only partial support for separate voices. Our coders found it relatively simple to discover a voice whose decisions are rationalized in a justice model as Gilligan (1982) describes it. ("An education is much more valuable in the long run, and it's worth the trouble of struggling for a few years.") In addition, there were voices rooted in relational concerns. ("In every relationship, people must learn to give and take in order for the relationship to work.") We also found a voice concerned with communication. ("The use of counselors is more accepted these days and can help people focus on their hidden agendas and true needs and wants as well as finding ways to communicate.")

Although three categories emerged from our data that seemed to overlap with Gilligan (1982), our data indicate a position contrary to Gilligan's. We would argue that justifications made in terms of the good of the relationship are also hierarchical in nature. Arguments based on the principle that the maintenance of the relationship is of greater value than any alternatives are appealing to the formal logic of fairness just as arguments in the hierarchical voice do. Gilligan's (1982) theoretical position fails to acknowledge that concern for the relationship may be substituting one hierarchical value for another. However, the category we observed concerned with communication processes does seem to differ from a hierarchical voice. Gilligan (1982) includes this emphasis on process with the feminine voice. For example, in discussing Amy, one of her respondents, Gilligan (1982) notes . . . "her solution to the dilemma lies in activating the network by communication" (pp. 30-31). In Gilligan's (1982) work and our own studies there is the suggestion that those respondents who were concerned with the communication processes were more likely to go outside the boundaries of the question as posed and seek creative solutions. In further discussing Amy, Gilligan (1982) describes the interviewer's concern:

It immediately becomes clear that the interviewer's problem in understanding Amy's response stems from the fact that Amy is answering a different question from the one the interviewer thought had been posed. (p. 31)

In our data a similar re-interpretation of the problem occurred when a respondent questioned the premises of the situation rather than tackling the problem posed by it. ("This is not something to decide in a committee.")

Although in constructing her theory Gilligan (1982) conducted many interviews, in illuminating her points she discusses individual cases at length. We have tried to extend Gilligan's (1982) work to see if these examples are generalizable in the aggregate. Despite finding prototypical individual examplars of Gilligan's (1982) voices in our study (A female: "In every relationship, people must learn to give and take in order for the relationship to work"; A female: "Somehow Terry must persuade Pat that going back to school is right for both of them"; A male: "It might not be the best thing for the marriage, but it appears to be the logical and rational way to go.") her identification of two voices with biological sex does not hold. While it appears that separate voices do exist, it is possible that their explanation depends on more complex variables than biological sex. Gender may not be an isolated trait. The "masculine" and "feminine" voices might be created by contextual variables, and a theoretical perspective should take this into consideration.

Any study's findings are limited by the methodology employed. In this study, the use of a hypothetical situation and a pen and paper self-report may make the results less robust than those from a more naturalistic setting. Further, the use of multivariate statistics in the future might enable researchers to more readily tap the richness of the data. A final problem could be that the subjects were not randomly sampled.

Different choices for rationalization reveal different ways of seeing the world. We plan to continue pursuing this line of research since our results indicate that both men and women utilize a language that expresses an ethic of care and a language that expresses a concern for rules. That both men and women may speak the same language and that what prompts a person to speak in process terms, or relational terms, or hierarchical terms may be more complex than biological sex, suggests fruitful future research.

References

Baggio, M.K., and Neilson, E.C. (1976). Anxiety correlates of sex-role identity. Journal of Clinical Psychology 32, 619-623.

Bardwick, J.M. (1971). Psychology of Women: A study of bio-cultural conflicts. New York: Harper and Row.

Bem, S. (1974). The measurement of psychological androgyny. Journal of Consulting and Clinical Psychology 42, 155-162.

Bem, S. (1976). Probing the promise of psychological androgyny. In A. G. Kaplan and J.P. Bean (Eds.), Beyond sex-role stereo-types: Readings toward a psychology of androgyny. Boston: Little, Brown and Company.

Bem, S. (1975). Sex-role adaptability: One consequence of psychological androgyny. Journal of Personality and Social Psychology 31, 634-643.

Berzins, J.J., Welling, M.A., and Wetter, R.E. (1978). A new measure of psychological androgyny based on the personality research form. Journal of Consulting and Clinical Psychology 46, 126-138.

Brouwer, C., Gernitsen, M., and Dellaan, D. (1979). Speech dif-ferences between women and men: On the wrong track? Language in Society 8, 33-50.

Certner, B. (1973). Exchange of self-disclosures in same-sexed groups of strangers. Journal of Consulting and Clinical Psychology 40, 292-297.

Chelune, G.S. (1976). Reactions and male and female disclosure at two levels. Journal of Personality and Social Psychology 34, 1000-1003.

Frost, J. and Wilmot, W. (1978). Interpersonal conflict. Dubuque, Iowa: William G. Brown.

Gaudreau, P. (1977). Factor analysis of the Bem Sex Role Inven-tory. Journal of Consulting and Clinical Psychology 42, 155-162.

Gilligan, C. (1982). In a different voice. Cambridge, Mass.: Harvard University Press.

Greenblatt, L., Hasenauer, J.E., and Freimuth, V.S. (1980). Psychological sex type and androgyny in the study of communication variables: Self-disclosure and communication apprehension. Human Communication Research 6, 117-129.

Gross, R., Baltis, N., Small, A., and Erdwins, C. (1979). Factor structure of the Bem Sex Role Inventory and the Personal Attributes Questionnaire. Journal of Consulting and Clinical Psychology 47, 1222-1224.

Guetzkow, H. (1950). Unitizing and categorizing problems in coding qualitative data. Journal of Clinical Psychology 6, 47-58.

Heibrun, A.E. (1976). Measurement of masculine and feminine sex role identities as independent dimensions. Journal of Consulting and Clinical Psychology 44, 183-190.

Holsti, O.R. (1969). Content analysis for the social sciences and humanities. Reading, Mass.: Addison-Wesley Publishing Company.

Jourard, S., and Lasakow, P. (1958). Some factors in self-disclosure. Journal of Abnormal and Social Psychology 5, 221-231.

Kohlberg, L. (1969). Stage and sequence: The cognitive-development approach to socialization. In D.A. Goslin (Ed.), Handbook of socialization theory and research. Chicago: Rand McNally.

Kohlberg, L., and Kramer, R. (1969). Continuities and discontinuities in child and adult moral development. Human Development 12, 93-120.

Konsky, C. (1978). Male-female language attributions in the resolutions of conflict. Paper presented at the Speech Communication Association Convention, Minneapolis.

Konsky, C., and Murdock, J. (1982). Research on male and female language behavior: A methodological analysis for women's caucus. Paper presented at the Central States Speech Association Convention, Milwaukee.

Kramarae, C. (1981). Women and men speaking. Rowley, Mass.: Newberry House.

Lott, B., Spence, J.T., and Helmreich, R.L. (1979). The many faces of androgyny: A reply to Locksley and Colten. Journal of Personality and Social Psychology 37, 1032-1046.

Mabry, E. (1976). Female-male interaction in unstructured small group setting. Paper presented at the Speech Communication Association Convention, San Francisco.

Martin, J., and Craig, R. (1980). Linguistic sex differences during initial interaction. Paper presented at the Speech Communication Association Convention, New York.

McClelland, D.C. (1975). Power: The inner experience. New York: Irvington.

Montgomery, C.L., and Burgoon, M. (1977). An experimental study of the interactive effects of sex and androgyny on attitude change. Communication Monographs 44, 130-135.

Morgan, B.S. (1976). Intimacy of disclosure topics and sex differences in self-disclosure. Journal of Sex Roles 2, 161-166.

Pearson, J.C. (1980). A factor analytic study of the items in three selected sex-role instruments. Psychological Reports 47, 1111-1118.

Pearson, J.C. (1981). Sex, sex-roles, and rhetorical sensitivity. Paper presented at the Western Speech Communication Association Convention, San Jose, Calif.

Pederson, D., and Higbee, K. (1969). Self-disclosure and relationship to the target person. Merill-Palmer Quarterly 15, 213-220.

Putnam, L. (1982). In search of gender: A critique of communication and sex-roles research. Women's Studies in Communication 5, 1-9.

Rancer, A.S. and Baukus, R.A. (1984). Discriminating males and females on belief structures about arguing. Paper presented to the annual Communication, Language and Gender Conference, Oxford, Ohio.

Ricker-Ousiankina, A., and Kusmin, A. (1958). Individual differences in social accessibility. Psychological Reports 4, 391-406.

Riverback, W.H., III. (1971). Self-disclosure patterns among adolescents. Psychological Reports 28, 35-42.

Rosenkrantz, P., Vogel, S., Bee, H., Broverman, I., and Broverman, D.M. (1968). Sex-role stereotypes and self-concepts in college students. Journal of Consulting and Clinical Psychology 32, 287-295.

Selltiz, C., Wrightsman, L., and Cook, S. (1976). Research methods in social relations. New York: Holt, Rinehart and Winston.

Spence, J.T., Helmreich, R., and Stapp, J. (1975). Ratings of self on sex-role attributes and their relation to self-esteem and conceptions of masculinity-femininity. Journal of Personality and Social Psychology 32, 29-39.

Strodtbeck, L., and Mann, R. (1956). Sex-role differentiation in jury deliberations. Sociometry 19, 3-11.

Swacker, M. (1975). The sex of the speaker as a sociolinguistic variable. In B. Thorne and N. Henley (Eds.), Language and sex: Differences and dominance. Rowley, Mass.: Newberry House.

Terhune, K.W. (1970). The effects of personality in cooperation and conflict. In P. Swingle (Ed.), The structure of conflict. New York: Academic Press.

Turner, L.H., and Henzl, S.A. (1984). Language utilized in rationalizing conflict decisions: Is there a different voice? Paper presented at the Conference on Communication Language and Gender, Oxford, Ohio.

Weigel, R., Weigel, V., and Chadwick, P. (1969). Reported and projected self-disclosure. Psychological Reports 24, 283-287.

Zimmerman, D.H., and West, C. (1975). Sex-roles, interruptions and silences in conversation. In B. Thorne and N. Henley (Eds.), Language and Sex: Differences and dominance. Rowley, Mass.: Newberry House.

Imagine this situation:

Pat and Terry have been married for six years and live in a three bedroom home in a suburb of Chicago. Pat works as an executive for a small public relations firm, providing the couple with 3/4 of their $40,000 income. Terry works as an administrative assistant for a small college, providing the remaining 1/4 of their income. Terry has recently expressed a desire to go back to school, but Pat has strong objections.

Pat claims that Terry's income is essential to the couple's financial security. Their two car payments and mortgage payment would be almost impossible to make on just one income. Pat feels Terry has a good job with strong possibilities for advancement. Terry is also responsible for many home chores, and Pat is unsure who will pick these up if Terry is too busy with school. Pat is unwilling to volunteer to do Terry's work as well as what Pat already does around the house.

Terry thinks the couple could survive on only Pat's income for the three years that the program would take. They have around $7,000 in savings. Additionally, Terry has been offered a scholarship which would cover the cost of the tuition plus provide a stipend of $2,000 per year. Terry wants to go back to school because the present job is neither challenging nor interesting, and Terry believes that after completing this program, the salary possibilities in the new career would increase the couple's income significantly.

Imagine this situation:

XYZ Airlines is a large airline with its home base in Chicago. It currently employs 750 people and serves 30 cities. XYZ has decided to discontinue service to two cities due to money constraints. The discontinuation will result in the layoff of 50 employees. The layoff will take place in two months. The company plans to help in relocation and to offer a severance settlement for those laid off. The company is relying upon the advice of two executives, Jones and Smith, to determine how to communicate the layoff plans to the employees.

When Smith and Jones meet, it is obvious that they disagree radically concerning the best possible approach to take. Jones believes that best business practices dictate keeping the layoff secret for as long as possible. Smith believes that best business practices dictate informing the employees immediately.

CHAPTER 12

THE INFLUENCE OF GENDER ON NEGOTIATION SUCCESS IN ASYMMETRIC POWER SITUATIONS

Marjorie Keeshan Nadler, Miami University
Lawrence B. Nadler, Miami University

INTRODUCTION

Reported inequities in gender-related success patterns in American corporations highlight the need to explore women's ability to negotiate successfully within their work organizations. Estimates of the gender salary gap range from women earning 31 percent to 38 percent less than men (Changing Times, 1984). Similarly, Linden asserts that women managers and administrators earn only 52% of their male counterparts wages (Linden, 1981). In addition to wage inequities, women have been limited in gaining entry to managerial or executive positions. Harris (1978) indicates that in 1940, only four percent of company executives were women; by 1978, this figure had not topped six percent. As Larwood, Wood, and Inderlied (1978) state, women managers perform as credibly as men. However, women have not been successfully integrated into positions of power and authority in business (Terborg, Peters, Ilgen, Smith, 1977). Koehn (1976) points out that while women comprise over one-third of the work force, only five percent are in middle management and less than two percent are business executives. Clearly, women experience considerable difficulty in earning promotions to management level positions, receiving equal pay for performing the same work as men, and possibly even selling their ideas and gaining recognition for their work. While various reasons (e.g., lower need for income, interruptions for child-rearing, and the nature of their occupations) have been advanced to account for these disparities, it appears that a gap still exists. As Changing Times (1984) reports, "most researchers agree that anywhere from one-third to one-half of the earnings gap can be explained by male-female differences in work experience, job tenure and advanced training ... but that still leaves a so-called residual gap (p. 10)."

We contend that obtaining raises, promotions, and other forms of organizational support are at least partially related to the individual's negotiation ability and that women are at a negotiation disadvantage relative to men. This paper will briefly examine the research on the role of sex-role stereotypes and role prescriptions, self-concept and personality factors, and orientations toward negotiation situations and present the results of an experimental study examining the role of gender and power in an organizational negotiation situation.

SEX-ROLE STEREOTYPES

A primary aspect of negotiation outcomes involves sex-role stereotypes and related role prescriptions. In any communication situation, individuals possess expectations and make predictions regarding the other person's cognitive, affective, and behavioral states. These predictions, in turn, allow the individual to guide his/her own behavior to obtain more favorable communication outcomes. In negotiation, the argumentative process culminating in agreement is significantly dependent upon behavioral predictions based on the participants' expectations (Reiches and Harral, 1974). Reiches and Harral predicted that more successful negotiators would make more accurate estimates of their opponents' dispositions, with the results generally suggesting that this hypothesis is quite tenable. Reiches and Harral conclude that "the dimension of prediction appears closely related to the negotiated outcome (p. 42)." An interesting illustration of the connection between expectations and behavior involves self-fulfilling prophecies. Here, an individual's expectations of the other person's behavior, based upon stereotypical judgments, produce actions which are likely to reinforce those role-based predictions. If managers expect less of female subordinates, they are likely to receive less. Some studies have demonstrated this relationship with regard to on-the-job training. According to Zellman (1976), employers are often reluctant to offer on-the-job training to female employees. Further, Stewart (1982) asserts that women may be given different task assignments than men, preventing exposure to experiences which may promote advancement. In fact, she states that "stereotypic prejudgment is especially acute in the area of promotions." According to Fink (1982), studies depict the perception that males are better suited to and more capable of assuming management positions. In fact, Bowman, Worthy, and Grayson (1965) report that managers do not perceive women as having the decision-making skills or competitive aggressiveness needed for these positions. Instead, women are viewed as too emotional for managerial positions (Orth and Jacobs, 1971; Schein, 1973). This lack of training and exposure to critical experiences reinforces the prophecies by ensuring that females will be unprepared to assume managerial roles.

In a negotiation setting, sex-role stereotyping can increase the likelihood of women obtaining negative outcomes relative to men. This assertion is supported by the literature on gender-related norm violations. As Grotjahn (1957) states, "the women of our contemporary scene have to be careful, because any show of aggression, open or disguised, is taken by every man in our competitive culture as a challenge...to which he has to rise." This point, thought somewhat overstated, still possesses relevance. As Sereno and Weathers (1981) maintain, women are caught in a conflict between traditional female roles and new emerging behavioral alternatives. They frequently encounter the following double bind: if they conform to norms of passivity and dependence, they might fail to attain desired outcomes; on the other hand, if they act assertively, they risk the consequences associated with any norm deviation. While cultural conditions are changing, Sereno and Weathers accurately observe that "in the midst of this social change, women often find themselves in anxiety-provoking situations for which they do not have effective responses (p. 2)."

Nieva and Gutek (1980) note that competent males are rated more positively than equally competent females. Thus, the expectations of male success and skill in completing tasks lead to greater awareness and recognition of that success. Sex-role stereotypes would not lead observers to expect the same level of success for females. Thus, recognition and corresponding rewards (i.e., raises, promotions) are harder for women to attain and require greater effort to ensure recognition. Unfortunately, Viega (1977) reports that female patterns run counter to achieving this objective. While men plan ahead to achieve career objectives, women tend to feel that if they work hard they will be promoted. Henning and Jardim (1977) argue that women wait to be chosen rather than seeking promotions and recognition. Hoffman and Reed (1981) reported that men were twice as likely to express overt interest in being promoted. Thus, females often start out with stereotypes counterproductive to success in organizational negotiation situations and fail to attempt actively to deal with those issues.

SELF-CONCEPT AND PERSONALITY FACTORS

A second set of relevant variables involves self-concept and personality factors. Certainly, the existence of sex-role stereotypes exerts strong influence on how women view themselves in communication situations, especially intraorganizational negotiation settings. These perceptions, in turn, affect the manner in which women present themselves and the outcomes they obtain. For example, Bentley (1982) identifies a lack of confidence in their own abilities as a factor which inhibits women from entering upper management. A related factor entails women's fear of success. According to Horner (1968), females are often motivated to avoid success, believing that femininity and intellectual achievement are desirable, but mutually exclusive goals. In other words, women often modify their behavior to be more socially acceptable, even if certain goals must be sacrificed in the process. Athanassiades (1974) suggests that exclusion from informal networks may make women feel less free to express disagreement and to provide input into organizational decision-making. In addition, Nadler and Nadler (1984) examined personality and self-concept dimensions relevant to negotiation/bargaining situations. Females reported less confidence and less assertiveness in negotiation situations, as well as more emotional responses than males. Clearly, these self-perceptions and personality manifestations influence a woman's cognitive and behavioral orientation in communication situations.

ORIENTATIONS TOWARD NEGOTIATION

The awareness of sex-role stereotypes and behavioral expectations, and the formation of one's self-concept, influence the individual's orientation toward negotiation and conflict situations. In turn, the person's orientation determines negotiation success. Bentley (1982) identifies the lack of risk-taking and assertive behaviors as limiting factors in women's entry into high level management positions. According to Lange and Jakubowski (1976), women are often non-assertive because they believe assertive behavior will be construed as aggressive and masculine. Further, interactants' concerns exert strong influence on behavioral patterns in conflict or negotiation settings. We suggest that gender differences exist in perceptions of situational factors in negotiation settings. For instance, females may be more concerned with relational consequences than males. In fact, Bean (1970) found that females do show greater inclusion and affection needs in bargaining situations, while males more frequently display dominance and achievement orientation. Baird and Bradley (1979) reported that these patterns carry over into management styles. They found that female managers were perceived to give more information about other departments, to place more emphasis upon interpersonal relationships, to be more responsive to subordinates' ideas, and to be more encouraging of subordinates' efforts than male managers.

Marr (1974) found that female subjects exhibited significantly greater conciliatory behavior than male subjects in a study examining orientation and threat in group interaction. Baird (1976) observes that females are predominantly cooperative while males behave more competitively in conflict situations. Here, females voluntarily give their opponents a greater share of available resources, less frequently make initial offers more favorable to themselves, and tend to make final offers which provide opponents with a large share of rewards (Gamson, 1964).

Nadler and Nadler (1984) studied male and female orientations to negotiation in an organizational setting. Subjects were presented with several organizational negotiation settings and were asked to explain how they would approach these situations. One situation of concern to the current study involved a hypothetical job performance evaluation. Subjects were asked what percentage pay raise they ideally wanted, thought was realistic, and would minimally settle for given that the company's average pay raise would be six percent and the subject received a very good evaluation. On all three items, males had significantly higher expectations. Subjects were also asked to predict their supervisor's view concerning the employees' ideal pay increase, realistic raise level, and minimum acceptable salary gain. Again, males had significantly higher expectations concerning their supervisor's bargaining stance for all three items. Thus, the results of this study would suggest that males approach organizational negotiation settings in a more personally advantageous manner than females.

THE STUDY

It is clear that negotiation skills can affect organizational outcomes and that there are differences in the way males and females operate in these situations. The current study was designed to develop the line of inquiry started by the authors. As our interest lies in the impact of gender on negotiation behavior in professional organizations, and as this context typically involves asymmetric power relationships, it is also necessary to consider the individual's power position within the negotiation situation.

METHODOLOGY

This section describes the methodology employed to study the interrelationships of gender, power, and negotiation processes and outcomes. A 2 X 2 design with unequal cell sizes was utilized in manipulating two between-group variables: sex of supervisor and sex of subordinate.

In analyzing the relationship of these variables to negotiation processes and outcomes, a realistic bargaining situation was enacted. Specifically, subjects were randomly assigned to dyads, such that one person played the role of a supervisor in the "ACME Corporation" and the other person assumed the position of a subordinate. Subjects were provided with relevant information concerning their role and were asked to try to reach agreement regarding the percentage of the subordinate's pay increase for the upcoming fiscal year. In this manner, the position power manipulation was performed, with the supervisor occupying the high power position and the subordinate being placed in the low power position. As subject variables, gender of the subject and gender of his/her negotiation partner were easily operationalized and constituted the other bases for random assignment. Thus, each subject was placed within one of the four experimental conditions.

THEORETICAL RATIONALE AND HYPOTHESES

The theoretical predictions stemmed from the extant literature base and previous research endeavors by the experimenters concerning gender, power position, and negotiation. As noted earlier, several factors, including sex-role stereotypes, self-concept dimensions, and behavioral orientations toward conflict and negotiation can mediate against the relative effectiveness of women versus men in bargaining situations. As a result, the following experimental hypotheses regarding behavioral orientations were advanced:

H1: Females will make initial offers significantly more advantageous to their negotiation partner than will males.

H2: Females will make final offers significantly more advantageous to their negotiation partner than will males.

H3: Females will obtain negotiation outcomes significantly less personally advantageous than will males.

H4: Females will receive less advantageous initial offers than will males.

H5: Females will receive less advantageous final offers than will males.

Further, the literature concerning self-concept and personality dimensions as well as previous research findings (e.g., Nadler and Nadler, 1984) were the basis for the following predictions:

H6: Females will perceive themselves as less successful than will males at the conclusion of the negotiations.

H7: Females will perceive themselves as less confident than will males in regard to the negotiation session.

H8: Females will perceive themselves as less assertive than will males in regard to the negotiation session.

H9: Females will perceive themselves as more emotional than will males in regard to the negotiation session.

Although no gender differences were anticipated regarding satisfaction with the negotiation outcome, this variable was studied because of its possible interaction with other dependent measures. Specifically, Nadler and Nadler's (1984) research found that although females had lower expectation levels than males, they were equally satisfied with projected negotiation outcomes. Thus, an examination of this factor should provide a more thorough picture of gender-based differences in negotiation. Similarly, an item concerning fairness of negotiation outcome was included for this purpose.

Another set of analyses focused upon the interaction of subjects' gender and power position. Based upon the literature review, it was expected that male supervisors would obtain more beneficial outcomes than would female supervisors. Specifically, we advanced the following hypotheses:

H10: Male supervisors will suggest lower pay raises initially for the subordinate than will female supervisors.

H11: Male supervisors will suggest lower pay raises at the conclusion of negotiations for the subordinate than will female supervisors.

H12: Male supervisors will produce lower final pay raises for the subordinate than will female supervisors.

Additionally, it was anticipated that female subordinates would receive lower pay increases than would male subordinates. As a result, the following predictions were made:

H13: Female subordinates will receive lower pay raise offers initially than will male subordinates.

H14: Female subordinates will receive lower pay raise offers at the conclusion of negotiations than will male subordinates.

H15: Female subordinates will receive lower final pay raises than will male subordinates.

H16: Higher initial demands will be made of female versus male supervisors.

H17: Higher final demands will be made of female versus male supervisors.

H18: Higher initial demands will be made by male versus female subordinates.

H19: Higher final demands will be made by male versus female subordinates.

H20: Male supervisors will make lower initial offers to female versus male subordinates.

H21: Male supervisors will make lower final offers to female versus male subordinates.

A final area of analysis entailed interpersonal perceptions within the negotiation situation. In particular, comparisons were made concerning how each person viewed himself/herself versus how his/her negotiation partner viewed the person along the following dimensions: fairness of negotiation outcome, confidence, assertiveness, and emotionality. While no specific predictions were advanced, these comparisons possess theoretical interest and have been included for this reason.

SAMPLE

The sample consisted of 174 undergraduate students enrolled in the Basic Interpersonal Communication course at Miami University during the Fall, 1984 semester. Subjects, who were randomly assigned to one of the four experimental conditions, were placed into dyads involving the following combinations: Male Supervisor-Male Subordinate, Male Supervisor-Female Subordinate, Female Supervisor-Female Subordinate, and Female Supervisor-Female

Subordinate. The respective cell sizes for these dyad combinations were 20, 20, 22, and 25 pairs. These dyads were run in seven classroom situations which ranged from 12 to 14 pairs.

PROCEDURES

In beginning the experiment, subjects were provided with the following information:

> We would like to request your voluntary participation in a communication study. Specifically, we are interested in how people negotiate and we expect that this is an area of interest to you, as you have probably already encountered negotiation situations (such as buying a car) and will need to bargain in many personal and professional contexts when you graduate. In this regard, we are interested in negotiation within an organizational setting. As you probably realize, negotiation can be important in obtaining raises and promotions, receiving choice job assignments, and selling your ideas to upper management. So, we are going to present you with a realistic bargaining situation and ask you to negotiate the best possible outcome. We will pair people into negotiation dyads, such that one person will be a supervisor and the other person will be his/her subordinate. The situation is that the supervisor is completing the subordinate's annual job performance appraisal and is consulting with the subordinate to try to reach agreement concerning the percentage pay increase for the upcoming fiscal year. As the supervisor, you should be concerned with balancing the demands to be fair to the employee and prudent with the company's money. As the subordinate, you should try to obtain the greatest possible pay increase. In a moment we will provide you with more specific information regarding your role and, after pairing people together, you will have up to twelve minutes to try to reach an agreement. Please realize that although this is not a real-life situation, it is very realistic. So, please try to put yourself into the role and do the best possible job of obtaining a desirable outcome. Do you have any questions before we begin?

At this point, subjects were told that copies of the class roster were obtained beforehand for the purpose of facilitating the creation of dyads. In actuality, an additional purpose of this action was to permit random assignment to the experimental conditions. Thus, students' names were called in pairs, with the first person called playing the supervisor role and the second individual assuming the subordinate position. The role-related instructions (see Appendix A) were then disseminated. After subjects had an opportunity to read them, they were again given a chance to ask questions. At this point, the dyad pairs were formed and the twelve minute negotiation session began.

At the conclusion of the negotiation period, subjects were requested to respond to a sixteen item questionnaire which assessed their behaviors in and responses to the experimental situation. After responding to the dependent measures, which are described below, the questionnaires and role instructions were collected (within each dyad, members' questionnaires were stapled together to permit later comparative analyses) and subjects were debriefed. Specifically, they were told the nature, impetus, and purpose of the study, asked not to talk about the experiment with friends, and given an opportunity to ask questions. They were told that the results would be made available to them through their instructors and they were thanked for their participation.

DEPENDENT MEASURES

The first dependent measure entailed whether the dyad reached agreement concerning the percentage pay increase in the allotted time period. Next, subjects were asked five questions concerning negotiation offers in this organizational bargaining situation. Specifically, they were asked to indicate the initial and final percentage pay increases advocated by both parties during negotiations. Also, subjects indicated the agreed upon pay raise (assuming one existed) which culminated the bargaining session. The next six questions focused on perceptions about oneself and the final negotiation outcome. For these items, semantic differential scales were utilized. Subjects were asked how fair they though the final outcome was and how satisfied they were with it. Also, they were asked to assess how successful, confident, assertive, and emotional they were during the negotiation session. Finally, four semantic differential items were employed regarding perceptions of the subject's negotiation partner. These scales concerned how fair they believed the other person thought the final outcome was, as well as the perceived confidence, assertiveness, and emotionality levels of their bargaining partner. As discussed earlier, these items were included to allow comparison of interpersonal perceptions. A fundamental communication tenet is that our perceptions of fellow interactants influence our communication behavior with them. In a bargaining situation, these perceptions could influence negotiation strategies and tactics, thereby having impact on bargaining success.

DATA ANALYSIS

All but one statistical test involved performing an analysis of variance with unequal cell sizes. The sole exception was whether an agreement was reached; this variable was examined using the Chi-Square test. Differences were assessed between groups on the independent variables via the SPSS-X computer program.

RESULTS

This section describes the experimental results as they relate to the theoretical predictions concerning the impact of sex of supervisor and sex of subordinate on negotiation processes and outcomes. To facilitate data interpretation, a value of 1 reflects a male and a value of 2 indicates a female for the gender variables, while a value of 3 denotes a supervisor and a value of 4 indicates a subordinate for the position power dimension. In all instances, an alpha level of .05 is employed to determine statistical significance of results.

The first item involved the percentage of dyads reaching final agreement in each of the experimental conditions. As 85 of 87 negotiating pairs reached an agreement, no significant differences occurred for this dependent measure. Neither sex of supervisor, sex of subordinate nor their interaction exerted any influence on the ability to reach a final agreement.

The second measure entailed the percentage of the final agreement reached by each dyad. While no main effects were obtained, the interaction of subjects' gender and position power was statistically significant (Table 1). Specifically, male subordinates received higher outcomes than female subordinates, while male supervisors produced lower outcomes for their subordinates than did female supervisors. This finding is consistent with the experimental hypotheses. Further, subjects were delineated into four categories (Combination 1= Male Supervisor, Combination 2= Female Supervisor, Combination 3= Male Subordinate, Combination 4= Female Subordinate) to examine this dependent measure more precisely, as the initial analysis lumped all male supervisors and male subordinates, as well as all female supervisors and female subordinates, together. The "Combination" by partner's gender interaction was statistically significant (Table 2). Male supervisors yielded higher outcomes to male versus female subordinates, whereas female subordinates obtained higher outcomes with female versus male supervisors. Although most cell means were remarkably similar, the lowest final outcomes occurred in the male supervisor-female subordinate conditions. Again, this pattern provides support for the experimental predictions.

The third item focused upon the percentage of the initial offer made by the subject. The main effect for position power was statistically significant for this measure (Table 3). As subordinates made average initial demands of 9.14 percent and supervisors made average initial offers of 7.03 percent, it is evident that these roles were enacted in a realistic manner. While these averages show the mean negotiation range for the bargaining situation, they are quite obvious and lend no support to the experimental hypotheses. The "Combination" variable also produced a statistically significant difference (Table 4). Specifically, male supervisors made higher initial offers than did female supervisors, while male subordinates made higher beginning demands than did female subordinates. Although the "Combination" by partner's gender interaction was not significant, an analysis of the cell means (Table 5) reveals that the lowest initial offers were made by female supervisors toward female partners (subordinates). This finding explains the surprising nature of the first part of the "Combination" effect, as male supervisors do not yield more to all of their subordinates; instead, female supervisors are particularly tough when negotiating with female subordinates. Finally, the latter part of the "Combination" effect provides support for the theoretical predictions.

The fourth question dealt with the beginning pay increase advocated by the subject's partner. A main effect for power was obtained (Table 6), such that when the subject was the supervisor, he/she received an average initial demand of 9.27 percent from the subordinate, whereas he/she received a mean starting offer of 7.02 percent from the supervisor when playing the subordinate role. Again, this result neither supports nor fails to support the experimental hypotheses. A related observation regarding this finding is that it closely resembles the results for the preceding question. Although slight mean differences exist in subjects' reports of the pay raises they suggested initially versus their negotiation partners' beginning offers, it is evident that very little perceptual distortion existed concerning these offers. The "Combination" variable also yielded a main effect for partner's beginning offer. As Table 7 indicates, when the subject was a female versus a male supervisor, their partner (subordinate) made slightly higher average initial demands. Further, when the subject was a male versus a female subordinate, the negotiation partner (supervisor) made higher average initial offers. These results are congruent with the theoretical expectations.

The fifth item involved the subject's final suggested pay increase and produced three significant interaction effects. The first interaction effect entailed subject's gender and position power (Table 8). Male subordinates made higher final demands than did female subordinates, while female supervisors made higher final offers than did male supervisors. This pattern provides support for the experimental hypotheses. Also, it is interesting to note that this interaction did not appear for subjects' initial offers. Thus, it appears that the process of negotiation served to magnify gender differences in relation to supervisor-subordinate roles. The second significant interaction effect involved the subject's gender and the negotiation partner's gender. Basically, higher final offers were advanced by subjects in same-sex versus mixed-sex dyads (Table 9). While this finding is quite interesting, it was not predicted at the outset of the study. Finally, there was a significant interaction between "Combination"

and partner's gender (Table 10). Male supervisors made higher
final offers with male versus female subordinates and female
subordinates obtained higher final offers from female versus male
supervisors. Again, this interesting result was not anticipated
beforehand.

The sixth measure focused upon the level of the negotiation
partner's final suggested pay increase. The only significant
result involved the interaction of "Combination" and partner's
gender (Table 11). In this instance, males versus females
advanced higher final demands with male supervisors, while male
supervisors offered less with female versus male subordinates.
These findings are consistent with the experimental predictions.

The next six items examined the subject's self-perceptions in
various areas pertinent to the negotiation process. These factors
included perceived success in the negotiation situation, fairness
of the bargaining agreement, and satisfaction with the final
outcome. Additionally, we tapped the subject's self-perceived
degree of confidence, assertiveness, and emotionality. No effects
were obtained for any of these dependent measures.

In addition to self-perceptions, interpersonal perceptions
were measured regarding the negotiation partner's assessment of
outcome fairness, confidence, assertiveness, and emotionality.
The only significant result was a main effect for subject's gender
on the perceived confidence dimension. As Table 12 depicts,
female subjects perceived their partner as more confident than did
male subjects. While the mean scores (5.35 for males and 5.69 for
females on a seven-point scale) were high for both groups, this
difference could partially explain the negotiation differences for
gender reported earlier.

The final set of items involved a comparative analysis of
subjects' and negotiation partners' perceptions regarding their
assessment of fairness of the negotiation outcome and levels of
confidence, assertiveness, and emotionality. These factors
produced no significant differences for any of the independent
variables.

FURTHER DATA ANALYSIS

The preceding examination of the experimental results
revealed that some significant differences existed for the
independent variables for the negotiation process and outcome
measures, with the personality dimensions yielding virtually no
significant findings. Although support for the experimental
hypotheses is obviously limited, one aspect of the study, which
could have had a bearing upon the experimental findings, should be
mentioned. This aspect is the instruction set given to subjects
at the beginning of the study. Specifically, we instructed

subordinates to obtain the greatest percentage pay increase possible, while we told supervisors to be fair but to exercise fiscal concern for their company. Although these directions were given to reduce ambiguity and provide structure for subjects, who otherwise might have lacked sufficient information to conduct the negotiation role play in a meaningful manner, it is quite possible that this instruction set entailed more information than a person would have or generate in a real-life negotiation situation. In other words, we believe that subjects may have enacted certain behaviors to follow the experimenters' instructions regardless of their normal orientation in negotiation situations. Thus, the instruction set may have overridden subjects' normal behavior patterns. If this contention is valid, then the impact of the directions would likely have been greatest at the outset of the negotiation session. Specifically, the initial offers by each subject and his/her negotiation partner would have been affected by the instruction set. Thus, by holding these factors constant, it is possible to control for the impact of the directions. In this manner, any new significant differences, that might have been obscured otherwise, have an opportunity to emerge in a more complete test of the experimental hypotheses. Therefore, this section presents the results of this covariate analysis.

As discussed earlier, the second measure involved the percentage of the final agreement reached by each dyad. Once again, the interaction of subject's gender and position was significant, such that male subordinates received higher outcomes than female subordinates and male supervisors produced lower outcomes for their subordinates than did female supervisors. The covariate analysis yielded two other interactions, between subject's and partner's gender as well as between partner's gender and position power. In the first interaction (Table 13), higher final outcomes were obtained in same-sex versus mixed-sex dyads. For partner's gender and position power (Table 14), supervisors gave higher pay increases to male versus female subordinates, while subordinates received higher raises from female versus male supervisors. This finding is consistent with the experimental hypotheses. The interaction of "Combination" and partner's gender was duplicated, as male supervisors provided higher raises to male versus female subordinates and female subordinates obtained higher outcomes with female versus male supervisors. Additionally, a main effect for "Combination" was obtained using the covariate analysis (Table 15). Male supervisors gave lower pay increases than did female supervisors, whereas female subordinates received lower outcomes than did male subordinates. Again, this pattern provides support for the theoretical predictions.

The next measure involved the subject's final suggested pay increase. The two interaction effects obtained earlier (i.e., subject's gender by position power and subject's gender by partner's gender) were also produced by the covariate analysis.

Additionally, a main effect for subject's gender occurred (Table 16), such that female subjects produced higher pay increases overall than did male subjects. While this finding may be surprising, it should be recalled that supervisors and subordinates, working for opposite goals, are lumped together. Thus, a further delineation of gender by position power is needed to interpret this result. As Table 8 indicates, this finding is primarily a function of female supervisors providing higher outcomes than male supervisors, regardless of the negotiation partner's gender. This finding, then, actually offers support for the experimental predictions. The interaction of "Combination" and partner's gender (Table 10) was replicated, such that male supervisors made higher final offers to male versus female subordinates and female subordinates obtained higher final offers from female versus male supervisors. Additionally, a main effect for "Combination" (Table 17) occurred, with male supervisors making lower final offers than female supervisors and female subordinates making lower final demands than male subordinates. This pattern is also congruent with the theoretical expectations.

The covariate analysis yielded additional effects for the level of the negotiation partner's final suggested pay increase. Whereas the original analysis of variance produced a "Combination" by partner's gender interaction (Table 11), three other effects were identified. First, a main effect for partner's gender occurred (Table 18), such that higher final offers were made by partners when the negotiation partner was female versus male. Also, the subject's gender by partner's gender interaction was significant, as the negotiation partner made higher final offers in same-sex versus mixed-sex dyads (Table 19). Another interaction effect encompassed subject's gender and position power (Table 20). When the supervisor was female versus male, the subordinate partner made higher final demands; when the subordinate subject was male versus female, the supervisor partner made higher final offers. Thus, considerably greater support was garnered for the experimental hypotheses via the covariate analyses.

The covariate analysis produced only two effects regarding the self-concept and personality dimensions. The main effect for subject's gender on the "confidence of partner" factor (Table 12), such that female subjects perceived their partners as more confident than did male subjects, was reported earlier. An additional main effect, for partner's gender on the "assertiveness of partner" dimension (Table 21), was also obtained. Interestingly, subjects perceived their partner as more assertive when the partner was female versus male. Clearly, this finding is not consistent with the experimental hypotheses.

DISCUSSION

This section examines the experimental results as they relate to the theoretical predictions. Also, limitations of the study are identified and discussed to provide a fuller interpretation of the results. Finally, directions for future research in this area are advanced.

Generally, the results concerning negotiation processes and outcomes supported the experimental hypotheses. Although the independent variables had no impact on the dyads' ability to reach an agreement, the dependent measures concerning initial and final offers by the subject and his/her partner, as well as the level of the final agreement, yielded many statistically significant results. For example, hypotheses 12 and 15 predicted that male supervisors would produce lower pay raises for their subordinates than would female supervisors, while female subordinates would receive lower pay increases than would male subordinates. This pattern was supported by the interaction of subject's gender and position power for the second dependent measure. Interestingly, the lowest final outcomes were accrued in the male supervisor-female subordinate conditions. As this gender mix is the most frequently occurring combination in the organization, these results possess tremendous practical significance for professionals in these organizations.

The processes by which a final outcome was produced are important and also yielded several significant results. For instance, hypothesis 1 stated that females would make higher initial offers to their partners than would males. The "Combination" effect for the third and fourth dependent measures supported this prediction, as male subordinates displayed higher initial demand levels and female supervisors made higher initial offers to male versus female subordinates. This latter finding also partially supported hypothesis 4, as female subordinates received lower initial offers than did male subordinates. Hypothesis 10, however, was not supported, as male supervisors did not suggest lower pay raises initially than female supervisors. A closer examination of the data revealed, though, that this pattern resulted from female supervisors being especially tough toward female subordinates. Again, as male supervisor-female subordinate pairs predominate in organizations, this overall pattern indicates that females encounter a negotiation disadvantage.

Hypotheses 13, 16, and 18 suggested that female subordinates would receive lower offers initially than would male subordinates and that higher initial demands would be made of female versus male supervisors. The "Combination" effect for the fourth dependent measure fully supported these predictions. Clearly, negotiators make gender-related distinctions concerning their bargaining partner and these distinctions are translated into behaviors which serve to benefit males more than females.

Hypotheses 11, 17, and 19 stated that male supervisors would suggest lower final pay raises than female supervisors, higher final demands would be made of female versus male supervisors, and higher final demands would be made by male versus female subordinates. For the fifth dependent measure, the interaction of subject's gender and position power supported the first and third of these predictions. Thus, males advanced final offers, in the supervisor and subordinate roles, which were more personally advantageous than females' offers.

The sixth dependent measure (percentage of partner's final offer) permitted a test of hypothesis 21. As the interaction of "Combination" and partner's gender, such that male supervisors offered less to female versus male subordinates, was significant, this prediction was supported by the experimental results.

The covariate analysis provided additional support for the theoretical predictions. For example, hypothesis 3, which stated that females would obtain poorer negotiation outcomes than males, was buttressed by the main effect for "Combination" for the second dependent measure. Specifically, male supervisors yielded lower pay increases than did female supervisors, while female subordinates received lower pay raises than did male subordinates. Further, hypothesis 2 (females would make more advantageous final offers to their partners than would males) was supported by the "Combination" effect for the fifth dependent measure. Here, male supervisors made lower final offers than female supervisors and female subordinates made lower final demands than male subordinates. Overall, the level of support for the negotiation process and outcome items was quite high.

The theoretical predictions concerning personality and self-concept items were completely unsupported by the experimental results. In other words, no gender differences were exhibited concerning self-perceptions of success, confidence, assertiveness, or emotionality. For the interpersonal perception items, the only difference involved the confidence dimension, such that females viewed their partners as more confident than did males. It should be noted that the covariate analysis yielded a main effect for assertiveness, such that subjects rated female versus male partners higher on this dimension. This overall pattern, however, provides no support for the theoretical predictions. Also, the perceptual comparison items, while similarly possessing theoretical interest but entailing no experimental predictions, produced no significant results.

In interpreting the experimental results, a few limitations of the study should be considered. First, the data were gathered in a classroom setting and the presence of other negotiating pairs could have influenced what transpired in each dyad. As real negotiations typically occur in private, this factor could have influenced the experimental results. Also, the experimental situation involved a role play, which differs greatly from an actual negotiation situation. While the instruction set attempted to set a realistic tone, and while most subjects appeared interested and motivated, this situational factor should be acknowledged. Similarly, the amount of information provided to subjects may have been significantly less than they would possess in an actual negotiation situation. For example, the ego-involvement with their job, their knowledge of prior accomplishments, and their relationship with their supervisor all represent information points which would be far richer in an actual bargaining setting. Finally, the situational constraints mediated against analyzing the communicative content of negotiations. Instead, we had to rely upon self-report data to measure negotiation processes (i.e., offers) and outcomes.

While this experiment accomplished its objectives in demonstrating some important gender-related differences in organizational negotiation behavior, more research is needed to examine this situation further. Whereas this study focused on asymmetric power situations (vertical communication), future research should also examine symmetric power transactions (horizontal communication). Also, the research focus might be expanded to consider psychological rather than just biological sex. In making recommendations to male and female negotiators, this distinction should be considered. Further, the instruction set, which may have limited the experimental results, could be varied to determine whether "training" can and does influence negotiation behavior. Finally, it is important to move from the laboratory setting to the organizational environment, where these communication processes are particularly important.

REFERENCES

Athanassiades, J. C. (1974). An investigation of some communication patterns for female subordinates in hierarchial organizations. Human Relations, 27, 195-209.

Baird, J. E., Jr. (1976). Sex differences in group communication: A review of relevant research. The Quarterly Journal of Speech, 62, 179-192.

Baird, J. E., Jr. and Bradley, P. (1979). Styles of management and communication: A comparative study of men and women. Communication Monographs, 46, 101-111.

Bean, F. (1970).Social role, personality, and interpersonal bargaining between the sexes. Unpublished doctoral dissertation, Duke University.

Bentley, N. W. (1982, October). An historical perspective: Where did the mentor system come from and how has it affected women to date? Fifth Annual Communication, Language and Gender Conference, Ohio University.

Bowman, G. W., Worthy, N. B. and Grayser, S. A. (1965). Problems in review: Are women executives people? Harvard Business Review, 43 (4), 14-28, 164-178.

_____. (1984). Why do women earn less than men? Changing Times, April, 10.

Fink, C. (1982). Perceptions of women's communication skills related to managerial effectiveness. Fifth Annual Communication, Language and Gender Conference, Athens, Ohio, October.

Gamson, W. A. (1964). Experimental studies of coalition formation. Advances in Experimental Social Psychology, 1, 82-110.

Grotjahn, M. (1957). Beyond Laughter. New York: McGraw-Hill.

Harris, M. (1978). One-upwomanship: Six books on women executives. Money, 7, 118, 120.

Henning, M. and Jardim, A. (1977). The Managerial Woman. New York: Pocket Books, 1977.

Hoffman, C. and Reed, J. S. (1981). The strange case of XYZ corporation. Across the Board, 19, 27-38.

Horner, M. S. (1968). Sex differences in achievement motivation and performance in competitive and non-competitive situations. Unpublished doctoral dissertation, University of Michigan.

Koehn, H. B. (1976). Attitude: The success element for women in business. Journal of Systems Management, 27, 12-15.

Lange, A. J. and Jakubowski, P. (1976). Responsible Assertive Behavior: Cognitive Behavioral Procedures for Trainers. Champaign, Illinois: Research Press.

Larwood, L., Wood, M. M., and Inderlied, S. D. (1978). Training women for management: New problems, new solutions. Academy of Management Review, 3, 584-593.

Linden, F. (1981). Women's work. Across the Board, 18, 68-70.

Marr, T. J. (1974). Conciliation and verbal responses as functions of orientation and threat in group interaction. Speech Monographs, 41, 6-18.

Nadler, L. B. and Nadler, M. K. (1984, March). Communication, gender, and negotiation: Theory and findings. Eastern Communication Association Conference, Philadelphia, Pennsylvania.

Nieva, V. F. and Gutek, B. A. (1980). Sex effects on evaluation. Academy of Management Review, 5, 267-276.

Orth, C. P. and Jacobs, F. (1971). Women in management: Pattern for change. Harvard Business Review, 49 (4), 139.

Reiches, N. A. and Harral, H. B. (1974). Argument in negotiation: A theoretical and empirical approach. Speech Monographs, 41, 36-48.

Schein, V. E. (1973). The relationship between sex role stereotypes and requisite management characteristics. Journal of Applied Psychology, 57, 95-100.

Sereno, K. K. and Weathers, J. (1981). Impact of communicator sex on receiver reactions to assertive, nonassertive, and aggressive communication. Women's Studies in Communication, 4, 1-17.

Stewart, L. P. (1982, May). Women in management: Implications for communication researchers. Eastern Communication Association Convention, Hartford, Connecticut.

Terborg, J., Peters, L., Ilgen, D., and Smith, F. (1977). Organizational and personal correlates of attitudes toward women as managers. _Academy of Management Journal_, _20_, 89-100.

Viega, J. F. (1977). Do managers on the move get anywhere? _Harvard Business Review_, _59_ (2), 20-38.

Zellman, G. L. (1976). The role of structural factors in limiting women's institutional participation. _Journal of Social Issues_, _32_ (3), 33-46.

INSTRUCTIONS FOR SUBORDINATE

You have worked for the ACME Corporation for one year and
you have just been given your first annual performance evaluation,
which was very good overall. Your supervisor informed you that
the company's average pay raise for the upcoming fiscal year will
be 6 percent and that employees who received above average
evaluations should receive somewhat greater raises, while employees with below average performance evaluations will get
somewhat smaller raises. Overall, though, the average salary
increase will be 6 percent for the company. Your supervisor, in
trying to determine the amount of your raise, wants to discuss
the performance evaluation with you and get some idea of the pay
increase you feel you deserve. You will be given 12 minutes to
negotiate with your supervisor and to try to convince the supervisor to give you the raise you feel you deserve. If you do not
reach a mutually agreed upon decision in this time frame, you
will have no further say in the matter and your supervisor will
make the final decision for you.

INSTRUCTIONS FOR SUPERVISOR

Employee X (your dyad partner) has worked for the ACME
Corporation for one year and you have just given them their first
annual performance evaluation, which was very good overall. The
company's average pay raise for the upcoming fiscal year will be
6 percent, with employees who receive above average evaluations
receiving somewhat greater raises and employees with below average
performance evaluations receiving somewhat smaller raises.
Overall, though, you must average 6 percent in assigning pay
raises to your set of subordinates. In trying to determine the
amount of employee X's raise, you want to discuss the performance
evaluation with them and get their input concerning the raise.
You will have 12 minutes to negotiate with employee X to try to
get them to accept your recommendation (as you are concerned with
the satisfaction level of this valued employee). If you do not
reach a mutually agreed upon decision in this time frame, you
will have to exercise your authority and make the final decision
for employee X.

TABLE 1
PERCENTAGE OF FINAL AGREEMENT

Variable	Sum of Squares	Df	Mean Square	F	Sig. of F
Gender of Subject X Power	572.920	1	572.920	4.03	0.047

CELL MEANS

Power

		Sup.	Sub.
	Male	7.80	8.16
Gender of Subject	Female	8.23	7.87

TABLE 2
PERCENTAGE OF FINAL AGREEMENT

Variable	Sum of Squares	Df	Mean Square	F	Sig. of F
Combination X Gender of Partner	1466.481	3	488.827	3.505	0.017

CELL MEANS

Gender of Partner

		Male	Female
	1	8.11	7.36
Combination	2	8.17	8.34
	3	8.24	8.23
	4	7.48	8.36

TABLE 3
PERCENTAGE OF SUBJECT'S BEGINNING OFFER

Variable	Sum of Squares	Df	Mean Square	F	Sig. of F
Power	16489.641	1	16489.641	48.79	0.000

CELL MEANS

Power

Sup.	Sub.
7.03	9.14

TABLE 4
PERCENTAGE OF SUBJECT'S BEGINNING OFFER

Variable	Sum of Squares	Df	Mean Square	F	Sig. of F
Combination	17552.061	3	5850.687	17.312	0.000

CELL MEANS

Combination

1	2	3	4
7.23	6.89	9.35	8.94

TABLE 5
PERCENTAGE OF SUBJECT'S BEGINNING OFFER

		Gender of Partner	
		Male	Female
	1	7.22	7.23
	2	7.16	6.67
Combination	3	9.45	9.24
	4	8.65	9.15

TABLE 6
PERCENTAGE OF PARTNER'S BEGINNING OFFER

Variable	Sum of Squares	Df	Mean Square	F	Sig. of F
Power	19307.950	1	19307.950	59.61	0.000

CELL MEANS

Power

Sup.	Sub.
9.27	7.02

TABLE 7
PERCENTAGE OF PARTNER'S BEGINNING OFFER

Variable	Sum of Squares	Df	Mean Square	F	Sig. of F
Combination	19436.314	3	6478.771	20.00	0.000

CELL MEANS

Combination

1	2	3	4
9.23	9.30	7.13	6.91

TABLE 8
PERCENTAGE OF SUBJECT'S FINAL OFFER

Variable	Sum of Squares	Df	Mean Square	F	Sig. of F
Gender of Subject X Power	655.733	1	655.733	4.44	0.037

CELL MEANS

Power

		Sup.	Sub.
	Male	7.74	8.23
Gender of Subject	Female	8.23	7.95

TABLE 9
PERCENTAGE OF SUBJECT'S FINAL OFFER

Variable	Sum of Squares	Df	Mean Square	F	Sig. of F
Gender of Subject X Gender of Partner	564.585	1	564.585	3.83	0.050

CELL MEANS

Gender of Partner

		Male	Female
	Male	8.17	7.85
Gender of Subject	Female	7.87	8.27

TABLE 10
PERCENTAGE OF SUBJECT'S FINAL OFFER

Variable	Sum of Squares	Df	Mean Square	F	Sig. of F
Combination X Gender of Partner	1440.997	3	480.332	3.33	0.021

CELL MEANS

Gender of Partner

		Male	Female
	1	8.11	7.36
	2	8.17	8.34
Combination	3	8.24	8.23
	4	7.48	8.36

TABLE 11
PERCENTAGE OF PARTNER'S FINAL OFFER

Variable	Sum of Squares	Df	Mean Square	F	Sig. of F
Combination X Gender of Partner	1354.520	3	451.507	3.10	0.028

CELL MEANS

Gender of Partner

		Male	Female
	1	8.29	7.59
	2	8.25	8.46
Combination	3	8.07	8.17
	4	7.39	8.28

TABLE 12
PERCEPTION OF PARTNER'S CONFIDENCE

Variable	Sum of Squares	Df	Mean Square	F	Sig. of F
Gender of Subject	5.130	1	5.130	3.941	0.049

CELL MEANS

Gender of Subject

Male	Female
5.35	5.69

TABLE 13
PERCENTAGE OF FINAL AGREEMENT

Variable	Sum of Squares	Df	Mean Square	F	Sig. of F
Gender of Subject X Gender of Partner	386.312	1	386.312	7.786	0.006

CELL MEANS

Gender of Partner

		Male	Female
Gender of Subject	Male	8.13	7.85
	Female	7.87	8.23

TABLE 14
PERCENTAGE OF FINAL AGREEMENT

Variable	Sum of Squares	Df	Mean Square	F	Sig. of F
Gender of Partner X Power	215.584	1	215.584	4.345	0.039

CELL MEANS

Power

		Sup.	Sub.
Gender of Partner	Male	8.17	7.81
	Female	7.94	8.19

TABLE 15
PERCENTAGE OF FINAL AGREEMENT

Variable	Sum of Squares	Df	Mean Square	F	Sig. of F
Combination	479.532	3	159.844	3.221	0.025

CELL MEANS

Combination

1	2	3	4
7.80	8.23	8.16	7.87

TABLE 16
PERCENTAGE OF SUBJECT'S FINAL OFFER

Variable	Sum of Squares	Df	Mean Square	F	Sig. of F
Gender of Subject	208.552	1	208.552	4.008	0.047

CELL MEANS

Gender of Subject

Male	Female
8.01	8.09

TABLE 17
PERCENTAGE OF SUBJECT'S FINAL OFFER

Variable	Sum of Squares	Df	Mean Square	F	Sig. of F
Combination	614.612	3	204.871	3.937	0.010

CELL MEANS

Combination

1	2	3	4
7.74	8.23	8.23	7.95

TABLE 18
PERCENTAGE OF PARTNER'S FINAL OFFER

Variable	Sum of Squares	Df	Mean Square	F	Sig. of F
Gender of Partner	212.055	1	212.055	4.028	0.047

CELL MEANS

Gender of Partner

Male	Female
8.02	8.15

TABLE 19
PERCENTAGE OF PARTNER'S FINAL OFFER

Variable	Sum of Squares	Df	Mean Square	F	Sig. of F
Gender of Subject X Gender of Partner	348.917	1	348.917	6.63	0.011

CELL MEANS

Gender of Partner

		Male	Female
	Male	8.18	7.96
Gender of Subject	Female	7.86	8.29

TABLE 20

PERCENTAGE OF PARTNER'S FINAL OFFER

Variable	Sum of Squares	Df	Mean Square	F	Sig. of F
Gender of Subject X Power	241.646	1	241.646	4.590	0.034

CELL MEANS

Power

		Sup.	Sub.
Gender of Subject	Male	8.01	8.12
	Female	8.33	7.85

TABLE 21

PERCEPTION OF PARTNER'S ASSERTIVENESS

Variable	Sum of Squares	Df	Mean Square	F	Sig. of F
Gender of Partner	6.457	1	6.457	4.014	0.047

CELL MEANS

Gender of Partner

Male	Female
5.08	5.49

CHAPTER 13

COOPERATIVE BEHAVIOR BY FEMALE NEGOTIATORS;

EXPERTS OR MASOCHISTS?

Deanna F. Womack, Northern Illinois University

Two contradictory explanations have been advanced to account for the research findings regarding the effect of gender on communication. On one hand, scholars have noted the prejudice against women evident in social forms such as language.

> The overall effect of "women's language" . . . is this: it submerges a woman's personal identity, by denying her the means of expressing herself strongly, on the one hand, and encouraging expressions that suggest triviality in subject matter and uncertainty about it; and, when a woman is being discussed, by treating her as an object -- sexual or otherwise -- but never a serious person with individual views. . . .
> The ultimate effect of these discrepancies is that women are systematically denied access to power, on the grounds that they are not capable of holding it as demonstrated by their linguistic behavior . . .and the irony here is that women are made to feel that they deserve such treatment, because of inadequacies in their own intelligence and/or education. (Lakoff, 1975, p. 7).

The first trend evident in gender research was to identify women's verbal and nonverbal behavior indicating powerlessness and thus perhaps even provoking unequal treatment.

Recently a new trend has emerged, as evident in such work as Carol Gilligan's In A Different Voice (1982). Researchers following this trend have reconceptualized feminine values as equal or superior to those of men. Cheris Kramer (1974) notes that verbal behavior is not inherently strong or weak but that our culture is biased to interpret sex differences in favor of men. Citing the work of Miller (1976), Gilligan argues that women have a different psychological structure and morality from men. Instead of being pathological, women's psychic structures contain, "the possibilities for an entirely different (and more advanced) approach to 'living and functioning.' . ."(Miller, p. 83). Thus, Gilligan calls for "a psychology of adulthood which recognizes that development does not displace the value of ongoing attachment and the continuing importance of care in relationships" (p. 170).

Campbell has chosen the oxymoron, the rhetorical figure of paradox and contradiction, as the most appropriate metaphor for femininity in our culture (1973, p. 84). The oxymoron seems also to characterize the research about women's communication.

The present investigation attempted to test two contradictory explanations for women's conforming (Eagly, 1978) or cooperative behavior. In response to Putnam's call for studies of behavior that "evolve from contextual constraints" (1982, p. 7), I chose to examine cooperativeness in the negotiation setting. The results of the experiment indicate that, while women's verbal behaviors in negotiations differ from those of men, they are reflective of different constructs of the negotiation situation. Neither view is inherently functional or dysfunctional. It appears that verbal and nonverbal indicants of powerlessness found in women in studies of the 1970s are no longer descriptive of female behavior.

Cooperative Behavior by Female Negotiators

Gender is perhaps the most frequently studied independent variable in the negotiation literature. Yet there is ample evidence for three conflicting conclusions: females are more cooperative negotiators than males; males are more cooperative than females; and gender has no effect on cooperation or competition (Rubin and Brown, 1975). This body of research using the game theory paradigm is further complicated by the frequent use of Prisoner's Dilemma as the experimental game and by having subjects play against noncontingent experimental strategies rather than real opponents. Both of these experimental artifacts induce negotiators to behave competitively (Komorita, 1965). Bargainers are also frequently asked to play Prisoner's Dilemma against a tit-for-tat experimental strategy. In such a case, the game is biased toward a completely cooperative strategy (Kahn, Hottes, and Davis, 1971). Thus, not only are results from such studies contradictory, but the methodologies used are biased, making it even more difficult to draw accurate conclusions.

Rubin and Brown conclude that the contradictory results in the negotiation literature are explained by the finding that females are more sensitive than males to interpersonal cues such as: gender of the other bargainer and of the experimenter, attractiveness of the other, availability of communication, equity, and cooperativeness of the other. They believe that,
Males . . . orient themselves not to the other, but to the impersonal task of maximizing their own earnings. When earnings can best be maximized through the use of a competitive strategy, males tend to compete; on the other hand, when a cooperative strategy seems most likely to maximize own earnings, males cooperate (1975, p. 173).
Therefore, by being more sensitive, females may harm themselves by receiving lower payoffs from negotiations.

In fact, empirical research by Womack (1981) and by Nadler and Nadler (1984) indicates that females expect to receive less of the possible rewards in a negotiation than do males. Female subjects, both students and adults, studied by Womack expected to pay and were willing to pay higher prices in a hypothetical used car negotiation than were males. Female students studied by Nadler and Nadler expected to receive lower starting salaries and lower salaries after five years' experience than did males. They also had lower ideal, realistic, and minimum expectations of raises in response to a hypothetical job performance evaluation than males (p. 29). As Nadler and Nadler illustrate by their gender-based model of negotiation (1984), cognitive, affective, and behavioral orientations influence both process variables, such as language use and nonverbal behavior, and output variables, such as raises and promotions. To summarize, research indicates that females have expectations of negotiation outcomes which are less favorable to themselves than to their counterparts and that females may adopt bargaining strategies which result in less favorable outcomes than do males' strategies.

Conflicting Interpretations of Women's Bargaining Behavior

Two recent publications present contradictory interpretations of the finding regarding women's cooperative negotiation behaviors. These interpretations follow the lines of reasoning of the two interpretive trends in gender research presented in the introduction.

Greenhalgh, Gilkey and Pufahl (1984) hypothesized that women (or those with feminine orientations according to the 1974 Bem Sex-Role Inventory) desire to foster rather than risk the continuity of the relationship with the other party. Through questionnaires and analyses of videotaped negotiations, they found that feminine bargainers differed significantly from masculine ones in holding continuous rather than episodic perspectives on the relationship with the other negotiator, in being more willing to compromise, and in being less willing to attempt to deceive the other. Although feminine negotiators were slightly more likely to make empathic inquires, the difference was not significant.

Greenhalgh, Gilkey, and Pufahl (1984) argue that women may be more effective negotiators than men in business settings because of their continuous perspective. Women's tendencies to view the negotiations as merely one episode of a long-term relationship cause women to refrain from more competitive negotiation behaviors which may result in higher payoffs in the negotiation at hand but which would impair future relations with their counterpart. This study, then, is representative of the trend toward viewing feminine values as alternative or superior to masculine ones.

Natalie Shainess's book, <u>Sweet Suffering: Woman as Victim</u> (1984), considers submissive behavior in women to be masochistic. Masochism has two components: feelings and communication behavior. The masochistic person is:

> fearful of others, filled with self-doubt, and utterly unable to resist, refuse, offend or insist on limits. The masochist's feeling of guilt is all-pervasive, her stream of apologies constant, her capacity for self-punishment and self-denial seemingly endless. She does not dare to question, too quickly takes things at face value, too readily accepts someone else's premise. She is dependent upon the wishes, whims, and judgments of any authority figure. If you were to ask a masochist to define her own best interests, she would not know where to begin (p. 5).

Shainess mentions seventeen verbal and nonverbal behaviors which indicate masochism. These include apologizing, being unwilling to ask questions or to challenge the premises of the other, using equivocal language, revealing too much about oneself, being unable to change the direction of an encounter, refraining from direct eye contact, and capitulating, or accommodating the other. Shainess argues that these behaviors reveal women's systems of self-punishment.

> While men also suffer from the masochistic syndrome, it is much more common among women. . . .It is because women in our society bear such liabilities as inferior social and economic status, lesser biological strength, and reproductive handicaps that masochism is a special problem for them. In nearly four decades of practice as a psychiatrist and psychoanalyst, I have all too frequently encountered masochism in women and only occasionally in men. Both women and men may have early experiences that dispose them to masochistic behavior, but the cultural elements that continually reinforce masochistic behavior in women are largely absent for men. Women, in this sense, experience a real double whammy. Many emerge from their childhoods with a damaged sense of self. Then the culture in which they live ratifies that distorted image rather than helping them to repair the damage. And the odds are longer for women in their struggle to overcome masochism (p. 3).

Six of Shainess' seventeen communication behaviors seem likely to occur during negotiations. They are: (1) apologizing; (2) being unwilling to ask questions or to challenge the premise of the other; (3) revealing too much about one's own needs, or "spilling," overexplaining; (4) being unable to take control of conversation and to change the subject; (5) using equivocal language or language that indicates hesitation or lack of self-assurance; and (6) exhibiting nonverbal behaviors such as slouching posture, avoiding eye contact, and frequent head-nodding.

Dysfunctional Communication Behaviors by Women Negotiators

(1) Shainess claims that women and other masochists frequently apologize because they have low self-esteem, they feel they are always wrong, and they believe apologizing will deflect verbal aggression and hurt. Shainess recounts the story of a woman who apologized when Shainess dropped a postcard in an elevator. The woman apologized for not picking up the postcard for Shainess, then apologized for apologizing when Shainess remarked that there was no reason why the other woman should pick up Shainess's postcard. Shainess's hypothesis appears consistent with Lakoff's contention that women are superpolite and deferential in conversation (1975, p. 65).

(2) Lakoff's observation also seems to explain Shainess's second category of verbal behavior, reluctance to challenge the other's premises or to ask questions. Shainess presents an extreme characterization of such behavior. She believes a state of

> hypno-suggestibility . . . causes the masochist to accept whatever the other person says as correct just as surely as if she had been hypnotized into believing it. Totally paralyzed by the power and the idea of the other person, she loses any ability to think for herself and allows the other's viewpoint to be imposed on her immediately and totally. Having accepted the premise of the other, the masochist will then rationalize why it is so as a means of justifying her acceptance (p. 41).

This behavior begins as a defense mechanism when weak children are told by parents they are wrong. The child believes the powerful parent must be right; she denies her own behavior or responses because she feels she must be in the wrong. This feeling also leads the masochist to avoid questioning the other since, says Shainess,

> asking a question is the equivalent of returning the serve in a tennis game, putting the ball into the opponent's court, and forcing him to respond. Response, of course, is what the masochist fears. . . . She also has no confidence in herself and her own views. Asking a question, returning a serve, feels dangerous and she avoids it (p. 45).

Clifton and Lee's (1976) finding that women are more likely than men to internalize negative feelings, become "hurt," and to doubt themselves supports this interpretation (McMillan, Clifton, McGrath and Gale, 1977).

Lakoff's explanation of women's use of tag questions is similar. Tag questions in certain contexts, "provide a means whereby a speaker can avoid committing himself and thereby avoid coming into conflict with the addressee" (1975, p. 17). Empirical research indicates that women do use more tag questions when men are present than when men are absent and that use of inappropriate tag questions by low-status individuals is viewed negatively (McMillan et. al., 1977).

(3) Spilling, or excessive self-revelation and explanation, constitutes the third type of verbal behavior proposed by Shainess. She writes, "Insecure about her own power, the masochist feels she has no right to keep her own counsel, no right to maintain a self-contained position. So she believes she can ward off harm by a stream of words, the way a fire hose directed at an attacking dog can keep him at bay" (p. 51). Shainess's illustration of spilling takes place in a negotiation context. When quoted a price by a salesman, a female buyer replied, "That's about what we can pay, . . . but I'd like you to do better" (p. 51). The buyer then gave a lengthy explanation of why her company could afford the asking price. As Shainess notes, this response gave the seller every reason to remain firm.

(4) The academic literature provides specific support for Shainess's fourth and fifth categories of verbal masochism, inability to control conversations or to change the subject, and use of equivocal language. Shainess discusses inability to control the topic of conversation in the context of criticism directed at women such as a remark that a woman has gained weight. Instead of responding briefly, then changing the subject, the woman explains at length the problems she has been having.

Empirical research has related conversational control to interruptions. Zimmerman and West observed that retarded minimal responses and repeated interruptions by a speaker were followed by topic change. They concluded, "We view the production of both retarded minimal responses and interruptions by male speakers interacting with females as an assertion of the right to control the topic of conversation reminiscent of adult-child conversations where in most instances the child has restricted rights to speak and to be listened to" (1975, p. 124). McLaughlin, Cody, Kane, and Robey (1981) and Henley (1977) also discuss men's control of conversations.

(5) Shainess's discussion of word use centers on patterns of extreme language found in masochistic persons. She mentions the

use of bipolar adjectives such as black and white and such words as totally, completely, and absolutely to an extent far beyond "what the situation calls for" (pp. 58-59).

Quite the opposite finding is abundantly documented in the academic literature. Two of the studies conducted by Crosby and Nyquist (1977) indicated more frequent use of hedges such as "I guess" by women. However, the effect of gender was confounded by that of role differentiation in their experiments. Swacker (1975) found that women preceded their use of numbers by approximations such as about fifty percent of the time. Thus, the use of equivocal language is viewed as characteristic of women by academicians, while Shainess believes extreme language is typical of masochists.

(6) Shainess describes an array of nonverbal behaviors characteristic of the masochistic style. They include avoidance of eye contact, frequent head-nodding (to indicate how agreeable women are), crying, and slouching posture rather than "erect self-assurance" (p. 59).

Empirical research into women's nonverbal behavior confirms that women nod more than men (Rosenfeld, 1966) and maintain more eye contact than males (Baird, 1976). Weitz (1976) found that women adapted their nonverbal behavior to fit male needs, producing more dominant nonverbals with submissive men and more submissive nonverbals with dominant males. This adaptiveness might produce either an advantage or disadvantage during negotiations. If the male were submissive, females would likely dominate, but they would react submissively to a dominant male. This prediction is similar to Shainess's assertion that masochistic behaviors are revealed when the masochist feels threatened. Knapp (1978, p. 228) summarizes Mehrabian's research by concluding that high-status persons are associated with nonverbal behavior including less eye gaze, postural relaxation, greater voice loudness, and more expansive movements and postures. It is important to interpret nonverbal behavior in context, since deliberate avoidance of eye contact and posture slumped in self-consciousness rather than relaxation are mentioned by Shainess as indicative of masochism.

In addition to the six categories of masochistic verbal and nonverbal behaviors suggested by Shainess, four other categories of verbal behaviors were included in the present study because they have been tested in the negotiation context. Greenhalgh, Gilkey, and Pufahl (1984) hypothesized that feminine bargainers would (7) make more empathic inquiries intended to learn the other party's point of view and would (8) refrain from interrupting or (9) attempting to deceive the other. Of these three hypotheses, only attempted deception was significantly different for masculine and feminine negotiators, even though

225

feminine bargainers did make more empathic inquiries and interrupt less frequently. Although Rogers and Jones (1975) found no difference in interruptions, there is much evidence in the gender-difference literature confirming that males interrupt females (Eakins and Eakins, 1978; Zimmerman and West, 1975).

(10) Threats were included as the tenth category of verbal behavior because they are frequently discussed in the negotiation literature and have been found to be related to expected selling prices in previous research involving bargaining for a used car (Womack,1981). Consistent with Shainess's analysis, "masochistic" females are expected to threaten less because of their feeling of powerlessness and fear of their opponent (Rubin and Brown, 1975, p. 288).

Although empirical researchers avoid Shainess's extreme characterization of women's behavior as masochistic, they generally confirm her predictions for female behavior. If Shainess's analysis is correct, women's sensitivity to interpersonal cues and their willingness to be flexible or cooperative in negotiations stem not from inner strength nor from a continuous rather than episodic view of the negotiations (Greenhalgh,Gilkey and Pufahl, 1984), but from inner weakness. Thus, women's cooperative behavior is not an advantage but a liability if it results from an inability to structure negotiations to seek high payoffs for themselves. The experiment described below was an attempt to test these two contradictory explanations of female negotiating behavior.

Hypotheses

Based on Shainess's analysis and the gender-difference and negotiation literature, seven experimental hypotheses were formed. The first three concern the prediction that women are more cooperative than men: (1) Females will expect to pay higher prices for a used care than will males; (2) Females will be willing to pay higher prices than males before breaking off negotiations if the other party does not agree to their price; and (3) The difference between the expected selling price and the highest price bargainers are willing to pay before breaking off negotiations will be greater for females than males. The third hypothesis predicts that women have a more flexible bargaining range than do men. The fourth and fifth hypotheses are related to the predictions of cooperativeness for females. (4) Females will be more likely than males to settle negotiations within a given time limit, and (5) Males will be perceived as more forceful than females by an independent observer of the negotiations. The last two hypotheses regard specific predictions of the verbal and nonverbal behaviors discussed earlier: (6) Females will exhibit significantly more verbal characteristics of the masochistic style than will males, and (7)

Females will exhibit significantly more nonverbal characteristics of the masochistic style than will males, in a negotiation situation.

Methods

The hypotheses were tested by comparing and contrasting the behaviors of fifteen female and fourteen male participants in a mock negotiation involving a used car. The twenty-nine participants were graduate and undergraduate students attending a small, private eastern college. Since some researchers (Crosby and Nyquist, 1977) have argued that gender differences in language use are actually reflective of different roles, male and female participants were asked to play the same role, that of a used car buyer bargaining against a forceful male used car seller.

In advance of the mock negotiation, participants were presented information about the wholesale value of the car ($2,000), the seller's asking price ($3,000), and the seller's and buyer's need to agree to the transaction. Participants were asked to indicate the price they most expected to pay for the car (Expected Selling Price) and the highest price they would be willing to pay without breaking off negotiations (High Price) on a scale of prices ranging from $2,000 to $3,000 at $50 intervals. They also explained why they chose a particular price as most likely, what strategy they planned to use against the seller, and what they planned to say to the dealer to persuade him to sell them the car at their Expected Selling Price. The seller was described as the owner of a small used car lot, so the buyer would not be likely to expect to take the car to him for service or to deal with him again for several years. Thus, the situation presented an episodic rather than a continuous buyer-seller relationship. Participants also completed a modified form of Crockett's (1965) Role Category Questionnaire. They were asked to describe someone they liked of any age and either gender as if telling a friend who did not know the person about him or her. Participants were allowed three minutes to write their descriptions. Demographic data were also collected.

Several days after completing the questionnaire, participants came for individual appointments to be videotaped while negotiating with the used car seller for fifteen minutes. The seller was one of two male confederates. Both confederates were experienced actors. The sellers had been instructed to be forceful and aggressive, even threatening, toward the buyer, conditions which Shainess claims evoke a masochistic response in self-punishing individuals (1984, p. 39).

After the fifteen-minute time period had elapsed, or buyer and seller had agreed on a price before the time signal, participants filled out a brief questionnaire regarding their perception of the seller's forcefulness as a manipulation check. Results indicated that participants found the seller to be forceful (X = 4.586 on a 5-point scale ranging from 5 = strongly agree to 1 = strongly disagree) and aggressive (X = 4.207 on a similar 5-point scale).

Data Analysis

Each of the participants' impressions was coded for number of constructs according to the procedure specified by Crockett, Press, Delia, and Kenny (1974). Ten percent of the descriptions were randomly selected and scored by a trained coder unconnected with the experiment. Interrater reliability measured by Pearson correlation was 1.00. The number of constructs was used as a predictor variable in the multiple regression equations which tested the seven hypotheses. Expecting Selling Price and Highest Price participants were willing to pay before breaking off negotiations were coded in dollar values ranging from $2,000 to $3,000 as indicated on the questionnaire. Range was computed by subtracting Expected Selling Price from High Price for each participant.

Videotapes were coded for verbal and nonverbal behaviors indicative of the ten categories suggested in the literature. Shainess' complete set of masochistic behaviors was not evident; neither was it possible to form a combined masochism score from participants' behaviors. Instead, a coding scheme which combined behaviors mentioned by Shainess (1984) with those found by empirical research on gender differences was constructed. The coding scheme consisted of nine categories of verbal behavior and one category of nonverbal behavior. These were: (1) apology; (2) being unwilling to ask questions or to challenge the premise of the other; (3) spilling, overexplaining, or revealing too much about one's own needs; (4) being unable to take control of conversation and to change the subject; (5) using equivocal or hesitant language; (6) making empathic inquiries or statements; (7) interruptions; (8) attempted deceptions; (9) threatens; and (10) nonverbal behavior. With the exceptions noted below, each category was scored on a five-point Likert-like scale ranging from "very often" to "very seldom" or on a dichotomous scale for the presence or absence of the behavior. Threat was scored according to three levels: no threat, weak threats (i.e., a statement that the buyer would go elsewhere to buy the car), and strong threats (i.e., a threat to report the seller to the Better Business Bureau). The tapes were also coded on Likert-like scales for the buyer's forcefulness, whether or not the (confederate) seller was more forceful than the buyer, and whether or not they settled the deal and at what price. A cluster of nonverbal behaviors was examined and each videotape scored as reflecting aggressive, defensive, or neutral nonverbals on the part of the buyer.

A trained coder unconnected with the experiment scored ten percent of the videotapes. Inter-rater reliability as measured by Pearson correlation was .81. Inter-rater reliability for the nonverbal category was 1.0. Because of the length and richness of the tapes and the fact that raters were asked to make judgments about the frequency of participants' behaviors rather than counting each specific occurrence, the reliability was considered sufficient to proceed to further analysis. The categories of apology and threat were not subjected to further analysis because apologies and threats were made so infrequently by bargainers.

A series of multiple regression equations was computed using the SPSS statistical package for the PDP11 computer (Morrison, 1982). The independent variables were age, gender, education, full-time job, previous bargaining experience, how forceful the seller was perceived by the buyer, how aggressive the seller was perceived by the buyer, whether or not the participant was a U.S. citizen, and number of constructs scored on the cognitive complexity measure. Gender, whether or not the buyer currently held a full-time job, whether or not the buyer had had previous bargaining experience for a major purchase such as a house or car, and whether or not the buyer was a U.S. citizen were coded as dichotomous dummy variables. Education, full-time job, and the seller's forcefulness and aggressiveness as perceived by the buyer were coded as ranging from values of 1-8 (age), 1-6 (education) and 1-5 (forcefulness and aggressiveness). Cognitive complexity scores ranged from 3 to 14 with a mean value of 7.76.

Thirteen separate regression equations were estimated, one predicting each of the dependent variables.

Results

HYPOTHESES 1, 2, 3, and 4

Females were expected to pay higher Expected Selling Prices, Highest Price before breaking off negotiations and to have broader Ranges than males. The mean Expected Selling Price of the car was $2,575.86, and the mean Highest Price before breaking off negotiations was $2,765.52. Expected Selling Prices ranged from $2,250 to $2,800; High Price varied from $2,250 to $3,000. Range, the difference between High Price and Expected Selling Price, varied from $0 to $500.00. Females were also expected to be more likely to settle within the fifteen-minute time limit than males. In fact, eleven of the twenty-nine participants settled with the seller. The average price at which they settled was $2,911.36, about $330.00 more than the average Expected

229

Selling Price. The discrepancy between actual and expected selling price averages indicates that, when bargaining against a forceful and aggressive male seller, participants were willing to pay approximately $300.00 more than they had expected. There was no statistical difference between males' and females' propensities to settle within the time limit. Actual selling price was not investigated since the confederates were told in advance to settle only within a very narrow range. The regression equations predicting Expected Selling Price, High Price, and Range did not yield statistically significant F-scores. Therefore, Hypotheses One through Four were rejected; males and females did not differ on Expected Selling Price, High Price, Range, or Propensity to Settle.

HYPOTHESES 5, 6, and 7

Hypothesis Five predicted that females would be perceived by the coder as less forceful than males. Hypotheses Six and Seven predicted that females would be more likely than males to exhibit the verbal and nonverbal indices of masochism selected for analysis. Each verbal measure was predicted with a separate multiple regression equation. In general, the results of the experiment were not as expected. The percentage of variance explained by the independent variables varied from thirty-five percent to sixty-nine percent, with the Frequency of Interruption having the lowest percentage of explained variance and Conversational Control and Empathic Statements having the highest percentages. (See Table One for complete results.)

Overall, Gender entered the stepwise multiple regression equations on about the fifth iteration. (See Tables Two through Nine.) Specifically, Gender was the second strongest predictor of Empathy, fourth of Buyer Control of the Conversation, and fifth of Accepts the Premise of the Seller and Is Too Self-Revealing. Gender was the sixth strongest predictor of Use of Equivocal Language and Buyer's Forcefulness. It did not enter the equations predicting Attempted Deception, Interruptions and Nonverbal Behavior. Therefore, Hypothesis Seven, Females will exhibit significantly more nonverbal characteristics of the masochistic style than will males, was rejected.

Not only was gender found not to predict the expected dependent variable in many cases, but the relationship between gender and the dependent variables predicted was often in the opposite of the hypothesized direction. For example, females were _less_ likely to show Empathy, to Accept the Premise of the Seller, and to be excessively Self-Revealing than were males. They were more likely to Control the Conversation and to be perceived by the coder as Forceful. The only result found in the expected direction was that women were more likely to use Equivocal Language than were males. Thus, Hypotheses Five and

Six were also rejected. Females were not perceived as less forceful than males, nor did they use more indicants of verbal masochism.

Discussion

In an effort to explain these surprising results, crosstabulations were computed using SPSS to see whether or not Gender was related systematically with a pattern of Age, Bargaining Experience, and Education, other independent variables which frequently entered the equations. While gender was not systematically related with age and education differences, about half the women had had bargaining experience. Twice as many males reported bargaining experience as reported no previous experience. It may be that more experienced negotiators are more likely to be Empathic, to Accept the Premises of the Seller, and to be excessively Self-Revealing. However, research by Womack (1980) indicated that professional negotiators were generally less cooperative than non-professionals, a finding which would lead to the hypotheses that were rejected. Males ought to be more competitive than females if they are more experienced, according to previous research.

Next, interviews were conducted with participants, who were asked to explain their negotiation behavior and their analysis of the seller and the situation. The interviews provided the information which best helps to explain the findings of the study. Females tended to view the situation as a "contest" between themselves and a used car dealer who was trying to take advantage of them. They were determined to remain firm and not to give in to the dealer. One woman reported a trip to shop for a car with her mother. The student perceived her mother to be quite weak and yielding, giving in to the seller and accepting his claims as true without questioning them. The student said she was determined not to behave like her mother during the experiment. Several women reported feeling quite angry at the seller.

On the other hand, men tended to admire the seller. Instead of feeling insulted by the seller's forcefulness, they interpreted it as a sign of his great financial need. They apparently felt that if they did not concede, the seller would eventually agree to sell the car at a lower price, "because he was really hungry." These gender differences did not vary with age; both graduate and undergraduate males and females analyzed the situation similarly.

There is mixed empirical evidence regarding response to threat. Chammah's dissertation, reported by Baird (1976), indicates that promises are most effective for inducing cooperation in females. Males cooperated when confronted with

231

threats, as was the case in the present study. However, there is also evidence that female performances suffer and male performances improve in competitive situations (Baird, 1976). If the goal was to obtain the highest possible payoff for the bargainer (i.e., the lowest selling price), males' verbal strategies for doing so were not those one might expect, but were those generally associated in the literature with powerlessness.

One final hypothesis which might account for the findings is that males were more Empathic and exhibited the rest of the verbal behaviors mentioned above because they were better able to take the perspective of the male seller. Although no measure of perspective-taking was obtained in the present study, cognitive complexity has been related to perspective-taking ability in the literature (Delia, Kline and Burleson, 1979). Women were more cognitively complex than men in the present study, with a mean score of 8.67 compared to 6.79 for males. This result is consistent with other research into cognitive complexity (Crockett, 1965). Thus, while women had greater ability to take the perspective of the seller, they challenged the premises of the seller rather than making empathic inquiries about his needs.

It is also important to interpret the one finding in the predicted direction, that women used more Equivocal Language than did men. While one normally thinks of equivocal language as indicative of uncertainty and thus weakness, in negotiations uncertainty may help to conceal one's real goals from the opponent. Careful review of the videotapes indicated that this is in fact what happened in the present study. Women appeared tentative, not in their attitude toward the seller or his asking price, but on topics such as how much they could afford to pay for the car. Thus, in this case, equivocal language was connected with negotiating strength rather than weakness.

Conclusion

The results presented and analyzed above indicate that women's negotiating behaviors were unlike those reported in studies of the 1970s, both in terms of cooperativeness and of verbal and nonverbal indicants of powerlessness usually associated with women. The differences between men's and women's behavior in the present study are best explained by their different construals of the bargaining situation and of the seller. In general, men behaved as women were expected to. Further research is required to confirm these findings and to determine whether or not males' constructions of used car negotiations with male sellers consistently differ from those of women. More research is also needed to determine whether the unexpected behavior of men and women in this study was due to the gender of the seller, a male, and whether or not the used car situation calls forth unique or typical construals of negotiation contexts. It appears likely that, with the continuing changes in society, the older findings regarding women's "powerless" communication behaviors will no longer hold true, either because women are gaining in self-esteem and in the battle against sexism, or because more women will be determined to "win" in situations where social stereotypes indicate they will be taken advantage of.

It seems impossible to test the two interpretations of women's behavior that were the original focus of this study. Whether or not a particular behavior, such as equivocal language, is indicative of powerlessness or power cannot be assessed outside the context in which it occurs. Furthermore, the effectiveness of any particular behavior in negotiations depends on the goal of the bargainer. As Greenhalgh, Gilkey and Pufahl (1984) note, an episodic as contrasted with a continuous perspective of the negotiation leads bargainers to different goals. A bargainer with a continuous perspective may be judged as effective if she decides to "lose the battle in order to win the war," to yield in a particular negotiation in order to maintain a good relationship which will influence future negotiations. Even within the same time perspective, effectiveness must be judged by what the bargainer attempts to accomplish. In the experimental situation, women may have sacrificed the possibility of a quick settlement in favor of maintaining their identities as "firm bargainers." It is not for the researcher to determine the comparative utility of projecting a particular image of oneself versus reaching an agreement, however favorable or unfavorable. The value of gender research in negotiation lies in relating particular verbal and nonverbal behaviors to the accomplishment of different goals as chosen by the bargainers themselves.

References

Baglan, T., & Nelson, D. (1982). A comparison of the effects of sex and status on the perceived appropriateness of nonverbal behavior. Women's Studies in Communication, 5, 29-38.

Baird, J., Jr. (1976). Sex difference in group communication: A review of relevant research. Quarterly Journal of Speech, 62, 179-192.

Bem, S. (1974). The measurement of psychological androgyny. Journal of Consulting and Clinical Psychology, 42, 155-162.

Bradley, P. (1981). The folk-linguistics of women's speech: An empirical examination. Communication Monographs, 48, 73-90.

Campbell, K. (1973). The rhetoric of women's liberation: An oxymoron. Quarterly Journal of Speech, 59, 84.

Clifton, A., & Lee, D. (1976). Self-destructive consequences of sex role socialization. Suicide, 6, 11-22.

Crockett, W. (1965). Cognitive complexity and impression formation. In B.A. Maher (Ed.), Progress in experimental personality research, (Vol. 2, pp. 47-90). New York: Academic Press.

Crockett, W., Press, A., Delia, J., & Kenny, C. (1974). The structural analysis of the organization of written impressions. Unpublished paper, Department of Psychology, University of Kansas.

Crosby, F., & Nyquist, L. (1977). The female register: An empirical study of Lakoff's hypotheses. Language in Society, 6, 313-322.

Delia, J., Kline, S., & Burleson, B. (1979). The development of persuasive communication strategies in kindergartners through twelfth-graders. Communication Monographs, 46, 241-256.

Eagly, A. (1978). Sex differences in influenceability. Psychological Bulletin, 85, 86-116.

Eakins, B., & Eakins, R. (1978). Sex differences in human communication. Boston: Houghton-Mifflin.

Gilligan, C. (1982). In a different voice: Psychological theory and women's development. Cambridge: Harvard University Press.

Greenhalgh, L., Gilkey, R., & Pufahl, S. (1984). Effects of sex-role differences on approach to business negotiations. Paper presented at the meeting of the Academy of Management, Boston.

Henley, N. (1977). Body politics: Power, sex, and nonverbal communication. Englewood Cliffs, NJ: Prentice-Hall.

Kahn, A., Hottes, J., & Davis, W. L. (1971). Cooperation and optimal responding in the prisoner's dilemma game: Effects of sex and physical attractiveness. Journal of Personality and Social Psychology, 17, 267-279.

Knapp, M. (1978). Nonverbal communication in human interaction (2nd ed.). New York: Holt, Rinehart, & Winston.

Komorita, S.S. (1975). Cooperative choice in a prisoner's dilemma game. Journal of Personality and Social Psychology, 20, 160-165.

Kramer, C. (1974, June). Folklinguistics. Psychology Today, pp. 82-85.

Lakoff, R. (1975). Language and women's place. New York: Harper Colophon.

McLaughlin, M., Cody, M., Kane, M., & Robey, C. (1981). Sex differences in story receipt and story sequencing behaviors in dyadic conversations. Human Communication Research, 7, 99-116.

McMillan, J., Clifton, A., McGrath, D., & Gale, W. (1977). Women's language: Uncertainty or interpersonal sensitivity and emotionality? Sex Roles, 3, 545-559.

Miller, J. (1976). Toward a new psychology of women. Boston: Beacon Press.

Morrison, S. (1982). SPSS-11: The SPSS-11 batch system for the DEC PDP-11 (2nd ed.). New York: McGraw-Hill.

Nadler, L., & Nadler, M. (1984). Communication, gender and negotiation: Theory and findings. Paper presented at the meeting of the Eastern Communication Association, Philadelphia.

Putnam, L. (1982). In search of gender: A critique of communication and sex-roles research. Women's Studies in Communication, 5, 1-9.

235

Rogers, W., & Jones, S. (1975). Effects of dominance tendencies on floor holding and interruption behavior in dyadic interaction. Human Communication Research, 1, 113-132.

Rosenfeld, H. (1966). Approval-seeking and approval-inducing functions of verbal and nonverbal responses in the dyad. Journal of Personality and Social Psychology, 4, 597-605.

Rubin, J., & Brown, B. (1975). The social psychology of bargaining and negotiation. New York: Academic Press.

Shainess, N. (1984). Sweet suffering: Woman as victim. New York: Bobbs-Merrill.

Swacker, M. (1975). The sex of the speaker as a sociolinguistic variable. In B. Thorne & N. Henley (Eds.), Language and sex: Difference and dominance (pp. 76-83). Rowley, Mass.: Newbury House.

Weitz, S. (1976). Sex differences in nonverbal communication. Sex Roles, 2, 175-184.

Womack, D. (1980). Bargaining orientations of professional negotiators: A game theoretic perspective. Unpublished masters thesis, University of Kansas.

Womack, D. (1981). Orientations to conflict and their consequences for negotiating behavior. Unpublished doctoral dissertation, University of Kansas.

Zimmerman, D. H., & West, C. (1975). Sex roles, interruptions and silences in conversations. In B. Thorne & N. Henley (Eds.), Language and sex: Difference and dominance (pp. 105-129). Rowley, Mass.: Newbury House.

TABLE 1

Dependent Variable: Buyer's Forcefulness

Multiple R	R Square	Degrees of Freedom	F	Significance Level
.76180	.58034	10, 18	2.48916	.05

Independent Variables	B	Beta	Std. Error B	F
Bargaining Experience	1.361998	.47746	.60976	4.989
Seller was Aggressive	-.6385667	-.27684	.49869	2.441
Education	.2612929	.25346	.25999	1.010
Foreign Citizen	-1.607200	-.34839	.82860	3.762
Seller was Forceful	.4419597	.21090	.33148	1.778
Gender	.4813309	.17120	.50642	.903
Which Confederate	-.5982906	-.20974	.48911	1.496
Full-time Job	-.7201533	-.22910	.76687	.882
Age	.1940037	.17573	.27534	.496
Cognitive Complexity	.1763636	-.03324	.09842	.032

Female = 1; Male = 0.

TABLE 2

Dependent Variable: Buyer's Unwillingness to Ask Challenging
Questions

Multiple R	R Square	Degrees of Freedom	F	Significance Level
.67894	.46096	7, 21	2.56541	.05

Independent Variables	B	Beta	Std. Error B	F
Seller was Forceful	-.9327873	-.39841	.38069	6.004
Education	-.5368002	-.46608	.28427	3.566
Age	.2773575	.22487	.31401	.780
Bargaining Experience	-.8410415	-.26390	.60984	1.902
Gender	-.5640978	-.17958	.54621	1.067
Which Confederate	.5511831	.17295	.55454	.988
Full-time Job	.6863886	.19545	.78773	.759

Female = 1; Male = 0.

TABLE 3

Dependent Variable: Excessively Self-Revealing

Multiple R	R Square	Degrees of Freedom	F	Significance Level
.64624	.41763	6, 22	2.62945	.05

Independent Variables	B	Beta	Std. Error B	F
Education	-.3649555	-.37143	.16420	4.940
Seller was Forceful	-.5845141	-.29264	.33324	3.077
Which Confederate	.7263360	.26715	.45327	2.568
Cognitive Complexity	.1654617	.32717	.09017	3.367
Gender	-.7137852	-.26636	.47006	2.306
Seller was Aggressive	.3090751	.14059	.36629	.712

Female = 1; Male = 0.

TABLE 4

Dependent Variable: Controlling the Conversation

Multiple R	R Square	Degrees of Freedom	F	Significance Level
.80331	.64531	9, 19	3.84085	.01

Independent Variables	B	Beta	Std. Error B	F
Bargaining Experience	1.433221	.44564	.58795	5.942
Age	.1612136	.12952	.27776	.337
Which Confederate	-.9682680	-.30107	.48664	3.959
Gender	.2467233	.07784	.50457	.239
Seller was Forceful	.5567475	.23565	.33392	2.780
Seller was Aggressive	-.7338284	-.28218	.40898	3.219
Education	.3364232	.28946	.25662	1.719
Cognitive Complexity	.1155180	.19310	.09921	1.356
Full-time Job	-.6222605	-.17558	.73367	.719

Female = 1; Male = 0

TABLE 5

Dependent Variable: Equivocal Language

Multiple R	R Square	Degrees of Freedom	F	Significance Level
.75961	.57701	9,19	2.87981	.05

Independent Variables	B	Beta	Std. Error B	F
Seller was Forceful	-.7455194	-.36358	.31423	5.645
Seller was Aggressive	.9951348	.44027	.35724	7.760
Which Seller	-.8781780	-.31416	.45559	3.715
Education	-.4965149	-.49151	.23063	4.635
Foreign Citizen	1.296409	.28678	.75834	2.922
Gender	.3495552	.12688	.45917	.580
Age	.1373488	.12696	.25686	.286
Full-time Job	.1130177	.03669	.71613	.025
Cognitive Complexity	.9419356	.01812	.09261	.010

Female = 1; Male = 0.

TABLE 6

Dependent Variable: Empathy

Multiple R	R Square	Degrees of Freedom	F	Significance Level
.83617	.69917	10, 18	4.18353	.01

Independent Variables	B	Beta	Std. Error B	F
Cognitive Complexity	.2450548	.80528	.04779	26.296
Gender	-.5411217	-.33559	.24590	4.842
Seller was Aggressive	-.3080316	-.23285	.19845	2.409
Full-time Job	-1.550893	-.86028	.37237	17.347
Age	.4010999	.63350	.13370	9.000
Foreign Citizen	-.5798817	-.21917	.40234	2.077
Seller was Forceful	.1589028	.13222	.16095	.975
Which Seller	-.2825240	-.17269	.23749	1.415
Bargaining Experience	.3402985	.20801	.29608	1.321
Education	-.1814343	-.03069	.12624	.021

Female = 1; Male = 0.

TABLE 7

Dependent Variable: Interruptions

Multiple R	R Square	Degrees of Freedom	F	Significance Level
.59755	.32517	4, 24	2.89119	.05

Independent Variables	B	Beta	Std. Error B	F
Bargaining Experience	1.144855	.35819	.57865	3.914
Age	.2887443	.23343	.21263	1.844
Foreign Citizen	1.062977	.20565	.90377	1.383
Which Seller	-.604092	-.18898	.54626	1.223
Seller was Forceful	.4239234	.18054	.39687	1.141

TABLE 8

Dependent Variable: Attempted Deception

Multiple R	R Square	Degrees of Freedom	F	Significance Level
.68530	.46964	7, 21	2.65650	.05

Independent Variables	B	Beta	Std. Error B	F
Age	.4333968	.35641	.27580	2.469
Bargaining Experience	.5757242	.18323	.58675	.963
Cognitive Complexity	-.1365694	-.23367	.10100	1.829
Education	.3279238	.28879	.28081	1.364
Foreign Citizen	-.5940538	-.11691	.87613	.460
Seller was Forceful	.2521596	.10924	.37328	.456
Which Seller	-.3415326	-.10870	.51720	.436

TABLE 9

Dependent Variable: Nonverbal Behavior

Multiple R	R Square	Degrees of Freedom	F	Significance Level
.73548	.54093	9, 19	2.48759	.05

Independent Variables	B	Beta	Std. Error B	F
Seller was Aggressive	-.5739969	-.45991	.22041	6.782
Seller was Forceful	.3256563	.28720	.18144	3.221
Education	.2146839	.38488	.13956	2.366
Foreign Citizen	-.9693081	-.38832	.45076	4.624
Full-time Job	-.8923301	-.52464	.41906	4.534
Cognitive Complexity	.7941946	.27662	.05133	2.394
Bargaining Experience	.2595742	.16817	.31803	.666
Age	.9626078	.16115	.15157	.403
Which Seller	-.9656575	-.06256	.26929	.129

CHAPTER 14

WOMEN, MEN AND PERSONAL SALES: AN ANALYSIS
OF SEX DIFFERENCES IN COMPLIANCE GAINING
STRATEGY USE

John Parrish Sprowl, University of Connecticut

Job performance in personal sales, perhaps
more so than in any other profession, depends upon the
communication style, skills and ability of the
individual sales representative. Yet, despite the
centrality of human communication to successful task
function, a striking dearth of research focused upon
sales communication has been conducted up to this
point. The purpose of the present study is to begin
filling the void by exploring the effects of both the
sales representative's and the target consumer's
biological gender upon the persuasive strategy choice
of the salesperson. First, the paper discusses the
importance of exploring the effects of biological
gender in personal sales. Secondly, relevant
persuasive strategy research is outlined. Finally, the
study method, results and discussion are presented.

In part, the role of biological gender is
important in personal sales because of the increasing
number of women entering the sales field. While women
have long held the majority of the lower paying retail
sales positions (e.g. department store clerks and food
service personnel), they have traditionally been absent
both in higher level and paying sales positions. In
the last decade, however, the employment mix in this
profession has been rapidly changing. Carter and
Bryant (1980) illustrate the dramatic change when they
report that:

> Demand for women in industrial
> sales and related areas is
> increasing. As an example,
> Computer Sciences Corporation of
> El Segundo, California, had but
> four female marketing and customer
> service representatives in 1973.
> Five years later, however, one of
> its sales divisions went to 50
> women and a 200 person staff.
> Xerox hired over 1200 people for
> sales jobs in 1977 and 419, or 31%

were women, and IBM has doubled its female salesforce since 1974. In addition, the percentage of women selling insurance increased from 2% of all life insurance salespeople in 1972 to 12% in 1978.

U.S. Labor Department statistics indicate that 70.4% of the entire retail salesforce was women and that only 7.6% of the 850,000 wholesale and manufacturer sales representative jobs were held by women in 1977. However, according to a _Business Week_ survey released in early 1979, the picture is changing rapidly. Women now hold corporate sales jobs in steel, aluminum, lumber, and other traditionally male-only industries. The Aluminum Company of America has a 190 person salesforce and 10% are women. A recent study of chemical and printing companies showed that 14 companies employed 36 industrial saleswomen in 1972. In the same industry, 43 companies employed 402 female industrial sales representatives. The increase is over 1100% (p. 23).

Due to the increasing number of women in sales, their performance versus men becomes a natural concern for sales management professionals. For example, if males and females perform differently, then training and development programs need to be assessed with respect to these differences. Furthermore, since women are relative newcomers to the upper echelons of the sales field, special consideration must be given to adjust both males and females to any differences which may exist. Such efforts should allow practitioners to tap the best sales abilities and behaviors of both sexes.

A second reason for examining the biological gender differences in salespeople is to provide a substantive, scientific basis for assessing performance independent of any traditional stereotypes which may exist. Many people believe that one sex is inherently

superior to the other in sales ability and such
attitudes constitute a serious potential for
unnecessary and unethical discrimination against both
sexes. The following is one example of such an
attitude, cited in Carter and Bryant (1980) which
places women as superior to males in sales positions:

> D.D. Miller, Board Chairman of
> Rumrill-Hoyt, Inc., of Rochester,
> NY believes that women are often
> better sales representatives than
> men. He advocates business
> publications hiring more women as
> sales representatives and, speaking
> at a meeting of the American
> Business Press, he said, "Women are
> often far better prepared, far more
> organized, and do a far better
> follow-up job, and think a lot
> faster on their feet than do their
> male counterparts (p. 24).

In contrast, Swan and Futrell (1978) report that many
sales managers believe that women may not perform in
the sales role quite as well as men. In either case,
little research examining the communication of males
and females in sales has been conducted which might
lend support to the respective claims of both
positions.

A more fundamental question of concern to scholars
is not so much whether or not one sex possesses sales
skills superior to the other, but do they do it
differently, and if so, how are they different? A
simple test or tests of differences between the sexes
is important to people exploring the nature of human
relations in the professional as well as the social
realm. Because sales is fundamentally a persuasive
undertaking, a natural starting point in sales
communication research is to explore the effects of
biological gender upon sales strategy use. To begin
this endeavor, since such research in sales has not
been conducted in the past, the recent strain of
research in communication examining compliance gaining
strategy choice will be reviewed because it is of
direct relevance to the present discussion.

Compliance gaining strategies have been defined as "a form of symbolic behavior designed to shape or regulate the behavior of others" (Schenk-Hamlin, Wiseman and Georgacarakos, 1982). Stated differently, compliance gaining strategies are message plans which people develop to induce a set of behaviors in others which they might not have otherwise evoked. Sales agents, for example, attempt to induce a potential customer to become an actual customer via the use of one or more compliance gaining strategies. Research in this area has been of two fundamental types known as taxonomic, which is designed to identify the potential number of strategies one might engage in any given persuasive situation, and message efficacy, which includes investigations with respect to variables affecting the invocation of the various strategies by persuaders.

Taxonomic research, while the subject of much investigative and theoretical work as of yet has not resulted in an agreed upon exhaustive list of potential compliance gaining strategies (Falbo, 1977; Marwell and Schmitt, 1967; Wiseman and Schenck-Hamlin, 1981). Although the researchers have employed different underlying logics in their compilations of strategies, none has been able to derive a complete taxonomy as evidenced by the disparate content of each effort. The purpose of this investigation is not one of taxonomic development but nonetheless such research impacts upon any study of strategy use because any research is bound by the response alternatives of the people considering the potential list of strategies. Consequently, rather than employing a single taxonomy, this study utilizes 27 strategies derived from Marwell and Schmitt (1967) and Falbo (1977). This list is probably not exhaustive but it captures a broader range of persuasive behaviors than any single taxonomy. Since all of the strategies are measured by single indicant items such an integration is a simple procedure.

Aside from the above taxonomic research, several people have conducted message efficacy research with a variety of variables. Cody, Woelfel and Jordan (1983) provide a review of a broad range of studies, not germane to the present effort, investigating the nature of several situation and personality variables involved in the choice of compliance gaining strategies by persuaders. Their review suggests that such variables deserve further investigative efforts.

Research exploring gender effects upon compliance gaining strategy use has been reported by Burgoon, Dillard, Koper and Doran (1984). They utilize the Marwell and Schmitt taxonomy and measure biological gender effects of the persuader with both a summative (a measure of likelihood use with the taxonomy as a whole) and a nonsummative approach (a measure of use likelihood utilizing each strategy as a separate dependent variable). They discover no significant effect with the summative approach, however, differences in use likelihood with two strategies were found with the nonsummative tests. Males were more likely to use aversive stimulation while females rated higher in likely use on the liking strategy. They conclude that the nonsummative results warrant further investigation into biological gender differences "in other samples that are more diverse in terms of age and education" (p. 12).

This study comprises one such investigation called for by Burgoon et al., however, several important differences besides the nature of the population must be noted. First, rather than creating narrative situation stories where the respondents are asked which strategies they might use, as most of the research in this area has done, the current effort asks salespeople to indicate which strategies they actually used in a real sales situation. Secondly, the salespeople responded to the sixteen Marwell and Schmitt (1967) items as well as eleven additional strategies from the Falbo (1977) taxonomy (see Table 1). Finally, and perhaps most importantly, the sex of the target consumer is considered as well as the sex of the agent. If biological gender is a factor in compliance gaining strategy use, then the biological gender of every person involved should be considered.

In summary, while previous research has examined the effects of biological gender in compliance gaining strategy use, no such effort has been made in personal sales. The purpose of this study is to begin filling the void in this area. Towards this end, the following research questions are posited:

RQ1: Does biological gender affect the degree to which salespeople use a compliance gaining strategy?

RQ2: Does sex of target affect the degree to which salespeople use a compliance gaining strategy?

RQ3: Does the interaction of biological gender and sex of target affect the degree to which salespeople use a compliance gaining strategy?

RQ4: Are there clusters of compliance gaining strategies which differentiate salespeople based upon biological gender?

RQ5: Are there clusters of compliance gaining strategies which differentiate salespeople based on the sex of the target?

RQ6: Are there clusters of compliance gaining strategies which differentiate salespeople based on the interaction of biological gender and sex of target?

Sample and Procedure

Subjects for this study were 204 salespeople, representing 90 businesses, including 70 from the automobile industry (28 dealers), 59 from the insurance industry (39 agencies), and 75 from the real estate industry (23 agencies). Data was collected over a six-week period in cities which range in size from under 2,000 to over 500,000 people.

The sample includes 56 females (10 from insurance; 46 from real estate) and 148 males (70 from the automobile industry, 49 from insurance and 29 from real estate). A wide range of ages is represented, with 15% of the sample under 30, 29% from 30-39, 31% from 40-49, 21% from 50-59, and 6% from age 60 and over. In addition, all levels of education are represented, from people with only a partial high school education to those with graduate degrees. Sales training and experience levels are also broad based with 20% of the sample having had no formal sales training and a range

248

of experience levels from just hired to those with over ten years in the sales profession.

To secure a response from subjects the researcher entered each business and contacted someone from the sales staff and requested permission to have all the salespeople on duty respond to the study questionnaire. Each subject was given the questionnaire which required them to respond to several demographic items and then instructed them to recall their most recent initial customer contact which had lasted at least fifteen minutes. Following this, the subjects responded on a seven-point Likert-type scale ranging from definitely did use to definitely did not use for each compliance gaining strategy.

Operational Definitions

Biological gender--
There were two levels, male and female.

Sex of Target --
There were three levels of sex of target: female, male and a male/female pair. This was done because the above commodities are often purchased by couples rather than single individuals.

Compliance Gaining Strategies--
This variable was measured via a 27-item instrument with each item containing a strategy, definition and a seven-point Likert-type scale ranging from definitely did use to definitely did not use. The scale is an adaptation of Marwell and Schmitt's (1967) scale with eleven additional items derived from the Falbo (1977) scale. This represents a comprehensive list of strategies derived from the literature concerned with the taxonomic development of compliance gaining strategies.

Statistical Analysis

The analysis of variance (ANOVA) model was used to answer research questions 1, 2, and 3. Twenty-seven separate 3 x 3 ANOVAs were performed, each using a different compliance gaining strategy as the dependent variable. To account for any correlation between the

strategies (dependent variables), alpha was set at
.0025 for each ANOVA, resulting in a total alpha of
.054.

To answer research questions 4, 5, and 6, a 3 x 3
multivariate analysis of variance (MANOVA) was
performed. A Multiple Discriminant Analysis (MULDIS)
was used as a post hoc test to locate differences among
the groups identified in the MANOVA. Alpha for the
MANOVA/MULDIS was set at .05.

Results

Research question one asked if biological gender
affects the degree to which salespeople use compliance
gaining strategies. The results of the ANOVAs revealed a significant main effect for biological gender
on eleven of the twenty seven strategies. Group
differences, representing greater use by males, are
found with promise ($F = 16.93$, $df = 1$; $p < .001$),
positive expertise ($F = 13.03$; $df = 1$; $p < .001$), pre-
giving ($F = 17.00$; $df = 1$; $p < .001$), positive
altercasting ($F = 23.88$, $df = 1$, $p < .001$), compromise
($F = 13.05$; $df = 1$; $p < .001$), emotion target ($F =
14.58$, $df = 1$, $p < .001$), hinting ($F = 11.02$, $df = 1$, $p
< .001$), persistence ($F = 18.62$, $df = 1$, $p < .001$),
thought manipulation ($F = 13.18$, $df = 1$, $p < .001$),
evasion ($F = 12.31$, $df = 1$, $p < .001$), and fait
accompli ($F = 21.79$, $df = 1$, $p < .001$).

Research question two asked if sex of target
affects the use of compliance gaining strategies. The
results of the ANOVAs revealed no significant main
effects for the sex of target independent variable.

Research question three asked if an interaction
between biological gender and sex of target affects the
use of compliance gaining strategies. The results of
the ANOVAs revealed no significant interaction between
these two variables.

Research question four asked if clusters of
compliance gaining strategies exist which differentiate
salespeople based upon biological gender. Results from
the MANOVA revealed a significant one-way main effect
for biological gender (Wilks $F = 2.57$, $df = 27/172$, $p <
.00013$).

Research question five asked if clusters of
compliance gaining strategies exist which differentiate
salespeople based upon the sex of target. Results from
the MANOVA revealed no significant main effect for sex
of target (Wilks $F = 1.10$, $df = 54/344$, $p < .297$).

Research question six asked if clusters of compliance gaining strategies exist based upon the interaction of biological gender and sex of target which differentiate salespeople. Results of the MANOVA revealed no significant difference from the interaction of these two variables (Wilks F = 1.12, df = 54/344, p < .27).

The MULDIS revealed one significant discriminant function (x = 63.82, df = 27, p < .0001). The items loading highest on this function were positive altercasting (.54) and fait accompli (.51). This function was not labeled; the reason will be discussed below. Centroids were computed for each group on the significant function. The female centroid was -1.0, the male centroid was .39.

Discussion

Both the nonsummative and the summative results indicate clear differences between men and women sales representatives with respect to compliance gaining strategy use. Surprisingly, however, the sex of the target consumer appears to have no effect upon compliance gaining strategy use. In toto, the findings in this study suggest males engage a larger number of strategies than females when attempting to sell a product. While the results offer no absolute explanation as to why the differences between men and women sales representatives exist, they provide grounds for speculation and suggestions for future research.

Unfortunately, thematic continuity appears to be lacking when the group of strategies which differentiate men and women in this study are examined. In the nonsummative (ANOVA) data, the strategies are neither all prosocial (evasion, thought manipulation) anti-social (positive expertise, positive altercasting), verbally aggressive (hinting, emotion target) or similar in style (compromise, persistence). Furthermore, although the summative data (MANOVA/MULDIS) produces a significant difference, the discriminate function does not provide a consistent theme (positive altercasting, fait accompli). The top eleven strategies loading on the discriminate function are the same as those uncovered in the nonsummative data with loadings ranging from .47 to .54. Thus, while the differences between male and female sales representatives are pronounced, the rationale for these differences is unclear.

Irrespective of why the differences exist, the results indicate that women and men approach the task of selling quite differently. Given that in each case men respond with higher use, they appear to utilize a broader spectrum of compliance gaining strategies when confronting a customer than does a woman sales agent. The respective approach of each seems to occur no matter what the sex of the target consumer happens to be in the selling situation. One proposition suggested by these findings is that males use the "shotgun" approach to customer adaptation, which is consistent with male sex role socialization. In other words, men tend to be task rather than relationship focused, thus they will do whatever it takes to get the job done, but are not quite certain as to how this should be accomplished when the task is relational in nature. Women, on the other hand, probably utilize no one strategy more so than another, but are more accurate in deciding which strategy is the best approach in any given sales situation. To decide which is better is a case of pure speculation, since both sexes seem to be able to accomplish the task of selling. However, the differences may be a good illustration of the concept of equifinality, two alternative approaches achieving the same end.

A note should be made concerning these results vis a vis the Burgoon et al. (1984) study. They failed to detect the number of strategy differences in either the summative or the nonsummative approach. The inconsistent findings of the two studies may be explained by a myriad of reasons. First, obviously the samples are different, suggesting greater sampling of non-college student populations is necessary in the future. Secondly, the present study utilized a larger strategy list thereby allowing more differences to be detected. Third, salespeople were asked to respond to the strategies based upon actual use rather than likelihood of use. Jackson and Backus (1982) suggest that the stories used to generate likely use responses may confound the results of compliance gaining strategy studies. Finally, sales professionals may simply view strategy use differently than other people. All of these differences point to the need for further study and replication in compliance gaining strategy research.

Biological gender appears to be an important variable in the assessment of sales communication practices. Aside from a need for replication, future research should continue to explore the nature and extent of the differences between women and men in sales occupations. Some key areas include success measures, communication satisfaction, nonverbal differences, argument construction and use, differences in the sexes with respect to the type of sales position and the effects of psychological gender orientation. This list is by no means exhaustive, however, it points to the paucity of research in an important organizational and vocational area.

The results of the present study indicate great differences between women and men sales representatives, but provide little explanation as to why these differences exist. Men use eleven of the strategies to a greater degree than women when the data is analyzed with each strategy as a separate dependent variable and appear to use more strategies overall when they are scored in a summative manner. More needs to be understood concerning these differences as more women enter the profession. In addition, sales training needs to be conducted with a strong consideration for these differences if it is to help all salespeople improve their performance. At this point the gender gap in sales communication can be considered neither good nor bad, but it certainly should not be ignored.

TABLE
Compliance Gaining Strategies

1. <u>Promise</u> - (Definition: You offered to reward the customer for buying your product/service).

2. <u>Threat</u> - (Definition: You threatened the customer with negative consequences if s/he did not buy the product/service).

3. <u>Positive Expertise</u> - (Definition: You told the customer that your expertise about the product/service allows you to assure him/her that s/he would benefit by your service/product).

4. <u>Negative Expertise</u> - (Definition: You told the customer that your expertise about the product/service allows you to assure him/her that s/he would suffer negative consequences by not purchasing your product).

5. <u>Liking</u> - (Definition: You acted friendly and helpful to get the customer in a "good frame of mind" so that s/he would buy your product).

6. <u>Pre-giving</u> - (Definition: You somehow rewarded the customer before you tried to sell him/her your product/service).

7. <u>Aversive Stimulation</u> - (Definition: You somehow punished the customer and made it clear that the punishment would cease if and only if s/he bought your product/service).

8. <u>Debt</u> - (Definition: You told the customer that s/he should buy your product because of past favors you have done for him/her).

9. <u>Moral Appeal</u> - (Definition: You suggested to the customer that it would be immoral not to purchase your product).

10. <u>Positive Self-feeling</u> - (Definition: You told the customer that s/he would feel better about him/herself if s/he bought your product/service).

11. Negative Self-feeling - (Definition: You told the customer that s/he would feel worse about him/herself if s/he did not buy the product/service).

12. Positive Altercasting - (Definition: You pointed out that a person with good qualities would buy your product/service).

13. Negative Altercasting - (Definition: You pointed out that only a person with bad qualities would refuse to buy your product/service).

14. Altruism - (Definition: You stressed how badly you needed for the customer to purchase your product/service).

15. Positive Esteem - (Definition: You pointed out that people would think better of the customer if s/he bought your product/-service).

16. Negative Esteem - (Definition: You pointed out that people would think badly of the customer if s/he refused to buy your product/service).

17. Compromise - (Definition: You told the customer that you would be willing to give a little if s/he would give a little in order to sell your product/service).

18. Deceit - (Definition: You used flattery or lies in your attempts to sell your product/service to the customer).

19. Emotion-agent - (Definition: You used your facial expressions in your attempts to sell your product/service).

20. Emotion-target - (Definition: You tried to influence the emotions of the customer to help you sell your product/service).

21. Hinting - (Definition: You used indirect attempts to get the customer to buy your product/service).

22. <u>Persistence</u> - (Definition: You continued to repeat your attempts to sell your product/-service throughout your conversation with the customer).

23. <u>Reason</u> - (Definition: You used rational argument to sell your product/service).

24. <u>Simple Statement</u> - (Definition: You used matter of fact statements without supporting evidence or threats to sell your product/-service).

25. <u>Thought Manipulation</u> - (Definition: You tried to make the customer think that your ideas were his/her ideas).

26. <u>Evasion</u> - (Definition: You tried to hide the strategies you used from the customer).

27. <u>Fait Accompli</u> - (Definition: You were determined to sell your product/service, regardless of what the customer said).

References

Burgoon, M., Dillard, J., Koper, R., and Doran, N. (1984). The impact of communication context and persuader gender on persuasive message selection. Women's Studies in Communication, 7 (Spring) 1-12.

Carter, R.N., and Bryant, M.R. (1980). Women as industrial sales representatives. Industrial Marketing Management, 9, 23-26.

Cody, M.J., and McLaughlin, M.L. (1980). Perceptions of compliance-gaining situations: A dimensional analysis. Communication Monographs, 47, 132-48.

Falbo, T. A multidimensional scaling of power strategies. (1977). Journal of Personality and Social Psychology, 35, 537-47.

Jackson, S., and Backus, D. (1982). Are compliance-gaining strategies dependent on situational variables? Central States Speech Journal, 1982, 33, 469-79.

Magnusson, D. (1971). An analysis of situational dimensions. Perceptual and Motor Skills, 37, 851-67.

Schenck-Hamlin, W.J., Wiseman, R.L., and Georgacarakos, G.N. (1982). A model of properties of compliance-gaining strategies. Communication Quarterly, 30, 92-100.

Swan, J.E., and Futrell, C.M. (1978). Men versus women in industrial sales: A performance gap. Industrial Marketing Management, 7, 369-373.

Weinstein, E.A., and Deutschberger, P. (1963). Some dimensions of altercasting. Sociometry, 26, 454-66.

SECTION FOUR

THE COMMUNICATIVE INFLUENCE OF GENDER ON POLITICS AND CULTURE

POLITICAL DISCOURSE REVISITED: THE LANGUAGE OF WOMEN IN POLITICS
AND WOMEN IN POLITICS OF LANGUAGE

Rita M. Miller, Clarkson University

Ellen Goodman (1984), reporting the results of a study
conducted by the National Women's Political Caucus, explains that
the average voter has "tended to vote for men and only voted for
women when they were more qualified than the men." The same
study suggests that male candidates are still perceived as more
capable of dealing with budgetary matters and stress and as
better public speakers. Women are perceived as more
understanding, organized and able to bring a fresh outlook to a
political office.

The results of the NWPC study raises some interesting
questions about the language of women holding political office.
Do women politicians speak a variety of language distinct from
men? If women do speak similar to men, why are they perceived as
less able public speakers? If women in political office do speak
a unique variety of language, why do they? How does this
difference, whether real or perceived, influence voters?

This chapter is an attempt to begin to answer some of those
questions about the nature of political women's language. The
problems of language use that are faced by women in politics will
be studied through the politician's descriptions of their own
language and their perceptions of how their language is viewed by
those who decide if they remain in political office.

Few studies in the past have been concerned with political
women's language, although many have been concerned with
political women. One of the genres, the "how I got there story,"
uses the actual language of the politicians as data, but the
focus is on the women themselves. Lamson (1968; 1979) has two
books which are made up of several short biographies of women who
have crossed the political barrier. Diamond (1977), Kirkpatrick
(1974; 1976), and Mandel (1981) exemplify another type of study;
these draw a composite sketch of women in politics based on
interviews or questionnaires. All three of these writers give
valuable insight into campaign strategy and how women do talk
about the political process. Other genres of literature include
how groups of women can gain more access to political power
(Tolchin and Tolchin, 1983; Gelb and Palley, 1982; Klein, 1984)
and studies of the behavior of women voters (Randall, 1982;
Sapiro, 1983). Margolis (1980), as a part of a larger project,
discovered that women's talk, while they were working for a town
committee, "involved an exchange of information." Men's talk was
usually "an attempt to influence another person."

Although none of these studies is a systematic analysis of the language of women in politics, they are of interest as they usually mention the dual and conflicting expectations that are placed on political women. It would appear that one problem for women in politics concerns the existing cultural expectations for men and women.

Traditionally, women have been given the jobs of tending the home, caring for the children, and protecting the family morals. Men were given the public sphere and all of its problems. This rigid public/private split, once seemingly mandated by beliefs about the destiny of biology, may now appear to have broken down since women are now running for and being elected to public office in record numbers.

However, as the NWPC study has already indicated, the specter of this public/private system still influences voter expectations for how a politician should sound. Obviously, there are no easy answers to striking a balance between cultural expectations and personality. Any candidate must look at his or her own strengths and weaknesses, as well as what the voting public wants and what the office requires. But women politicians need to balance two contradictory sets of expectations, since the culturally approved traits for a politician are closer to the expectations for men and since men have traditionally been politicians.

Kirkpatrick (1974) found that the state legislators she studied were aware of this conflict of social expectations. One woman reported "I work overtime at being feminine in every way in actions and in manner of speech," while another commented,"...too much aggressiveness is not acceptable in a woman." Gloria Steinem sums up the dilemma of political women the best: "If you are assertive and aggressive enough to do the job, you're unfeminine and therefore unacceptable; if your're not aggressive you can't do the job – and in either case, good-bye" (quoted in Mandel, 1981, p. 43).

What women in politics find themselves in is a "double bind." According to Bateson (1972) when an individual is in a double bind "every move he [or she] makes is the common-sense move in the situation as he [or she] correctly sees it at that moment, his [or her] every move is subsequently demonstrated to have been wrong by the moves which other members of the system make in response to his [or her] 'right' move." Since politicians in our culture have traditionally been men, male behaviors have been associated with elected office. If women act like politicians, they might seem to be behaving as men and therefore they are behaving inappropriately for women. They can't win because the system won't allow it. By way of illustration consider the 1982 Congressional campaign of Barney

Frank and Margaret Heckler. Both were incumbents forced to run against each other due to redistricting. The campaign was expensive and explosive. Both Frank and Heckler ran a series of negative ads and at times the discourse more closely resembled a barroom brawl than intelligent argument. Heckler lost, although she had a large lead early in the campaign. An "unidentified liberal political pro" quoted in the <u>Boston Phoenix</u> (1982) best summed up the campaign and the situation of women in politics by remarking, "It's sad but true... If you're a man and pull this stuff, you're tough. If you're a woman you're a bitch."

Double binds exist for women in everyday language. Lakoff (1974) was among the first to discuss the implications of a double bind for women and their language. Although a great deal of Lakoff's research has been brought into question, there does seem to be a consensus that women are not rewarded for the same types of language that men are rewarded for. Lakoff explains: "if he [any man] speaks (and generally behaves) as men in his culture are supposed to, he generally gains people's respect. But whichever course the woman takes - to speak women's language or not to - she will not be respected. So she cannot carry out the order, and the order is transmitted by society at large; there is no way to question it, no one even to direct the question to." Kuykendall (1980) has also discussed the implications of double binds for women. Although her conclusion is that all speakers must deal with these "linguistic dilemmas" since all speakers must adapt to a variety of situations and audiences, she does argue that "speakers can break their double binds only if they can identify them."

Certainly these attitudes about the social role of women and the expectations for language carry over to political women and their language. Both the politicians and the people they represent (or those that they hope to represent) have notions about how women should speak and how politicians should speak. The politician's language -- via speeches, advertisements, campaign literature, press conferences, debates -- is a very important element for the voters to weigh when they cast ballots. But do voters place the woman politician in a double bind because she is conforms to certain linguistic expectations?

In order to identify if these "linguistic dilemmas" do exist for women in politics, I decided to go to the experts --- the women themselves. My actual study was designed to be descriptive and exploratory. Data were collected through questionnaires and depth interviews. Both parts of the study were set up to answer the following research questions.

Research Question One: How do women in politics speak while acting in their public capacity? Are they aware of their speech? Have they made changes in their public language or in their voice?

Research Question Two: How do women in political office view their private language? Is it different than their public language?

Research Question Three: What do women in politics describe as political language? Do they see it as more distinctly male-associated than female-associated? Do they see differences between men's and women's languages?

The questionnaires were mailed to sixty women selected from a stratified random sample of the politicians listed in the 1983 National Women's Political Caucus' Directory of Elected Women Officials. The study was divided into two parts. The first part listed forty-five adjectives taken from the Bem scale. The subjects were asked to indicate how often they felt their languages reflected these qualities. Each word was to be ranked on the following scale: 1-almost never, 2-rarely, 3-sometimes, 4-frequently, and 5-very often. The respondents were also asked to respond for their public language, their private language, and how often they felt their constituents expected this type of language. Seven of these were returned (11.6%). The mean score for each characteristic was tabulated, and the results are shown in Table 1.

The second part of the questionnaire asked more specific questions about their public and private languages. Four of these were returned.

The study also consisted of four interviews. All of these women had held or do hold office on the local level. Their ages ranged from 25 to 60; two were members of a city council, one was a town meeting member, and one was a city treasurer. Their educational backgrounds, interests, and political histories all varied. They turned out to be a very eclectic group, and one rich with information on how the political process works. Each interview followed a schedule, and was audio-taped. The interviews lasted from 30 minutes to 90 minutes.

The data collected supplied some interesting responses to my research questions. Each question will be discussed below. All of the data from each source are included in the discussion.

Research Question One: How do women in public office speak? These self-reports indicated an interesting mosaic of responses. The numerical responses indicated several male-associated qualities, several neutral qualities, and several female-associated qualities. The terms that these women felt either frequently or very often described their public language were self-reliant, helpful, independent, conscientious,

264

assertive, happy, analytical, sympathetic, decisive, compassionate, sincere, self-sufficient, warm, friendly, leader-like, individualistic, and tactful. Other terms offered in the extended questionnaire were friendly, low-key and knowledgeable. The interviews also show that these were the qualities that women saw themselves projecting. Three of the women interviewed suggested that they liked to portray themselves as logical and informed. The fourth woman interviewed called her public style "simple and to the point." Three of the four women interviewed also suggested that their language also consisted of asking questions in addition to being knowledgeable. The questions asked are not because the women aren't aware of the topic under discussion, but because they feel a need to know all that is possible about the issue.

It appears from the data that women in politics have an awareness of their language. This awareness comes in part because they know others listen to them. One woman responded that she was aware of her language, "but not as much as I should be." One other responded, "I have learned...to be brief and not have possible double meanings." All four of the politicians interviewed spoke of nervousness while first in office. The nervousness stemmed from being in a new situation and in one case because of her own attempts to end sexist remarks made about her.

Most of the women indicated that the way they speak has changed some since they first entered office. One remarked that she tries to gear her language so that her constituents will understand her. Another woman responded that she tried to be more forceful. There were comments, especially from those women who were interviewed, that they felt self-conscious of the way that they spoke. One woman spoke with a marked regional variety and had asked others to do speaking for her in the past, since she felt that people would not listen to what she was saying. Another woman, whose voice has been affected by asthma, also remarked that she was very aware of "sounding like I'm going to burst into tears." The most interesting comment came from the woman who had not been opposed in ten years in office. She remarked that, "If I really had to go out and wage a campaign, I think I'd have to stop and think...." She went on to say that her insecurity about her public speaking would probably prevent her from seeking another term if she was opposed.

Research Question Two: How do women in public office view their private language? In brief, it appears that they don't see their private language as much different than their public language. The same descriptors that applied to their public language also applied to their private. Tender, soft-spoken and moody all made a gain of one point, but none of these were used to describe how they frequently spoke. Most of the women made comments like, "not much difference. I'm apt to say what I think or believe so long as it doesn't hurt anyone." The only exception to what many would say in private but not in public was swearing, although one woman commented that she does slip and swear in public from time to time. Among those women interviewed only one woman spoke of using her public voice in private, and when probed to explain the differences between the two she could only describe her public language as "more explanatory." One woman, who had originally said there was no difference in her speaking styles, commented that with her friends she could "say a whole lot less...but in Town Meeting, I just tried to be as logical as possible, because...through the years you learn that [being] irrational and yelling and just getting upset about things and spewing out rhetorical statements doesn't convince anybody."

Research Question Three: What do women in politics describe as political language? Do they see it as more male-associated than female-associated? Do they think that women speak differently from men? The numerical studies show no clear differences between how the politicians actually speak (or how they view their own speech) and how they feel they would expect anyone in political office to speak. Most interesting here is the rating <u>masculine</u> received from politicians. They felt their constituents expected any politician to almost never sound <u>masculine</u>. They also rated both their own public and private speech as almost never sounding <u>masculine</u>. The most interesting comments about language and general difference came from the interviews.

Two rather unexpected issues emerged from the interviews related to how the women viewed political language. The first was the general consensus among the women that women did speak differently from men. Three of the four women openly discussed differences between women's discourse and men's.

--- "We're [women] used to it [being open and friendly in conversation]. We're used to having to do it to get our point across. Otherwise, we're criticized for being aggressive, unpleasantly so.., So, I think we learn to use that."

--- "Men are more self-conscious about using sort of flowery, caring language... They, like, always have to be logical... I think women deal with much more human issues... I think women are much closer to what life is about. I think men have become very...abstract...it's like dinosaurs. They're going to have to die out...it's like this whole way of thinking that's becoming extinct, or if it doesn't we will. Women deal with children, they deal with the very basics of life. That leads to a different understanding."

266

--- Women are always better than men... I just feel that's true,
but I can't give you an example... It's the mother instinct,
taking care of children...

A second issue that emerged in the interviews was the role
of morality in public office and public discourse. One woman
openly labeled herself a "reformer" and added "I wish it weren't
necessary to reform. I wish people would behave like they were
supposed to." This woman got her start in politics during the
Eugene McCarthy campaign. She remarked, "I had no problem being
a queen for Gene, 'cause I'd never been dirty." Her strong views
of moral issues extend to city policies and local business
interests. While discussing a building that had added 2000 sq.
ft. without permission of the council, she said, "I said that
they should have to devote, not all of the new space, but some
portion of it to a social service use for nothing for awhile.
That this would be a moral and appropriate way to show companies
that they couldn't pull the wool over the city's eyes and get
away with it." Another woman, a city treasurer, said the most
important advice she could give to any other city treasurer was
to "be honest." Her discussion of what made a good public
speaker also showed her concern with moral issues. "...I think
the mayor does a good job...he gives a very honest presentation,
I mean, I think it's what he feels...he speaks from the heart."

Another woman, while discussing a speech given by a fellow
member of Town Meeting said, "I thought he was good because I
felt like he was genuine and sincere in his concerns about the
town." Women in politics seem to have a concern about people
being honest and saying what they feel. Good political discourse
is that which truly reflects the wishes of the people. The
fourth woman interviewed stressed how important it was for all
the members of the board of Selectpersons to work together. She
stressed that "getting people to talk together" was very
important in city government. She said, "I don't enjoy the
confrontational style that some people seem to enjoy...I really
don't think that it's effective. In that style...very frequently
there is less room for compromise and if you don't come out with
compromise you haven't achieved very much." Finally, she
concluded that all politicians need to "listen...We have to keep
talking and we have to keep listening to each other. If we
don't, it'll be chaos."

It seems that this preliminary look at the nature of
political women's discourse suggests several things. First, it
appears that women in politics are aware of their language and
are not making major changes to alter how they sound. These
women also reported that they did not significantly change their
language when they shifted from a public to a private situation.
If Lakoff is correct in her assumptions about women's language,
then a new type of discourse is being used in the world of

politics. If Lakoff's definition of women's language is not being used by these women, then these women should be in a double bind situation or the double bind is not applicable to these women. It appears to me that these women do speak as women since most clearly identified the distinction between men and women's discourse. Their reticence to alter their language tends to indicate that these women want to be themselves – language and all. Yet few mentioned double bind situations. Whether they have merely escaped them or whether the problem has been overstated needs to be further investigated. However, it does stand to reason that as more diverse types of people, those other than white males, become involved in politics, voter perceptions and expectations will change to include visions and sounds of politicians who are different.

Second, I was very intrigued with the low value given to masculine as a characteristic for self-reports of public discourse, private discourse and what the constituents expected. This certainly needs to be checked against male politicians. Do they think that their constituents don't want them to sound masculine? And do the constituents agree that this is not an appropriate political style?

Finally, the issue of the moral nature of political discourse is also compelling. This would be interesting to check against not only male self reports but also against actual voter expectations. Remember that voters perceive women politicians to be more moral than their male peers. This may be a case where the folk myths about women being "better" have carried over to the voter or it may be a case where the woman politician's discourse is more centered around arguments based on morality than expediency, cost, or tradition. Gilligan (1982) has recently begun to discover that women's moral logics are constructed in ways distinct from men's. If this is the case, then their discourse would be different to reflect this distinct view.

Women in this country have only been able to participate in electoral politics for less than a century and they did not begin to run for office in sizeable numbers until 25 years ago. Social progress takes time. While it is still too early to make predictions about the impact women will have on political discourse, this study seems to indicate that women in politics do not see their language as a limitation to their performance.

REFERENCES

Bateson, G. (1972). The group dynamics of schizophrenia. In *Steps to an ecology of mind*. New York: Ballantine Books.

Boston Phoenix. (1982, November 2). p.7.

Diamond, I. (1977). *Sex roles in the state house*. New Haven: Yale University Press.

Gelb, J., and Palley, M.L. (1982). *Women and public policies*. Princeton: Princeton University Press.

Gilligan, C. (1982). *In a different voice: Psychological theory and women's development*. Cambridge, Massachusetts: Harvard University Press.

Goodman, E. (1984, 16 February). Winning votes for women. *Boston Globe*, p. 25.

Kirkpatrick, J. (1974). *Political woman*. New York: Basic Books.

Kirkpatrick, J. (1976). *The new presidential elite*. New York: Basic Books.

Klein, E. (1984). *Gender politics: From consciousness to mass politics*. Cambridge, Massachusetts: Harvard University Press.

Kuykendall, E. (1980). Breaking the double binds. *Language and style, 13*(4), 81-93.

Lakoff, R. (1975). *Language and woman's place*. New York: Harper & Row.

Lamson, P. (1968). *Few are chosen*. Boston: Houghton Mifflin Company.

Lamson, P. (1979). *In the vanguard*. Boston: Houghton Mifflin Company.

Mandel, R. (1981). *In the running: The new woman candidate*. New Haven: Ticknore & Fields.

Margolis, D. (1980). The invisible hands: Sex roles and the diversity of labor in two local political parties. In D. Stewart (Ed.), *Women and local politics*. Metuchen, New Jersey: The Scarecrow Press, Inc.

Randall, V. (1982). *Women and politics*. New York: St. Martin's Press.

Sapiro, V. (1983). The political integration of women. Urbana, Illinois: University of Illinois Press.

Tolchin, S. and Tolchin, M. (1973). Clout-womanpower and politics. New York: Coward, McCann & Geoghegan.

TABLE I

Mean Scores For Questionnaire Responses
1 = almost never, 2 = rarely, 3 = sometimes, 4 = frequently, 5 = very often

Language Characteristics	*	public language	private language	how often do your constituents expect this
self-reliant	(m)	4.42	4.57	4.57
yielding	(f)	2.42	3.00	2.28
helpful	(a)	4.14	4.28	4.71
cheerful	(f)	4.42	4.14	4.28
moody	(a)	1.28	2.14	1.28
independent	(m)	4.57	4.71	4.14
shy	(f)	1.14	2.00	1.28
conscientious	(a)	4.71	4.71	4.85
affectionate	(f)	2.57	4.28	2.28
theatrical	(a)	2.00	1.42	2.33
assertive	(m)	4.00	3.85	4.42
flattering	(a)	3.42	3.14	3.00
happy	(a)	4.14	4.14	4.00
unpredictable	(a)	2.28	2.28	2.00
forceful	(m)	3.71	3.42	4.28
feminine	(f)	3.00	3.28	3.14
analytical	(m)	4.42	4.41	4.14
sympathic	(f)	4.00	3.71	3.85
jealous	(a)	1.00	1.71	1.28
sensitive	(f)	3.57	4.00	3.42
decisive	(a)	4.42	4.14	4.57

* The Bem scale assigns a gender association with most words.
  f = female, m = male, a = androgynous or neutral

gentle	(f)	2.66	3.33	2.82
conventional	(a)	3.57	3.00	3.57
compassionate	(f)	4.00	4.14	3.83
sincere	(a)	4.85	4.41	5.00
self-sufficient	(m)	4.85	4.42	4.71
soothing	(a)	3.00	3.28	2.28
conceited	(a)	1.57	1.7.	1.85
dominant	(m)	3.28	3.14	3.14
soft-spoken	(f)	3.14	2.17	3.28
masculine	(m)	1.3	1.5	1.15
warm	(f)	4.14	3.71	4.14
solemn	(a)	2.71	2.28	2.71
tender	(f)	2.00	3.00	2.14
friendly	(a)	4.28	4.42	4.57
aggressive	(m)	2.85	2.85	3.14
gullible	(f)	1.28	1.85	1.00
leader-like	(m)	4.42	4.14	5.00
child-like	(f)	1.28	1.71	1.00
individualistic	(m)	4.28	4.28	4.28
harsh	(a)	1.42	1.57	1.28
unsystematic	(a)	1.42	1.57	1.14
competitive	(m)	2.85	3.14	3.57
tactful	(a)	4.14	3.17	4.71
ambitious	(m)	3.14	3.57	3.14

CHAPTER 16

CAMPAIGN 1984: THE FERRARO FACTOR
The Politics of Pragmatism and Prejudice

William G. Davey and Michael E. Mayer
Arizona State University

To most Americans, the nomination of Geraldine Ferraro was a striking political innovation. In the transition from a loosely structured conceptualization to an idea whose time had come, the actual selection, nomination, and candidacy of Geraldine Ferraro was a complex process of symbolic influence and the restructuring of political expectations in presidential politics. In much the same way as John Kennedy broke the religious barrier, Ferraro's candidacy was a fundamental reform of our political system. The historic reform of shattering the gender barrier made the Ferraro candidacy much more than a bold strategy designed to transform a faltering Mondale campaign into a credible claim to the presidency. Indeed, political analysts, candidates, party power brokers, and average Americans freely offered their perspectives on the Ferraro factor.

For communication scholars, the import of this nomination assumes a largely symbolic nature. It is a complex set of symbolic acts that may well impact on the long-term character of American presidential politics. This paper explores this symbolic nature by focusing on the motivating factors surrounding the nomination, the impact of the feminist influence, and the communication strategies involved with the finance and abortion issues.

Brenda Robinson Hancock (1972) argued that the radical feminist movement began in 1967-1968 with students and social activists who had promoted solidarity through the power of sisterhood and naming men the enemy. The movement was also associated with the New Left, and generated several manifestos which negated capitalism and men. Consciousness-raising became a common method to identify the causes of women's inferior position and exploitation. The perceived radicalism associated with women's liberation movement has helped to create a social reality among some that links contemporary feminist behavior with the movement of the sixties. Despite an extensive evolution of goals, Ferraro had to counter the numerous stereotypes originally generated by opponents of the early fight for women's rights and resurrected by current opponents. During the campaign, media recalled their early perceptions of feminists as "just chicks with personal hangups" (Willis, 1970, p. 57).

In contrast, the National Organization for Women (NOW) was formed by mostly professional women to promote equality in the workplace. This reformist brand of feminism stressed quality and competence as its goals. NOW has worked actively within the system to affect public policy, and while it still promotes and adheres to the power of unity among women, it also has targeted institutions and persons who promote sexist practices that limit a woman's ability to access the benefits of society.

Although frequently perceived as a singular construct by the media, there is no evidence in the historical development of feminist thinking to support this view. The differing orientations presented by groups of women have impacted significantly on the development of the feminist movement. Joan Kelly (1984) perhaps presented a more realistic view of feminism when she wrote:

> In the United States, we oscillate between participating in, and separating from, organizations and institutions that remain alienating and stubbornly male dominant. We are pulled in one direction by a Marxist-feminist analysis of the socioeconomic bases of women's oppression, and in another direction by a radical feminist focus on male control of women's bodies as a key to patriarchy. Our differences have not hampered the ad hoc coalitions formed around struggles for abortion and protection against sterilization abuse; for affirmative action, maternity leave, and daycare; for the Equal Rights Amendment and the right of sexual preference. But differences in theoretical position do affect our broader social commitments and political alliances. They affect our conception of the scope of the women's movement; its relation to issues of race and class; and specifically, whether or how to join with what are still male-dominant movements to inequities stemming from an imperialist organization of the world economy and society. (p. 55)

Other feminist writers have clearly articulated goals for the women's movement. Nancy Reeves (1982) for example suggests three goals for the new woman: "First is the claim to full participation in all fields of work, including politics and government; second, the right to equal training and to equal pay; third, the pressure for institutional change that would rationalize the double burden of personal and public responsibilities" (p. 17).

The Ferraro candidacy and ensuing campaign were permeated with adherence to the pro-abortion posture of both radical and moderate feminism, the power of unity among women, and the identification with women's rights as a legitimate goal of society. In addition to the tension created between radical and reformist feminism, the distinctions inferred by those outside the movement (specifically the popular opinion media) acted as motivation for the communication which took place within the campaign. The major symbolic importance of the Ferraro factor occurred because of her unique position as the first female vice-presidential candidate.

To understand the impact of the Ferraro factor, it is necessary to investigate Walter Mondale's motivation for her selection. A review of the popular literature suggests three major motives: 1) The nomination of Ferraro was a political payoff to the Feminist Movement; 2) The nomination would help restructure Mondale's image from unimaginative to bold and innovative; and 3) Ferraro might well appeal to traditionally Democratic ethnic groups, as well as some others, who abandoned the party for Reagan in 1980.

The most frequently mentioned motivation for the Ferraro candidacy was the payoff for feminist support. To some extent, Mondale encouraged the pressure from the feminists, especially the National Organization for Women. NOW endorsed Mondale early in the campaign and "ecstatically welcomed his promise to seriously consider a woman" for his running mate (Morganthau, 1984b, p. 22). Although the movement for a woman vice-president began as early as October 1983 (Ferraro, 1985, pp. 60-84; O'Reilly, 1984), Mondale's promise to the NOW convention in late June 1984 led to intense lobbying for a woman nominee. Morganthau (1984b, p. 22) reported that "NOW approved a resolution threatening a floor fight in San Francisco if Mondale's nominee were unacceptable." In fact, Church (1984a) indicated that Mondale's interview process led NOW not only to threaten a floor fight, but to claim that a floor fight might be won. Even Ferraro indicated before her nomination that "she would allow her name to be placed in nomination as a 'symbolic gesture' if Mondale selected a man" (Doerner, 1984c, p. 17). As a result, some argued that Ferraro's selection was a result of such pressure. Columnist Meg Greenfield posited that "[F]anaticism . . . was precisely what got the whole business going in the first place" (1984, p. 72). In an editorial, The Nation asserted that "she owes her candidacy to the Women's movement--not, perhaps, to organized Feminism or to any single ideological drive of the last many years, but rather to the radical expansion of possible roles for women in America" (1984). While some viewed the selection of a woman as unrealistic, many believed that NOW was exercising appropriate political influence. Suffice it to say that Ferraro never underestimated the role which the feminist movement had in developing her candidacy, and her positions on the issues were due to her feminist perspective (Ferraro, 1985, pp. 132-38).

Although pressure from the feminist movement clearly motivated Mondale to select a woman as his vice-presidental nominee, the second consideration was to improve Mondale's image as an imaginative leader. In early 1984, Berg argued that Mondale was too traditional and unimaginative to select a woman as his running mate. In a Time cover story on potential female nominees, Dianne Feinstein doubted "Mondale would even seriously consider a female running mate" (Doerner, 1984e, p. 27). While such attitudes continued to prevail during Mondale's vice-presidential interviews (Shapiro, 1984c), reporter Lance Morrow quoted a political consultant who asserted that if Mondale ". . . is 20 points down, he may say it's time to roll the dice. That's where Ferraro comes in at convention time" (1984, pp. 21-22). Others indicated the potential that ". . . the right woman might bring a feeling of something fresh and new to a campaign that so far has sounded like a large, heavy suitcase being tumbled, slow motion, down an interminable flight of stairs" (Morrow, 1984, pp. 19-20). When the Ferraro selection was made, Church and Magnuson (1984) indicated Mondale and his aides found that a bold stroke, even if it were risky, was needed after Mondale's loss in the California primary. Morganthau (1984c, p. 16) reported the Ferraro nomination had ". . . quelled the complaints of those who said Walter Mondale lacks imagination and daring." Morganthau further indicated that Reagan aides ". . . conceded that Mondale had, at the least, stabilized his floundering candidacy with the bold choice . . ." (p. 20). Even the conservative opinion magazine National Review begrudgingly wrote that "Walter Mondale, perhaps for the first time in his political career, has done something interesting . . ." and that "the choice of a woman in itself does add a touch of color to an otherwise drab Mondale operation . . ." (1984b, p. 13).

The third possible motive for Ferraro's nomination was related to the need to energize his campaign to appeal to traditional Democratic voters who deserted the presidential ticket in 1980. Ferraro was perceived as helping with as many as four demographic groups. Morganthau wrote that "Mondale aides believe . . . she can catalyze the women's vote" (1984a, p. 23). More interestingly, some thought Ferraro would appeal to ethnic blue-collar voters. Newsweek reported that "the other goal is tougher: recapturing voters who went Republican in 1980. Many are ethnic Americans from blue-collar backgrounds: the Democrat's flag and family imagery, together with Ferraro's Catholic, Italian-American heritage, should help" (Morganthau, 1984a, p. 24). Church, writing for Time (1984c, p. 20) added that "well educated suburbanites [who] may be attracted to her as a symbol of new ideas and new departures in politics . . ." and "[v]oters under 40, who in recent polls seemed to be turning heavily toward Reagan." The net effect of her nomination was to ". . . give the Democrats new hope in New Jersey, Connecticut, Ohio, Illinois, and Michigan. They also hoped to make some inroads in Reagan's western turf--in Oregon and Washington . . . and perhaps in California as well" (Morganthau, 1984a, p. 24).

Despite the controversy associated with the Ferraro nomination, some evidence indicated the gambit might be successful in appealing to voters who might otherwise vote Republican. Feminist Mim Kelber (1984) argued that three polls, including two from

1983, indicated that a woman would increase Democratic votes. NOW President Judy Goldsmith argued that a woman in the vice-presidential slot ". . . appeared to mean the margin of victory" (O'Reilly, 1984, p. 29). More traditional politicians such as Speaker of the House Tip O'Neill and Governors Mario Cuomo of New York and Richard Celeste of Ohio also supported a woman candidate (Morrow, 1984). New York City Mayor Ed Koch bubbled that "A woman on the ticket would bring more women, and not just women. It would attract young people because of the idea of a breakthrough. Let me tell ya [sic], it's better than chicken soup" (Morrow, 1984, pp. 18-19). Initially, the nomination of Ferraro appeared successful. Polls taken between the announcement of the nomination and the end of the Democratic convention gave the Democrats reason to cheer the selection. Mondale's campaign chair James Johnson stated ". . . that 'tracking' polls showed a rise in the popularity of the ticket every night of the convention, with an especially sharp jump of 10 to 15 points after the nominees' speeches on Thursday. The same tracking polls showed that during the convention, more men 50 and older changed their mind than in any other category" (Church, 1984c, p. 20). Other polls also concurred. The first Newsweek poll after the Ferraro announcement showed the Democratic ticket within six points of Reagan and Bush (Morganthau, 1984c). One week later, the same poll showed the Democrats ahead by two points, although this effect was attributed to the afterglow of the convention (Morganthau, 1984a).

While effective political lobbying by feminist groups opened the door for a female candidate, Ferraro's qualifications secured the nomination for her (Stanley, 1984). Her record in New York and Washington illustrated a personal and professional competence. After a supposedly elaborate scrutiny of press clippings, voting records, financial disclosure statements, and other public records, Mondale aides proclaimed there were "no skeletons in her closet" (Morganthau, 1984c, p. 20). Despite this proclamation, Ferraro encountered three major difficulties during the campaign: 1) gender issues and ideological tension; 2) finances; and 3) abortion. Several analysts suggested her finances may have been her ultimate skeleton.

Gender and Ideological Tension

For the first month, it appeared that balancing the ticket on gender was not problematic. However, as in past elections where balancing variables such as region, religion, ideology, etc., helped secure nominations, these variables often became central issues in the campaign. So it was for Geraldine Ferraro. For the first time, gender permeated discussions of the candidate and the substantive issues. Ferraro's alignment with feminist backers precipitated tension concerning the issues of finances and abortion. Ferraro was expected to assume a pro-abortion posture and to articulate at least a moderate feminist perspective on the issues. In addition, she was expected to be competent, independent, and articulate in her interpersonal relations with feminists and the Mondale organization. These expectations were in sharp contrast to the dependency she articulated regarding her finances and the differences in her public and personal posture on abortion. In addition, Ferraro suffered an array of sexual innuendos based on stereotypes espoused by opponents of feminism and communicated by media representatives eager to make gender an issue in the campaign. We begin with the issue of sexism because in many ways this issue impacted on all others.

Gender affected several technical aspects of the campaign in addition to the overt and strategic use of sexual slurs. The fact that Ferraro was female led to difficulties for the press and members of both the Democratic and Republican campaigns. Gender permeated the norms of interaction which developed with the press. Time (Andersen, 1984) reported that Gregory Fossedel of the Wall Street Journal was booed when he demanded that she answer a question about her finances at a news conference. It is difficult to recall such behavior in a previous national campaign.

The press faced unique problems due to the combination of Ferraro's sex and the inability of the English language to generate equality in titles. One major problem was what to call Ferraro. The New York Times insisted on labeling Ferraro "Miss," partially because the Times refuses to use the title "Ms." When Ferraro objected, the Times began to call her Mrs. Ferraro, which led Times columnist William Safire to comment, "It breaks my heart to suggest this, but the time has come for Ms." (Time, 1984, p. 105). Although some papers dealt with the problem by referring to Ferraro only by her surname, some readers found this objectionable (Time, 1984). In contrast, public opinion magazines apparently took pleasure in the name controversy. The conservative National Review (1984b; W.F. Buckley, 1984) tended to refer to her as Mrs. Ferraro. More interestingly, the perceived liberal New Republic used a variety of appellations. The first article after the nomination consistently referred to her as Mrs. Zaccaro (Breslin, 1984). The lead for New Republic's article on her financial difficulties began, "she says Ferraro, and he says Zaccaro . . ." (1984, p. 5). Both magazines used terms indicating that Ferraro was inextricably tied to her mate, an occurrence rare in political reporting.

The press also had difficulty selecting items to report about Ferraro. Newsweek (Mathews, 1984) opened its story on Ferraro's nomination noting that she wore a size 6 dress, causing one incensed reader to demand Reagan and Bush's suit sizes so that she could make an informed choice (Eng-Wong, 1984). Newsweek did a special story on the impressions that Italian-American women had of Ferraro (J. Buckley, 1984). It is difficult to imagine a male vice-presidential candidate treated in the same fashion. Reporters do not typically concern themselves with suit sizes, nor does the press normally do stories on the way demographic groups similar to the candidate perceive the candidate.

Geraldine Ferraro's nomination also caused difficulties for both party organizations. The Democratic problems were limited to developing "an etiquette for running mates of opposite sexes. They do not kiss, hug, or even join hands in the classic raised-arm political salute" (Alpern, 1984, p. 20). While the Democrats were limited to issues of etiquette, the Republicans had a more complex form of symbolic difficulty in dealing with Ferraro. It is unclear if these statements were generated overtly, but the very existence of multiple embarrassing double entendres suggests sexist intent. For example, Reagan's campaign director Ed Rollins evaluated the nomination by saying that "Geraldine Ferraro may be the biggest bust politically in recent history" (Doerner, 1984d, p. 17). Vice President Bush committed a similar gaffe when he evaluated his debate with Ferraro by boasting that "we tried to kick a little ass last night," a statement which he dismissed as "an old Texas football expression" (Shapiro, 1984e, p. 29). Other Republicans made more clearly sexist comments. Barbara Bush referred to Ferraro as "That $4 million. . . . I can't say it, but it rhymes with rich" (Doerner, 1984b, p. 31). Although Bush claimed that the unspoken word was witch, most listeners probably thought of a word similar to the one used by Bush's press secretary Peter Tenfly, who speculated that Ferraro might appear "too bitchy" in the vice-presidental debate (Doerner, 1984b, p. 31). These remarks, regardless of the extent of their sexist intent, would have been interpreted differently, or in some cases would have been rephrased if Ferraro had not been female.

Despite the denial that the previous comments were overtly sexist, they clearly called attention to Ferraro's gender. The lack of stability in the norms of interaction during the campaign also caused potentially discriminatory acts, both inadvertent and overt. Rather innocent were the occurrences such as the presentation of a wrist corsage to Ferraro before she spoke at a fund raising dinner (Doerner, 1984a). Blatant exploitation of gender was more common. Columnist George Will, who speculated that Ferraro and her husband had not paid their fair share of taxes, generated a denial from Ferraro and a demand for an apology. Will's apology, however, consisted of a dozen pink roses accompanied by a note that read, "Has anyone told you that you are cute when you're mad?" (Andersen, 1984).

In addition to the sexist attitudes of some politicians and media personalities, at least parts of the electorate also contributed to the sexism. It was argued: Women were unfit for leadership positions; women were unbalanced during their monthly cycle; and women belonged at home. Symptomatic of the leadership issue were the comments of one woman who called a Boston radio station and demanded to know, ". . . what business a woman has in the White House" (Morganthau, 1984c). An Italian-American woman added, "A woman is not strong enough to be running the country. I would never want her as President, even if she is Italian" (J. Buckley, 1984). Florence Robinson of Memphis went so far to say, "I'm a liberated woman, but I don't think a woman should be running things in Washington" (Thomas, 1984a, p. 42). Interestingly, all these statements were from women from specific groups to which Ferraro was supposed to appeal. The generic attitude against women in leadership positions may be best expressed in the campaign experience of Roxanne Conlin, the Democratic nominee for Governor of Iowa in 1982: "The sort of thing one does is campaign at grain elevators. I'd walk in and say, 'Hi, I'm Roxanne Conlin and I'm running for Governor.' People would stand there, like 'you're kidding.' One man just laughed for five minutes straight" (Morrow, 1984, p. 21).

Perhaps the most serious sexist line of argument made prominent during the campaign concerned the spurious correlation of psychological instability and the menstrual cycle. As Dr. Edgar Bernan phrased it, every month women were subject to a "raging hormonal imbalance" (Morrow, 1984, p. 21). A woman called a radio talk show wanting to know if Ferraro had "been through menopause yet" (Morganthau, 1984c, p. 20). Time (Morrow) dismissed those concerns because women in office have not behaved differently from men, they had passed menopause anyway, and that men such as Richard Nixon and Lyndon Johnson had behaved rather bizarrely when they were in office. Despite Time's attempt to counter the argument, the condescending tone and the parenthetical comment on menopause leads us to believe that the media assisted in perpetuating this fallacy, and that indeed some members of the electorate harbored this belief.

The final sexist objection to Ferraro's nomination was the feeling that a woman's place was in the home. Two groups voiced this opinion. The religious right objected on biblical grounds. As Greg Dixon, the former national secretary for the Moral Majority, stated, "I think God had a plan for men to be responsible for affairs of government. The Bible just teaches that the head of the man is Christ, the head of the woman is man, and that's God's order of things. God has made the woman, biologically and psychologically, keeper of the home. It is rare to find a woman to stand up to the rigor of politics" (Morrow, 1984, p. 21). The Democrats tended to trivialize the impact of the religious right as they expected few votes from this group anyway.

The second "home" objection came from labor union members and this attitude gave the Democrats great concern. Ohio labor consultant Don Switzer explained his perceptions of labor's view: "Labor people have that old macho attitude. They want a woman who stays in the home and the man outside working. It's a real serious problem if you have a woman Vice-President" (Morrow, 1984, p. 24). Oral historian Studs Terkel disagreed, "The issue is dead. The guys in the bar have been conditioned by idols like Barbara Stanwyck. Now they're ready for a Gerri Ferraro or a Pat Schroeder" (Morrow, 1984, p. 21). While this controversy was never resolved, polls indicated that Reagan gathered substantially more union support than in 1980 when he gained an almost even split with Carter (Tifft, 1984).

Finances

The controversy over Ferraro's finances arose suddenly, developing from a minimal mention in the news magazines on August 20 to a cover story two weeks later. Shapiro (1984b, p. 20) reported that the excitement over Ferraro's nomination turned to "agony . . . as Geraldine Ferraro desperately struggled to prepare answers to dozens of questions about her tangled finances and those of her husband, New York real-estate entrepreneur John Zaccaro." The substantive issues involving finances were three: 1) congressional disclosure forms; 2) the legality of her 1978 campaign contributions; and 3) appropriate payment of taxes (Chaze, 1984). The substance of the arguments relating to finances was eventually determined to be minimal. On the question of exempting Zaccaro's finances on congressional disclosure forms, Cifelli (1984) argued that Ferraro may have broken congressional rules. However, most mitigated the impact of the infraction, suggesting the rules require that "you have two separate refrigerators" (Andersen, 1984, p. 16). The congressional campaign financing issue had been resolved by having Ferraro sell her interest in a building at a substantial profit to her partner, who, in turn, sold the building to Zaccaro. Despite the fact that, according to Ferraro, the deal did not look legal or ethical, it was legal (Chaze, 1984). As for their tax bill, Zaccaro and Ferraro paid approximately 40% of their income in taxes, which U.S. News (Chaze) noted was more than most people in their bracket paid. Additionally, Ferraro and Zaccaro voluntarily paid back taxes resulting from "an accountant's error" on the 1978 real estate deal. In the end, The Nation editorialized that the flap over Ferraro's finances might be nothing more than a blip (1984, p. 131). As the campaign progressed, however, J. Buckley (1984, p. 12) indicated that "the euphoria that swept the [Italian] neighborhood [in Boston] in July has faded somewhat, due in part to the well publicized financial problems with Ferraro. . . ." In analyzing the campaign as a whole, Doerner (1984a, p. 84) argued that "[H]er campaign never fully made up for the loss of momentum caused by the financial crisis. . . ."

While it is clear that Ferraro's financial situation did not help the campaign, the symbolism associated with this issue required the Democrats to alter strategy by negating the "sleaze" factor, raising questions about Mondale's leadership, and questioning Ferraro's competence because of her sex.

Upon claiming the nomination in June, Mondale had planned to attack Reagan on what the Democrats saw as "the disregard for propriety, if not the rule of law. More than thirty Reagan appointees have been investigated for one thing or another" (Thomas, 1984b). Ferraro's financial difficulties, however, negated whatever benefit the Mondale campaign might have hoped to obtain from the "sleaze" factor (New Republic, 1984; Shapiro, 1984b). Ironically, both the mainstream liberal and conservative press argued that Mondale and Ferraro had been caught in the reforms pushed through by the liberal Democrats after the Watergate scandal (National Review, 1984a; New Republic, 1984).

Perhaps more importantly, the flap over Ferraro's finances brought Mondale's leadership into question. The financial difficulties effectively negated the "bold leadership" factor that motivated Mondale to select Ferraro in the first place. The difficulties occurred despite the fact that Mondale supposedly had scrutinized carefully potential vice-presidential candidates. During the selection process, Mondale wanted to make certain that his "choice has an unassailable personal history that will stand up under harsh media scrutiny" (Beck, 1984, pp. 37-39). However, the financial review of potential running mates had been conducted in only two days. In fact, one Mondale aide indicated the campaign could have done a better job if they had spent more time on the disclosure process (Church, 1984b). Goldman described the entire episode by suggesting that the "derelictions were more nettlesome than grave, but Mondale's men had too little time for detailed financial inquiries and so were not armored against trouble when it came" (1984, p. 83). Although Ferraro's problems were not considered sufficient to cause her removal from the ticket, the difficulties symbolically accentuated questions about Mondale's leadership ability. The liberal opinion magazine New Republic, which might have been expected to be sympathetic to Mondale and Ferraro, raised the leadership issue by arguing that the vice-presidential selection process was flawed. "Apparently, the Mondale people failed even to look at the Ferraro financial forms on file in the House of Representatives. For Mr. Mondale, the doubts raised have nothing to do with ethics or propriety but with competence" (New Republic, 1984, p. 6). As expected, the Republicans used Ferraro's finances to attack Mondale's ability to run the nation. Senator Paul Laxalt was typical of the Republican position when he asked, "If Walter Mondale can't even run his own campaign, how in the world can we expect him to successfully negotiate with the Soviets?" (Walsh, 1984, p. 26). Thus, the leadership issue which had been softened by the Ferraro nomination was in turn negated by her tangled finances.

The final symbolic effect associated with Ferraro's finances can be tied to the previous discussion of gender. Cifelli indicated that the controversy over the finances in Ferraro's initial congressional campaign would not have occurred if she had lived in a community property state such as California where ". . . she could have allowed him [Zaccaro] to finance her campaign openly--[as] Jane Fonda . . . [had for] the 1976 Senate campaign of her husband, Tom Hayden. . . ." (Cifelli, 1984, p. 136). In addition, Ferraro and Zaccaro had ". . . paid an extra $6,000 to $7,000 to file [income taxes] separately in hopes of keeping Zaccaro's business out of the public eye" (Quinn, 1984, p. 69). This strategy failed to prevent the disclosure of his business ventures because Ferraro had benefited from his holdings. Symbolically, the difficulties over Ferraro's finances demonstrated that she was a female who was viewed as dependent upon her spouse. The Nation editorialized that ". . . [T]he larger society still holds standards and maintains laws that do not recognize women as equal partners in the business world or independent political actors-- . . . . If John Zaccaro ran for office with a wife safely at home and a business all to himself, it would be hard to put together the scandal that has been inflicted unfairly on Geraldine Ferraro" (1984, p. 132). Oddly enough, Ferraro herself contributed to the perception of dependency. After Zaccaro initially refused to release his financial statements, Ferraro attempted to explain his actions with a statement that not only demonstrated her dependency but also accentuated her ethnicity: "If you've ever been married to Italian men, you know what it's like" (Shapiro, 1984b). In the minds of at least some voters, the statement violated the traditional value of dependence that Italian women are supposed to accept. One Italian-American woman suggested that Ferraro had "belittled" her husband (J. Buckley, 1984).

Thus, while Ferraro's finances presented the Republicans with a minimally effective substantive issue, the symbolic effects were more significant. The finance issue enhanced doubts about Mondale's competence, and negatively emphasized both her gender and ethnicity.

Abortion

The final substantive issue to cause difficulty for Ferraro was abortion. In an interview with Vogue (Henry, 1984, p. 721) Ferraro explained her position on abortion: "I was raised in a convent; and if I were to become pregnant, I would never have an abortion, even at my age. . . . However, if I were to become pregnant as a result of rape, I'm not sure I'd be so righteous. That decision would have to be mine, with nobody telling me what to do." Prior to her nomination and throughout the campaign, Ferraro attempted to differentiate her personal position on abortion from her political stance. Stanley (1984, p. 24) explained Ferraro's position as ". . . pro-choice as a matter of public policy; as a matter of conscience, she is against abortion. 'I'm a Catholic,' she says, 'and I accept the teachings of my faith.' But in fact, Ferraro admits that she is not against abortion in cases of rape and has mixed feelings about the problem of pregnancy in young girls."

While the abortion issue plagued both Mondale and Ferraro, the controversy was perhaps more telling in Ferraro's case because her position was not congruent with the position of her church. The disparity between her position and that of the Roman Catholic Church began in June, prior to becoming Mondale's running mate, when New York Archbishop John O'Connor stated: "I don't see how a Catholic in good conscience can vote for a candidate who explicitly supports abortion" (Shapiro, 1984d, p. 26). Although Catholic bishops later urged the clergy to refrain from supporting political candidates, the issue arose again when O'Connor attacked Ferraro for misrepresenting the Catholic position as not monolithic. This attack, which Ed Magnuson (1984) of _Time_ called almost gratuitous, was based on a 1982 letter Ferraro had circulated. While she referred to individual Catholics who did not agree with the Church's position, O'Connor was referring to Catholic doctrine (Magnuson). In effect, he had misrepresented Ferraro's position to other members of the Church hierarchy, and sustained the attack on her abortion position. Archbishop Bernard Law of Boston further stated, "Voters should make abortion the critical issue of the campaign" (Shapiro, 1984d, p. 26). After Ferraro had given a speech in heavily Catholic Scranton, Pennsylvania, Bishop James Timlin sharply attacked her attempt to separate her public duties from her religious views as "absolutely ridiculous." He likened her abortion stance to the slavery issue. "'You can't say,' Timlin argued, 'I'm personally opposed to slavery, but I don't care if others down the street have them'" (Magnuson, 1984, p. 26).

Although Catholic Democratic office holders Senator Ted Kennedy and Mario Cuomo, who oppose imposing the Church's moral teachings on the country as a whole, defended the pro-choice position (Magnuson, 1984), the controversy had two negative effects on the Democratic campaign. First, the entire religious issue, of which abortion was a major part, deflected the Democrats from the substantive issues they had hoped to emphasize. Second, the difficulties with the Church hurt the ticket with traditional Catholic voters. As one Italian-American woman from Boston phrased it: "She shouldn't be arguing with the Church" (J. Buckley, 1984, p. 12). While the abortion issue, and the attendant controversy with the Catholic Church undoubtedly cost votes, the Ferraro campaign staff felt that the confrontation was "inspired by the candidate's sex." One aide claimed that "Teddy Kennedy has the same position on abortion, yet he was never attacked by the hierarchy in 1980" (Doerner, 1984a, p. 85).

Election results presented some curious findings. The result that occurred with union voters (an almost even split for Reagan), also occurred with the other groups to which Ferraro was supposed to appeal: 55% of the women, 54% of Italian-Americans, and 56% of Catholic voters supported Ronald Reagan (Shapiro, 1984a; Tifft, 1984). Time reported that "Republican strategists believe Ferraro, a Catholic, lost votes by tangling with Catholic Bishops over abortion" (Thomas, 1984a). The results for young professionals were even worse—67% selected Reagan (Thomas, 1984a). On the whole "Ferraro failed to become what Walter Mondale, perhaps naively, desperately hoped she would: An electoral alchemist who would transform the lead of his campaign into White House gold" (Doerner, 1984a, p. 84). Not only did Ferraro fail to help Mondale win votes, exit polls indicated that her presence on the ticket only led 16% to be more likely to vote for the ticket. In contrast, 26% said it made them less likely to vote for Mondale-Ferraro. The responses of women were only marginally better with 19% more likely and 24% less likely (Thomas).

While hindsight revealed to her campaign manager, John Sasso, that early estimates of Ferraro's ballot-box appeal were unrealistic (Doerner, 1984a), Mondale chose to ignore ample evidence that the Ferraro nomination would be an unsuccessful gambit. Both Mashek of U.S. News (1984) and Morrow of Time (1984) reported a poll that indicated a female running mate for Mondale would gain some younger women voters, but lose older men voters. National Review (1984b, p. 11) reported that politicians, at least initially, agreed "the Ferraro elevation despite all the publicity, left the political professionals who were milling around the San Francisco hotel lobbies with the collective impression that her presence on the ticket would probably amount, when all is said and done, to a wash, or, possibly, a slight minus. . . ."

In reviewing the evidence, one quickly acquires the impression that in many ways Geraldine Ferraro was a victim of circumstances. While she had hoped to focus on issues, she was forced to devote significant time to gender-based matters. It is clear that Mondale viewed Ferraro as a savior archetype hoping that she would miraculously redeem his ailing campaign. Mondale expected Ferraro to conform to unrealistic expectations. He expected her to appeal to significantly diverse demographic audiences; to project an image which represented traditional values. In many ways he expected her to be merely perfect—because perfection may have been the only way to save his candidacy.

The pragmatics of the campaign, however, created different demands for Geraldine Ferraro. She was forced to react to endemic sexism from the media, the political organizations, and some members of the electorate. This problem was especially difficult for Ferraro to counteract. Linguist Julia Penelope (1982) suggests six basic classes of arguments against eradicating sexist

285

usage in English. Among these are denial, creativity, trivialization, and esthetic reasons. When sexism in the campaign seemed overt, it was denied; when it was allegedly spontaneous, it was attributed to creativity or esthetic turns of phrases; when it was challenged, it was pronounced trivial. When Ferraro attempted to object, she was criticized for whining and unduly complaining. Ferraro felt she was victimized by the gender issue. It served to deflect attention from the substantive issues of the campaign. More importantly, it forced Ferraro to adopt victimage type responses. Burke (1945) suggests that people develop vocabularies that are selections of reality. Ferraro's reality transformed from opposing Republicans to defending herself. The campaign deteriorated to prolonged discussions of abortion, finances, and gender. Ferraro was unable to maintain control of the issues discussed in the campaign. The dissonance caused by the contrast of her personal and public posture on abortion resulted in a totally nonproductive fight with the Church whose position demanded conformity.

In the end, the Ferraro factor served to illustrate the pervasiveness of institutional sexism in presidental politics. Geraldine Ferraro became acutely aware of a lack of infrastructure able to accommodate a woman vice-president. One can speculate that she anticipated this. What she did not anticipate was the aggressive position of her church, the prejudices expressed by her opponents, the media, and the electorate. Ferraro revolutionized the political process because she was first, and the opening of the door appears to be the biggest impact of the Ferraro factor--a fact we should not underestimate.

References

Alpern, D.M. (1984, July 30). The Ferraro magic. Newsweek, pp. 20-21.

Andersen, K. (1984, September 3). Show and tell. Time, pp. 14-18.

Beck, M. (1984, June 18). Mondale's veepstakes. Newsweek, pp. 37-39.

Berg, D. (1984, March). A woman in 84? No way. Vogue, pp. 146, 151.

Breslin, R. (1984, August 6). Mrs. Zaccaro of Queens: Beyond the land of Archie Bunker. New Republic, pp. 15-16.

Buckley, J. (1984, October 1). Ferraro's mixed blessing. Newsweek, p. 12.

Buckley, W.F. (1984, September 7). Tiresome Democratic distractions. National Review, pp. 12-13.

Burke, K. (1945). A grammar of motives. New York: Prentice-Hall.

Chaze, W.L. (1984, September 3). Fresh facts about smoldering questions. U.S. News, p. 26.

Church, G.J. (1984a, July 16). Aiming for a good show. Time, pp. 10-13.

Church, G.J. (1984b, September 3). Hoping for a fresh start. Time, pp. 22-23.

Church, G.J. (1984c, July 30). Now for the real fight. Time, pp. 18-22.

Church, G.J., & Magnuson, E. (1984, July 23). A break with tradition. Time, pp. 12-16.

Cifelli, A. (1984, September 17). The high price of disclosure. Fortune, pp. 135-136.

Doerner, W.R. (1984a, November 19). A credible candidacy and then some. Time, pp. 84-85.

Doerner, W.R. (1984b, October 22). Co-stars on center stage. Time, pp. 30-31.

Doerner, W.R. (1984c, July 9). Mondale's demanding suitors. Time, pp. 12, 17.

Doerner, W.R. (1984d, August 6). The Gipper strikes back. Time, pp. 16-17.

Doerner, W.R. (1984e, June 4). The pride of San Francisco. Time, pp. 26-27.

Eng-Wong, V.L. (1984, August 6). The Mondale-Ferraro ticket [Letter to the editor]. Newsweek, p. 7.

Ferraro, G.A. (1985). Ferraro: My story. New York: Bantam.

Goldman, P. (1984, November/December). 'An exciting choice'--Then a clumsy gaffe. Newsweek, pp. 81-86.

Greenfield, M. (1984, July 23). Ferraro's debt to the noisy ones. Newsweek, p. 72.

Hancock, B.R. (1972). Affirmation by negation in the women's liberation movement. Quarterly Journal of Speech, 58, 264-271.

Henry, S. (1984, September). Geraldine Ferraro--The first [Interview with Geraldine Ferraro]. Vogue, pp. 721, 790-791.

Kelber, M. (1984, June 2). Why the Democrats need a woman V.P. The Nation, pp. 664-666.

Kelly, J. (1984). Women, history, & theory. Chicago: The University of Chicago Press.

Magnuson, E. (1984, September 24). Pressing the abortion issue. Time. pp. 18-20.

Mashek, J.W. (1984, June 18). Next question: Where's the veep? U.S. News, pp. 33-35.

Mathews, T.M. (1984, July 23). A team player. Newsweek, pp. 22-24, 27-28.

Morganthau, T. (1984a, July 30). A running start. Newsweek, pp. 18-25.

Morganthau, T. (1984b, July 16). Can Mondale pull it together? Newsweek, pp. 20-23.

Morganthau, T. (1984c, July 23). Making history. Newsweek, pp. 16-21.

Morrow, L. (1984, June 4). Why not a woman? Time, pp. 18-22.

O'Reilly, J. (1984, July 30). Smiles, tears, and goose bumps. Time, p. 29.

Penelope, J. (1982). Two essays on language and change: I: Power and the opposition to feminist proposals for language change; II: John Simon and the "Dragons of Eden." College English, 44, 840-854.

Quinn, J.B. (1984, September 17). Not so tender traps of marriage. Newsweek, p. 69.

Reeves, N. (1982). Womankind: Beyond the stereotypes (2nd ed). New York: Aldine Publishing Company.

Shapiro, W. (1984a, November/December). America: Reagan country. Newsweek, pp. 4-8.

Shapiro, W. (1984b, August 27). Furor over Ferraro finances. Newsweek, pp. 20-22.

Shapiro, W. (1984c, July 2). Mondale kicks off the race for no. 2. Newsweek, pp. 20-22.

Shapiro, W. (1984d, September 17). Politics and the pulpit. News-week, pp. 24-27.

Shapiro, W. (1984e, October 22). Shoot-out at gender gap. News-week, pp. 29-30.

Staff. (1984, September 1). Ferraroblip [Editorial]. The Nation, pp. 131-132.

Staff. (1984a, September 21). Nemesis. National Review, pp. 17-18.

Staff. (1984b, August 10). The Ferraro factor. National Review, pp. 13-14.

Staff. (1984, September 10). The reform petard. New Republic, pp. 5-7.

Staff. (1984, August 20). It's no Ms-tery, call me Mrs. Time, p. 105.

Stanley, A. (1984, June 4). The rising star from Queens. Time, pp. 24-25.

Thomas, E. (1984a, 19 November). Every region, every age group, almost every voting bloc. Time, pp. 42, 45.

Thomas, E. (1984b, June 18). Tackling the teflon president. Time, pp. 20-21.

Tifft, S. (1984, 19 November). Despite an all out effort, labor comes up short. Time, p. 66.

Walsh, K.T. (1984, September 3). Ferraro weathers the storm -- What next. U.S. News. pp. 25-27.

Willis, E. (1970). Letter to a critic. In S. Firestone & A. Koedt (Eds.), Notes from the second year. New York: Radical Feminists, p. 57.

CHAPTER 17

CANDIDATE IMAGE, VOTER VALUES, AND GENDER
AS DETERMINANTS OF VOTER PREFERENCE
IN THE 1984 PRESIDENTIAL CAMPAIGN

Jerry Allen, University of Bridgeport; Kathleen M. Long, University of New Haven; Joan O'Mara, University of Bridgeport; Ben Judd, University of Bridgeport.

The vice presidential bid of Geraldine Ferraro has given observers the opportunity to scrutinize the gender gap in the political arena. Despite the Reagan landslide in 1984, the gender gap was credited as a significant factor in political races in Michigan, Illinois, Missouri, Massachusetts, and Vermont (Dowd, 1984).

Communication researchers will no doubt examine all phases of this contest to see if communication variables differ when the candidate for a major political office is a female.

REVIEW OF LITERATURE

Traditionally communication researchers have viewed candidate image largely in one of two ways: (1) As a variable completely under the control of the communicator, and subject to manipulation by persuasion; or (2) as a variable controlled by the voters' selective biases, and subject to partisan resistance to change. In recent years, several problems have been associated with both the "stimulus-response" and "limited effects" models (Blumler & McLeod, 1974; Becker, McCombs, & McLeod, 1975). The current trend is to view voters as being creatively active in processing candidates' messages in search of information to fulfill varied social and psychological needs (Blumler & McQuail, 1969; Becker, McCombs, & McLeod, 1975; Sanders, 1975; Sanders & Pace, 1978; Blumler, 1978; Sanders & Kaid, 1981). Thus, while candidate image continues to generate considerable interest among those who study political communication (Kraus & Davis, 1976; Nimmo & Savage, 1976), it is suggested that orientation toward a particular candidate may be based upon the voters' desires to fulfill a variety of complicated needs (DeVries & Tarrance, 1972; Atwood & Sanders, 1975). The fulfilling of these needs becomes the motivation for evaluating candidates. Therefore, analysis of voter value of orientations may yield insight into the support of a particular candidate in fulfilling these needs.

Considerable evidence exists that voters' perceptions of the attributes of a candidate, or candidate image, is related to voter preference. Although the early studies of voter behavior did not use the specific term "candidate image," they examined something very much like candidate image when they discussed candidate appeal, candidate personality and where voters think the candidate stands on issues. The first voting studies found that selective exposure, buttressed by partisan influences, accounted for more votes than did persuasive strategies (Lazarsfeld, Berelson, & Gaudet, 1948; Berelson, Lazarsfeld, & McPhee, 1954). However, it has been contended that candidate image is a factor in such selectivity (Nimmo, 1976; Post, 1983). This was verified by Sherrod (1968) who found in the 1968 presidential campaign that voters with a preferred candidate selectively perceived that candidate's position on issues to make it consistent with their own positions. Other studies have indicated that fluctuation in voter attitudes is significantly related to candidate image variables.

In many studies, researchers have tested candidate image as a gross univariate variable, and conclusions as to its influence in the voting decision have been mixed. However, some of the investigations of media influences indicate that voters' evaluations of candidates are multidimensional (Kokkeler, 1972; Sanders, et al., 1972; Allen, 1975; Atwood & Sanders, 1975). Several earlier studies operationalized candidate image multidimensionally and used semantic differentials and factor analysis to account for the significant influence of voters' evaluations of candidates in making voting decisions (Stricker, 1963; McLeod, Wackman, Hurt & Payne, 1965; Rosenbaum & McGinniss, 1969; Weisberg & Rusk, 1970). More recently, Bowes and Strentz (1978) examined several components of stereotyping, and found that viewers of the 1976 television debates between Ford and Carter were more influenced by the candidates' attributes than by issues.

Support for studying the influence of source variables in combination, or multidimensionally is found in recent research literature (McGuire, 1969; Lashbrook & McCroskey, 1972; Wheeless, 1974). Andersen and Todd-Mancillas (1978) found homophily effective in measuring attitudes toward public figures, and Hellweg (1979), using multidimensional scaling, reports that dimensions of credibility were more predictive of voters' concept of "ideal candidate" than dimensions of homophily. Barnett and his associates (1976) used longitudinal tracing of changes in attitude to make predictions about voting behavior, and advocated the need to use multidimensional analysis to improve campaign communication research.

Andersen and Kibler (1978) operationalized source valence as multidimensions of credibility, homophily, and attraction, and found this combination of variables was highly predictive of voter preference in a Democratic primary for the United States Senate. Interestingly, while the full eight-variable model accounted for 61.6 percent of the variance in voter preference, attitude homophily alone accounted for 58 percent of that variance. Post (1983) replicated the Andersen and Kibler study, in a local election, and concluded that the multidimensional measurement of competence and attitude homophily are effective in predicting voter preference.

Allen, O'Mara and Judd (1985) examined the dimensions of candidate image, either singularly or in combination, to determine if these variables were predictive of voters' choice of a gubernatorial candidate when at least one was female. The voters in this study were moderately influenced by the image of the candidates, but sex of the voter was not a factor in the evaluation of image.

Rokeach theorized that there is a linear, sequential relationship between values, attitudes and behavior. Rokeach and his colleagues (1973) have tested his theory of value, attitude, and behavioral change in a variety of settings -- one-to-many, group, and computer-simulated communication -- utilizing both laboratory and field methodologies. The dependent variables of value, attitude, and behavioral change have been studied using diverse topics and issues as subject matter -- political campaigns, a survey of changes in American values over a four-year period, personal therapy, and attitudes toward civil rights movements, Viet Nam, environmental issues, smoking, health-related issues, etc. It would seem to fulfill the requirements of those who maintain that theories of communication should be applied in the "real world" (Clevenger, 1969; McCroskey, 1971), in a variety of communication contexts -- interpersonal, relational, social, and mass settings (Becker, 1969, 1971; McCroskey, 1971; Berg, 1972; Miller & Burgoon, 1978; Allen, 1978; Wheeless, et al., 1983). Of special interest are the findings of Rokeach (1971) that groups of individuals' hierarchies of values are predictive of support for individual candidates.

Therefore, the multidimensional measurement of communicator image has been found to be predictive of receiver evaluation in political campaigns. With the exception of the Allen, O'Mara and Judd (1985) study, such research has been concerned exclusively with voters' evaluations of male candidates. Rokeach's value preferences as predictors of voter support for a particular candidate warrant further investigation.

An increasing number of females are becoming candidates at all levels of government, and the findings of studies of male candidates should be applied with caution. In fact, there are probably compelling reasons for believing that female candidates are evaluated differently than men. Even the initial selection of women to be candidates by party leaders may be based upon dimensions of competence and personality that are different than those that are used in the selection of male candidates. Questions such as the following emerge: Does image or candidate evaluation play a more or less important role when a female and male candidate are opposing each other? Is image a more crucial variable for the female or the male candidate? Are different value preferences predictive of voter support for either a female or male candidate?

RESEARCH QUESTIONS

Many political observers believe that the selection of a woman, Geraldine Ferraro, as a candidate for Vice President closed the gender gap in politics and that the 1984 presidential race will, therefore, have a lasting impact (Dowd, 1984). The study reported here was undertaken to determine if the dimensions of candidate image, either singularly or in combination, and/or voters' gender and/or value preferences were predictive of voters' support for a female candidate on a presidential ticket. The following research questions were examined:

1. Are different dimensions of candidate image predictive of voters' support for female as opposed to male candidates?
2. Is sex of the voter predictive of evaluation of the candidates when at least one of the candidates is female?
3. Are differences in value orientations predictive of voters' support for political candidates when at least one candidate is female?

METHODOLOGY

Trained undergraduate interviewers collected data on 297 subjects picked at random from the telephone directories of Greater New Haven and Bridgeport, CT. Subjects called were asked to respond to a 21 item Likert-type survey designed to measure source valence.

Subjects were also asked to rank the 18 items of the Rokeach Value Scale (Rokeach, 1973). In addition to this data, subjects were asked to supply information relative to educational level, gender, and age. Surveying was done two months before the general election.

Previous studies have demonstrated that source valence composed of constructs of credibility, attraction, and homophily, is relevant to the evaluation of communication sources in a variety of contexts, including political campaigns (Lashbrook & McCroskey, 1972; Andersen & Todd-Mancillas, 1974; McCroskey, Richmond & Daly, 1975; Andersen & Kibler, 1978; Hellweg, 1979; Post, 1983). In this study, as in studies by Andersen and Kibler (1978) and Post (1983), four dimensions of credibility were examined.

The dimensions of credibility were competence, sociability, character, and extroversion. Two dimensions of competence were analyzed -- social attraction and physical attraction. Also, two dimensions of homophily -- attitude and background -- were examined as in previous studies. Previous studies have demonstrated that these dimensions have high reliability and contruct validity. Therefore, the independent or predictor variables were source credibility, homophily, and attraction, and the criterion variable was voter preference. Each subject was asked, "If the election were held today, and Geraldine Ferraro and George Bush were the presidential candidates for whom would you vote?" Only voters who indicated a preference for one of the two named candidates and who completed the values survey were used in the final analysis reported here.

After subjects had supplied data relative to candidate image and demographics, the Rokeach Value Scale was explained. Subjects were told that it would take about twenty minutes to complete. If the subject agreed to participate, the Value Scale was mailed to him or her. One hundred and twenty-six subjects returned completed scales, and were used in the analysis reported here.

Data on candidate image was analyzed using the MANOVA procedure, and the rank data of the Rokeach Value Scale was analyzed by the nonparametric Kruskal-Wallis (one-way analysis of variance) Test.

RESULTS

An examination of Table 1 reveals that Geraldine Ferraro and George Bush were perceived as different on all the variables except social attitude and physical attraction. George Bush was perceived as more competent, and as being of higher character. Subjects also believed his attitudes to be more homophilous with theirs. However, Ms. Ferraro was seen as more sociable, extroverted, and coming from a background which was more homophilous with that of the respondents.

Dimensions of candidate image differentiated among supporters of Ferraro, Bush, and undecided voters (Table 2). Supporters of Bush evaluated Ferraro as significantly lower on all dimensions than did either Ferraro supporters or undecided voters. Supporters of Bush believed him to be superior on all qualities. He was rated much higher by his supporters in terms of competence, sociability, and character.

Ferraro was seen by her supporters as much more sociable, more extroverted, higher in character, and having a background more similar to theirs. Also her supporters evaluated Bush lower on all dimensions. It is noteworthy that the evaluation

295

of the two candidates in terms of competency was less extreme for Ferraro supporters than for Bush supporters.

Undecided voters were very similar to Ferraro supporters in most evaluations. However, they perceived less background homophily with Geraldine Ferraro than did those who indicated that they would vote for her.

Females evaluated Ferraro higher on all dimensions, except background homophily than did males. Males evaluated Bush higher on all dimensions of candidate image than did females. Male and female evaluations of candidate image were significantly different in terms of competence, sociability, character, and attitude homophily. However, there was not significant inter-action among sex, image, and voter preference. This indicated that while females were perceiving Ferraro's image as more positive, not enough were willing to vote for her to make a difference.

It is important to note that while sociability accounted for very little variance (six percent), the other dimensions of credibility -- competence, extroversion, and character -- accounted for approximately 25-30 percent of the variance in candidate evaluation. The dimensions of homophily -- attitude and background -- accounted for a slight amount of the variance in candidate image, while the dimensions of attraction -- social and physical -- were responsible for less than five percent of that variance (Table 1).

In terms of making a voting decision, the dimensions of credibility again accounted for the most variance. In fact, competence provided 60 percent of the variance in voting prefer-ence. Sociability provided 40 percent of that variance, and extroversion and character provided 30 and 24 percent, respec-tively. In terms of perceived homophily, attitude homophily accounted for 16 percent of the variance and background homophily accounted for 33 percent of the variance in voting choice.

Attitude homophily provided 33 percent of variance in candidate evaluation as far as sex was concerned. Competence, sociability, and social attraction were all significant, but accounted for less than 15 percent of the variance contributed to candidate evaluation by sex. Background homophily, physical attraction, social attraction, and extroversion provided almost no variance as far as the impact of sex on candidate evaluation.

The Kruskel-Wallis Test for analysis of variance of ranked data indicated there were differences in the ranking of those who indicated a preference for Bush or Ferraro, or were undecided (Table 4). Undecided and Ferraro voters placed more priority on sense of accomplishment than did Bush voters (x^2=8.65,

$p < .02$). Those supporting Ferraro ranked equality slightly higher than those supporting Bush, but both Bush and Ferraro voters felt that equality was a significantly more important value than did those voters who were undecided ($x^2 = 5.92$, $p < .05$). Freedom was considered more important by those undecided or supporting Ferraro than those supporting Bush ($x^2 = 8.04$, $p < .02$). National security was a more significant priority to Bush supporters than it was to either Ferraro supporters or those who were undecided ($x^2 = 6.25$, $p < .05$). Self-respect ($x^2 = 6.46$, $p < .04$) and wisdom ($x^2 = 7.36$, $p < .03$) were more important values for undecided and Ferraro voters than for those supporting Bush. Interestingly, world at peace was significantly less important to undecided voters than it was to those who opted for one of the two candidates ($x^2 = 8.65$, $p < .02$).

DISCUSSION

Candidate image variables reflected by dimensions of credibility, attraction, and homophily were predictive of candidate evaluations. In this case the male candidate, George Bush, was evaluated more favorably than the female candidate, Geraldine Ferraro, and subjects indicated that such evaluations did affect their voting behavior. In fact, one variable, credibility, accounted for 60 percent of the variance in voting behavior. Sex of the voter was a consideration in voters' evaluations of the candidates, but had little impact on voting behavior. Two-thirds of the females in the study indicated that they would vote for George Bush.

While certain values did differentiate between the male and female candidates (e.g., national security), it is difficult to know whether these were predictive of gender differences or artifacts of Republican-Democratic, conservative-liberal influences.

The results of this study indicate that candidate image was significant in predicting voting preference, and there was some evidence of a gender issue when at least one of the candidates is female. The gender gap was credited with making a difference in several local and state political races in 1984 (Dowd, 1984). Given the increasing number of women seeking elective office, there is a need to further investigate the extent to which image politics may be a factor for female candidates.

297

REFERENCES

Allen, J.L. (1975). The impact of media and candidate image. Paper presented at the New England conference on the study of political communication, Amherest, MA.

Allen, J.L. (1978). Persuasion through self-confrontation: An experimental study of value, attitude, and behavior change initiated by interpersonal and mass media. Unpublished doctoral dissertation, Southern Illinois University-Carbondale.

Allen, J.L., O'Mara, J. and Judd, B. (1985). Changes in the evaluation of female candidates from Ella Grasso to Geraldine Ferraro. Paper presented at the annual meeting of the International Communication Association, Honolulu, HI.

Andersen, P.A. & Kibler, R.J. (1978). Candidate valence as a predicator of voter preference. Human Communication Research, 5 4-14.

Andersen, P.A. & Todd-Mancillas, W.R. (1978). Scales for the measurement of homophily with public figures. Southern Speech Communication Journal, 43, 169-179.

Atwood, L.E. & Sanders, K.R. (1975). Perception of information sources and likelihood of split ticket voting. Journalism Quarterly, 421-428.

Barnett, G.A. (1976). Campaign communication and attitude change: A multidimensional analysis. Human Communication Research, 2, 227-244.

Becker, S.L. (1969). The impact of the mass media on society. In R. Wiman & W.C. Meirkeny (Eds.), Educational media: Theory into practice. Columbus, OH: Charles E. Merrill.

Becker, S.L. (1971). Rhetorical studies for the contemporary world. In L. Bitzer and E. Black. (Eds.) The prospect of rhetoric. New York: Prentice-Hall.

Becker, L.B., McCombs, M.E., & McLeod, J.M. (1975). The development of political cognitions. In S.H. Chaffee (Ed.). Political communication. Beverly Hills, CA: Sage Publishing Company.

Berelson, B., Lazarsfeld, P., & McPhee, W. (1954). Voting. Chicago: Univeristy of Chicago Press.

Berg, D.M. (1972). Rhetoric reality and mass media. Quarterly Journal of Speech, 58, 255-263.

Blumler, J.G. (1978). The role of theory in uses and gratifications study. Political Communication Review, 3, 1-10.

Blumler, J.G. & McLeod, J.M. (1974). Communication and voter turnout in Britain. In T. Leggart (Ed.). Sociological theory and survey research. Beverly Hills, CA: Sage.

Blumler, J.G. & McQuail, D. (1969). Television in politics: Its uses and influence. Chicago: University of Chicago Press.

Bowes, J.E. & Strentz, H. (1978). Candidate images: Stereotyping and the 1976 debates. In B.D. Rubin (Ed.). Communication Yearbook 2. New Brunswick, NJ: Transaction Books.

Clevenger, T. (1969). Research methodologies in speech communication. In L. Barker and R. Kibler. (Eds.) Conceptual frontiers in speech communication. New York: Speech Communication Association of America.

Devries, W. and Tarrance, V.L. (1972). The ticket-splitter. Grand Rapids, MI: Eardmans.

Dowd, M. (1984). Reassessing women's political role: The lasting impact of Geraldine Ferraro. The New York Times Magazine, December.

Hellweg, S. (1979). An examination of voter conceptualizations of the ideal political candidate. The Southern Speech Communication Journal, 44, 373-385.

Kokkeler, L.A. (1973). Communication variables, candidate image and voting behavior: A study of influence in the 1972 presidential and gubernatorial elections. Unpublished doctoral dissertation, Southern Illinois University-Carbondale.

Kraus, S. & David, D. (1976). The effects of mass communication on political behavior. University Park, PA: Pennsylvania State University Press.

Lashbrook, V.J. & McCroskey, J.D. (1972). Source valence: An improved conceptualization. Paper presented at the annual meeting of the Western Speech Communication Association, Honolulu, HI.

Lazarfeld, P.R., Berelson, B.R., and Gaudet, H. (1948). The people's choice. New York: Columbia University Press.

Miller, G.R. and Burgoon, M. (1978). Persuasion research: Review and commentary. In Ruben, R.D. (Ed.). Communication Yearbook 2. New Brunswick, NJ: Transaction Books.

McCroskey, J.C., Richmond, V.P. and Daly, J.A. The development of a measure of perceived homophily in interpersonal communication. Human Communication Research, 1975, 1, 323-332.

McCroskey, J.C. (1971). Speech communication research of the 70's: Six priority areas - research in persuasion and attitude change. Paper presented at the annual conference of the Speech Communication Association.

McGuire, W.J. (1969). The nature of attitudes and attitude change. In G. Lindzey & E. Aronson (Eds.). The handbook of social psychology, Vol. 2 (2nd ed.). Reading, MA: Addison Wesley.

McLeod, J.M. Wachman, D., Hurt, W.H., & Payne, H.W. (1965). Political conflict and communication behavior in the 1964 political campaign. Paper presented at the Association for Education in Journalism Convention, Syracuse, NY.

Nimmo, D. & Savage, R.L. (1976). Candidates and their images. Pacific Palisades, CA: Goodyear Publishing Company.

Post, D.J. (1983). Candidate image and source valence: Predicting the outcome of a local primary election. Unpublished Master's Thesis, West Virginia University.

Rokeach, M. (1971). The measurement of values and value systems. In Abcariam, G. and Soule, J.W. (Eds.) Social psychology and political behavior. Columbus, OH: Charles Merrill.

Rokeach, M. (1971). The nature of human values. New York: The Free Press.

Rosenbaum, L.L. and McGinniss, E. (1969). A semantic differential analysis of concepts associated with the 1964 presidential election. Journal of Social Psychology, 78, 227-235.

Sanders, K.R. (1975). A critique of contemporary approaches to the study of political communication. In R. Davis (Ed.), Proceedings of the Speech Communication Association Summer Conference, 1975. Falls Church, VA: Speech Communication Association.

Sanders, K.R. & Kaid, L.L. (1981). Political rallies: Their uses and effects. Central States Speech Journal, 32, 1-11.

Sanders, K.R. & Pace, T.J. (1977). The influence of speech communication on the image of a political candidate: "Limited effect" revisited. In B.D. Rubin (Ed.), Communication Yearbook 1. New Brunswick, NJ: Transaction Books.

Sanders, K.R., Pace, T.J., McNeil, K., & Dybvig, E. (1971). The impact of communication media on candidate image. Unpublished paper, Center for Communication Research, Southern Illinois University-Carbondale.

Sherrod, D.R. (1972). Selective perception of political candidates. Public Opinion Quarterly, 35, 127-138.

Simons, H.W. (1973). Interpersonal perception, similarity and credibility. In C.D. Mortensen and K.K. Sereno. (Eds.). Advances in communication research. New York: Harper and Row.

Stricker, G. (1963). The use of the semantic differential to predict voting behavior. The Journal of Social Psychology, 59, 159-167.

Weiberg, H. and Ruck, J. (1970). Dimensions of candidate evaluation. American Political Science Review, 104, 1167-1185.

Wheeless, L.R. (1974). The effects of attitude, credibility, and homophily on selective exposure to information. Speech Monographs, 41, 329-327.

Wheeless, L.R., Barraclough, R., and Stewart, R. (1983). Compliance-gaining and power in persuasion. In R. Bostrom (Ed.). Communication Yearbook 7. Beverly Hills, CA: Sage.

TABLE 1

OVERALL MEAN IMAGE EVALUATIONS
OF THE 1984
VICE PRESIDENTIAL CANDIDATES

(n = 126)

Dimension	Ferraro	Bush	F	R^2
Competence	3.33	3.82	12.30**	.25
Sociability	3.73	3.54	2.93	.06
Extroversion	3.62	3.28	16.02*	.32
Character	3.39	3.82	11.83**	.24
Social Att.	3.02	3.22	1.29	.03
Phy. Att.	3.46	3.32	1.69	.03
Attitude Hom.	2.86	3.35	8.19**	.16
Backgrd. Hom.	2.85	2.57	4.29****	.09

*$p < .0001$
**$p < .001$
***$p < .01$
****$p < .05$

TABLE 2

OVERALL MEAN IMAGE EVALUATION OF THE 1984
VICE PRESIDENTIAL CANDIDATES
BY CANDIDATE PREFERENCE

Dimension	Evaluation for Ferraro			Eval. for Bush			F	R^2
	Pref. for Ferraro (n=44)	Pref. for Bush (n=57)	Undec. (n=24)	Pref. for Ferraro (n=44)	Pref. for Bush (n=57)	Undec. (n=24)		
Competence	3.92	2.98	3.54	3.42	4.19	3.38	15.25*	.60
Sociability	4.23	3.53	3.69	3.23	3.78	3.27	10.18*	.41
Extroversion	3.95	3.47	3.64	3.10	3.41	3.15	7.50**	.30
Character	4.15	2.92	3.73	3.58	4.13	3.35	23.22*	.24
Social Att.	3.65	2.63	3.27	2.62	3.62	2.92	11.55*	.03
Physical Att.	3.65	3.33	3.58	3.12	3.60	2.88	8.15**	.33
Attitude Hom.	3.92	2.13	3.49	2.54	3.92	2.82	37.77***	.16
Backgrd. Hom.	3.65	2.57	2.69	2.38	2.62	2.65	8.38**	.33

*p < .0001
**p < .001
***p < .01
****p < .05

303

TABLE 3

OVERALL MEAN IMAGE EVALUATIONS OF THE 1984
VICE PRESIDENTIAL CANDIDATES
BY VOTERS' SEX

Dimension	Eval. of Ferraro		Eval. of Bush		F	R^2
	Males (n=55)	Females (n=71)	Males (n=55)	Females (n=70)		
Competence	3.04	3.42	4.26	3.68	6.27****	.13
Sociability	3.54	3.80	3.82	3.44	5.16****	.10
Extroversion	3.62	3.62	3.50	3.21	1.82	.04
Character	3.11	3.49	4.21	3.69	6.04****	.12
Social Att.	2.96	3.04	3.79	3.04	2.80	.04
Physical Att.	3.36	3.50	3.64	3.21	2.93	.06
Attitude Hom.	2.14	3.10	4.00	3.13	16.33*	.33
Backgrd. Hom.	3.07	2.77	2.75	2.51	.0030	.00

*$p < .0001$
****$p < .05$

TABLE 4

1984 VICE PRESIDENTIAL STUDY

MEAN VALUE RANKINGS BY SEX AND VOTING PREFERENCE[1]

Value	Overall mean rank (n=126)	Sex		Voting Preference		
		Males (n=55)	Females (n=71)	Ferraro (n=44)	Bush (n=55)	Undecided (n=24)
Comfortable Life	9.3	8.6	9.5	8.1	9.8	9.00
Exciting Life	11.3	10.6	12.6	11.1	12.3	9.80
Sense of Accomplishment	9.5	10.7	9.3	8.3	10.7	8.4
World at Peace	6.1	6.7	3.9	5.8	4.3	8.92*
World of Beauty	13.1	12.2	13.4	13.6	12.6	13.7
Equality	10.39	10.1	9.5	10.7	9.1	13.6*
Family Security	5.4	4.7	5.9	6.5	4.8	6.2
Freedom	6.4	5.6	5.5	5.3	5.7	8.92*
Happiness	5.8	5.9	6.2	6.3	5.9	4.9
Inner Harmony	9.2	11.1	9.1	10.2	9.5	6.6
Mature Love	8.9	8.3	9.6	9.6	8.8	7.9
National Security	10.4	9.5	9.3	10.8	8.5	13.5*
Pleasure	11.9	10.8	12.5	12.0	11.8	11.2
Salvation	14.2	14.7	13.0	14.4	13.1	14.4
Self-respect	7.6	9.1	7.9	7.3	9.0	5.8*
Social Recognition	13.3	13.8	13.6	12.5	14.4	12.9
True Friendship	7.5	8.6	8.1	8.1	8.4	6.9
Wisdom	10.0	10.5	11.3	9.9	11.7	8.1*

[1] smaller numbers are higher rank

*p<.05

305

CHAPTER 18

GENDER AND THE PRESS: AN UPDATE

Pamela Schroeder Kingsolver, Missouri Western State College
Harold V. Cordry, Central Missouri State University

In 1818, when the grammarian William Cobbett undertook to explain the etymology of pronouns in his Grammar of the English Language, he devoted but one short paragraph to gender. Pointing out that the only changes to express gender occur in third person singular -- "he," "she," and "it" -- he remarked that it was hardly necessary for him to explain the circumstances under which each was to be used.

Indeed, there was a time when the gender of pronouns was a simple matter, but for American newspaper and magazine editors of the 1970s and '80s, the question of gender and other points of usage associated with the issue of sexism have become highly problematical. Some feminists, for example, have exerted considerable pressure on editors to dispense with the generic "he" and to replace it with "he or she," "they," "he/she," or even "s/he"; they have urged that nouns containing the suffix "-man" not be used; they have lobbied against the use of such gender-specific words as "coed," "aviatrix," and "poetess"; and they have vigorously protested against such terms as "lady lawyer" and "woman doctor."

On the whole, editors have appeared to be more receptive to arguments regarding stereotypes and stereotypical thinking than they have been to attempts directed specifically at altering the way they use language, for while editors themselves tend to be highly prescriptive in matters of language, they are at the same time, most of them, highly resistant to prescription.

Nevertheless, it is evident to anyone who reads the periodical press that a number of editors have adopted certain of the changes in grammar and usage proposed by feminists. Some measure of the extent to which these proposals have been adopted may be inferred from the results of a series of small surveys conducted annually since 1979 by Prof. Richard L. Tobin of Indiana University and published in The Quill magazine. The surveys, each of which consisted of 10 questions, dealt with usage in general, but five of them included questions relating to gender:

1. "Spokesperson" or "spokesman"? --In Tobin's 1980 survey, 56.8 percent of the respondents (newspaper and magazine copy chiefs) preferred "spokesman."

2. "Ms." --In both his 1981 and 1984 surveys, Tobin asked editors whether they accepted the title "Ms." Responses in 1981 indicated 57.3 percent acceptance, but by 1984 the acceptance level had dropped sharply to 28.4 percent, leading Tobin to conclude that "Ms." was "on its way out."

3. "His" or "his or her"? -- In his 1982 survey, Tobin asked copy chiefs whether they would accept "his" in the sentence "A student should take his time on this important exam" or change it to "his or her." Responses indicated that 54.9 percent of the editors preferred the generic "his."

4. "Chairperson" or "chairman"? -- Tobin found in his 1983 survey that only 29.6 percent of the copy editors accepted "chairperson," and in reporting this fact he observed that "The influence of the women's movement upon language appears to be lessening. . . ."

While it may indeed be true that the feminists' influence on language is waning, it seems necessary to determine first of all precisely what the extent of feminist influence is. To this end, the authors undertook to design a survey that not only would provide up-to-date statistics on a variety of points of usage but also would yield comparatively detailed information relating to editors' attitudes toward the generic "he."

Methodology

In January 1985, copies of questionnaires consisting of questions addressing 79 points of usage, including five relating to the generic "he," were mailed to the chief copy editors at 97 newspapers and 108 magazines published in the United States. The survey sample was restricted to general consumer publications with circulations in excess of 130,000, but several smaller publications commonly regarded as "elites" -- publications distinguished by exceptionally high editorial standards and quality -- were included as well. Also included were Editor & Publisher and Folio, the trade publications of the newspaper and magazine industries. Of the 205 questionnaires sent out, 120 were completed and returned, for a success rate of 58 percent.

The survey questions, which called for "yes" and "no" answers, were worded in such a way as to elicit responses that would reflect the policy of the publications rather than the personal preferences of the individual editors. Analysis of the responses was carried out by tabulating "yes" and "no" answers to each question for all respondents and for newspapers and magazines individually. A z ratio analysis was performed on the totals to test for statistically significant differences from a point of group ambivalence, or a 50-50 split. A .05 level of significance was set. In addition, a chi-square analysis was performed to determine whether the "yes"-"no" distribution for magazines versus newspapers was significantly different. (See table 1.) Cross-tabulations were also performed on selected responses in order to reveal relationships between attitudes toward the generic "he" and usage in general. (See table 2.)

Following are the gender-related questions included in the survey:

1. Does your publication allow the use of a plural pronoun following "one," as in "One may do so if <u>they</u> wish"?

2. Does your publication allow the use of a plural pronoun following "each," as in "Each player is responsible for <u>their</u> own equipment"?

3. Does your publication prefer "he or she" to the generic "he"?

4. Does your publication prefer "his or her" to the generic "his"?

5. Does your publication accept the generic "he" but prefer to avoid it by restructuring?

Results

The survey responses revealed that 42 percent of the newspapers and 54 percent of the magazines prefer "he or she" and "his or her" to the generic "he" and "his." Using a z ratio for a 5 percent level of significance, however, we found that each group is statistically evenly divided on the issue.

Although comments were not solicited, a number of editors wrote brief explanations in the margins. The chief copy editor of the magazine <u>Health</u>, for example, answered "no," but added: "We always use 'she.' We're a women's magazine." <u>Outdoor Life</u>'s chief copy editor, on the other hand, attributed the reason for his "no" to the magazine's "90 percent male readership." One magazine editor who answered "yes" added, "Within reason," and another who responded in the affirmative said: "Unless it's too cumbersome -- too many repeats. In that case we'd go with 'he.'" Still another magazine editor -- this one anonymous -- declared a preference not only for "she" but for "the generic 'she'" (?).

In regard to the question of accepting plural pronouns with the antecedents "each" and "one," the response was

TABLE 1

SURVEY RESPONSES TO QUESTIONS RELATING TO GENERIC "HE"

Question	Mag. Responses Yes	No	Z	Newsp. Responses Yes	No	Z	Chi Square	Total Responses Yes	No	Z
1. Does your publication allow the use of a plural pronoun following "one" as in "One may do so if 'they' wish"?	1	48	-23.74	1	65	-32.25	0.258	2	113	-39.59
2. Does your publication allow the use of a plural pronoun following "each" as in "Each player is responsible for 'their' own equipment"?	3	47	-13.01	2	64	-22.26	0.101	5	111	-24.23
3. Does your publication prefer "he or she" to the generic "he"?	27	23	0.57	27	37	-1.27	1.133	50	60	-0.56
4. Does your publication prefer "his or her" to the generic "his"?	27	23	0.57	27	37	-1.27	1.133	50	60	-0.56
5. Does your publication accept the generic "he" but prefer to avoid it by restructuring?	38	8	5.84	55	12	6.85	0.032	98	20	9.00

overwhelmingly negative, with 98 percent of all respondents rejecting "they" following "one" and 96 percent rejecting "their" following "each." Again, there was no significant difference between newspapers and magazines. Marginal comments ranged from a large metropolitan paper's "Hell no!" to the admission by the copy chief of The Nation that she was "considering a break with the rule. . . ."

Most interesting was the response to the question "Do you accept the generic 'he' but prefer to avoid it by restructuring?" To this 83 percent of the magazine editors and 82 percent of the newspaper editors responded "yes."

Analysis of Cross-Tabulations

In assessing the results of the survey, the authors hypothesized -- rather belatedly -- that reluctance to adopt changes in usage advocated by feminists was not necessarily a result of sexism or of a lack of empathy for the women's movement but that it was to some extent attributable to a concern for maintaining standards. Indeed, editors who adhere to strict standards of usage are almost by definition slow in accepting change. They are slow to accept new words, slow to give up on fading distinctions, and slow to accept new uses for old words.

Accordingly, in order to test this hypothesis, we undertook to compare responses on the gender questions to responses on various other questions on which the positions of language purists are well-known. Earlier research has shown, for example, that language conservatives continue to resist the use of "contact" as a verb and that they oppose the use of "claim" as a synonym for "assert," of "sustain" as a synonym for "suffer" (as in "sustain injuries"), and of "over" in place of "more than." As we expected, the respondents who insisted on these and other similar distinctions unanimously rejected use of plural pronouns with singular antecedents.

We also suspected that the respondents who said they continue to prefer the generic "he" to "he or she" would align themselves more closely with the purists than would those respondents who prefer "he or she." To test this hypothesis, we selected seven questions involving points of usage on which the purists have made their views quite clear: (1) misuse of "claim" for "assert," (2) misuse of "contact" as a verb, (3) misuse of "over" for "more than," (4) misuse of "partially" for "partly," (5) misuse of "anxious" for "eager," (6) misuse of "die from" for "die of," and (7) misuse of "sustain" for "suffer." The findings, however, reported in Table 2, reveal no dramatic patterns. Respondents who prefer the generic "he" are more resistant to misuse of "over," "partially," and "die from," but only by a margin of 8-10 percent. On the remaining issues, the percentages of acceptance and rejection in the two groups are essentially identical.

Discussion

Given the findings that, first, only about half of the editors surveyed preferred "he or she" and "his or her" to the generic alternatives, and, second, that more than 80 percent of those who do prefer them also prefer to restructure, it is clear that only a small percentage of the editors -- about 10 percent -- have accepted "he or she" and "his or her" without reservations.

In marginal comments, no respondents argued in favor of the generic "he," nor did anyone argue against "he or she" or "his or her" for any reason other than stylistic considerations. It is probably safe to infer from the findings and from the nature of the marginal comments that most editors are less than enthusiastic about "he or she" and "his or her" not because they disagree with the feminist argument against using the generic "he" but primarily because the alternatives the feminists propose are cumbersome and unwieldy.

Neologisms such as "he/she" and "s/he" would be more easily manageable in type, but at this point no major publications have adopted them, nor are they likely to do so, considering the overwhelming opposition among the respondents to such comparatively small compromises as "each" followed by "their" and "one" followed by "they."

Another factor that probably accounts to a large extent for the editors' responses is the influence of The Associated Press Stylebook and Libel Manual. The stylebook (1984) has no entry under "he or she," but its position on the generic "he" is made clear in the entry under "his, her": "Do not presume maleness in constructing a sentence, but use the pronoun 'his' when an indefinite antecedent may be male or female: 'A reporter attempts to protect his sources.' (Not 'his or her' sources. . . .)" The entry ends with the following advice: "Frequently, however, the best of choice is a slight revision of the sentence: 'Reporters attempt to protect their sources.'" Presumably the same prescription applies to the generic "he." The significance of this is that the AP stylebook is used by most newspapers and many magazines. Of the 120 respondents to the survey, for example, 57 said they followed AP style. The percentage among smaller papers would be even greater. Moreover, many "house" stylebooks, even at large publications, are patterned very closely on the AP stylebook.

TABLE 2

POSITIONS ON SELECTED POINTS OF USAGE BY POSITION
ON GENERIC "HE"

Usage	Prefer "he or she"		Prefer generic "he"	
	Yes (N)	No (N)	Yes (N)	No (N)
Do you accept "claim" for "assert"?	53.8% (28)	46.2% (24)	55% (33)	45% (27)
Do you accept "contact" for "get in touch with"?	84.6% (44)	15.4% (8)	86.4% (51)	13.6% (8)
Do you accept "over" for "more than"?	32.7% (17)	67.3% (35)	22% (13)	78% (46)
Do you accept "partially" for "partly"?	77.6% (38)	22.4% (11)	69.5% (41)	30.5% (18)
Do you accept "anxious" for "eager"?	25% (13)	75% (39)	25.4% (15)	74.6% (44)
Do you accept "die from" for "die of"?	48.1% (25)	31.9% (27)	39% (23)	61% (36)
Do you accept "sustain" for "suffer"?	49% (25)	51% (26)	52.5% (31)	47.5% (28)

Editors could, of course, establish their own exceptions to AP style, and some of the respondents clearly have done so. One reason not to introduce an exception, however, is that all AP copy received by a subscriber is already edited to conform to AP style, and many newspapers, particularly small ones, run wire copy unedited. Thus, either the AP copy would have to be edited or the editor would have to tolerate style inconsistencies between local and wire copy, and most editors have a low tolerance for style inconsistencies. Thus it seems likely that feminists will not see much progress toward further rejection of the generic "he" unless AP itself initiates a style revision.

One obvious question to be addressed in later research is how many newspapers and magazines that use the AP stylebook have deviated from AP's style on generic pronouns -- how many, in short, prefer "he or she" and "his or her." Researchers might also try to determine the extent to which the so-called "generic 'she'" has been adopted by women's publications. Finally, how much restructuring is being done -- not only in publications preferring "he or she" but in others as well? Comparing the frequency of generic pronouns in publications today with their frequency in, say, the 1950s would provide a strong indicator of the extent to which editors are in fact restructuring. It may be, for example, that even editors who say they prefer the generic "he" are using it less often than in the past. It might also be interesting to move away from the editor's desk and survey reporters and staff writers. After all, at least part of whatever restructuring is being done takes place not at the level of the editor but at the level of the writer.

Bibliography

French, Christopher W., Eileen Alt Powell, and Howard Angions,
    eds. <u>The Associated Press Stylebook and Libel Manual</u>. New
    York: The Associated Press, 1984 (106).

Tobin, Richard L. "Usage Survey No. 4." <u>The Quill</u>, March
    1983 (5).

Tobin, Richard L. "Usage Survey No. 5." <u>The Quill</u>, March
    1984 (5-7).

Tobin, Richard L. "Usage Survey No. 6." <u>The Quill</u>, April
    1985 (9-10).

Tobin, Richard L. Personal letter.

CHAPTER 19

THE IMPACT OF SEX AND BLACK IDENTIFICATION
ON EVALUATIONS OF COMMUNICATOR STYLE:
IMPLICATIONS FOR ORGANIZATIONAL SENSE-MAKING

by

Mark Carnius Cox, Ph.D.
California State University-Chico

Introduction

Adapting Norton's (1978) viewpoint, the researcher who wants
to establish an organizational communication theory must deal not
only with what is communicated, but with the way it is
communicated. However, as society has transformed real or
imagined racial differences in communicator style into
stereotypical expectations and, in some cases, mandates for
behavior, the prevailing tendency has been to restrict
discussions of factors that may influence the way blacks
communicate to historical and linguistic analyses of 'Black
American English' (BAE). This article represents a movement away
from this trend. As such, it attempts to discern effects of
gender and black identification perceptions of communicator style
among black people.

The paper is divided into the following sections. First, a
rationale for the following investigation is presented. This is
followed by a description of the communicative significance of
gender, black identification, and communicator style. Third,
specific research questions for this investigation are presented.
Next, the methods and procedures used to collect and analyze data
are discussed. Finally, the conclusions and implications of the
research to organizational sense-making are outlined.

Rationale

The approach to exploring communicator style in the present investigation is significant for several reasons. First, the results of this study may help explain consequences of certain interpersonal encounters inside the work place. It is reasonable to assert that how black people interact within and make sense of organizational environments generally, at least in part, is a function of what they think of themselves and other black people. Hence, the extent to which communicator style similarities and differences exist among blacks may account for many consequences of intra- as well as interracial interaction on the job.

Second, centering on black identification may provide a level of information about interpersonal and organizational communication behavior that, heretofore, has remained unexplored. Today, for example, the scholarly literature is replete with studies that suggest the primary way to understand blacks is to focus on the ways they differ from their white counterparts. Yet, though studies from this isolated, segmented approach have told us a great deal about how blacks are unlike whites and vice versa, our knowledge about blacks and communicative phenomena remains limited. Also, focusing on interracial differences alone makes it difficult to assess whether differences are due to a specific type of individual or a category of race/sex grouping or some other confounding variables in the context.

Finally, to suggest that blacks can be understood only in relation to whites defines black communication experiences in the context of the status quo which may serve only to perpetuate existing stereotypical expectations. The present investigation, however, in some ways attempts to uncover effects of "psychological race" among blacks which may have more significance to communication study than biological racial differences.

Gender, Black Identification and Communicator Style

Sex Differences and the Communicator Style Construct

Norton (1978, 1983) defines communicator style as "the way one verbally and paraverbally interacts to signal how literal meaning should be taken, interpreted, filtered, or understood." In other words, language refers to the words, style suggests what one **does** with the words. In a detailed analysis of the construct, Norton (1978) isolates nine independent variables (dominant, dramatic, animated, open, contentious, relaxed, friendly, attentive, and impression leaving) and one dependent variable (communicator image) which define the domain of communicator style. In subsequent research, Norton and Robinson

(1980) included five additional variables (serious, quiet, loud, humorous, and flexible) that will be used to frame the present investigation. Operational definitions for each of these variables are contained in Table 1.

Montgomery and Norton (1979) exposed many subtle differences in communicator style of men and women. Specifically, their results suggest that males see themselves as more precise, dramatic, and impression leaving. Females, on the other hand, evaluate themselves as more animated and friendly. In addition, these researchers found that the "communicator image" for females was predicted by friendly, impression leaving, dominant and open. Yet, male communicator image was best predicted by dominant, friendly, open, relaxed, contentious and impression leaving style variables.

The present investigation is different from previous style research in at least two ways. First, this study is not as general as previous examinations of style since it will focus only on black men and women. However, based upon Montgomery and Norton's study, a tentative axiom is that black women would evaluate certain aspects of their communicator style differently from black men and vice versa. Second, the present research will examine whether sex and black identification interact to influence reported communicator style. It is reasonable to assert that gender and black identification would affect perceptions of communicator style since both are communicative phenomena; how they operate depends on the interaction between the self and others. Hence, the purpose of this research is to discover the extent to which, if at all, sex differences and racial group identification influence how black people perceive communicator style.

Black Identification and Communicator Style

Black identification occurs to the extent that black people express loyalty and similarity to and membership or affiliation with one another (Cox, 1985a). As such, black identification is intricately linked to communicator style since a person may exaggerate his/her voice and other stylistic devices to either highlight or understate expressions of the identification. Black identification can be classified into two kinds of communicative behaviors -- expressions that a person is given and the expressions that a person gives off. In terms of expressions given, according to Miller (1963), communication in social interaction provides the basis from which perceptions of the self or identity are formed. As Hilgard (1944) explained, "the self (i.e., identity) as a social product has full meaning **only** (emphasis added) when expressed in social interaction." Since style is inextricably linked to one's expressions and creates expectations about literal meaning (Norton, 1983), it can be concluded that a black person's racial group identification, at least in part, is a function of the messages and styles of others in the environment.

Likewise, black identification involves expressions that are given off. For example, the pronouns used to describe the self (i.e., I, me) in conjunction with the mode or style of expression provide persons with a linguistic means of distinguishing themselves from the environment (Miller, 1963). On the other hand, pronouns like "we" and "our" may signal overall association with a social group and/or unit. Hence, blacks may be said to identify with one another to the degree that they distinguish themselves in use of language and style from other black people. In the following sections, a review of relevant black identification literature is presented and the perspective of the phenomenon in the present research is described.

Review of Relevant Literature

Stages of Black Identification

Social science scholars have tended to conceptualize black identification as steps, states, levels or stages of "Black Consciousness Development" (Cross, 1971, 1973; Toomer, 1975; Butler, 1975; Milliones, 1980). One of the premier stage theory conceptualizations was formulated and tested by Cross (see Hall, Freedle, & Cross, 1972). Cross (1971) hypothesizes that there exists a series of stages through which blacks must pass to encounter "blackness" in themselves. Several theorists have attempted to validate Cross' model with varied results (Hall et al., 1972; Cheek, 1972; Williams, 1975).

In addition, Cross' original theory has generated other black identity models (see Thomas, 1971; Milliones, 1980). However, since most of them are deeply rooted in Cross' formulation, they also share some of its conceptual and empirical limitations. First, it seems that researchers have failed, generally speaking, to develop the black identification construct theoretically before attempting to measure the phenomenon. It is apparent from a review of the literature, for example, the black identification has been conceived as synonymous with "black consciousness." Merging these constructs, however, may cause us to overlook unique conceptual qualities of identification.

Second, using stage theories as principle indices of black identification implies that blacks experience a sort of mystical -- albeit "transcendental" -- movement towards higher stages of consciousness. Even though this perspective may be heuristic, one might conclude that blacks at lower levels of consciousness are "abnormal" as compared to those at higher consciousness levels. In addition, most of the past studies lack strong evidence of the reliability and validity of the scales used to measure black identification. Obviously, real knowledge of the phenomenon cannot advance until such evidence is made available.

Furthermore, the degree to which a black person identifies with his/her racial group has been seen in most studies as a response to and/or a consequence of a black person's beliefs, attitudes, and intentions towards whites (see Lessing & Zagorin, 1972; Banks, 1970). However, as revealed in previous research, black people tend to separate their attitudes toward whites from their "identification" with blacks (Cox, 1985b).

Finally, the movement between stages is not adequately explained in previous literature. For example, researchers have failed to account for half or backwards moves on each stage of black identification. Hence, due to all of these limitations, stage development theories were considered conceptually unappealing to guide this research.

Dimensions of Black Identification

Adapting Patchen's (1970) schemata, the dimensions of black identification that will be used in this study can be described as follows. First, membership or affiliation characterizes a black person's sense of belonging to and feelings of accountability to others within his/her racial group. For the purposes of this investigation, the membership component will be termed "brother- and/or sisterhood" among black people.

The second dimension of black identification, loyalty, involves expressions of enthusiasm of membership in the black race. Statements like, "It makes me feel good when blacks call me their 'brother' ('sister')," and "I enjoy helping other blacks become successful," reflect the loyalty component of black identification.

Finally, Patchen's last dimension of identification, similarity, is especially important to black identification. In this case, similarity refers to a black person's evaluation of him/herself in relation to other black people, groups, or subunits who are black. Declarations such as, "On the whole, my problems and the problems of most black people are the same," and "I see myself the same as most black people" reflect the similarity component.

In addition to adapting Patchen's schemata, feelings of black identification will be conceived as curvi-linear rather than in stages. In other words, in the present study, racial group identification among blacks will be considered to exist in varying degrees as opposed to "steps" of consciousness development. It is believed that this orientation will help overcome many of the previously discussed conceptual pitfalls.

Research Questions

In light of the preceding rationale and review of pertinent research, this project was undertaken to investigate possible effects of gender and black identification on reported communicator styles of blacks. Specifically, the following questions structure this research:

1. Do black males and females differ significantly in their reported communicator styles?

2. Do gender and black identification interact to affect reported communicator styles?

Method and Procedures

Settings, Subjects and Procedures

Data were collected from black employees at three Midwestern universities: Purdue University, Indiana University-Purdue University at Indianapolis (IU-PUI), and the University of Illinois at Champaign, Urbana. There were 1,312 questionnaires distributed, and the 271 useable measures represent an approximate 21% return rate. Of the 271 respondents, there were 185 (68%) women and 86 (32%) men.

Participants in this study received cover-letters and copies of the Black Identification Questionnaire (BIQ) and the Communicator Style Measure (CSM) Shortened Version through each university's campus mail system. Upon completing the scales, participants were asked to return the questionnaires to specific campus drop-off sites. Depending upon the degree of assistance offered by university officials and other implicit and explicit restrictions placed upon this project, subjects received questionnaires if their names: (1) appeared on public lists of black university employees (i.e., telephone directories, partial listings of minority employees); or (2) were on computer-generated lists of black faculty and staff employees at each campus.

Measures

Communicator Style Measure (CSM)

In the present study, communicator style was measured by using a shortened version of Norton's Communicator Style Measure (CSM) using only the style descriptor, namely the adjectival label (Table 2). This version of the measure has good structural reliability (see Norton and Robinson, 1980). Fourteen style variables were used on the CSM shortened version, with a five-point Likert-type scale ranging from "Describes Me Well" to "Does Not Describe Me Well."

Black Identification Questionnaire (BIQ)

The BIQ (Table 3) is an eleven-item instrument developed by the author specifically for this investigation. The scale, a result of an extensive literature review of the phenomenon, produced a Cronbach alpha of .89. The three-stage pilot, data-collection and analysis process for the measure has been reported previously, (Cox, 1985b)

The BIQ measure includes Likert-type scales designed to measure two subscales of the black identification construct: "Brother-/Sisterhood" and "Loyalty/Similarity". Subjects respond to items along a five-point scale indicating strong agreement to strong disagreement. In the present study, scores were added to obtain a total BIQ score and negatively worded items were reversed scored. Finally, two levels of black identification (low, high) were achieved using a median-split of the subjects' responses.

Statistical Analyses

The effects of gender and black identification on perceptions of communicator style were investigated using the following types of analysis: First, t-tests were used to determine if means of the communicator style variables differed significantly for black males and females. Second, a multiple discriminant analysis was computed to determine if a linear combination of variables could distinguish between the sexes. Finally, analyses of variance (ANOVA)'s were used to uncover possible interaction effects among the variables.

Results

Question #1: Do black males and females differ

323

significantly in their reported communicator styles?

T-tests were computed to assess the significance of mean differences between scores on these variables. Significant differences between the means of the two groups were found for **dramatic**, **attentive**, and **argumentative** (see Table 4). In addition, to provide a clearer indication of sex differences, a stepwise, multiple discriminant analysis was also computed.

The discriminant analysis was performed to determine if application of some linear combination of variables could discriminate between the sexes. The resulting linear combination produced significant between-group differences (X^2 = 15.661, p < .001). Table 5 presents the stepwise solution for the variable data set. The best discriminating variables were **dramatic** and **attentive**. Based upon these analyses, then, in general black males see themselves as being dramatic and argumentative communicators. Black females, on the other hand, tend to report being attentive.

Question #2: Do gender and black identification interact to affect reported communicator styles?

Analysis of variance results indicated significant main effects for sex and the following style variables: **dramatic**, **attentive**, **argumentative**, and **flexible** (see Tables 6, 7, 8, and 9, respectively). A particularly important finding of these ANOVA's is the consistent emergence of three style subconstructs as best distinguishing between black males and females. T-test analysis of means, however, indicates the differences in flexible style scores between men and women only approached statistical significance.

In addition, three significant two-way interaction effects were obtained for sex, black identification, and the following variables: **friendly**, **open**, and **quiet**. Basically, these results tend to suggest that sex and black identification do interact to influence evaluations of communicator style. Newman Keuls (NK) post hoc analysis was computed for each interaction to explore the significance of the differences between the sexes.

First, Newman Keuls post hoc analysis revealed that black males with low black identification scores ($\bar{x}$ = 4.61, n = 28) evaluated themselves as significantly more friendly communicators than black females with low black identification scores ($\bar{x}$ = 4.46, n = 91). Concomitantly, black males with high black identification scores ($\bar{x}$ = 4.29, n = 35) rated themselves as significantly less friendly communicators than black females with high black identification scores ($\bar{x}$ = 4.73, n = 64), (see Table 10, Figure I).

A second interaction effect emerged for the open communicator subconstruct. Specifically, NK analysis showed black males with low black identification scores ($\bar{x}$ = 4.36, n = 28) reported higher openness scores than black females with low black identification scores ($\bar{x}$ = 3.92, n = 91). On the other hand, black males with high black identification scores ($\bar{x}$ = 3.77, n = 35) perceived themselves to be significantly less open communicators than black females with high black identification scores ($\bar{x}$ = 4.23, n = 62), (see Table 11, Figure II).

Finally, post hoc analysis suggests that black men with low black identification scores ($\bar{x}$ = 2.83, n = 29) reported to be significantly less quiet than black females with low black identification scores ($\bar{x}$ = 3.14, n = 90). However, black males with high black identification scores ($\bar{x}$ = 3.54, n = 35) rated themselves to be significantly more quiet than black females with high black identification levels ($\bar{x}$ = 3.02, n = 63), (see Table 12, Figure III).

Discussion and Implications

According to Weick (1979), organizational sense-making involves, at least in part, imposing one's cause map on the world in order to understand human activity. As Weick explains, cause maps "allow the person to interpret what goes on in a situation and **express** herself in that same situation and be understood by others," (p. 132). Since style gives form to the content of expressions (Norton, 1983), it is reasonable to suggest that communicator style is an enduring component of organizational sense-making.

This study provides evidence to suggest that subtle communicator style differences exist between black males and females. Generally speaking, black males report to be mostly dramatic and argumentative communicators, whereas black females see themselves as primarily attentive. These results are significant for at least two reasons. First, previous organizational researchers who have focused on black people have tended to group males and females together as one homogeneous group. However, though this research has been heuristic, such capricious grouping has tended to simplify (at best) and/or ignore (at worst) the significance and complexity of intragroup communication among blacks in organizational contexts. The results indicate that intra-racial differences may need to be addressed when doing organizational research.

Second, Norton (1983) suggests that the way people are managed via a superior's communicator style may determine specific attitudes and behaviors. Hence, since communication activity may influence the motivation and productivity of others (Lewis et al., 1982), style differences between black males and females, in a tentative way, may offer an alternative in exploring the relationship between worker productivity and motivation in organizations.

In addition, this study indicates, at least tentatively, that sex and racial group identification interact to influence reports of communicator style among black people. Specifically, black males with low black identification scores see themselves as significantly more friendly and open and less quiet than black females at the same level of black identification. Concomitantly, black females with high black identification scores report to be significantly more friendly and open and quieter than black males at high black identification levels.

Interestingly, these results suggest that for black males, generally speaking, black identification may dilute communicative activity in organizational settings while having an intensifying effect for black females. Davis and Watson (1982) address this issue when they find:

> "In some companies it was the women who were the splashers, because the men were either tired or felt that career advancement was an individual thing and that any identification with a group, especially a disrespected racial group, could do their careers more harm than good," (p. 128).

Black identification and sex interacting to influence reports of communicator style have several important consequences for organizational sense-making. First, these results tend to demonstrate that racial group identities are **not** left outside organizational doors; they continually influence and are influenced by communicative activity inside and outside the work place. Second, the relationship between black identification, sex and communicator style illuminates the delicate balance that exists for those who must maintain multiple identity group memberships in organizations. Based upon these results, it is reasonable to assert that the extent to which either one's sexual or racial group identity is altered may directly influence how black people make sense of organizational environments.

Finally, these results indicate that black people have not, as of yet, reconciled the issue of racial group identification among themselves. In organizational contexts, then, differences in reported black identification may help explain the consequences of many intra- and interracial interactions. The prospects for future research efforts in this area are promising.

TABLE 1
Operational Definitions
of Communicator Style Subconstructs

Dominant

The dominant communicator tends to take charge in social situations. This individual tends to control conversations and is generally authoritative in group interactions.

Dramatic

The dramatic communicator manipulates, exaggerates fantasies, stories, metaphors, rhythm, voice and other stylistic devices to highlight or understate content.

Lively/Animated

A lively/animated communicator provides frequent sustained eye-contact, uses many gestures and facial expression. The animated communicator actively uses postures and body movements to exaggerate or understate the content.

Impression Leaving

Impression leaving centers around whether the person is remembered because of the communicative stimuli which are projected. Impression leaving is related to perceptions and thought processes, initial encounters, and total interactions in dyads.

Relaxed

The relaxed communicator can be described as "calm and collected," and relatively free from nervousness and anxiety in his/her communication. This individual comes across as a relaxed speaker when under pressure.

Attentive

The attentive communicator makes certain that the other person knows that he/she is being listened to. This individual deliberately uses paraverbal regulators and sustains eye contact during conversations.

Open

Behavior associated with the open subconstruct includes communicative activity which is characterized as being conversational, expansive, affable, gregarious, unreserved, unsecretive, somewhat frank, possibly outspoken, definitely extroverted, and obviously approachable.

Stylistically, the open communicator readily reveals personal information about the self in communicative interactions.

Friendly

Friendly communicators range from being simply "unhostile" to "deeply intimate" in their communicative interactions. This individual is usually judged as well-liked in group and interpersonal situations.

The friendly communicator interacts easily with strangers and is generally considered to be very sociable.

Contentious/Argumentative

The contentious communicator is usually quick to challenge others in disagreements. This person becomes very upset when he/she has to drop an argument that is unresolved. This person rarely withdraws from verbal confrontation.

Precise

The precise communicator is the person who phrases comments exactly. This person usually insists upon proof for arguments. The precise communicator requires accurate definitions in communicative interactions. This person can always repeat to someone else exactly what was meant.

Serious

The serious communicator is a "strictly business" interactant. This person usually engages in minimal amounts of small talk. Stylistically, the serious communicator is more formal than informal in their communicative interactions.

Quiet

Behavior associated with the quiet communicator includes less conversation and very reserved. The quiet communicator is also less audible during communicative interactions.

Loud

Loud communicators usually communicate at high volumes. These individuals interrupt conversations and usually obtain the attention of others in group settings easily.

Humorous

The humorous communicator deliberately includes jokes within his/her communication. This individual employs stories, anecdotes, and witty remarks to explain or emphasize content.

Flexible

The flexible communicator is best described as a compromiser. This individual readily acquiesces rather than confronts. The flexible communicator is easily persuaded by other individuals. These persons are often described as submissive, docile, and affable.

Good Communicator

The good communicator subconstruct is best described as an "umbrella" variable for all of the elements which have been heretofore discussed.

Because of the intensely perceptual nature of this variable, no attempt will be made to define this subconstruct within this paper. However, this subconstruct is important in that it will serve as an anchor for other variables to be analyzed in this and other articles.

TABLE 2
The Communicator Style Measure (CSM)
Shortened Version

INSTRUCTIONS: The following items describe the way people communicate. Indicate the degree that the item accurately describes your communicator style. Circle "5" if the item really describes you well, "4" if it describes you moderately well, "3" if you do not know whether the item describes you or not, and "2" if the item does not describe you. Circle "1" if you believe that the item really does not describe you well.

	DOES NOT DESCRIBE ME WELL		?	DESCRIBES ME WELL	
DOMINANT	1	2	3	4	5
RELAXED	1	2	3	4	5
FRIENDLY	1	2	3	4	5
OPEN	1	2	3	4	5
ARGUMENTATIVE	1	2	3	4	5
DRAMATIC	1	2	3	4	5
LIVELY/ANIMATED	1	2	3	4	5
ATTENTIVE	1	2	3	4	5
IMPRESSION LEAVING	1	2	3	4	5
SERIOUS	1	2	3	4	5
QUIET	1	2	3	4	5
PRECISE	1	2	3	4	5
HUMOROUS	1	2	3	4	5
FLEXIBLE	1	2	3	4	5
LOUD	1	2	3	4	5
GOOD COMMUNICATOR	1	2	3	4	5

331

TABLE 3
The Black Identification Questionnaire (BIQ)

IDENTIFICATION SIGNALS FEELINGS OF ACCOUNTABILITY, BELONGING, AND
ASSOCIATION WITH A PERSON AND/OR GROUP. IDENTIFICATION CONSISTS
OF BOTH VERBAL AND NON-VERBAL CLUES. BLACK PEOPLE MAY VARY
GREATLY IN THE AMOUNT AND KINDS OF IDENTIFICATION THEY MAY HAVE
WITH ONE ANOTHER.

EACH OF THE FOLLOWING STATEMENTS REPRESENT DIFFERENT DIMENSIONS
OF BLACK IDENTIFICATION. READ EACH STATEMENT CAREFULLY. DECIDE
HOW MUCH YOU DISAGREE OR AGREE WITH THE STATEMENT AND CIRCLE THE
APPROPRIATE RESPONSE.

PLEASE DO NOT RESPOND THE WAY YOU THINK A BLACK PERSON SHOULD.
RATHER, YOUR ANSWERS SHOULD BE AS HONEST AS POSSIBLE AND REFLECT
YOUR PERSONAL FEELINGS. THERE ARE NO RIGHT OR WRONG ANSWERS.

1. On the whole, my beliefs and
   the beliefs of most black
   people are very much alike.   NO   no   ?   yes   YES

2. I have nothing in common with
   most black people.   NO   no   ?   yes   YES

3. Things that matter to black
   people also matter to me.   NO   no   ?   yes   YES

4. I truly believe that black
   people are my "brothers" and
   "sisters."   NO   no   ?   yes   YES

5. I see myself the same as most
   black people.   NO   no   ?   yes   YES

6. I identify with black people.   NO   no   ?   yes   YES

7. I dislike openly showing
   "brother"/"sisterhood" to
   black people.   NO   no   ?   yes   YES

8. I would describe myself as
   being like most black people.   NO   no   ?   yes   YES

9. I like being with black people. NO   no   ?   yes   YES

332

10. Blacks who have "made it" should help other blacks become successful.　　　NO　　no　　?　　yes　　YES

11. I would describe black people as my "brothers" and/or "sisters."　　　NO　　no　　?　　yes　　YES

12. I feel emotionally related to black people.　　　NO　　no　　?　　yes　　YES

13. I almost never call black people my "brothers"/ "sisters."　　　NO　　no　　?　　yes　　YES

14. I do not feel emotionally related to black people.　　　NO　　no　　?　　yes　　YES

15. Sometimes, I have trouble talking to black people.　　　NO　　no　　?　　yes　　YES

16. It makes me feel good when blacks call me their "brother"/ "sister."　　　NO　　no　　?　　yes　　YES

17. On the whole, my problems and the problems of black people are the same.　　　NO　　no　　?　　yes　　YES

18. I feel accountable to black people for many of the things that I do.　　　NO　　no　　?　　yes　　YES

19. I truly believe that race is rarely discussed among my white co-workers.　　　NO　　no　　?　　yes　　YES

20. I strongly identify with black people.　　　NO　　no　　?　　yes　　YES

21. It is hard for me to get close to most black people.　　　NO　　no　　?　　yes　　YES

22. I do not enjoy helping black people.　　　NO　　no　　?　　yes　　YES

23. I talk about how I am like most black people.　　　NO　　no　　?　　yes　　YES

24. I almost never see myself as a
    black person.   NO   no   ?   yes   YES

25. I truly believe that black
    people should help other black
    people.   NO   no   ?   yes   YES

26. I enjoy representing black
    people.   NO   no   ?   yes   YES

27. I have very little in common
    with most black people.   NO   no   ?   yes   YES

28. Being black is only a small
    part of who I am.   NO   no   ?   yes   YES

29. It is really important for me
    to be black.   NO   no   ?   yes   YES

30. Things that matter to most
    black people also matter to me. NO   no   ?   yes   YES

31. Generally speaking, my values
    and the values of most black
    people are the same.   NO   no   ?   yes   YES

32. I often find it difficult to
    relate to black people.   NO   no   ?   yes   YES

334

TABLE 4
T-test Analysis
Sex by Communicator Style Variables

Variable Name	Sex	N	Style Mean	t	DF	2-Tail Prob.
Argumentative	Women	158	2.37	2.19	114.04	.031
	Men	63	**2.79**			
Dramatic	Women	157	2.36	2.74	113.63	.007
	Men	63	**2.87**			
Attentive	Women	157	**4.32**	2.32	108.73	.022
	Men	64	4.03			

TABLE 5
Multiple Discriminant Analysis
Stepwise Solution

Step	Variable	Change in Raos V
1	Dramatic	7.3*
2	Attentive	7.4*
3	Lively/Animated	1.7

*$p < .01$ for changes in Raos V

TABLE 6
Analysis of Variance
The Effect of Sex and Black Identification
on "Dramatic" Style

Source of Variation	Sum of Squares	DF	Mean Squares	F
Main Effects	17.192	2	8.596	5.603
Sex	10.472	1	10.472	6.826*
Black Identification	4.507	1	4.507	2.938
2-way Interactions	1.549	1	1.549	1.009
Sex x Black Identification	1.549	1	1.549	1.009
Explained	18.740	3	6.247	4.072
Residual	325.255	212	1.534	
Total	343.995	215	1.600	

----

*$p < .05$

337

TABLE 7
Analysis of Variance
The Effect of Sex and Black Identification
On "Attentive" Style

Source of Variation	Sum of Squares	DF	Mean Square	F
Main Effects	3.076	2	1.538	2.252
Sex	3.003	1	3.003	4.397*
Black Identification	.213	1	.213	.311
2-way Interactions	.128	1	.128	.187
Sex x Black Identification	.128	1	.128	.187
Explained	3.203	3	1.068	1.564
Residual	142.042	208	.683	
Total	145.245	211	.688	

*$p < .05$

TABLE 8
Analysis of Variance
The Effect of Sex and Black Identification
On "Argumentative" Style

Source of Variation	Sum of Squares	DF	Mean Square	F
Main Effects	8.414	2	4.207	2.456
Sex	7.232	1	7.232	4.222*
Black Identification	.501	1	.501	.292
2-way Interactions	.483	1	.483	.282
Sex x Black Identification	.483	1	.483	.282
Explained	363.099	212	1.713	
Total	371.995	215	1.730	

*$p < .05$

TABLE 9
Analysis of Variance
The Effect of Sex and Black Identification
On "Flexible" Style

Source of Variation	Sum of Squares	DF	Mean Square	F
Main Effects	3.085	2	1.543	1.876
Sex	3.081	1	3.081	3.746*
Black Identification	.085	1	.085	.104
2-way Interactions	.239	1	.239	.291
Sex x Black Identification	.239	1	.239	.291
Explained	3.324	3	1.108	1.347
Residual	176.840	215	.823	
Total	180.164	218	.826	

*$p < .05$

TABLE 10
Analysis of Variance
The Effect of Sex and Black Identification
On "Friendly" Style

Source of Variation	Sum of Squares	DF	Mean Square	F
Main Effects	1.305	2	.652	1.346
Sex	1.034	1	1.034	2.132
Black Identification	.429	1	.429	.885
2-way Interaction	3.753	1	3.753	7.742*
Sex x Black Identification	3.753	1	3.753	7.742
Explained	5.058	3	1.686	3.478
Residual	102.776	212	.485	
Total	107.833	215	.502	

*$p < .05$

TABLE 11
Analysis of Variance
The Effect of Sex and Black Identification
On "Open" Style

Source of Variation	Sum of Squares	DF	Mean Square	F
Main Effects	.089	2	.045	.041
Sex	.017	1	.017	.016
Black Identification	.080	1	.080	.073
2-way Interactions	8.636	1	8.636	7.895*
Sex x Black Identification	8.636	1	8.636	7.895
Explained	8.725	3	2.908	2.659
Residual	231.900	212	1.094	
Total	240.625	215	1.119	

---

*$p < .005$

TABLE 12
Analysis of Variance
The Effect of Sex and Black Identification
On "Quiet" Style

Source of Variation	Sum of Squares	DF	Mean Square	F
Main Effects	1.578	2	.789	.417
Sex	.548	1	.548	.289
Black Identification	.831	1	.831	.439
2-way Interactions	7.871	1	7.871	4.158*
Sex x Black Identification	7.871	1	7.871	4.158
Explained	9.449	3	3.150	1.664
Residual	406.971	215	1.893	
Total	416.420	218	1.910	

---

*p $<$ .05

343

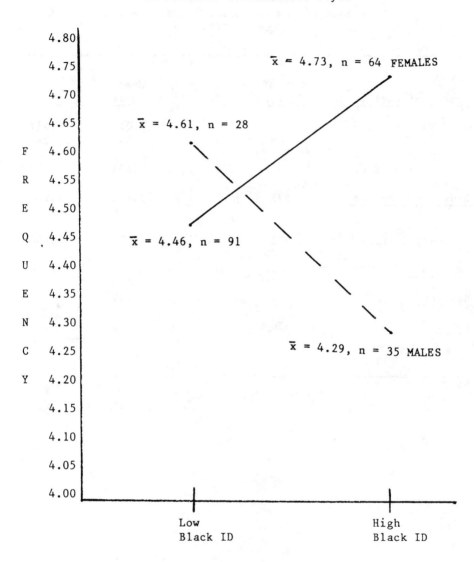

Figure I: Effect of Black Identification and Sex
on FRIENDLY Communicator Style

$\bar{x}$ = 4.73, n = 64 FEMALES

$\bar{x}$ = 4.61, n = 28

$\bar{x}$ = 4.46, n = 91

$\bar{x}$ = 4.29, n = 35 MALES

Low
Black ID

High
Black ID

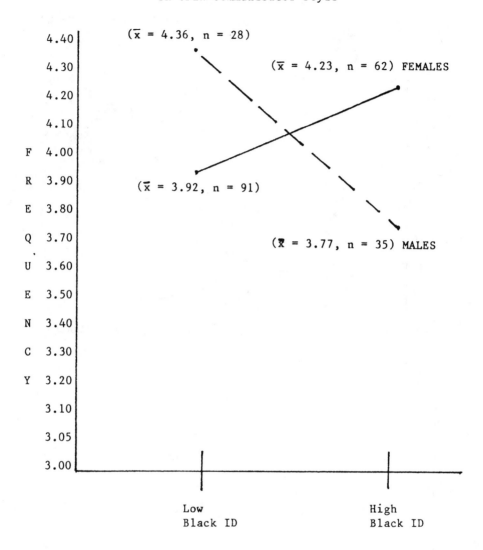

Figure II: Effect of Black Identification and Sex
on OPEN Communicator Style

($\bar{x}$ = 4.36, n = 28)

($\bar{x}$ = 4.23, n = 62) FEMALES

($\bar{x}$ = 3.92, n = 91)

($\bar{x}$ = 3.77, n = 35) MALES

F   4.40
    4.30
    4.20
    4.10
F   4.00
R   3.90
E   3.80
Q   3.70
U   3.60
E   3.50
N   3.40
C   3.30
Y   3.20
    3.10
    3.05
    3.00

Low   High
Black ID   Black ID

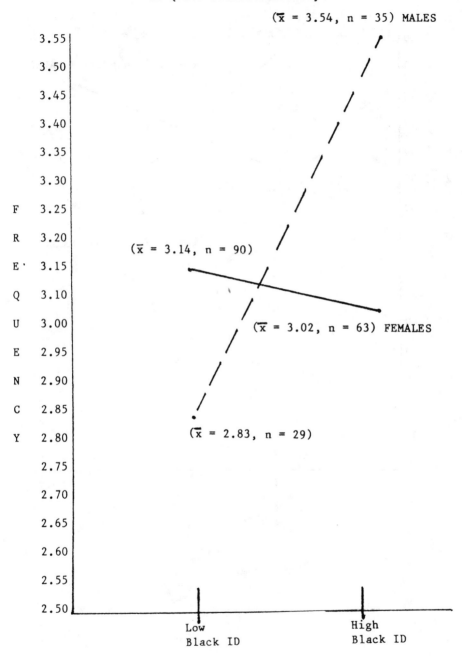

Figure III: Effect of Black Identification and Sex
on QUIET Communicator Style

($\bar{x}$ = 3.54, n = 35) MALES

($\bar{x}$ = 3.14, n = 90)

($\bar{x}$ = 3.02, n = 63) FEMALES

($\bar{x}$ = 2.83, n = 29)

F
R
E·
Q
U
E
N
C
Y

3.55
3.50
3.45
3.40
3.35
3.30
3.25
3.20
3.15
3.10
3.00
2.95
2.90
2.85
2.80
2.75
2.70
2.65
2.60
2.55
2.50

Low
Black ID

High
Black ID

BIBLIOGRAPHY

Banks, W. (1970). The changing attitudes of black students. Personnel & Guidance Journal, 48, 9-20.

Butler, R. (1975). Psychotherapy: Implications of a black consciousness model. Psychotherapy: Theory, Research & Practice, Winter, 12(4), 407-411.

Cheek, D. (1972). Black ethnic identity as related to skin color, social class, and selected variables. (Doctoral dissertation, Temple University, 1972).

Cox, M. (1985a, February). An interpretive approach: Studying the communicative experiences of blacks in organizations. Paper prepared for presentation at the Western Speech Communication Association Convention.

Cox, M. (1985b). The development of a black identification questionnaire: Implications for communication in business and the professions. Unpublished manuscript. California State University-Chico.

Cross, W. (1971). The negro-to-black conversion experience. Black World, 118-137.

Davis, G., & Watson, G. (1982). Black life in corporate america: Swimming in the mainstream. New York: Doubleday.

Hall, W., Freedle, R., & Cross, W. (1972). Stages in the development of black awareness: An exploratory investigation. In R. L. Jones (Ed.), Black Psychology, (pp. 256-265). New York: Harper & Row.

Hilgard, E.R. (1944). Human motives and the concept of the self. American Psychologist, 4, 374-382.

Lessing, E., & Zargarin, S. (1972). Black power ideology and college students' attitudes toward their own and other racial groups. Journal of Pesonality and Social Psychology, 21, 61-73.

Lewis, M., Cummings, H. & Long, L. (1982). Communication activity as a predictor of the fit between worker motivation and worker productivity. In M. Burgoon (Ed.). Communication Yearbook 5 (pp. 473-503). New Jersey: Transaction Books.

Miller, D. (1963). The study of social relationships: Situation, identity, and social interaction. In Sigmund Koch (Ed.). Psychology: A Study of A Science. Study II. Empirical Substructure and Relations with Other Sciences (pp. 639-679). New York: McGraw-Hill.

Milliones, J. (1980). Construction of a black consciousness measure: Psychotherapeutic implication. Psychotherapy: Theory, Research and Practice, 17, 175-182.

Montgomery, B. & Norton, R. (1981). Sex differences and similarities in communicator style. Communication Monographs, 48, 121-132.

Norton, R. (1978). Foundation of a communicator style construct. Human Communication Research, 4, 99-112.

Norton, R. (1983). Communicator Style: Theory, Applications, and Measures. Beverly Hills: Sage.

Norton, R. & Robinson, D. (1980). Communicator style in career decisions. Paper presented at the meeting of the Speech Communication Association in New York, N.Y.

Patchen, Martin. (1970). Participating, Achievement, and Involvement on the Job. Englewood Cliffs: Prentice Hall,

Thomas, C. (1971). Boys no more. Beverly Hills, CA: Glencoe Press.

Toomer, J. W. (1975). Beyond being black: Identification alone is not enough. Journal of Negro Education. Summer, 44(3), 432-440.

Weick, K. (1978). The social psychology of organizing. Reading, Mass.: Addison-Wesley Publishers.

Williams, I. (1975). An investigation of the developmental stages of black consciousness. (Doctoral dissertation, University of Cincinnati, 1975).

SECTION FIVE

GENDER COMMUNICATION PEDAGOGY

CHAPTER 20

TEACHING THE COLLEGE COURSE ON GENDER
DIFFERENCES AS BARRIERS TO CONFLICT
RESOLUTION

Deborah Borisoff, New York University
Lisa Merrill, Hofstra University

INTRODUCTION

The numbers of women and men who are required to work together as colleagues has increased dramatically during the past decade. As a result of professional proximity, many gender-related problems and strategies for behavior have emerged as issues for serious consideration.

A major issue that requires closer scrutiny is how conflict management may be affected by gender. Although the ability to handle conflict is often a part of courses that deal with communication, most existing training programs ignore strategies in the communicative behavior of women and men that affect the ability to deal with confrontation and with conflict resolution.

In this chapter, we explore first, how women's communication styles have traditionally been a barrier to effective conflict management. Second, we examine how the strategies for understanding cross cultural communication may parallel and lead to a greater awareness of how women communicate. This knowledge, in turn, can be applied to women's conflict management styles. Third, we present current research that regards the natural communication styles of women as an asset in conflict resolution. Fourth, we discuss the implications of gender as a factor in conflict management and posit new ideas for continued research in the field of gender and conflict resolution.

GENDER AND ITS IMPACT ON CONFLICT STYLE

In Joyce Hocker and William Wilmot's book on interpersonal conflict (1985), the authors mention that the Chinese character for conflict is comprised of two different symbols superimposed: one is the symbol for danger while the other signifies opportunity, and how both of these features are exacerbated when one broadens her or his framework to include a cognizance of the role gender plays in understanding, and,

351

hopefully ameliorating conflict.

Much of the traditional research on conflict resolution has developed from a perception that conflict is the expressed struggle between individuals over differing goals, or divergent means to achieve goals. Using a game-theoretical model, one could say that the participants (or players) in conflict each desire to win or at least to maximize their gains and minimize their losses.

We contend, however, that when the players are different sexes, the participants frequently find that they are not playing the same game. Different norms, rules and values apply to each sex, and for each even the notion of winning or losing takes on different connotations. Therefore, when considering gender as a factor in conflict management, it is necessary to look at some of the divergent sex-role stereotyped assumptions that have shaped each partner's view of the world and picture of her or himself.

One of the first variables in conflict is the differences in the goal, opinion or value that is expressed. Stereotypically expression is different for males and females. In our book, The Power to Communicate: Gender Differences as Barriers (1985), we contend that speech and voice are metaphors for power. Furthermore, women have been socialized to refrain from exercising their power of expression. Women have been taught to internalize a socially imposed stereotype of the ideal feminine communicator -- as one who is soft-spoken, self-effacing and compliant. Whether we have adopted these standards, or consciously struggled to resist this image of women, the mere existence of the socially sanctioned set of expectations means the act of communication, of expressing ourselves and the choice of what mode one employs to do so will mean something different for women than for men.

Let us briefly examine the obvious limitations of the stereotype. First, women have been encouraged to be soft spoken, rather than risk being considered strident, grating, nagging, or shrill. They are taught to employ a vocal tone that threatens no one, but may lack sufficient force or volume for effective or convincing speech.

Second, women are encouraged to be self-effacing. To some extent, women's messages are ignored, interrupted and not attended to because women are taught, according to Robin Lakoff (1975), to "talk like a lady," to use disclaimers, weak particles, tag questions, and to reflect uncertainty. When women do not employ these tactics, they may be accused of being unfeminine. However, if they do "talk like a lady" they risk not being taken seriously. Thus, women are acculturated to adopt communication strategies that are hyperpolite, and that are constructed to please by minimizing one's own skills, rather than to risk antagonizing one's audience.

In contrast, the stereotypically masculine communicator is direct, confrontational, forceful and logical. This model, however, is not as neutral and positive as it may appear. Unlike the explicit limitations in the feminine model, the masculine orientation suggests hidden problems that may impede the successful resolution of conflicts.

First, men are not encouraged to be effective listeners. All too often they interrupt other speakers, or take time, while others are speaking, to prepare their own responses rather than attending to the messages of others. Second, men are less likely to be self-disclosing, and they are more likely than women to make categorical assertions and sweeping claims. While this behavior appears more self-assured, in a conflict situation it can be an impediment to an open and honest exchange in which partners need to hear each other's point of view.

One problem with stereotypes is that they often limit what individuals believe they can or cannot do or feel in our culture. Thus gender roles and their resultant stereotypes limit us from without and inhibit us from within. A second problem with these stereotypes is that they subtly and sometimes not so subtly, influence decisions on hiring, promotion, interpersonal relationships, and on marital and familial relationships.

THE INTERRELATIONSHIP BETWEEN CROSS-CULTURAL COMMUNICATION AND CONFLICT RESOLUTION

Given the gender-related communication barriers to conflict resolution, how does one, then, get beyond her or his stereotyping and work toward an accurate analysis and resolution of conflict?

Some of the answers can be found in applying developing strategies that have been suggested by several colleagues in the field of cross cultural communication. Harry C. Triandis (1979), in his work "Interpersonal Behavior Between Cultures" has found that many of the problems individuals encounter in cross cultural exchanges are due to: 1) a lack of understanding of the causes of the other's behavior; 2) a lack of awareness of how the other person analyzes her or his environment; and 3) ignorance of what constitutes a reward for her or him. Each of these factors has particular implications for a study of gender. The implicit and explicit power differences between men and women and the considerable differences in the ways we have been taught to view the world, can, if ignored, produce severe barriers to the resolution of individual conflict.

Triandis (1979) also postulated that individuals react to the other depending upon the perceived characteristics of the other, the social situation in which the participants find themselves and on each person's implicit personality theory. Here again, gender differences may increase the likelihood of conflict. For example, if you are perceived as helpful and accommodating by colleagues who assume that you will willingly forego a new course that you have proposed, they may be surprised and angered when they see you tenaciously asserting the value of your proposal and thus acting in an uncharacteristic manner.

Men and women may find conflict heightened by differences in each person's notion of appropriate behavior for the other in a given social situation. For example, a husband who routinely interrupts and corrects his wife in public may react vociferously if she does the same to him in public, although he may tolerate her interruptions in private.

Last and most significant, conflict with another individual may be based largely on one's own implicit and unconscious personality theory, or how one believes people in general (or women and men in specific) should act. A potent example of how one's personality theory can emerge during conflict can be seen in the different connotations for power held by women and men. Power is one of the primary variables in any conflict situation. In 1969, D.C. McClelland reported in the <u>Journal of International Affairs</u> that people who were told they had high drives to achieve or affiliate derived great satisfaction in the feedback. If they were told they had a drive for power, however, they experienced guilt.

The acknowledgement of a desire for power is especially difficult for women. As psychotherapist Harriet Lerner (1986, p. 129) has established in her article "Female dependency in context: Some theoretical and technical considerations," "Women...learn that being an autonomous self-directed person is hurtful to others, especially men. Their dependent behaviors are often an unconscious 'gift' or sacrifice to those they love; it is the gift of giving up self so that the other can gain self."

However, to resolve a conflict successfully, participants must be willing and able to acknowledge their own self-directed goals. All too often, research on power has focused on "perceived authority" (Hocker and Wilmot, 1985, pp. 80-81). Studies on power may well be skewed by participants who respond to researchers by indicating who they think "should" be making decisions rather than acknowledging the actual power dynamics within the relationship. Women have been encouraged to exercise their power covertly rather than overtly. It is not uncommon for participants who feel that they have little or no socially sanctioned power to employ in conflict situations whatever power or influence they have in a passive-aggressive manner, using tactics that may be considered "tyranny of the weak."

If we return to our two male and female players in a standard conflict game, it is apparent that these individuals come to this exchange with widely divergent fields of experience. They may be using different modes of expression (i.e., direct vs. indirect) starting from a position of power that is acknowledged by each and socially sanctioned or denied by the participants themselves. Even the ultimate goal, the notion of what constitutes a successful outcome, will differ for each participant.

Given these disparities, how can we deal with conflict in which gender is a variable (albeit an often unacknowledged variable)? Cross cultural resolution specialists Edward Glenn, Robert Johnson, Paul Kimmel and Bryant Wedge (1981) have proposed a cognitive interaction model which may be adopted to these ends. According to Glen et al., "In many international situations conflict is generated less by conflicting interests than by diverging patterns of understanding." This premise, the difference between a conflict of interest and a conflict of understanding has particular application for a gender-based study of conflict. For example, if two faculty members have a disagreement over who should take the minutes at the faculty meetings, one might assume that they are experiencing a simple conflict of interest where neither actor wants to perform a disagreeable task. However, if the task of notetaking means something different to each partner, no solution will be fully satisfactory until each understands the other's connotations for the behavior. Glenn et al. suggest a shared system of ideas or epistemologies as a mediating structure in a conflict of understanding.

WOMEN'S COMMUNICATION STYLES AS INTERVENTION STRATEGIES TO CONFLICT RESOLUTION

In the previous sections, we considered how female modes of communication serve as barriers to resolving conflict. In this section, we present four examples of how the behavior of women can serve as effective intervention strategies for conflict management. In this way, we attempt to demonstrate how certain behavior patterns that are regarded as negative in one context can become positive attributes in another setting.

According to Roderick Gilkey and Leonard Greenhalgh (1984), "...experiments involving simulated negotiations show that predominantly feminine subjects tend to view transactions with the other party as one of the many interactions within a long-term relationship rather than a discrete event with no future ramifications, adopt flexible bargaining postures, and avoid tactics that are likely to impair interpersonal relationships." Their findings have important implications for how women approach conflict.

First, because women approach bargaining situations from the perspective of long-term relationships, women may take greater pains than men to arrive at satisfactory resolutions to problems in order to maintain the relationships. In their study, Gilkey and Greenhalgh found that men often regard bargaining situations as short-term and episodic in nature. Therefore, men, they feel, may not expend the same considerable and often fruitful efforts that women will expend in order to find an acceptable resolution to a disagreement.

Related to length of the relationship is how women view the quality of their relationships. In her research on how women approach relationships and moral dilemmas, Carol Gilligan (1982) found that mutuality, cooperativeness, and interdependence inform women's relationships with others and the choices they make in certain situations. If we accept Gilligan's findings and contrast them with the concern for competitiveness, independence and individualism that are attributed to men, we can suggest that women may extend themselves beyond merely solving the problem at hand to find a solution to a problem that will take into account maintaining the relationship.

One way that women and men attempt to maintain relationships during a conflict situation is to utilize their ability to read others' nonverbal communication. Women, however, may be better equipped to understand nonverbal language. Nancy Henley (1977) reported on women's and subordinates' nonverbal behavior and on their greater ability to interpret accurately the nonverbal behavior of others. She related this ability to their subordinate position in society, which makes it incumbent upon them to read accurately nonverbal cues.

The ability to interpret body language correctly, however, is a definite asset during the negotiation process, where the participants frequently attempt to mask their true feelings. In addition to the interpretive abilities reading nonverbal behavior might indicate, when women attend to others' communication, they reflect two important traits of a negotiator.

First, accurate responses to another's feelings reflects sensitivity to the other party. Second, without empathic bonds between the parties in conflict, the likelihood for reaching a satisfactory resolution is diminished. When women connect with the feelings and concerns of others -- even if they are not in agreement -- they are demonstrating empathy, which is essential for bargaining and negotiating to be truly successful.

In addition to being more sensitive to nonverbal cues than men, studies show that women are also extremely sensitive to verbal cues. This is manifest in such findings as those of Don Zimmerman and Candace West (1975) who discovered that women interrupt others far less frequently than men in mixed-sex dyads.

One way that individuals demonstrate that they are listening fully to others is by waiting for the other individual to complete her or his thought before asserting their own views. In a conflict situation, it is important for the parties concerned to feel that they are being fully listened to. It is important for individuals to be allowed to express their concerns and frustrations in an honest and open manner. If under such circumstances women adhere to their tendency not to interrupt others, those individuals involved in a conflict may respond positively within an environment that allows them to air their views in an open and hopefully productive way.

Beyond being sensitive to the verbal cues of others, it is equally important for women to use their own verbal strategies appropriately and effectively. When Robin Lakoff (1975) discussed the interrelationship between women's tentativeness and their use of language, she was demonstrating how such language use could represent women in a negative and weak light. Certainly this is true in cases where forthrightness and assertiveness are required. However, in many negotiation settings, it is often advantageous to present an unbiased appearance which noncommital or open-ended language use can communicate.

Although current research is beginning to indicate that women's attitudes toward relationships and patterns of behavior can facilitate the negotiation process, there still lingers the perception that being a woman and being strong within the organization are mutually exclusive. For example, in her discussion of womens' conflict styles, Linda Putnam (1983) cautions that women in professional settings often feel trapped between risking assertiveness and being labelled with a negative masculine stereotype (such as 'ball buster,' 'castrating bitch,' 'pushy,' etc.), and sitting back, thereby perpetuating such equally disturbing feminine labels as 'incompetent,' 'a pussycat,' 'nonassertive,' etc. These stereotypes are so powerful, in fact, that they are often used as a justification to hinder the professional progress of women entering and moving up in executive positions.

Similarly, in a recent article in Working Woman, Basia Hellwig (1985) reported that executive consulting firms identified 73 potential chief executive officers who are women. Research presented by the consulting firms reflects the allegation that many women do not fare as well as men in positions of authority because they are considered to be too emotional and passive to deal effectively with conflict.

However, the articles goes on to report that many placement firms have found that women in authority positions use a collaborative approach to problem-solving with colleagues and staff. According to Kenneth Thomas and Ralph Kilmann (1977), the collaborative style is often desirable in routine situations because collaboration frequently leads to a win-win outcome which is an extremely productive result of conflict resolution.

When individuals are involved in training others in the strategies and techniques of conflict management, it is important to explore how the communication behavior of both women and men can be a barrier to effective conflict management. It is equally important to look at how their communication styles can be employed in conflict resolution.

CONCLUSION

Understanding the causes and dynamics of conflict is essential because conflict remains a potential and natural consequence of individual beliefs, goals and attitudes. In order to maximize effectiveness in conflict resolution, and to decrease stress when dealing with conflict, it is equally desirable to develop a conflict management style that is both flexible and appropriate to the occasion.

Although in the current literature on appropriate behavior for women and men, writers are beginning to encourage the adoption of an androgynous mode of communication, gender remains an overlooked variable in the conflict resolution process. If we look at the traits of a good negotiator, we find that these qualities quite naturally conform to an androgynous model and do not belong exclusively to either sex. If these attributes include confidence, trust, flexibility, empathy, openmindedness, constructive suggestions and fairness, then there is no reason to assume that women who quite consciously adopt effective communication strategies in a given situation, will not be as successful as men in conflict resolution. Equally important, we must continue to consider the values upon which sex-role stereotyped behavior is predicated. Unless women and men can articulate for each other the belief system that each brings to a disagreement, a conflict of understanding will remain untenable.

POTENTIAL AREAS FOR CONTINUED RESEARCH RELATED TO GENDER AND CONFLICT

As long as differences in the behavior patterns and the communication styles of women and men continue to exist, the issue of gender needs to be considered when studying conflict resolution.

Here, we present five ideas for potential investigation. While these points by no means exhaust the areas for research, they are meant to stimulate further consideration that will help to illuminate the intricate relationship between gender, communicative behavior and conflict resolution.

1. Research on international negotiation reveals that conflicts often occur because people from different nations approach problem solving in distinct ways. For example, one group of people may employ deductive reasoning to solve problems while another nation will use the inductive method. Earlier we proposed the connection between cross cultural communication and gender issues in conflict management. More research is indicated that would address the processes and approaches that women and men use in a conflict -- particularly in the problem

solving stage.

2. Works on conflict seem to target three basic types of disagreement: goal, value and attitude. Consideration needs to be given to how women and men view the relative importance of goals, values and attitudes in their lives. For example, the attainment of power might have more meaning for one segment of the population. Fame might be more important to another group.

3. More empirical research is needed on how the verbal and nonverbal communication of women and men is expressed during conflict and on how gender affects resolving conflict.

4. Careful scrutiny of the conflict-mode instruments currently being used is recommended. Are the questions, the situations or the language used possibly biased toward one group?

5. We must be mindful of the changing roles and communication strategies of women and men and how these roles are received and perceived by society. Such changes will no doubt affect the way conflict is approached and handled in the future.

References

Borisoff, D. and Merrill, L. The power to communicate: Gender differences as barriers. Prospect Heights, Ill.: Waveland Press, 1985.

Gilkey, Roderick W. and Greenhalgh, L. "Developing effective negotiating approaches among professional women in organizations." Submitted to the Third Annual Conference on Women and Organizations, Simmons College, August, 1984.

Gilligan, C. In a different voice: Psychological theory and women's development. Cambridge, Mass.: Harvard University Press, 1982.

Glenn, E., Johnson, R., Kimmel, P., and Wedge, B. "A cognitive interaction model to analyze culture conflict in international relations." Conflict Resolution, XIV, no. 1 (1981): 35-48.

Hellwig, B. "The breakthrough generation: 73 women ready to run corporate America." Working Women, April, 1985.

Henley, N. Body politics: Power, sex and nonverbal communication. Englewood Cliffs, N.J.: Prentice Hall, 1977.

Hocker, J. and Wilmot, W. Interpersonal Conflict. Dubuque, Iowa: William C. Brown, 1978.

Lakeoff, H. Language and woman's place. New York: Harper and Row, 1975.

Lerner, H. "Female dependency in context: Some theoretical and technical considerations." In P. Reider and E. Hilberman (Eds.) The gender gap in psychotherapy. New York: Plenum Press, 1984, pp. 125-134.

McClelland, D.C. "The two faces of power." Journal of International Affairs, no. 24 (1969): 141-154.

Putnam, L. "Lady you're trapped: Breaking out of conflict styles." In J. Pilotta (Ed.) Women in organizations. Prospect Heights, Ill.: Waveland Press, 1983.

Thomas, K.W. and Killman, R.H. "Developing a forced-choice measure of conflict handling behavior: The 'mode' instrument." Educational and Psychological Measurement, no. 37 (1977): 309-325.

Triandis, H.C. "Interpersonal behavior across cultures." In G. Cross, J. Names, and D. Beck (Eds.) Conflict and human interaction. Dubuque, Iowa: Kendall/Hunt, 1979, pp. 35-48.

Semlak, W.D. Conflict resolving communication: A skill development approach. Prospect Heights, Ill.: Waveland Press, 1982.

Zimmerman, D. and West, C. "Sex roles, interruptions and silences in conversation." In B. Thorne and N. Henley (Eds.) Language and sex: Difference and dominance. Rowley, Mass.: Newbury House, 1975.

CHAPTER 21

TESTING A MODEL OF ORGANIZATIONAL SIMULATIONS:
THE INFLUENCE OF PARTICIPANT SEX AND SEX ROLE ON
PARTICIPATIVENESS[1]

Lea P. Stewart, Rutgers University

An organizational simulation is an instructional tool designed to model the functioning of a real-world organization (Lederman & Stewart, 1983). Students who participate in this type of simulation function as members of a simulated organization. They are assigned specific organizational roles and are expected to perform their duties in accordance with standard business practices. Two traditions meet in the study of such organizational simulations: the study of simulation and gaming and the study of organizational communication. The first tradition, simulation and gaming, has a long history. A great deal of research has been conducted on simulations and gaming (see Bredemeier & Greenblat, 1981 for a summary of some of this research). The results of much of this research, however, are inconclusive. For example, simulations may or may not be more effective than traditional instructional methods in changing a student's attitude toward a particular subject. The second tradition involved in researching organizational simulations is the study of organizational communication. Teachers of organizational communication increasingly are using organizational simulations to expose students to "real-world" communication phenomena. In addition, communication researchers have begun to use organizational simulations as data-gathering sites. Putnam and Sorenson (1982), for example, gathered data on equivocal messages in organizations as students participated in a modified version of the Hi-Fli Fireworks simulation (Pacanowsky et al., 1977).

Most of the research on organizational simulations comes from one or the other of these two traditions; yet, to fully understand the organizational simulation process, both of these traditions must guide research efforts. Organizational simulations are not organizations; thus, researchers need to consider the unique characteristics of simulations. In addition, students participating in an organizational simulation work together to form a functioning organization. Thus, researchers need to consider the organizational communication aspects of the situation to develop a clear understanding of what is occurring during the simulation. This chapter presents a model of organizational simulations which attempts to look at the simulation as both an organization and as a simulation and tests the model using an ongoing organizational simulation as a data collection site. The model is designed to clarify the relationships among the variables in an organizational simulation so that systematic research into each of these areas may be conducted. This model applies to internally parametered simulations in which the outcomes are not entirely predetermined by the designer of the simulation or the instructor using the simulation (Ruben, 1977).

THE MODEL

In this analysis, an organizational simulation is seen as a system of interacting individuals. The activity emitted by each individual is considered to be a reward (or punishment) for and a stimulus to the activity of other organizational members (after Homans, 1961, p. 52). A simulation is composed of individuals who both shape the interaction which occurs in the simulation and who are, in turn, shaped by it.

The simulation process may be divided into three phases: Pre-Interaction Conditions, Interaction Stages, and Results of the Interaction (see Figure 1).

PRE-INTERACTION CONDITIONS exist prior to the start of a simulation. Analogous to Ellis and Fisher's (1975) "structural variables," these variables can influence the final outcome of a simulation, but cannot fully account for it. Pre-interaction conditions include: the individual resources of participants in a simulation, conditions surrounding the formation of a simulated organization, and external limits imposed on a simulated organization.

Individual Resources of the organizational members are those variables which individuals bring to a simulation and which are unaffected by the interaction within a simulation. These include: age, sex, level of intelligence, educational level, personality characteristics, and past experiences. For example, older students or students with a great deal of employment experience may behave differently in a simulation or learn different things than younger, less experienced students.

Conditions surrounding the formation of a simulated organization include how a simulation is introduced to

Figure 1

A MODEL OF ORGANIZATIONAL SIMULATIONS

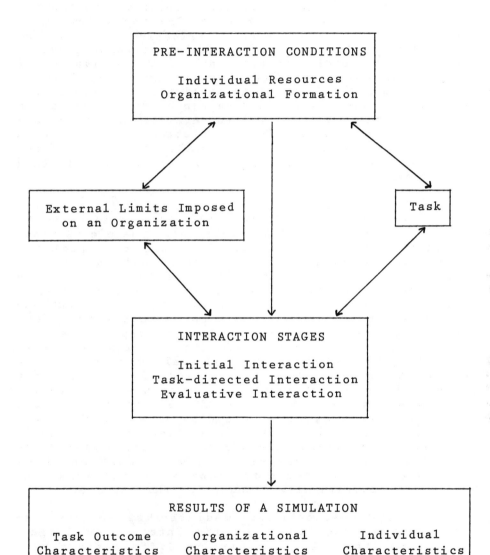

the students, what has preceded a simulation, and the attitude of the instructor toward using a simulation. In addition, these conditions also include why the participants chose to be part of this specific experience (for example, it was a class requirement, it was an opportunity to experience something new) and how the individuals define the situation for themselves (for example, to gain self-concept validation, as practice for future employment, or for socio-emotional interaction). These conditions also include the motivation of the individuals for participating in a simulation, that is, both the level of motivation for participating in a simulation and the motive behind participating in a simulation. For example, students who are enthusiastic about participating in a simulation and who have an instructor who encourages them may have a very different experience from unenthusiastic students fulfilling a course requirement.

Limits imposed on a simulated organization by external sources are conditions which are unaffected by the specific members of a simulation. These conditions include: rules for interaction, number of participants, amount of ambiguity in the situation, whether the interactions are competitive or cooperative, and pressures from outside the interaction such as time limits, deadlines, or a client waiting for the outcome of a simulation. Ruben (1977) notes that simulations have five characteristics: (1) participants cast in roles; (2) interactions between those roles; (3) rules governing the interactions; (4) goals with respect to which the interactions occur; and (5) criteria for determining the attainment of the goals and the termination of the activity. To the extent that roles, rules and goals are determined by an external source (for example, an instructor or a client of the organization), these variables are external limits imposed on the simulated organization. Again, each of these variables may influence the outcome of a simulation, but cannot individually account for the outcome.

The organization's task mediates between the Pre-Interaction Conditions and the Interaction Stages. [The term "task" is used here to differentiate this concept from an organization's "goal." The task is the product or service that an organization is designed to produce. A simulated organization may have numerous goals, for example, exposing students to organizational problems, training students in critical thinking, or giving students opportunities to use presentational skills.] The task may be defined for participants by

366

an outside source (for example, the designer of the
simulation) and, thus, would be considered a Pre-Interaction Condition. In another situation, the participants may decide on their own task during the initial
phases of their interaction. In this instance, deciding on the task would be considered part of the Interaction Stages. (Working on a task is conducted during
the Interaction Stages no matter when the participants
determine what their task will be.) Whether a task is
part of the Pre-Interaction Conditions or part of the
Interaction Stages, it can be analyzed in terms of type
and complexity. Tasks may be specific products or
services provided to clients. The particular task a
simulation is designed to accomplish mediates between
the Pre-Interaction Conditions and the Interaction
Stages. A simulated organization designed to sell t-
shirts, for example, may function differently than a
simulated organization that is "manufacturing" a mythi-
cal product.

There are three basic INTERACTION STAGES during an
organizational simulation: initial interaction, task-
directed interaction, and evaluative interaction.

The actual process of a simulation begins with
initial interaction. In this phase, participants in a
simulation begin to get acquainted, begin to develop a
sense of themselves as part of an organization. Participants decide on their task during this phase if a
task has not been assigned to them.

This get-acquainted phase is followed by specifically task-directed interaction. This is interaction directed mainly toward accomplishing a particular
task an organization is undertaking. The task-directed
phase may be relatively short or may last several
months.

Once the task is generally completed, the organizational members begin evaluative interaction. The
organizational members evaluate the solution to the
task they have been working on, the organization as a
functioning unit (including how well it has fulfilled
the member's individual needs while performing the
task), and how well each individual member performed as
seen by other members and by the individual member.
The majority of evaluative interaction occurs near the
end of a simulation, but this type of interaction can
also occur during initial interaction or task-directed
interaction as members perform an on-going evaluation
of an organization. An organization may have more than

one task or more than one subphase of a task to complete so it may move from task-directed interaction to evaluative interaction and back to task-directed interaction several times. Nevertheless, an organizational simulation always ends its interaction with evaluative interaction. Participants in an organizational simulation will engage naturally in evaluative interaction. In addition, the instructor using a simulation may spend time with the participants processing or debriefing their experiences during a simulation (Lederman, 1984). This processing time is considered evaluative interaction.

The RESULTS OF A SIMULATION are threefold: task characteristics, organizational characteristics, and individual characteristics. These are variables which are a direct result of organizational members' interaction. These three sets of variables can also influence, but not account for, each other.

Task outcome characteristics are analogous to what is commonly called productivity. For example, task outcome characteristics include the efficiency with which a task has been completed, the quality of a product, the number of tasks completed (if multiple tasks are desirable), and the time it has taken to complete a task.

Organizational characteristics are characteristics of an organization that have been determined by the interaction during the process of a simulation. These characteristics include: an organization's history, morale, leadership style, norms, and amount of cohesiveness.

Individual characteristics are those characteristics of organizational members that are a result of their experiences in a simulation, for example, individual roles, conformity to norms, interpersonal attraction of members, and amount of satisfaction with an organization, with the outcome of a simulation, and with their own behavior in a simulation. Each of these variables is a direct result of interaction during a simulation.

APPLYING THE MODEL TO AN ORGANIZATIONAL SIMULATION

SIMCORP (Lederman & Stewart, 1983) is an organizational simulation used in the Admistrative Communication course at Rutgers University. The model of organizational simulations described previously will be

examined using data collected during the running of the
SIMCORP SIMULATION. As noted previously, SIMCORP, like
all organizational simulations, is not an organization,
and it is more than a simulation. SIMCORP must be
studied as an organizational simulation to fully understand the communication processes which occur within
it.

Given the model described previously, research
could be conducted at any stage of the model. This
paper will examine the effects of Preinteraction Conditions (specifically biological sex and sex role of
participants) on the Results of the Simulation (specifically organizational characteristics and individual
characteristics). The organizational characteristic
examined is amount of participation; the individual
characteristic examined is desire for participation.

RATIONALE

Participation and desire for participation are
examined in this study because of their importance in
previous research. The study of participation within
organizations has a long and significant history. Recently there has been a call for more participation
within organizations. Authors such as Kanter (1983)
advocate increasing amounts of employee participation
to improve organizational performance. Little research, however, has specifically dealt with the responses of women to participation. As the number of
women working in significant roles within organizations
increases, the need for research in this area grows.

In an exploratory study, Harrison (1982) examined
sex differences in subordinate responses to participative decision making in a public welfare organization
and found no significant difference between females and
males in their desire to participate in decision
making. In addition, she found that females perceive
their current work environment as significantly more
participative than males do.

The research described in this chapter replicates
and extends Harrison's work using the employees in an
organizational simulation as the source of data. Both
sex of employee and sex role are examined in terms of
the following research questions:

1. Do employees in an organizational simulation
significantly differ in desire for participation based
on their sex?

369

2. Do employees in an organizational simulation significantly differ in desire for participation based on their sex role?

3. Do employees in an organizational simulation significantly differ in the amount of participation they perceive in their work environment based on their sex?

4. Do employees in an organizational simulation significantly differ in the amount of participation they perceive in their work environment based on their sex role?

METHOD

Procedure

Because of the relatively small number of participants in the SIMCORP SIMULATION each semester, this research is based on data collected during three iterations of the simulation. Mean responses to each measure were examined, and it was determined that responses during each iteration were not significantly different. Thus, data were combined for the three iterations.

SIMCORP "employees" were asked by one of the course instructors to complete a detailed questionnaire at the end of each semester. Responses were anonymous, although students were asked to indicate the position they held and the department they worked in. Questionnaires were completed during classtime and returned to an instructional aide who then gave the questionnaires to the instructor.

Participants

Useable questionnaires were returned by 124 SIMCORP employees (25 males and 99 females). Although no data were collected on age and educational level, most of the students enrolled in this course are either juniors or seniors.

Measures

Sex Role was measured using items from the Bem Sex-Role Inventory (Bem, 1974) with a seven-point response scale. Sex role was determined using the procedure suggested by Wheeless and Dierks-Stewart (1981).

The following items were summed to yield a score for "sensitivity": compassionate, eager to soothe hurt feelings, friendly, gentle, helpful, sensitive to needs of others, sincere, tender, understanding, and warm. The following items were summed to yield a score for "instrumental": acts as leader, aggressive, assertive, competitive, dominant, forceful, has leadership abilities, independent, strong personality, and willing to take a stand. A median split was used to yield respondents considered high or low in sensitivity or instrumentality.

Desire for Participation was measured by three questions developed by Mohr (1977) and used by Harrison (1982): (1) I have my own job to do, I would just as soon the manager did not try to involve me in making decisions; (2) People in positions like mine should be able to give their opinions about operations and policies at work, and not just carry out duties as assigned; and (3) Employees like myself should have a voice in deciding how their work will be organized. Responses on a seven-point Likert-type scale were recoded so that a high score indicated greater desire for participation. Responses to the three questions were summed to yield an index of desire for participation.

Perceived Participation was measured by asking respondents to indicate on a seven-point Likert-type scale how well each of the following items devised by Mohr (1977) and used by Harrison (1982) characterized their work situation at SIMCORP: (1) When some important matter comes up that concerns me, my manager seeks out my ideas on the question before a decision is made; (2) All in all, I have very little influence in supervisory decisions that affect my department in important ways; (3) Our manager is inclined to accept opinions of the department members in important decisions about job-related matters; (4) I get few opportunities, if any, to participate in supervisory decisions that affect the significant aspects of my job; and (5) If I had a suggestion for improvement to make, it would be difficult to get a real hearing on it from my manager. Responses to the questions were recoded so that a high score indicated greater participativeness. Responses to the five items were summed to yield an index of perceived participation.

RESULTS

Research question 1 was examined by a one-way analysis of variance comparing male and female responses to the measure of desire for participation. Males and females did not differ significantly in their desire for participation, $F(123) = 3.02$, $p = .085$. The mean score for males ($\underline{n} = 25$) was 13.44; the mean score for females ($\underline{n} = 99$) was 14.08.

Research question 2 was examined using a one-way analysis of variance to compare high and low sensitivity respondents' responses to the measure of desire for participation. High and low sensitivity respondents did not differ in their desire for participation, $F(123) = .57$, N.S. The mean response to the desire for participation measure was 14.06 for high sensitivity respondents ($\underline{n} = 62$) and 13.84 for low sensitivity respondents ($\underline{n} = 62$).

In addition, a one-way analysis of variance was used to compare high and low instrumental respondents' responses to the measure of desire for participation. There was no significant difference between high and low instrumental respondents' desire for participation, $F(123) = 1.17$, N.S. The mean response to the desire for participation measure was 14.11 for high instrumental respondents ($\underline{n} = 62$) and 13.79 for low instrumental respondents ($\underline{n} = 62$). Thus, high instrumental respondents did not desire participation more than low instrumental respondents.

Research question 3 was examined by a one-way analysis of variance comparing female and male responses to the measure of perceived participation. Males and females did not differ significantly in the amount of participation they perceived in the work environment, $F(123) = .17$, N.S. The mean response to perceived participation for males ($\underline{n} = 25$) was 26.72; the mean response for females ($\underline{n} = 99$) was 26.11.

Research question 4 was examined by a one-way analysis of variance comparing high and low sensitivity respondents' responses to the measure of perceived participation. High and low sensitivity respondents did not differ in the amount of participation they perceived in the work place, $F(123) = .96$, N.S. The mean response for high sensitivity respondents ($\underline{n} = 62$) was 26.81 and 25.66 for low sensitivity respondents ($\underline{n} = 62$).

In addition, a one-way analysis of variance was used to compare high and low instrumental respondents' responses to the measure of perceived participation. High and low instrumental respondents significantly

372

differed in the amount of participation they perceived in their work environment, $F(123) = 7.11$, $p < .01$. The mean response for high instrumental respondents ($n = 62$) was 27.76 and 24.71 for low instrumental respondents ($n = 62$).

CONCLUSION

Organizational simulations must be examined as both simulations and as organizations. The model discussed above indicates that organizational simulations consist of pre-interaction conditions, interaction stages, and results of the interaction. To examine pre-interaction conditions and results of the interaction, participants in the SIMCORP SIMULATION were asked to indicate their desire to participate in organizational decision making and the amount of participation they felt they were able to exercise. These results of the interaction were analyzed in terms of the pre-interaction conditions of sex and sex role of participants.

Analysis of the data collected in the SIMCORP SIMULATION indicates that males and females do not differ significantly in their desire to participate. These results are consistent with Harrison (1982). In addition, males and females do not differ significantly in the amount of participation they perceive in their work environment. These results contradict Harrison's (1982) results that females perceived their work environment as significantly more participative than males.

In terms of sex roles, high and low sensitivity respondents do not differ significantly in their desire to participate or in their perception of the amount of participation in their work environment. Instrumentality does, however, affect desire to participate. High instrumental respondents had a significantly greater perception of the amount of participation in their work environment. High and low instrumental respondents did not differ in their desire to participate in decision making, however.

This study supports the need to study organizational simulations as both simulations and as organizations. While this study supports Harrison (1982) in one area, it contradicts her results in another area. There is no difference between males and females in desire to participate in both real organizations and simulated ones. On the other hand, male and female participants in the SIMCORP SIMULATION did not perceive a differential amount of participation in their work environment, contrary to Harrison's social service agency employees. This difference in results may be accounted for by the fact that Harrison's respondents were "pure subordinates" with no supervisory authority. Respondents in SIMCORP came from all levels of the hierarchy and, thus, may have experienced more participation due to their level in the hierarchy. In addition, as an instructional methodology, organizational simulations encourage participation, and this fact may be reflected in these data.

In terms of sex role, high instrumental respondents believe that they participate more in decision making than low instrumental respondents. Thus, the pre-interaction condition of sex role significantly affects amount of participation of a participant in an organizational simulation, a result of the interaction.

Overall, it seems clear that organizational simulations are effective sites for data collection. In addition, it is clear that organizational simulations must be examined as both simulations and as organizations. This study sheds light on an area of concern in organizational communication--participation in decision making. Further research is needed to clarify the relationship between participation in decision-making and biological sex and sex role. This research will increase our knowledge of both organizational simulations and sex-role issues within organizations.

NOTE

1. I would like to thank Linda Lederman of Rutgers University for sharing her extensive knowledge of simulations with me. The model presented in this paper is more fully explained in Stewart (1983).

REFERENCES

Bem, S. L. (1974). The measurement of psychological androgyny. _Journal of Consulting and Clinical Psychology_, 42, 155-162.

Bredemeier, M. E., & Greenblat, C. S. (1981). The educational effectiveness of simulation games: A synthesis of findings. _Simulation & Games_, 12, 307-332.

Ellis, D., & Fisher, B. A. (1975). Phases of conflict in small group development. _Human Communication Research_, 1, 195-212.

Harrison, T. M. (1982). _Sex differences in participative decision making: An exploratory investigation_. Paper presented at the Fifth Annual Communication, Language and Gender Conference, Athens, OH.

Homans, G. (1961). _Social behavior: Its elementary forms_. New York: Harcourt Brace and World.

Kanter, R. M. (1983). _The change masters_. New York: Simon and Schuster.

Lederman, L. C. (1984). Debriefing: A critical reexamination of the post-experience analytic process with implications for its effective use. _Simulation & Games_, 15, 415-431.

Lederman, L. C., & Stewart, L. P. (1983). _The SIMCORP simulation participant's manual_. Princeton, NJ: Total Research Corporation.

Mohr, L. B. (1977). Authority and democracy in organizations. _Human Relations_, 30, 919-947.

Pacanowsky, M., with R. V. Farace, P. R. Monge, & H. M. Russell. (1977). _Instructor's guide to accompany communicating and organizing_. Reading, MA: Addison-Wesley.

Putnam, L. L., & Sorenson, R. L. (1982). Equivocal messages in organizations. _Human Communication Research_, 8, 114-132.

Ruben, B. D. (1977). Toward a theory of experience-based instruction. _Simulation & Games_, 8, 2.

Stewart, L. P. (1983). <u>Simulations and organizations:
     Research.</u> Paper presented at the Eastern Communi-
     cation Association, Ocean City, MD.

Wheeless, V. E., & Dierks-Stewart, K. (1981). The
     psychometric properties of the BEM sex-role inven-
     tory: Questions concerning reliability and validi-
     ty. <u>Communication Quarterly,</u> <u>29,</u> 173-186.

CHAPTER 22

TEACHING WOMEN AND COMMUNICATION:
ALTERNATIVE METHODS THROUGH VIDEOTAPE

Carol Valentine, Arizona State University

Courses related to women's communication are most typically offered as on-campus classes with the attending assets and liabilities. This paper outlines some existing alternatives. Following the development of the traditional course at Arizona State University in Tempe, Arizona, several additional course methodologies, relevant to distance education, were also developed.

First, a correspondence study version of the course was developed. This version permits enrollment of any approved student in a twenty-four lesson, three-credit course. Obviously, this version is designed for the off-campus student.

Second, a televised version of the course was prepared. Dr. Barbara Eakins, then at Arizona State, developed a televised version of the course. This iteration included lesson outlines, study questions and televised interviews with "big names" in the field of women and communication.

Third was a combination of the previously videotaped interviews and a more developed self-study guide. This version allowed students to view the tapes at home or in groups, answer study questions, and to add a new dimension to home study, i.e., the videotapes.

This paper stresses that such alternative delivery systems are both necessary and desirable. Further, with current technology, courses with even greater flair and flexibility can be prepared for the students not suited to or able to enroll in a traditional classroom taking a traditional class in "Women and Communication."

To begin, following the development of the traditional course at Arizona State University (ASU), several additional course methodologies were developed and still other alternatives could be developed.

First, the correspondence study version of the course is described in the Correspondence Bulletin:

This course explores women communicating. Both verbal and nonverbal communication are explored. Opportunities for in-depth study of related issues are available. (3 credits)

377

ASU correspondence courses are open to all students admitted to the University. Enrollees include working mothers, members of the military, traveling students, handicapped and others for whom sitting in an ASU classroom on any kind of regular schedule is either difficult or impossible. Still these students are anxious to earn credits, gain knowledge and work toward a degree. (See Correspondence Bulletin for details.)

ASU has gone further. A video series of interviews with various experts in the field of women and communication was produced. This series was shown on KAET-Channel 8, our state public broadcasting station. For several years the course was offered for credit through a combination of study questions and viewing the videotaped lectures on television.

A teaching assistant was assigned to grade the papers and handle the administration of the course. After several seasons, the televised course was dropped from programming, but the idea seemed to have much potential since many students were disappointed and sought to take the course including the video lectures.

So, when the course was dropped from the TV schedule, I proposed an expansion and combination of the correspondence and televised versions designed to meet student needs and requests. This version was conceived as a self-study system for studying "Women and Communication." The package included the lessons and the accompanying videotapes.

This resulting self-study package now allows for completion of the course, with the video component. All the student needs is access to a video tape player and for many students this is an easy problem to solve.

But let us look in some detail at the self-study version of the course. This is a "combo" course. It is designed to combine video and books. Each enrolled student is provided with a set of self-study questions, a list of required sixty-minute videos and procedures for ordering and returning the videotapes.

Study questions are based on both the video and the book learning. Some examples are attached.

This course option has several advantages. A combination video and literature program adds interest to otherwise traditional options. Combining video with books appeals to students who want more than just reading books and answering questions. One common complaint about correspondence courses is that they are unidimensional. Add some provocative and exciting videotapes to two or three fascinating books and this course delivery system becomes more appealing. This is one way to spice up correspondence offerings while adding additional information and visual contact with the instructor and others.

Beyond this option is the chance for remote groups to take the class together, to meet together, see the videos, discuss the videos, and work together on the material. This might sound like a description of a traditional class. There is, however, one interesting difference. The course outlines, questions, and tapes can be shipped to cities, towns, villages, and outposts. Students can learn from the best in the field even if they do not live in Champaign, Los Angeles, Ann Arbor, Lincoln, Athens, or other academic centers.

The extra dimension of ASU's "Women and Communication" courses appealed to the Women's Institute for Freedom of the Press. The course outline and concept was awarded the top prize for innovative women's programs. (Attached is some information about the wide-ranging and relevant offerings of this vibrant and related group.)

Now on to some other ideas. There are many other ways to teach about women, language, culture, gender and other relevant variables we find amusing, curious, interesting, and worthy of study.

Take films for example. There are several that raise interesting questions about relationships between women. Several raise questions about male-female relations. Still others raise additional questions about language, culture, and gender variables.

"Between Friends" is one illustration of this point. In this made-for-cable television film, Carol Burnett and Elizabeth Taylor work out a relationship. The relationship evolves. Students could be asked to analyze the development of this relationship between these two women and generalize to other woman-to-woman relationships.

There are still other variations on the traditional theme. Many of them deal with adapting our course offerings to accommodate new technology. Video tapes are no real innovation in terms of the existing possibilities, but they are in terms of increasing accessibility. Many people who do not have access to a university do have access to a VCR.

In summary, Arizona State University offers "Women and Communication" through various delivery systems. Correspondence study, televised courses, and videotaped lectures integrated into self-study courses are some options. These options are certainly not cited to be limiting. Instead they are cited to suggest alternative delivery systems for our very important messages.

379

INDEX / DIRECTORY OF WOMEN'S MEDIA

With today's communications system in the hands of a few individuals and corporations, permitting a minority to control the flow of information, it is more and more critical that new sources of information be opened up and that thought be given to the restructuring of the communications system. The Index/Directory of Women's Media provides both the network of existing women's media as well as ideas women have on the overall issues of restructuring the communications system.

The Directory, with nearly 500 periodicals and over 1,000 total entries in all the various categories, is an aid to networking and is published to increase communication among women, nationally and internationally.

With this resource, women, community groups and others with information can locate women's periodicals who will help get their information out. Writers can locate publishers, periodicals, and writers' groups. Presses can locate women's bookstores and vice versa. Film groups can contact distributors. Women with regular radio and TV programs can contact music groups for material.

Each group entry includes addresses, phone numbers, contact person, and 25 words about themselves.

Each individual entry in the section of Individual Media Women and Media-Concerned Women includes addresses, phone numbers, and a 15-word description.

So interesting are the various entries written by women around the globe that it makes fascinating reading simply to learn what women are doing -- apart from its usefulness as a directory of women's media.

Annual updating--the Directory is published each January 1-- assures the latest phone numbers and addresses.

The Index Section of the Directory indexes the bi-monthly Media Report to Women -- What Women Are Thinking and Doing to Build More Democratic Communications Systems. This annotated index of women's media activities and research provides a history of the women's media movement. It is a valuable resource for those who are studying the history of recent and current events. Only in Media Report to Women are the actions and thinking of women to bring change in the world's communications systems recorded systematically.

We at the Women's Institute for Freedom of the Press (WIFP), have been publishing the annual Index/Directory of Women's Media since 1975. In it, we index Media Report to Women to make that valuable material more accessible to those who are preparing programs, writing articles, making speeches, writing history, studying journalism and communication, and women's studies in all its disciplinary fields. Or for those who simply want to know what is happening in this world of communication because it so deeply affects the lives of all of us.

Martha Leslie Allen, Editor

Dear Martha:

"As the editor of Tradeswomen Magazine I can imagine the effort and time you must have put into putting together this directory. I know very well how projects like this sometimes cost us the painful exclusion of details in our personal lives, but let me assure you that the result of your efforts is spectacular. I have seldom been so excited about such a publication. Thank you for your concern for the networking needs of women!"

Sandra Marilyn
Editor, Tradeswomen Magazine

Are you, or do you know of, a women-owned and operated media that would like to be included in the upcoming edition? Or are you an individual media woman or media-concerned woman interested in a listing? Entries are free. Contact us for inclusion.

Author's note: The above has been copied with permission from Women's Institute for Freedom of the Press, 3306 Ross Place, NW, Washington, DC 20008. Information on the Directory can be obtained by writing to this address.

Sample Self-Study Lesson

Lesson #2: Male/Female Differentiation

Introduction

Our authors and the video tape seek to demonstrate the male bias of the English language and of our society. Miller and Swift claim that in our society the male-orientation is due to centuries of patriarchy where the language was designed to meet the needs of that patriarchy.

In the reading assignments we learn about masculine and feminine grammar in other societies and trace the history of male/female differentiation. From the historical we proceed to the anthropological and learn about relationships between language and culture. As Calvert Watkins wrote, language "is at once the expression of culture and part of it."

The video tape "On Becoming Female" combines historical, anthropological, sociological, and biological to present an integrated view of how we got where we are.

From birth on, parents and others in a child's environment prepare him or her to accept the appropriate sex role as interpreted by the culture. In the United States the socialization process to which the young are exposed includes an ever greater sex role differentiation. The extent to which this differentiation appropriately parallels the obvious biological differences between the sexes has become the subject of research. Findings to date have been summarized by Drs. Eleanor Maccoby and Carol Nagy Jacklin of Stanford University in their work, The Psychology of Sex Differences.

Among the specific sex differences these researchers have identified are the boys' greater ability at spatial visualization and girls' greater verbal ability. The latter seem to use that ability when displaying aggression while boys are more physically aggressive. But aggressive behavior in humans seems to be in good part a learned behavior; and submission is not found in girls to any greater degree than in boys. On the whole, researchers have found a lot of overlap and similarities for the sexes. Sex hormone differences have been studied in the laboratory, but precise measurements of significant differences by sex at various stages in life are as yet incomplete. Research also shows that while young children can identify boy toys and girl toys, any sense of their own sex remains hazy during early childhood. During those years, mothers seem not to treat their sons differently from their daughters. Comparable data on fathers is yet lacking.

American schools have contributed to sex role stereotyping. Counselors have reinforced the popular perceptions of sex differences by asking girls to leave science and mathematics to boys in high school and engineering, medicine, and law to men in college. Similar sex role stereotyping occurs in children's picture books and readers. Girls more often than not are portrayed as passive and acquiescing, while boys are shown as active, adventuresome, and initiating. Fathers represent a variety of occupations but mothers are shown almost exclusively in the home. Social studies textbooks, both verbally and pictorially, focus on males. Even teachers, according to researchers, address themselves more frequently to boys whose academic achievement they also are more likely to praise.

Boys find "success" through activity, often physical in nature. For girls, appearance and heterosexual relationships become important. At home they may be taught to seek their identity through marriage and motherhood. Later, for the high percentage of adult women in the labor force, identity may also come through their occupation.

To understand herself better, a woman may find that comparing her own socialization with what other women have experienced clarifies her present feelings and life style.

To counter the narrow sex role stereotyping of the past, parents may wish to express the same interest in their daughter's future educational and occupational plans as they have tradition- ally shown their son's. They can help girls to keep open many options rather than narrowing these down prematurely.

Reading Assignments

Key, _Male Female Language_, - "In the Beginning," pp. 11-21
Key, _Male Female Language_, - "Social Structures," pp. 22-29
Miller & Swift, _Words and Women_, - "Semantic Polarization," pp. 55-70

Viewing Assignment: Tape 1: "On Becoming Female"

Discussion Questions

(to be discussed with a group or responded to individually)

1. What kinds of observations of sex differences have been done in the past and by whom?

2. Give at least two reasons that Key offers as explanation for the fact that we do not have much information on actual male/female differences.

3. What are some explanations that Key says have been given as reasons for linguistic differences between males and females?

4. What point do you think Key is trying to make when she gives the example of Aztec language use concerning the pronouns and the "dual deity" of Ometeotl?

5. To what do you attribute male/female differentiation in language?

6. Why does Key believe applying findings from the study of animal behavior to human beings is "treacherous?"

7. Which of the basic physical differences between men and women which Key indicates are accepted among scientists do <u>you</u> consider most important? What is your reason for holding this opinion?

8. What is the meaning of the diagram on page 25 and Key's assertion that "these concepts can be handled better as a continuum rather than as a dichotomy"?

9. a. What does "male and female identification" have to do with the "principle of opposites" such as energy and inertia, Lord and flesh, etc., according to Key?

   b. What, generally speaking, does Key say that the psychological characteristics of females and of males are said to be in our society?

10. Describe the part words play in molding cultural assumptions.

11. What role do biological differences play in language?

12. To what extent does our common vocabulary contribute to social categorizing?

13. React to Margaret Fuller's observation about "what women need." (Miller and Swift, page 63).

14. Indicate examples of how words used to describe females have traveled a road that linguists call degeneration of meaning.

15. Margaret Mead wrote: "The existence in a given society of a dichotomy of social personality of sex-determined, sex-linked, personality, penalizes in greater or less degree every individual born within it." Explain this statement.

16. Why does Mead believe "masculine and feminine labels are even more destructive for a male who wants to depart from the cultural norm than they are for a female."

17. Take interesting issues raised by the video tape and discuss them with your group members or respond individually.

18. What do you suggest for parents who want to counter sex role stereotyping?

<u>Written Activities</u>   (to be written and submitted)

1. Summarize the conclusions of your group on the discussion questions.

2. Listen to the conversation around you and present five examples of how people's language choices say something about their cultural assumptions.

3. Illustrate points made in the reading with five examples from newspapers, magazines or your own experience.

4. Prepare a brief paper either agreeing or disagreeing with Watkin's statement that language "is at once the expression of culture and a part of it."

REFERENCES

Correspondence Study. Arizona State University Off-Campus Academic Services, Correspondence Study Office, Arizona State University, Tempe, AZ 85287.

Key, M.R. (1974). Male/female language. Metuchen, NJ: Scarecrow Press.

Maccobby, E.E., & Jacklin, C.N. (1974). The psychology of sex differences. Stanford, CA: Stanford University Press.

Media Report to Women. 3306 Ross Place, NW, Washington, DC 20008.

Miller, C., & Swift, K. (1977). Words and women. Garden City, NY: Anchor Doubleday.

On becoming a female. A 58-minute videotape. Department of Communication, Arizona State University, Tempe, AZ 85287.

Valentine, C.A. Women and communication: A self-study course. Off-campus Academic Services, Arizona State University, Tempe, AZ 85287.

Women's Institute for Freedom of the Press, 3306 Ross Place, NW, Washington, DC 20008.

CHAPTER 23

"SEE JANE FIGHT, WATCH DICK CRY."

DEVELOPING A UNIT ON SEX ROLES IN A COMMUNICATION CLASSROOM

Richard L. West, University of Northern Iowa

> Women have more strength in their looks than
> we have in our laws, and more power by their
> tears than we have by our argument.
> --Saville

> What a piece of work is a man! How noble in
> reason; how infinite in faculties; in form and
> moving; how express and admirable! In action
> how like an angel; in apprehension, how like
> a god; the beauty of the world--the paragon of
> animals!
> --Shakespeare

Throughout history, we have noted the existence of human sex role behavior. From the cave man, who it was assumed would sling his arrow and provide food for the table to his wife, who it was assumed would sling the dishes and cook it, sex roles have been present which are still characteristic of many contemporary males and females. Recently, however, social scientists are beginning to address the importance of educating students on the implications of both sexes maintaining such rigid role definitions and behaviors. This inquiry is indeed significant as it is becoming increasingly important for teachers to (1) acquaint themselves on the multi-faceted issue of sex roles and (2) be able to solicit discussion on the subject when such interaction is justified. One discipline where such discourse is warranted is the field of communication. Wilmot (1979), for instance, has accentuated the importance of roles when he explained that not only are roles shaped by transactions but also our transactions are shaped by our roles. This seems to suggest that roles are intricately related to the communication process. Since interpersonal communication involves responding to others as individuals, creating rules that govern certain interactions, and acquiring self-disclosive information (Adler, Rosenfeld, and Towne, 1980), an analysis of roles is both pertinent and necessary. With the foregoing in mind, the focus of this treatise is limited to sex roles and interpersonal communication. Specifically, the content of this paper will depict how a communication teacher can competently integrate a unit on sex roles into his/her classroom. As Carney and McMahon (1977) have remarked,

> Perhaps no area of change affects as many
> people or threatens as many varied relation-

ships as basic assumptions about sex
roles" (p.v).

One of the initial steps for any teacher preparing to employ
a unit on sex roles in his/her classroom is to review literature
relevant to the topic. A number of approaches are quite feasible
to explore. Some suggestions include: Socialization influences
(i.e., parents and peers), educational influences, differences in
language behavior of males and females, sex roles and personal
competence, and the stereotyping of sex roles (Appendix A).

Such initial research is appropriate as it provides an instructor the necessary basis from which to draw information both
for the content of the unit as well as for supplemental resource
material. Additionally, it is through such investigation that
the instructor gains a better insight into his/her own personal
attitudes regarding sex role literature. Furthermore, with a
library of research on sex roles at their grasp, students can secure evidential material which they can peruse should interest in
a particular area be provoked.

A second step for the communication teacher to take to teach
a sex role unit involves introspection. It is of great importance
that a teacher analyze personal attitudes toward sex roles and
their influences in our culture. The issue of sex roles can be a
very sensitive one in the classroom since "sex roles . . . cannot be studied without reference to sex inequality" (Stockard,
1980, p. xv). If sexes are "unequally valued and unequally rewarded" (Stockard, 1980, p. xv), it is inevitable that many students will develop adamant feelings on the subject. Thus, the
instructor must understand his/her own beliefs of sex role differences and their effect on the communication process. In addition,
that understanding must be reflected throughout the content of
the unit. Students, in turn, will recognize that the integration
of this unit is not based on personal biases and prejudices, but
on attempts to deal with "inequalities" that seem to be perpetu-
ated in social institutions, individual personalities, and cultural symbols.

While it is a significant step for the communication teacher
to examine his/her own attitudes regarding sex roles, it is also
essential that a third strategy occur: measuring student famil-
iarity/attitudes toward sex roles and how they function in interpersonal communication. Weitz (1977) has pointed out that a
child "will be dealt with differently by parents and other adults
and institutions as a function of sex and will model himself or
herself according to different standards, depending on sex" (p.
60). Clearly, this differential treatment functions to maintain
rigid perceptions of sex roles. Hence, it is the responsibility
of the instructor to assess students' views of male and female
sex roles. There are a number of ways in which to undertake such

388

an evaluation. Three methods include conducting classroom interaction, providing sex role measurement tools, and constructing
scenarios illustrative of pertinent subject matter.

In order for the classroom discussion to take place, an instructor might address the following concerns to students: family's influence on sex role acquisition; peer group effects on
assuming sex roles; the school's influences on males and females.
What is important to note is that the majority of the classroom
interaction should focus how students' reactions to sex role development have affected their interpersonal encounters. In most
cases, the classroom teacher should have little difficulty in
stimulating conversation. However, in many cases, such conversation may lead students to prematurely develop polarized attitudes regarding both sexes. For this reason, subsequent material
must be presented in order to obtain a student appreciation for
the applicability of sex roles to daily communication encounters.

What may be of particular value to assess student perceptions
of themselves is a variety of measuring instruments. One classic
measuring scale is the Bem Sex Role Inventory (BSRI) (Bem, 1974).
Briefly, the instrument requires subjects to indicate how well
each of the sixty masculine, feminine, and neutral items describe
their behavior. Students check along a seven-point scale ranging
from "never or almost never true" to "always or almost always
true." Such a self-report measure permits students to perceive
themselves in terms of possessing traditional masculine or traditional feminine characteristics, a combination of both (androgyny), or neither.

A second tool to measure sex role status is the Adjective
Check List (ACL) (Gough and Heilbrun, 1965). The ACL poses a
rather simple task: it asks the test-taker to select adjectives
from a list of 300 commonly used behavioral descriptors that are
self-characteristic. The ACL is quite flexible since it can be
used to examine individual adjectives that characterize particular
types of people.

The Personal Attributes Questionnaire (PAQ) (Spence and Helmreich, 1975) is a third sex role instrument that has attained
wide usage. The item format in the PAQ treats each of the stereotyped characteristics as a bipolar dimension, ranging from an
emphatic denial to a solid agreement. A five point rating scale
permits subjects to graduate their responses. Although additional
measuring scales are accessible to an instructor (Baucom, 1976;
Gough, 1957), and these instruments are not without problems,
these self-report devices allow both the instructor and student
the opportunity to engage in analyzing personal traits representative of a student's sex role.

Indeed, classroom discussion and sex role measurement are

valuable methods to utilize in the communication classroom in order to assess student attitudes. Yet, one technique also worthy of consideration is the construction of scenarios. An instructor might ask students to complete a story in order to acquire student attitudes that may be exemplified in the students' completion of that story. The following vignettes may be fruitful for analysis:

> Cathleen is the only woman in a five member group in her public speaking class. She has assumed the role of task leader, yet receives no cooperation from the men. Write an essay about how Cathleen should approach the situation.
>
> Steven and Carlton have been best of friends for ten years. During his freshman year of college, Steven auditioned for the cheerleading squad and made it. Because of the connotations of a male being a cheerleader, Carlton asks Steven to quit. Complete this story by discussing the interaction that takes place and how the issue is resolved.

This approach can be incorporated into the classroom at any time and is not necessarily restricted to a writing format. These scenes may be even more relevant to the student with a discussion following the writing portion of the exercise. Most likely, such stories will stimulate students to consider their own development as a man or a woman and examine the impact that sex role stereotypes have had on interpersonal situations.

Aside from researching sex roles, instigating self-analysis, and assessing student perceptions of the issue, a fourth step for the communication instructor to develop a sex roles unit relates to the actual introduction of the unit. It has been this writer's experience that typically, students are aware of sex roles that the media has presented. In fact, most students desire to engage in a significant amount of discussion regarding the issue. They tend to view the media as primarily responsible for the many rigid parameters of sex roles. However, beliefs and opinions begin to shift when the focus is on their past and present communication encounters. For instance, it is not uncommon that students will formulate certain feelings in the classroom on what competencies are necessary for either sex to possess in any interpersonal gathering. What was once perhaps a healthy classroom atmosphere can undergo a change as more tensions are stirred as a result of more "personal" issues (same-sex/opposite-sex responsibilities) being discussed. Many times, students do not realize their deep-rooted commitment to issues pertaining to sex roles. The instructor must recognize this and consistently reiterate that the goal of the unit is not necessarily agreement and/or consensus, but comprehension and applicability of issues. Thus, the instructor might emphasize student experiences. In doing so, he/she can foster student imput as well as implicitly encourage varied opinions of perspectives that may not have been gleaned in an atmosphere characterized by discord.

The communication teacher cannot, however, presume to have any positive classroom environment unless he/she maintains a strict sense of organization throughout the unit. This fifth step contributes substantially to the overall success of the unit. A sex roles unit is most beneficial to students when the instructor engages in a repertoire of methods. Aside from the traditional lecture format, other alternative teaching formats can be effective. Films (Appendix B), guest lectures, handouts, and classroom activities (Appendix C) are all appropriate strategies to use for instructional aids. The key to a productive and satisfying experience in class is not only instilling pedagogical principles to students but perhaps more important, providing students additional approaches which facilitate the understanding and explanation of those approaches.

To conclude this paper's analysis, two final arguments are germane. First, this unit will be perceived as time consuming and inappropriate by students in a communication classroom unless the instructor maintains a communication focus. He/She can achieve a positive student regard by emphasizing the influence that sex roles have on the communication process. Such an influence is important to examine as it may manifest how sex roles impose limitations on personal growth. Futhermore, if individuals desire less restricting norms governing their interactions (Aries, 1977), then perhaps exploring the sex roles of the interactions is resourceful.

A final argument pertains to evaluation of this unit. A multitude of evaluation methods are available to measure a student's knowledge of skill and sex roles in interpersonal communication. Generally, evaluation in terms of testing may incorporate either objective or essay questions as determined by the instructional approach. Essay examinations will determine the extent to which a student has knowledge and understanding of certain concepts previously discussed in class and will determine the student's ability to apply, analyze, synthesize and evaluate relevant information within the communication situation. To guarantee that all relevant content areas are covered, a number of short-answer questions would be preferable to one or two items requiring lengthy responses.

Interactions outside of the classroom provide ample opportunities for analysis and evaluation of communication concepts presented in the classroom. Although one does not readily accept televised episodes as true to life, some comedies and soap operas portray excellent examples of sex roles and their influences on interpersonal communication. Various adaptations of analysis papers remain useful tools to allow students to thoughtfully and logically analyze communication situations as a passive observer. Using this type of evaluation, cognitive as well as affective objectives may be determined (Appendix D).

Clearly, then, the issue of sex roles in a communication classroom is one needing attention and response. It might be added that a unit on sex roles has traditionally been incorporated in a basic psychology and sociology course (entire classes on the subject even exist in these two disciplines). Yet, Chafetz (1978) commented on its relevance to interpersonal communication by stating that ". . . roles encourage the dissolution of a variety of types of interpersonal relationships" (p. 177). To be sure, all competent interpersonal relationships should be characterized by both a knowledge of sex roles and their effects on the communication process in those relationships.

Appendix A

Selected References on Sex Roles and Interpersonal Communication

Adler, Ronald and Towne, Neil. (1978). Looking out/Looking in. New York: Holt, Rinehart, and Winston.

Berryman, Cynthia L. and Wilcox, James R. (1980). Attitudes toward male and female speech: Experiment on the effects of sex-typical language. The Western Journal of Speech Communication, 44, 50-59.

Bradley, Patricia Hayes. (1981). The folk-linguistics of women's speech: An empirical examination. Communication Monographs, 47, 73-90.

Broverman, Inge K., Broverman, Donald M., Clarkson, Frank E, Rosenkrantz, Paul S., and Vogel, Susan R. (1970). Sex-role stereotypes and clinical judgements of mental health. Journal of Consulting and Clinical Psychology, 34, 1-7.

Carney, Clarke G. and McMahon, Sarah L. (Eds.). (1977). Contemporary male/female roles. LaJolla, CA: University Associates.

David, Deborah and Brannon, Robert (Eds.). (1976). The forty-nine percent majority: The male sex role. Reading, MA: Addison-Wesley Publishing Co.

DeVito, Joseph. (1983). The interpersonal communication book. New York: Harper and Row.

Eakins, Barbara W. and Eakins, R. Gene. (1978). Sex differences in human communication. Boston: Houghton Mifflin.

Frances, Susan J. (1979). Sex differences in nonverbal behavior. Sex Roles, 5, 519-535.

Greenberg, S. (1978). Right from the start: A guide to non-sexist child rearing. Boston: Houghton Mifflin.

Kramarae, Cheris. (1981). Women and men speaking: Rowley, MA: Newbury House Publishers, Inc.

Kramer, Cheris. (1978). Sex differences in language. Psychology Today, 8, 82-85.

Lakoff, Robin. (1975). Language and women's place. New York: Harper and Row.

Pearson, Judy C. (1983). Interpersonal communication: Clarity, confidence, concern. Glenview, IL: Scott, Foresman and Company.

Pearson, Judy C. (1980). Sex roles and self-disclosure. Psychological Reports, 47, 640.

Sargent, Alice G. (1977). Beyond sex roles. St. Paul: West Publishing Company.

Sexton, Patricia C. (1969). The feminized male. New York: Vintage Books.

Thorne, Barrie and Henley, Nancy. (1975). Language and sex: Differences and dominance. Rowley, MA: Newbury House Publishers, Inc.

Weitz, Shirley. (1977). Sex roles: Biological, psychological, and social foundations. New York: Oxford University Press.

Selected Film Resources on Sex Roles and Interpersonal Communication*

Being a Boy--Being a Girl. KQED-TV: National Instructional TV
   Center. Masculinity and femininity are discussed as
   part of an individual's personality. Adults are shown
   helping children to learn their masculine and feminine
   roles. The concept of respect for people on the basis
   of differences is explored.

Different Folks. NVETA, AIT 1975. This film considers alternative sex roles in a family in which the mother is a
   veterinarian who produces most of the family's income
   and the father is a commercial illustrator for children's books who works at home and does most of the
   housework. The film helps adolescents deal with some
   of the current ambiguities in our culture about male
   and female roles. 16mm film, 15 minutes, color.

Faces of Women. LFA, FI. 1968. This animated film examines traditional and non-traditional roles of women. In rapid
   sequence and to a musical score, women are portrayed as
   adorned, mother, Amazon, and Eve. Some of the negative
   depictions provide a point for discussion. 16mm film,
   10 minutes, color.

Men's Lives: A Documentary Film about Masculinity in America.
   Antioch, 1974. This film re-examines masculinity and
   the socialization process. The pressures and motiva-
   tions that shape the roles and general behavior of men.
   The film received a great deal of national attention
   when it was first presented and it remains a controversial statement about men and women. 16mm, 43 minutes,
   color.

Sex Role Development. CRM Productions, 1974. This film examines
   some of the sex role stereotypes that exist in our culture. The tranmission of sex role stereotypes to children through the socialization process is included.
   Alternative approaches to socialization are considered.
   16mm film, 23 minutes.

Woman's Place. ABC News, 1973. This film examines women's traditional roles in society and illustrates how today's
   women are reexamining their roles and choices. 16mm
   film, 58 minutes.

*These film titles and brief synopses are adapted from the In-
structor's Manual of Gender and Communication, 1985. For an
excellent listing of additional film resources, contact the
Manual by Judy Cornelia Pearson.

Appendix C

Selected Activities on Sex Roles and Interpersonal Communication*

Sexual Stereotypes

Objectives: To identify specific behaviors and characteristics associated with males and females; discuss the validity of these stereotyped characteristics; indicate how their stereotyped perception influences their own behavior; and relate the specific discussion of sexual stereotypes to cultural and subcultural influences on perception.

Procedure: After a general discussion of stereotypes, divide the class into two groups; the males in one group and the females in the other. This activity is more effective when there are approximately equal numbers of males and females. Tell each group to compose a list of the likeable behaviors, characteristics, attitudes, and expectations of the other group, and another list of what they dislike about the other group. Each list should contain illustrative examples. After approximately fifteen minutes, the groups should face each other to read their lists and cite their examples. While one group is reading, the other group may not respond.

Class Discussion: After both groups have spoken, permit free discussion. The teacher should not participate in the discussion unless necessary. After a few minutes the students will usually conclude that their lists are stereotypes that don't really reflect _their_ attitudes or _their_ behavior toward the opposite sex.

At this point, the instructor should ask specific questions about the students' behavior toward the opposite sex (e.g., How many women have initiated a first date with a man? How do the men feel about having a woman pay the check? Do the men feel that they could succeed over a woman in most competitive situations?).

Empathic Listening

Objectives: To describe specific verbal and nonverbal behavior that demonstrates empathic understanding; demonstrate, in a discussion, their own ability to listen empathically; and discuss the effects of empathic listening on communication.

Procedure: Divide the class into groups of three or four. Each student should read the following statements and decide for himself or herself what the answers are. The group should then discuss each question and arrive at a consensus.
1. The next President of the United States should be a woman.
2. Women should refrain from smiling too much.
3. All students should be required to take a course on gender

and communication in order to graduate.

Each student should paraphase the comments of the person who just spoke before he or she is allowed to make any new comments.

Class Discussion: The class should discuss the exercise when all groups have reached their decision. The students should describe the behavior of the other students that indicated active listening and empathic understanding. Usually the students will identify body position and posture, eye contact, paraphrasing, asking probing questions, and words or gestures of affirmation, e.g., head nodding or saying "I see." The discussion should relate behavior indicating empathy to the factors that can create barriers to communication. The students should realize that empathy reduces the barriers to effective listening. They should also discuss their feelings during the discussion and the effect of empathic behavior on communication within the group.

Conversational Analysis

Objectives: To determine systematic patterns of female-male communication, to examine stereotypes about female-male conversational patterns, and to describe one's own perceptions of men and women in conversations.

Procedure: Assign half of the students in the class to conversational dyads. When possible, these dyads should be mixed-sex. Assign the other members of the class to be observers of the dyads. Two people should each observe one dyad. The conversational dyad members should not be told that which the observers will be examining. You may have the observers examine such areas as the topics that are most often discussed, who initiated the topics, who changed the topic, how the topic was changed, the kinds of topics that are discussed, whether stereotypical topics (women discussing clothing and relationships and men discussing automotive issues and politics) were discussed; how age, occupational background, or education affected topic choices; the use of tag questions, intensifying words, hedges, questions, qualifiers, modifiers, interruptions, overlaps, and humor.

Class Discussion: Have individual observers report on their dyads. Consider the differences that occurred from one dyad to another. How do you account for these differences? Did men behave in the way that the book suggests they might? Did women? Consider the effect these differences have on actual conversation.

*These activities are adapted from the Instructor's Manual of Gender and Communication, 1985, by Judy Cornelia Pearson. This and Beyond Sex Roles, 1977, by Alice G. Sargent are excellent sources to consider for additional exercises of sex roles and interpersonal communication.

Analysis Paper Topics for Sex Roles and Interpersonal Communication*

Self-Disclosure in Same-Sex and Mixed-Sex Groups

Sexism in the Classroom

Media Portrayal of Males and Females

Homophobia and Communication Breakdown

The "Language" of Sex Roles

Relationship Qualities of Males and Females

Gender Differences in Perception

Androgyny: The Ideal Mix?

Gossiping Women and Boring Men: Conversation Patterns of the Sexes

Friendships and Gender Differences

*These topics were investigated by students in my male/female communication class recently. Of course, a multitude of other subjects are accessible through teacher/student interaction, student/student interaction, and research in the area(s) of interest.

REFERENCES

Adler, Ronald, Rosenfeld, Lawrence, and Towne, Neil. (1980).
Interplay. New York: Holt, Rinehart, and Winston.

Aries, Elizabeth. (1977). Male-Female interpersonal styles in
all male, all female and mixed groups. In A. Sargent (Ed.),
Beyond Sex Roles. St. Paul: West Publishing Company.

Baucom, D.H. (1976). Independent masculinity and femininity
scales on the California Psychological Inventory. Journal
of Consulting and Clinical Psychology, 44, 876.

Bem, Sandra L. (1974). The measurement of psychological androgyny. Journal of Consulting and Clinical Psychology, 42.
155-162.

Carney, Clarke G. and McMahon, Sarah L. (Eds.). (1977). Contemporary male/female roles. LaJolla, CA: University Associates.

Chafetz, Jean. (1978). Masculine, feminine or human? Itasca,
IL: F.E. Peacock Publishers, Inc.

Gough, H.G. (1957). Manual for the California Psychological Inventory. Palo Alto, CA: Consulting Psychologists Press.

Gough, H.G. and Heilbrun, Alfred B. (1965). Manual for the Adjective Check List and the Need Scales for the ACL. Palo
Alto, CA: Consulting Psychologists Press.

Spence, Janet and Helmreich, Robert. (1978). Masculinity and
femininity: Their psychological dimension, correlates, and
antecedents. Austin: University of Texas Press.

Spence, Janet, Helmreich, Robert, and Stapp, Joy. (1975). Rating of self and peers on sex-role attributes and their relation to self-esteem and conceptions of masculinity and
femininity. Journal of Personality and Social Psychology,
46, 40-52.

Stockard, Jean. (1980). Sex roles. Englewood Cliffs, NJ:
Prentice-Hall, Inc.

Weitz, Shirley. (1977). Sex roles: Biological, psychological,
and social foundations. New York: Oxford University Press.

Abdel-Halim, A., 135
Abelson, R., 44, 45
Adams, K., 111
Adams, J., 127
Adler, R., 387
Aguiar, N., 27
Ajzen, I., 157, 164
Alexander, R., 3
Allen, J., 291, 292, 293
Alpern, D., 279
Amir, Y., 4
Andersen, K., 278, 279, 281
Andersen, P., 292, 294
Anderson, J., 156, 157, 166
Andler, C., 77
Applegate, R., 57
Aries, E., 105, 111, 391
Ashour, A., 128
Athanassiades, J., 191
Atwood, L., 291, 292
Backus, D., 252
Bagdikian, B., 62, 63
Baggio, M., 176
Baird, J., 4, 13, 19, 23, 127, 192, 225, 231, 232
Bales, R., 110
Ball, R., 27
Baltis, N., 176
Banks, W., 321
Bargh, J., 48
Barnes, R., 13
Barnett, G., 292
Baron, A., 4
Barrow, J., 128
Bartell, G., 76
Bartlett, K., 43
Bartol, K., 127
Basil, D., 3
Bass, B., 3, 127
Bateson, G., 262
Baucom, D., 389
Baukus, R., 155, 158, 159, 175
Bean, F., 192
Beasley, M., 57
Beck, M., 282
Becker, L., 291, 293
Bee, H., 177
Beinstein Miller, J., 109, 111, 119
Bem, S., 45, 176, 370, 389

Bentley, N., 191, 192
Berg, D., 293
Berger, C., 44, 46
Berkes, L., 133
Bernard, J., 76
Berryman-Fink, C., 3, 5, 127
Berzins, J., 176
Blank, A., 45
Blodgett, T., 43, 49, 50
Blumler, J., 291
Booth-Butterfield, M., 43, 46, 49, 50
Borisoff, D., 351
Bourke, D., 50
Bowers, T., 62
Bowes, J., 292
Bowman, G., 3, 190
Bradley, P., 4, 23, 127, 192
Brass, D., 4
Bredemeier, M., 363
Brenner, O., 3, 4
Breslin, R., 278
Bringle, R., 76, 77
Bromer, J., 3, 4
Broverman, D., 177
Broverman, I., 177
Brouwer, C., 175
Brown, B., 220, 226
Browning, C., 130
Bruning, N., 130, 135
Bryant, M., 243, 245
Bryson, J., 76, 77, 78, 79, 84
Buckley, J., 278, 280, 281, 283, 284
Burgoon, M., 130, 176, 247, 252, 293
Burleson, B., 232, 292
Burke, K., 286
Butler, R., 320
Buunk, B., 77
Burt, M., 43
Burtt, H., 90, 91, 92, 105
Butterfield, D., 3, 4
Campbell, K., 219
Carmen, B., 110
Carney, C., 387
Carpenter, S., 43
Carter, R., 243, 245
Carver, C., 113, 115, 121
Cashman, J., 127, 129
Caspi, A., 4
Certner, B., 175
Chadwick, P., 175

Chafetz, J., 392
Chanowitz, B., 45
Chaze, W., 281
Cheek, D., 320
Chelune, G., 84, 175
Christensen, E., 27
Church, G., 275, 276, 277, 282
Cifelli, A., 281, 283
Clanton, G., 75, 76, 77
Clevenger, T., 293
Clifton, A., 223
Cody, M., 224, 246
Collins, E., 43, 49, 50
Constantine, J., 76
Constantine, L., 76
Cook, S., 180
Cordry, H., 307
Courtright, J., 114
Cox, M., 317, 319, 321, 323
Craig, R., 175
Crino, M., 3, 4, 8, 127
Crockett, W., 227, 228, 232
Crosby, F., 225, 227
Cross, W., 320
Crumley, W., 62
Cushman, D., 45
Dachler, P., 129
Dallinger, J., 13
Daly, A., 60
Daly, J., 294
Danielson, K., 155
Dansereau, F., 127, 129
Davey, W., 273
David, D., 291
Davis, G., 326
Davis, T., 128
Davis, W., 220
Deakins, A., 89
Deaux, K., 80, 82, 130
Deckard, B., 57
Delia, J., 228, 232
Dellaan, D., 175
Denfield, D., 76
Derber, C., 105
DeSanctis, G., 3, 127
Dessler, G., 128, 129, 132, 133
Deutsch, F., 127
Devries, W., 291
Diamond, I., 261
Dierks-Stewart, K., 156, 157, 164, 370

McMillan, J., 109, 110, 224
McPhee, W., 292
McQuail, D., 291
Mead, M., 75
Merrill, L., 351
Millar, F., 114
Miller, C., 381, 383
Miller, D., 319, 320
Miller, G., 293
Miller, J., 219
Miller, R., 261
Milliones, J., 320
Minami, T., 129
Mitchell, T., 127, 128, 129, 130, 132
Mohr, L., 371
Montgomery, B., 156, 319
Montgomery, C., 176
Moore, H., 89, 90, 91, 92, 94, 96, 104, 105
Moore, L., 3
Morasch, B., 43, 47, 51
Morgan, B., 175
Morganthau, T., 275, 276, 277, 280
Morrow, L., 276, 277, 280, 281
Mosher, D., 75
Murdoch, J., 177
Nadler, L., 189, 191, 192, 194, 221
Nadler, M., 189, 191, 192, 194, 221
Natale, M., 109, 111
Neilson, E., 176
Neugarten, D., 43
Newcomb, T., 4
Nieva, V., 127, 191
Nimmo, D., 291, 292
Norton, R., 156, 317, 318, 319, 320, 323, 326
Nyquist, L., 225, 227
O'Connor, E., 127
O'Leary, V., 127
O'Mara, J., 291, 293
O'Reilly, J., 275, 277
Orth, C., 3, 190
Osborn, R., 135
Osterink, C., 89, 93
Pacanowsky, M., 363
Pace, T., 291
Palley, M., 261
Parkin, P., 127
Parrish Sprowl, J., 243
Parrish Sprowl, S., 75, 83
Patchen, M., 321, 322
Patterson, J., 62

Payne, H., 292
Paz, O., 27
Pearce, B., 45
Pearson, J., 105, 176, 395, 397
Penelope, J., 285
Peters, L., 3, 4, 5, 8, 127, 189
Pederson, D., 175
Peterson, P., 63, 64
Petty, M., 130, 135
Philipsen, G., 103
Pilliavin, J., 110
Platz, S., 127, 131
Pooyan, A., 127
Post, D., 292, 294
Powell, G., 3, 4
Press, A., 228
Pufahl, S., 221, 225, 226
Pulakos, E., 127
Putnam, L., 127, 175, 176, 177, 220, 358, 363
Quinn, D., 61, 62
Quinn, J., 283
Rancer, A., 155, 156, 157, 158, 159, 164, 175
Randall, V., 261
Ray, L., 76
Reed, J., 191
Reeves, N., 274
Reiches, N., 190
Reilly, T., 43, 46, 49, 50
Remland, M., 43
Rice, R., 14, 127
Richards, W., 14, 15
Richmond, A., 93, 105
Richmond, V., 294
Rickel, A., 3
Ricker-Ousiankina, A., 175
Rigny, A., 127
Riverback, W., 175
Roach, S., 77
Robey, C., 224
Robinson, D., 323
Robinson, R., 43
Rogers, L., 114
Rogers-Millar, L., 114
Rokeach, M., 293, 294
Rosen, B., 3
Rosenbaum, L., 292
Rosenberg, M., 79
Rosenfeld, H., 225
Rosenfeld, L., 387
Rosenkrantz, P., 176

Rosenthal, R., 131, 133
Rossi, A., 23, 24, 27
Ruben, B., 364, 366
Rubin, D., 133
Rubin, J., 112, 120, 220, 226
Rush, R., 59, 62
Rusk, J., 292
Ryder, R., 111, 112
Sadler, O., 109
Safran, C., 43
Sailor, P., 62
Saine, T., 110, 111
Sanchez de Rota, G., 28
Sanders, K., 291, 292
Sapiro, V., 261
Savage, R., 291
Sawyer, J., 49
Schaef, A., 82
Schamber, L., 64
Schank, R., 44, 45
Schein, V., 3, 127, 130, 190
Schenk-Hamlin, W., 246
Schmidt, F., 131
Schneer, J., 127, 128
Schriesheim, C., 132, 133
Schultz, B., 155, 156, 157, 166
Scott, W., 161
Sedney, M., 77, 80
Seebohm, M., 3
Seeds, D., 155
Selltiz, C., 180
Sentis, K., 44, 45
Sereno, K., 190
Severa, N., 77
Shafritz, J., 43
Shainess, N., 222, 223, 224, 225, 226, 227, 228
Shaklee, H., 44
Shapiro, W., 276, 279, 281, 283, 284, 285
Sharp, N., 64
Shaw, M., 13, 109
Sheier, M., 113, 115, 121
Sheperd, P., 155
Sherrod, D., 292
Shettel-Neuber, J., 76
Sherman, M., 105
Shingeldecker, P., 127
Shore, L., 127, 130
Siegel, S., 35
Small, A., 176
Smith, D., 49

Smith, F., 3, 189
Smith, L., 75, 76, 77
Smith, M., 128, 131, 133
Smith, P., 109, 111
Sollie, D., 105
Somers, A., 43
Sorenson, R., 363
Soskin, W., 105
Spaulding, C., 43
Spence, J., 389
Spence, T., 176
Staley, C., 166
Stanley, A., 277, 283
Stapp, J., 176
Stern, D., 62
Stewart, L., 190, 363, 368, 374
Stockard, J., 388
Stopeck, M., 127
Strentz, H., 292
Stricker, G., 292
Strodtbeck, F., 110, 175
Swacker, M., 175, 225
Swan, J., 245
Swap, W., 112, 120
Swift, K., 381, 383
Szilagyi, A., 132, 135
Talevich, T., 67
Tangri, S., 43, 50, 51
Tannen, D., 105
Tarrance, V., 291
Taylor, F., 27
Taynor, J., 3
Teismann, M., 75
Terborg, J., 3, 4, 8, 127, 189
Terhune, K., 175
Thomas, C., 320
Thomas, E., 280, 282, 285
Thomas, K., 358
Thornton, G., 127, 130
Tifft, S., 281, 285
Tobin, R., 307, 308
Todd-Mancillas, W., 23, 24, 27, 292, 294
Tolchin, M., 261
Tolchin, S., 261
Toomer, J., 320
Towne, N., 387
Trebing, J., 155
Trempe, J., 127
Triandis, H., 353, 354
Turk, J., 64